A New Land Beckoned

German Immigration to Texas,
1844-1847

A New Land Beckoned

German Immigration to Texas, 1844-1847

New and Enlarged Edition

BY CHESTER W. & ETHEL H. GEUE

CLEARFIELD

Reprinted for
Clearfield Company, Inc. by
Genealogical Publishing Co., Inc.
Baltimore, Maryland
2002

DEDICATION

This book
is dedicated
to those of our forefathers who
with thousands of other emigrants
left the German provinces in the 1840's
to seek new homes and better opportunities
in Texas.

Foreword

One would be hard pressed to fully explain the impact German immigrants have had on Texas. In the mid-1840's they came in substantial numbers and wielded such influence that the political, economic, and social life of Texas was materially altered by 1850. These Germans took an interest in education, were active in religious affairs, and founded literary and political societies to promote good fellowship. By 1861 they had founded at least five German language newspapers. Nor has their influence stopped. Descendants of these immigrants may still be found in the small communities along the coastal plain of Texas and in the beautiful hilly regions of the Edwards Plateau. In the beginning most of the Germans were farmers, but on the Edwards Plateau they rapidly became ranchers and sheepherders. Some presented themselves as merchants and shopkeepers. As Texas has become industrialized, the descendants have permeated the fiber of the cities, adding a distinctly German flavor. But in the agricultural areas a "German town" can still be recognized whether it be Doss in Gillespie County, Industry in Austin County, or New Braunfels in Comal County.

While good reasons existed for these people to leave their native land, the drama of journeying across the sea to settle in a new and unknown region cannot be stressed too much. The journey aboard ship was long and hard as disease, hunger, and death were constant companions that often reaped a heavy toll. Once in the new country untold dangers faced them, but they were a hearty race and although some fell by the wayside, others courageously survived. Even though much has been written about these pioneers, many details of the movement have not been heretofore understood.

Using the best research techniques of the historian—that of going to the source documents—Ethel and Chester Geue several years ago set about to better understand this German movement into Texas. Their research led them to the State Archives where they discovered the ship lists in the Colonization Papers; to the General Land Office Archives where the documents concerning land acquired by the Germans are kept; and to Germany, the land whence they came. The combination was especially correct. Ethel Geue has research ability to go with her intense interest in the subject while Chester possesses the talent to translate German into English. Both have unbounded energy and just as important, they have set aside sufficient time to do this job. It has been enjoyable to watch them work and to see the fruits of their labor.

All of the study is significant. So far as I can determine this is the first time the reports of Prince Solms have been translated and published in the English language. Their importance cannot be overestimated as they provide insight for the scholar into the operation of the German movement. Then comes the problem of the ship lists—that of listing correctly and indexing some four thousand names. Anyone with even the perfunctory knowledge of German names can readily appreciate that the task takes untold hours of patience, fortitude, and perseverance. Nor can the information on the German towns and ports be underestimated, because it provides data as important for the historian as the genealogist.

This book has been a labor of love by the Geues for which future students of the Germans in Texas must of necessity show their gratitude.

James M. Day
Director of State Archives

Preface

The largest colonization project in Texas history was the mass immigration of Germans to Texas in the years 1844-1847. Our interest in this movement began with a desire to learn more about our forefathers, some of whom were among this group.

Research in the early church records in New Braunfels revealed the fact that two of these forefathers died en route from Indianola to New Braunfels and were buried somewhere near Seguin. Others reached New Braunfels in 1845 and were among the earliest settlers. Further research showed that another became one of the wagon masters for the Verein. According to his obituary, he led the first wagon load of settlers across the Guadalupe River when New Braunfels was founded on March 21, 1845.

Records of another forefather showed only that he came from Württemberg. This was insufficient for tracing his lineage and it was necessary to search further. In a study of the well-preserved German Immigration Contracts in the General Land Office in Austin, Texas, we found that he came from Oberlenningen, Württemberg, and we learned something more. We found also that the nineteen volumes of immigration contracts contained the names of 2650 other German immigrants.

Would not these German Immigration Contracts help others in a search for information on their family if they were of German descent? We asked Karl Friedrich von Frank, genealogist in Austria, this question and his answer was "These Einwanderungs-Verträge (immigration contracts) in Austin are of predominant importance for locating immigrants over here, and I suggest that steps be taken to explore this important material." This was written in 1962 and our work began.

Other records were examined; and in the course of time new material was found. Translation of documents in the Verein and Wied Collections, located in the University of Texas Archives, added more information to the facts already known about the immigrants who came to Texas under the auspices of the Verein.

Many books, magazine articles, and newspaper columns

have been written about this movement. We have drawn on these sources to tell the story briefly. The compilation of data about the immigrants and the translations of Prince Solms's eleven reports sent from Texas, as well as the report made in Wiesbaden, we hope, will add to the information about this period in Texas history.

Since this has been primarily a research project, mostly about the people and their leaders, our search for data was concentrated in the State Archives, General Land Office, and the Archives of the University of Texas in Austin. Our sincere appreciation is expressed to the directors and staff in each place.

From the start Mr. James M. Day, Director of the State Archives, has been a most valued consultant. Mrs. Fischer Osburn, Archivist, suggested many sources that might yield the information that we were seeking. We are especially indebted to both of them.

In the University of Texas Archives Dr. Chester V. Kielman, Director, made available to us the Verein and Wied Collections recently acquired from Germany. Much valuable information was found in these. We sincerely appreciate this, as well as all the other help which he has given to us.

Mr. David Reeves of the General Land Office is due our gratitude for his help and advice in our study of the nineteen volumes of German Immigration Contracts which he has carefully preserved. His staff also was most co-operative.

Karl Friedrich von Frank, internationally known genealogist in Austria, has patiently corrected the spelling and given the location of the towns in Germany and Austria from which many immigrants came. His work has made our compilation far more correct, and we are deeply grateful.

Our good friend, Mr. Oscar Haas, historian of New Braunfels and Comal County, has given us permission to publish his English translation of ten of the eleven reports that Prince Solms made from Texas to the directors of the Verein in Germany. The eighth report and the Wiesbaden report were translated by Chester W. Geue. We are deeply indebted to Mr. Haas for the use of his translations and other valuable material.

We also wish to thank Mrs. Virginia H. Taylor, Director of the Spanish Archives Section of the General Land Office, for the use of the German Emigration Company land transfer contracts which were found and indexed by her.

Mrs. Edna Perry Deckler, President of the Texas State Genealogical Society, has given us both help and encouragement in the compilation of the information on the immigrants. We are truly grateful.

The arrangement of material and editing of our manuscript was made far better due to the careful reading of it by Mrs. Abby Moran, genealogist and former librarian of the Southwest and Genealogical Section of the Fort Worth Public Library. We are greatly indebted to her.

Colonel Harold B. Simpson offered suggestions which were of great value and we wish to extend our appreciation to him for these.

Without the advice, assistance, and encouragement of these and other interested persons, the compilation and editing of this material would have been far more difficult; with their interest and help, it was a real pleasure.

It is our hope that the research which we have done will be a source of help to future students of this movement and also to those seeking information about their forefathers who were among the German immigrants who came to Texas during the years 1844-1847.

Chester W. Geue
Ethel Hander Geue

The immigrant ship, *Herschel*, a sketch from a picture in the Museum at Fredericksburg, Texas.

Contents

Maps and Illustrations

Following Page 100

The Seal of the Mainzer Verein

The lone star on the seal was symbolic of the Republic of Texas. The bundle of arrows indicated the presence of Indians on the Fisher-Miller Grant, the destination of the German immigrants.

The Story of

The Mass Immigration of Germans
to Texas, 1844-1847

To a people faced with the problems of revolution and war, industrial inequality, and lack of opportunity for economic advancement, emigration to a new land seemed to offer a solution. Lack of political freedom and heavy taxation also caused much dissatisfaction. The industrial revolution of the eighteenth century had brought about the use of machinery which replaced handwork in many trades, with the result that many were left jobless. A large percentage of the people turned to farming and were scarcely able to eke out a bare existence. Conditions such as these made emigration seem very attractive to the people of Germany during the middle of the nineteenth century.

From letters and articles in newspapers the populace of Germany learned of better living conditions in the United States. Those who had come to the eastern shores of America had prospered after the first few hard years, and neat German and Dutch communities were numerous in New York, New Jersey, and Pennsylvania, a further incentive to emigration.

Colonization in Texas began with the coming of the Spanish missionaries. Despite all their labors, however, there were no more than two or three thousand white men, women and children in Texas when Mexico gained her independence from Spain in 1821. As a new nation, Mexico encouraged immigration by passing a colonization law in 1823. Stephen F. Austin was the only colonizer or empresario, as such men were called, until 1825 when the state of Coahuila, to which Texas was attached, passed a law which provided for contracts with other empresarios.

Under the Colonization Law of Coahuila a number of grants were made. Two were made with the Irish empresarios Power and Hewitson, and with McMullen and McGloin who brought settlers from Ireland and Mexico into the San Patricio area.[1] DeWitt settled several hundred families on land west of the Colorado River, and Sterling Robertson located six hundred families in the part of Texas west of the Brazos River. Other empresarios were Joseph Vehlein, Hayden Edwards, David Burnet, and de Zavala. By 1836 the white population of Texas had increased to 25,000 or 30,000. Grants made by Spain and Mexico to empresarios and individual settlers in Texas before 1836 amounted to 26,280,000 acres.[2]

In 1836 after the Battle of San Jacinto, Texas gained its freedom from Mexico. The war had taken its toll of lives and money, and the new Republic of Texas had only $55.68 in its treasury. Land was abundant, however, so the practice of awarding land grants seemed to be the best way to replenish its treasury. Taxes brought in on the land occupied by settlers of the grants would fill the need of the young Republic for revenue. During the ten years of its existence as a separate nation, Texas allotted 41,570,733 acres of land to pay debts, encourage settlement, and finance its operations.[3]

Early German settlers in Texas, such as Friedrich Ernst of Industry, in Austin County, wrote letters to friends and relatives in Germany telling about the free land to be obtained in Texas, the favorable climate, and the freedom from oppression. These letters found their way into the press in Germany with the result that many more Germans came to Texas during the 1830's. However, immigration on a large scale did not occur until after 1842 when the Mainzer Verein, or Society for the Protection of German Immigrants to Texas, was formed.

This "Verein zum Schutze deutscher Einwanderer in Texas," known to Germans in Europe and Texas by its shorter name "Verein," was organized on April 20, 1842 at Biebrich on the Rhine by a group of noblemen whose purpose was to secure land in Texas for Germans and other Europeans who wished to settle there, and to provide for their welfare.

The Verein, or Society, sent Prince Leiningen and Count Boos-Waldeck to Texas in 1842 to buy land. After a brief stay, Prince Leiningen went to Austin "to confer with President Houston about a land grant and concessions for the Society." Leiningen asked that the Society's colonists be exempted from taxation for a number of years, but President Houston could not grant the exemption nor would the Congress of Texas make any change in the colonization law to that effect.[4] Count Boos-Waldeck, in the meantime, searched for land and found a tract in Fayette County. He bought this and named it Nassau Farm in honor of the Duke of Nassau, Protector of the Society. The two men returned to Germany and each made a separate report to the directors. Prince Leiningen reported in favor of large scale colonization, but Count Boos-Waldeck advised against it since large scale colonization would require too large an outlay of money. The Society decided to go ahead with its plans and organized itself into a stock company with a capital of $80,000. A resolution was adopted declaring that its purpose was to protect the immigrant and aid him on his long journey from Germany to Texas and to secure for him a happy home in the land which he had adopted.[5]

The immigrants were promised inexpensive transportation from Germany to Texas and, after landing there, they were to have wagons to transport them to the land to be colonized. A house would be built for them, constructed after the customs of the country. Grain and implements were to be supplied for farming at a price less than that of the nearest market. Furthermore, the religious and educational needs of the settlers were to be taken care of by the Society. With such promises it was not difficult to procure emigrants for the proposed colony.

The first contract made by the Society for land in Texas was for the Bourgeois-Ducos grant. This grant had been secured on July 3, 1842 with the promise to settle four hundred families on the land within eighteen months. The time, therefore, had expired on December 7, 1843, four months before the contract was signed by the Society on April 7, 1844. Bourgeois had assured the directors of the Society that he could secure a renewal of his grant from the Republic of Texas.

Two men were dispatched to Texas to prepare for the arrival of the colonists, Bourgeois d'Orvanne as Colonial Director and Prince Carl of Solms-Braunfels as Commissioner-General. They landed at Galveston on July 1, 1844 and went from this city to Nassau Farm in Fayette County. The first of eleven reports that Prince Solms made to the directors of the Society in Germany was written from this place.[6] These reports are a source of detailed information on the work of the Society and Prince Solms in Texas.

It was not long before Prince Solms learned that the Bourgeois-Ducos contract had expired and could neither be renewed nor extended. "Thus he was temporarily the executive head of a colonization company without an acre of land except the plantation Nassau."[7]

The second contract for land in Texas was made with Henry

Fisher and Burchard Miller for what was to be known as the Fisher-Miller grant. The original application was made by Fisher and Miller on February 8, 1842 for land between the Colorado and Llano Rivers consisting of 3,800,000 acres of land. The application was approved by Sam Houston, at that time President of the Republic of Texas, with the order "Let the contract be made." This application proposed the settlement of one thousand German, Swiss, Norwegian, Swedish, and Danish families on the grant in eighteen months (Plate 8). A renewal of the contract, dated September 1, 1843, specified among eight other provisions:

1. the introduction of six hundred families and single men into Texas;
2. that each family should receive 640 acres and each single man over seventeen years of age should receive 320 acres of land for which each would get full title after having built a house and having kept fifteen acres under cultivation and in good fence;
3. that Fisher and Miller, upon request, could get title from the Republic of Texas for one-half of the land received by families and single men provided they had made such an agreement with the immigrants.[8]

On June 26, 1844 the Society bought an interest in the Fisher-Miller colonization contract with the provision that the Society take the place of Fisher and Miller in the contract and, after reimbursing itself for expenses, pay Fisher and Miller one-third of the profits from the sale of land. It provided also for the appointment of a colonial committee composed of six members, five from the Society with one vote each and Henry Fisher with three votes.

Before an account of the arrival of the first immigrants is given, this may be a fitting place to point out the disadvantages of the selection of the Fisher-Miller grant. In the first place the grant was almost three hundred miles from the coast of Texas. This required the immigrants to make a long tedious journey from the port of arrival. It was also one hundred miles west of Austin and one hundred and fifty miles from San Antonio, the only cities where supplies could be bought. Then, too, the land was not fertile, a fact which any of the members of the Society could have ascertained if an inspection of the lands had been made before the contract was signed. However, the great-

4

est barrier to settlement of the grant was the presence of Comanche Indians on the land. No immigrant could proceed to the land granted him until peace had been made with these Indians.

This, then, was the problem facing Prince Solms when he learned that three ships bearing 392 settlers were on their way to Texas. On November 22, 1844 Prince Solms arrived at Port Lavaca to inspect that area as a possible landing place for the immigrants. During the next several days he searched for a suitable harbor and fresh water. Both of these were found at Indian Point which he renamed Carlshafen, later called Indianola.

Henry Fisher had previously arranged for a small contingent of immigrants who came over on the Brig *Weser*. They arrived at Galveston in July, 1844 but Prince Solms left them there until he could secure another port of disembarkation nearer the center of Texas and the land which he hoped to secure for the first settlement.

Each Verein immigrant had signed an Immigration Contract (Einwanderungs Vertrag)[9] in Germany at the port of embarkation before he boarded the ship on which he would make the journey to Texas. This contract entitled him to 320 acres of land if he was a married man and 160 acres if he was single.

Having signed the Immigration Contract, the immigrant with his family and all his possessions boarded a ship, usually at Bremen or Antwerp, for the journey to Texas. There he felt sure that he would find freedom and a better life. Altogether about sixty ships from Europe brought more than 7000 immigrants to Texas during the years 1844, 1845, 1846, and part of 1847.[10]

The voyage over the Atlantic Ocean from Bremen or Antwerp to Galveston was long, usually requiring from two to three months. Enough water and food had to be taken aboard the vessels to supply the needs of the passengers for this length of time. Since these were sailing vessels, usually three-masted schooners, a storm or calm seas could cause a delay in the voyage. This often brought about a shortage of food and water or these became spoiled and scarcely fit for human consumption.

One vessel sailed from Antwerp on November 25, 1845 with 130 immigrants for Texas. This ship, the *Nahant*, was wrecked by a severe storm on the English coast. Its tragic story was told in a document preserved in the Verein Collection in the Archives of the University of Texas:

5

As many as 90 ships put into Torbay up to Tuesday owing to bad weather. Among the number was the *Nahant* of Boston, about 400 tons, from Ghent bound to Texas, having about 130 emigrants aboard, inclusive of 50 children.

The gale increased till about 2 A.M. with snow storms when the *Nahant* was driven on the rocks. - - - - - - The night was one of the most awful that can be imagined. The wind was howling and the waves roaring and lashing on the shores whilst shrieks of the poor creatures, with their helpless children, were heard imploring aid, the vessel rocking to and fro, her sides having been forced in and the hold filled with water.

The news of the vessel being on the rocks having reached the town, hundreds of persons crowded to the scene of distress and under the superintendence of Mr. Hingston, agent of Lloyd's, the vessel was boarded. Large baskets were slung on ropes which were fastened to the shore, and the passengers one by one were put in and safely landed.

As soon as the women and children were safe, the poor emigrants began to take out their goods. In a short time the spot was covered and they were given in charge of the coast guard. - - - - - - - - -

The Revds. Monsg. Hagg and Yarrington commenced making a subscription for them. It appears that seven men, besides the Master Mate and steward, were aboard to work the vessel, not more than one fourth the proper number.[11]

According to a list of passengers on board the *Timoleon*, another Verein ship,[12] many of those who were on the *Nahant* continued their voyage to Texas on this vessel. The *Timoleon* had left Antwerp on November 29, 1845, just four days after the *Nahant* had sailed.

The voyage of the large vessels ended at Galveston. Here a large ship, the *Karl Wilhelm*, was wrecked with a loss of one or two lives, according to a letter written by Victor Bracht in July, 1846.

In Galveston, as the immigrant left the large vessel to board a smaller one to go to Indianola, he and the members of his family, if any, were listed by D. H. Klaener, agent for the German Emigration Company, as settlers

who arrived here on the Brig _____, from Bremen [or Antwerp] for the German Emigration Company and who are hereby entered at the State Department of Texas as settlers on the Grant ceded to Messrs. Hry F. Fisher and Bd. Miller under the date Washington, Octbr 4, 1843, transferred to said company as per Contract of 24th of June, 1844, 9th Congress of 29 Janry, 1845.[13]

At Carlshafen or Indianola, the immigrant was probably greeted by many other people from his native land. This smaller port was often congested with those who were awaiting transportation inland. Indianola was 152 miles from New Braunfels, the destination of most of the immigrants. After a rest of a few days, the immigrant proceeded on his journey over roads which were only tracks left by wagons and horses that had passed the same route. Rivers and streams had to be forded and these were often at flood stage. At these times the trip had to be halted until ferries or rafts were built. In selecting a location for a camp several things had to be considered. For meals, water for cooking and wood for a fire were needed. The animals required good green grass if this could be found. For protection against an Indian attack, Prince Solms organized a company of twenty men. The immigrants traveled in a group or caravan of ten to twelve wagons headed by a leader who was chosen from the immigrants or they were led by an officer of the Society.

Prince Solms realized that it would be impossible to make the journey in one trip; therefore, he arranged for way stations along the route. The voyagers had encampments or "halting places" at Agua Dulce, Victoria, McCoy's Creek, Gonzales, and Seguin on the way to New Braunfels.[14]

In December 1844 Prince Solms learned that the Society's ships, the *Johann Dethardt*, the *Ferdinand*, and the *Hershel* had brought 292 immigrants. Among these were a physician, surveyor, engineer, carpenters, masons, millers, bakers, mechanics, and soldiers. Prince Solms hastened to meet them, as he wrote in his sixth report, dated 23rd December, 1844, in camp at Port Lavaca.[15]

The arrival of these immigrants made it imperative that a permanent place be selected as the first settlement for the colonists of the Society. Prince Solms considered several locations; but after an old settler, Johann Rahm, told him about a beautiful place about thirty miles from San Antonio known as "Las Fontanas," "the fountains" or springs, he decided that this would be the first settlement of the Society. Assisted by Dr. Ferdinand Lindheimer, Prince Solms purchased from Juan Veramendi and Rafael Garza a tract of land for the sum of $1,111. This land was situated on the banks of the beautiful Comal River, a clear stream fed by seven springs, and the banks of the Guadalupe River into which the Comal River flowed. It was a perfect location. Fresh clear water was abundant, wood for houses was available nearby, and the climate was mild. This ideal place was provided for the immigrants by Prince Solms while they were on the journey from Carlshafen. Brought by stages, these immigrants arrived at their first home in the new land. Encamped overnight on the east bank of the Guadalupe River, they crossed the river on the morning of Friday, March 21, 1845, led by Prince Solms. He then named the place New Braunfels after Braunfels, Germany, the ancestral home of the Solms family.

Each settler was immediately given a town lot and a ten acre tract, but this did not invalidate his right to the land which would be allotted to him when the Fisher-Miller grant could be surveyed. The settlers began at once to plant corn and potatoes on their farm land and to build their homes. Before the end of 1845 there were one hundred and fifty houses in New Braunfels. For protection against the Indians, a stockade was built on a bluff on the east bank of the Comal Creek. Later a fort was constructed which was called "Sophienburg" in honor of Princess Sophie, the fiancée of Prince Solms.

Less than two months after the founding of New Braunfels, Prince Solms returned to Germany. In his eleventh report to the directors of the Society in Germany, he wrote, "It is a cheerful sight to see this beauty spot of nature developing and the land becoming inhabited."[16]

Eleven reports were sent by Prince Solms to the directors of the Society in Germany during the ten months which he spent in Texas. A twelfth and final report was given to them in Wiesbaden after he returned to Germany in 1845. In this, Prince Solms summarized the entire colonization project in Texas from the time of his arrival until his departure:

Report made to the General Assembly held
at Wiesbaden on 28 July, 1845[17]

In May, 1844, the directors [of the Verein] requested that I go to Texas to establish the first settlement of the Verein. Although I felt flattered by the trust that was placed in me, I could not conceal from myself the difficulties to be met, difficulties which from my [later] personal experiences were even more serious than I had anticipated. From my many reports to the directors, the important details of the whole undertaking and the progress that is being made are well known. I will, therefore, give only a resumé of the whole undertaking.

Accompanied by Mr. Bourgeois d'Orvanne, I left Liverpool on May 19 [1844] and arrived in Boston on May 31.

8

Because of previous instructions I was able to continue my journey at the earliest possible date so that I arrived at Galveston on July 1. From here I immediately departed for Washington-on-the-Brazos, the seat of the [Texas] government where I had several satisfactory conferences with the then Secretary of State, Dr. Anson Jones.

From there I next went to Nassau Plantation [in Fayette County] from where, at that time and also later, I sent particular reports to the directors.

On July 16 I started from there on my trip to western Texas and specifically to San Antonio de Bexar. I am reminded that it was at this time the Verein became aware of the untrustworthiness of Mr. Bourgeois d'Orvanne; namely, that he had no land. It, therefore, became my next concern to acquire some land. In this search for land I intended to become more familiar with the grant of Mr. Bourgeois d'Orvanne so that I might know whether or not to ask for a renewal of this grant at the next session of Congress.

I devoted the months of July and August to looking at various areas of land, paying particular attention to the land, the soil, the climate, and the general surroundings. Indeed, I made it a point to pay particular attention to the latter.

On the 23rd of August, Mr. von Wrede arrived with dispatches for me from the directors. After terminating our affairs with Mr. Bourgeois d'Orvanne and though not in the best of health, I left for Nassau Plantation on the 27th, as instructed, to await there the arrival of Mr. Fischer.

On account of the protracted delay of his arrival, I decided to meet him in Galveston. Previously I had made a visit to Washington-on-the-Brazos where I had a conference with Dr. Anson Jones regarding the recent changes in our organization.

Finally on the 20th of October, the long awaited Mr. Fischer arrived, seemingly in no hurry. He needlessly spent several days in Houston. He let us wait nine days for him in Nassau where I had returned.

Finally on November 16th, I could start on the trip to Port Lavaca where I arrived on the 22nd. I made an inspection of the coast along the Bay and selected Indian Point as the place of debarkation. Here I made a plan for Carlshafen. I then boarded the schooner *Com Jack* on which I had spent eight days inspecting the various bays, and sailed for Galveston to welcome the emigrants.

Arriving there after severe storms, I found that the emigrants of the first ship had already left and had probably sailed past us during the night. However, twenty-two hours after my arrival, I was on board the *Alert* which, after repeated heavy storms, returned me to Lavaca. There I found that very few of the emigrants had landed. I welcomed them in the name of the Verein. Finally all the

9

emigrants arrived in Carlshafen and I assembled them in an encampment on the Agua Dulce on January 3 [1845].

In vain I had waited up to now for the means of transportation which Mr. Fischer had been instructed to supply. He had been provided with funds; and on the part of the directors in Germany, they had attempted to provide for all contingencies except this which could not have been foreseen; namely, that Mr. Fischer was lax in carrying out his responsibilities. As soon as I saw that Mr. Fischer had adopted American habits, I no longer depended on him but sought for advice wherever I could. This made it necessary for me to undertake another trip to Galveston, hoping at the same time to attend to necessary matters with the Congress. However, Mr. Fischer had already upset matters there to such an extent that, for the time being, nothing more was to be accomplished.

As soon as possible, I returned to the encampment and sent the emigrants in several groups to the encampment near Victoria and further on at McCoy's Creek. From here they were to go directly to the place of destination.

I myself rode ahead to San Antonio to conclude the purchase of the land at Comal Springs. I took along a few companions to reconnoiter the area, and if necessary to clear it of Indians.

I deliberately kept to myself my earlier suspicions and later definite reports of Mr. Fischer's intrigues and his behavior in the encampment where he sought to create resentment against me. Although all this was painful to me personally, yet I felt that he could not shatter the inborn trust of a German toward a German prince who was with them in a far away, strange, and wild land which was in the dizzy throes of new-found liberties.

On March 21st the first group of emigrants crossed the Guadalupe [River], followed by the wagons. After this the town was laid out, houses were built around the public square, gardens were planted, and fields were plowed.

On April 9th I started on the defenses of the fort, and on the 28th we dedicated it with the thunder of cannon. I named it Sophienburg and named the town New Braunfels. Local authorities were installed who assumed the duties of administering the town's affairs.

Until May 15 I awaited the arrival of my successor, Baron von Meusebach. On this day, however, I began my return journey, stopping in Gonzales where I expected the Baron to pass. After two days he finally arrived and accompanied me as far as Galveston from where I sailed for New Orleans on June 4th.

In the meantime I gave my successor both verbal and written accounts of all events and detailed information on things he needed to know, and especially on matters that had to be taken care of in the future.

Signed on the original   Carl Prince zu Solms

The directors of the Society had appointed Baron Ottfried Hans von Meusebach[18] as successor to Prince Solms, and he was still on his way to Texas when Prince Solms announced the date for his departure to be the 15th of May, 1845.

Late in May, Baron Meusebach arrived at New Braunfels after a long journey from New Orleans. The first situation that greeted him was a very unsatisfactory condition in the financial records of the Society. This was caused by the fact that "the commissioner-general [Solms], the treasurer, the doctor, and the engineer all had contracted debts in the name of the Society without making any record of them. They had signed promissory notes and had issued certificates of credit."[19] The books showed a debt of $20,000 and the creditors besieged Meusebach for the money owed them.

Anyone with less fortitude than John O. Meusebach, as he became known in Texas, would have returned to Europe immediately. The situation might even have been called dangerous since threats were made on his life. However, without delay Meusebach requested the treasurer to furnish him with a financial statement but he was told that this was impossible. Meusebach then "went to work on the books himself and in due time had them in respectable order. With order in the books and financial affairs of the company and by judicious business methods, he soon restored the confidence of the creditors."[20]

Another and a more serious situation faced Meusebach when he learned that several thousand immigrants were due to arrive at Carlshafen in November 1845. Knowing that such a large number could not be settled in New Braunfels, he decided to establish another way station on the road to the Fisher-Miller grant. Meusebach found a suitable place about eighty miles northwest of New Braunfels on the Pedernales River. According to Don Biggers, author of *German Pioneers in Texas,* "He is said to have been the first white man to visit that particular section of the Llano and Pedernales rivers country. At a considerable distance from the Fisher & Miller grant he selected a 10,000 acre tract. It was good land, well watered and with ample timber to supply the needs of the colonists."[21] The tract was surveyed and town lots made ready for the settlers. This new town was named Fredericksburg in honor of Prince Frederick of Prussia, a member of the Society.

Upon his return to New Braunfels Meusebach learned that four thousand immigrants would soon arrive at Galveston and that a credit of $24,000 had been provided for him in a New

Orleans bank. This amount probably seemed ample to the directors of the Society in Germany, but it was far from sufficient to transport four thousand immigrants over one hundred and fifty miles from the coast to New Braunfels, sustain them through the winter, build even the simplest log cabins, and provide them with food until they could raise a crop. The sum of six dollars per person was supposed to provide all of these things!

Between October 1845 and April 1846, thirty-six ships brought a total of 5,257 immigrants to Texas under the auspices of the Society. Meusebach secured the services of a Houston transporting company to move the immigrants from the coast to New Braunfels; but again he was faced with another very serious situation. Just as the work was started and after the first one hundred wagons had left Carlshafen, war broke out between the United States and Mexico in May 1846. The United States offered a much higher price to the private teamsters than Meusebach was paying with the result that the teamsters deserted Meusebach to work for the United States Army. Over four thousand immigrants were left at Carlshafen in tents or whatever shelter they could find to protect them from the sun and rain of the Texas spring and summer of 1846. Disease broke out among the immigrants already weakened by the long ocean voyage. It is estimated that four hundred died in Carlshafen or on the journey to New Braunfels. Many preferred to start the trip inland on foot rather than wait any longer in Carlshafen.

In their despair many men left their families to join the United States Army and go to Mexico.[22] Moritz Tiling in his book *The German Element in Texas* estimates that five hundred enlisted in the American Army, and more than two hundred perished on the way to New Braunfels from hunger, exposure, disease, and exhaustion.[23] Those who arrived at New Braunfels and the newly established town of Fredericksburg carried with them the germs of malaria, bilious fever, dysentery, and other diseases. A terrible epidemic broke out in every place traversed by or lived in by the immigrants; and over five hundred deaths were recorded in the summer of 1846.[24] It would be impossible to estimate the number of other deaths along the road or in remote places since many were buried on farms. In many instances every member of a family died. Many widows and orphans were left to be cared for by other settlers.

In New Braunfels Pastor Ervendberg sought to provide a

12

place for children made homeless by the epidemic and built the Waisenfarm or orphanage. A long shed was built on the banks of the Comal River for the many sick persons who came from Carlshafen and for those who had no one else to care for them in New Braunfels. Dr. Koester visited the sick daily but the disease claimed the lives of two or three each day in New Braunfels alone during the summer of 1846.

Dr. Ferdinand Roemer in his book *Texas*, based on his stay in Texas from December 1845 to April 1847, wrote, "It is certain that in the few summer months of the year 1846 more than one thousand out of the four thousand German immigrants, who had come to Texas in the fall of 1845 under the protection of the Mainzer Verein, died and not more than one thousand two hundred actually settled upon the land secured by the Verein."[25]

Due to the foresight of John O. Meusebach, many immigrants had left New Braunfels before the epidemic became severe. On April 23, 1846 the first immigrant wagon train left New Braunfels for the new settlement of Fredericksburg on the Pedernales River. There were about one hundred men, women and children in this group. After a trip lasting sixteen days, the settlers reached their new home. The date was May 8, 1846. The first task undertaken was the awarding of town lots to heads of families and single men. "Later these first arrivals received also an outlying ten-acre lot. The settlers who came later received only a ten-acre lot. By 1848 about 600 settlers had received ten-acre lots."[26] Cultivation of fields was started at once to assure a harvest before winter. Store houses were built before homes so that the supplies would be protected. One month after the first settlers arrived, a second wagon train brought many others.

Life was not pleasant in Fredericksburg during the first few months. The diseases that were brought from the coast claimed many lives during the summer and fall of 1846. In the epidemic of cholera in 1849, the Indians showed themselves to be real friends. They brought honey, meat, and bear fat to the colonists.

On March 1, 1847 John O. Meusebach once more performed a deed which helped the settlers very much. A few weeks before, accompanied by forty-five men, he had ventured into the lands of the Fisher-Miller grant in an attempt to make peace with the Comanche Indians. Wherever he was met by bands of Indians, he told them that his people had nothing but friendly feelings in coming to the land of the Comanche. A meeting of twenty Comanche chiefs was arranged for March 1, and the result was peace between the white man and the red man.[27] According to Dr. R. L. Biesele, foremost authority on the German immigration to Texas, "Meusebach's treaty with the Comanches in March, 1847 must ever be regarded as an achievement of incalculable value not alone for the Society but for the state of Texas as well."[28]

When peace with the Comanche Indians seemed assured, Meusebach resigned as commissioner-general of the Society in Texas, and Hermann Spiess was named as his successor. In the opinion of Dr. R. L. Biesele, "Meusebach had served the Society well and had done much for the welfare of the German settlers in West Texas. He had helped the settlements through many trying moments. It is probably not too much to say that his work in straightening out the Society's finances in Texas in 1845 and 1846 actually prevented the abandonment of the settlement of New Braunfels and made possible the founding of Fredericksburg and the continuance of the Society's colonization work."[29]

Peace with the Indians allowed the lands of the Fisher-Miller grant to be colonized. The Society founded five settlements on the grant: Castell, Leiningen, Schoenburg, Meerholz, and Bettina, but of these five Castell is the only town that has survived. A Latin settlement was started at Sisterdale, so named because the houses were built where the Sister Creek flowed into the Guadalupe River, fifty miles north of San Antonio. Here Nicolaus Zink, surveyor for the Society, built the first cabin in 1847. He was joined in 1848 by noblemen from Germany: Ottomar von Behr, Baron Westphal, Louis von Donop, and Louis von Breitenbach. Learned men also came to join this group: Professor Ernst Kapp, Edward Degener, Dr. Adolf Douai, Dr. W. I. Runge, Fritz Kraemer, August Siemering, and four members of the Dresel family. As a "Latin settlement" it lasted only two years, but it remains today a beautiful little village in the hill country north of San Antonio.

Other towns established later within the bounds of the Fisher-Miller grant, to name only a few of the larger ones, are: Mason, Boerne, Comfort, Llano, Brady, San Saba, and Paint Rock, where today Indian pictographs may still be seen. In these towns there are many descendants of the German immigrants who settled there in the 1840's. Ten counties were carved out of the 3,800,000 acres of the Fisher-Miller grant:

14

Llano, San Saba, McCulloch, Mason, Menard, Kimble Concho, Sutton, Tom Green and Schleicher.

By 1847 the Mainzer Verein or Society for the Protection of German Immigrants to Texas, was bankrupt. Several reasons may be given for its failure:

1. The land or grant selected by the Society was too far from the coast, a fact not taken into consideration by the noblemen in Europe who knew nothing about the transportation of thousands of immigrants over a distance of two hundred miles or more.

2. The grant was inhabited by Comanche Indians. Until peace was made with them, no land could be colonized. It was more than two years after the first group of immigrants arrived before they could proceed to the grant.

3. The War with Mexico in 1846, which caused a critical shortage in transportation at a time when thousands of immigrants were awaiting transportation from Carlshafen to New Braunfels.

4. The lack of sufficient funds for a project the size of the one planned. The original sum of $80,000 was far too small.

Without a doubt, the last named reason was the greatest cause of the failure of this project, so large in scope and so ill-planned. Tiling, in his book *The German Element in Texas*, states that "the surveying of the tract alone cost the Adelsverein about $80,000, in other words, the full amount for which it was capitalized."[30] Meager sums were sent for transportation and important needs of the settlers, but these were far too little to cover the additional costs of building houses, supplying implements and grain for farming, and animals for work on a farm. The whole venture was greatly under-financed for the magnitude of its original plan and promises.

The colonists, after the bankruptcy of the Society, were left to their own resources. Many were without finances and were even in debt. About all that the settlers of New Braunfels and Fredericksburg received from the Society was a town lot and a ten acre tract of land. Only a small percent had received transportation to New Braunfels and Fredericksburg. Without finances and in great need of money, most of the colonists "sold their certificates [land] for mere trifles, some certificates covering a section of land being sold for less than ten dollars each. Just a few held their certificates, located their land and became wealthy as a result."[31]

Victor Bracht, in his book *Texas in 1848*, reported in the fall of 1846, "New Braunfels has grown very much. It has two hundred and fifty houses and fifteen hundred permanent inhabitants, although at present there are three thousand persons here. Several beautiful houses are in the process of construction and a few are finished. Court meets regularly, and everything is running its regular course."[32] Concerning relations with the Indians, he wrote in August, 1847, "Santa Anna, the war chief of the Comanches, spent three days here with a number of his followers to have a good time. . . . He assured us that friendship for the Germans, which he esteemed very highly, should continue in the future as it has in the past."[33]

The Society, following its bankruptcy in 1847, no longer sent immigrants to Texas. Commissioner Spiess conducted its business in Texas under the title of the German Emigration Company. In 1852 Commissioner Spiess was succeeded by surveyor Ludwig Bene, the last representative of the Society for the Protection of German Immigrants to Texas. In September 1853 the company assigned all its properties and colonization rights to its Texas creditors.[34] A total of 7380 immigrants had come to Texas during the years 1844 through 1847, and the Republic of Texas granted 1,735,200 acres of land to these settlers.[35] Thus ended one of the greatest colonization projects in Texas history. The influx of Germans did not cease, however; they continued to come in large numbers, with the result that a great percentage of the population particularly of West Texas, is of German descent.

Now that the groundwork of colonization had been so heroically accomplished, it is interesting to contemplate the significance of it. What was the result of this mass immigration of Germans, and what was their mode of life in this new land?

Left to their own resources, there was no turning back. Each day brought new problems and the need to solve them. By accomplishing this, strong and determined characters were built. Industriousness and perseverance fulfilled the desire to build a new life in the beautiful hills to which they had come.

The necessities of life were supplied mostly by home gardens, hogs, and cattle. Those who had more land learned how to get more out of it; they produced plenteous crops of cotton, corn, wheat, and even tobacco. General merchandise stores carried practically all the necessities of life, from guns to ginghams.

Those who had skills used them to make a livelihood. Blacksmiths made tools and plow shares; often these men were also wheelrights and made wagons. Local leather tanneries came into existence and harness and saddle making became an important industry.

The difficulties of transportation from the port to the settlements had forced some to abandon good furniture and other household and farm equipment which they had brought from Europe. Some, of course, had come without any. Homemade furniture was first crudely made from cedar and oak which were in plentiful supply. Chairs were fitted with cowhide for seats. Homemade spinning wheels were used to spin cotton and wool yarn for clothing.

Those with special skills in wood working built simple foot-powered wood-turning lathes, and furniture making became another industry. Clay was found which was suitable for making sun-dried brick. Log houses were replaced by houses with frame work braced with timbers and filled in with mortar and brick. This type of construction, called "Fachwerk" was widely used in the homes of the early settlers.

The trek westward to the Fisher-Miller grant continued. Those who first established homes on their land were helpful to the ones that followed. This comradeship created small villages as more and more colonists sought homes on the land granted to them.

The need for education in these villages was met by highly educated men who helped to establish schools and became teachers. The first school was started by Hermann Seele in New Braunfels on August 11, 1845, just four months after the immigrants arrived.

Churches were begun almost immediately after the settlers came into a new location. Today the churches which have survived contain the best records of births, deaths, and marriages among the early settlers.

Agricultural societies were formed both for comradeship and for the purpose of assisting each other with the work in the fields. For relaxation and fellowship social clubs were created, such as the German Union for Texas in Houston.

The organization of singing societies such as the Germania and Liedertafel in New Braunfels filled a very important place in the lives of the people. Moritz Tiling, in his book *The German Element in Texas*, observed, "The German immigrants who came to Texas in great numbers from 1845 to 1850 brought along an invisible passenger 'Das deutsche Lied' (the German Song). It accompanied them westward on their weary march across the

broad prairies where many prospective settlers fell by the wayside from exposure and exhaustion, and established itself with
the sturdy pioneers on the beautiful banks of the Comal and
Pedernales, to cheer them in their daily toil and brighten their
evenings by the fireside."[36]

Several newspapers were established to bring the settlers
into communication with the world which they had left and to
acquaint them with their new land. Among these were the *San
Antonio Zeitung*, the *Freie Press für Texas*, the *New Braunfels
Zeitung* and *Texas Vorwaerts*. Writers of books of that period
include Victor Bracht, one of the immigrants from Dusseldorf,
who wrote about *Texas in 1848* using his own knowledge of life
in Texas at that time. Prince Karl of Solms-Braunfels gave
advice to immigrants in his book *Texas, 1844-1845*. Baron Meusebach told of his part in the Verein movement in a booklet titled
Answer to Interrogatories. Dr. Ferdinand Roemer who accompanied Meusebach on his trip into the Indian Territory wrote
about the geology of Texas in his book *Texas*.

Painters like Carl von Iwonski left permanent pictures of
early New Braunfels and other scenes in Texas. Doctors, such
as Dr. Wilhelm Remer and Dr. Theodore Koester, served their
communities in time of illness. Surveyors included in the list of
essential men were Nicolaus Zink, Carl Pressler, and Ludwig
Bene. Hermann Seele, Edward Degener, and others were prom-
inent in governmental service.

Many served the cause of the Confederacy when Texas decided to cast its lot with the Southern states. Although the Germans did not believe in slavery, they chose to support their
newly adopted state. Many units were organized in the German
communities which saw action on such battlefields as Gettys-
burg and Vicksburg. After the Civil War these men returned
and filled useful places in their home towns.

In the lands of the Fisher-Miller grant there is ample evidence of the success achieved by these Germans in the large
sheep and cattle ranches that were developed. Riding through
the beautiful hills and valleys, one can see on ranch gates such
names as Pehl, Preiss, Hopf, Rode, and Kothmann.

The immigrants brought to Texas by the Society developed
an allegiance to their new home. Within a few years most of
them had applied for or received their naturalization papers
which made them American citizens.

For Texas, most of them could say with Victor Bracht, "I
hope that I shall not be criticized too severely for often think-

18

ing and speaking like every other ardent Texan of his splendid
country.

'All for Texas and Texas forever'."[37]

NOTES

[1]Jerry Sadler, **History of Texas Land**, p. 6.
[2]**Handbook of Texas**, Vol. 2, p. 20.
[3]Jerry Sadler, **History of Texas Land**, p. 8.
[4]R. L. Biesele, **History of German Settlements in Texas, 1831-1861**, p. 67.
[5]**Ibid.**, pp. 83-86.
[6]Solms-Braunfels, Prince Carl of, **First Report**.
[7]Moritz Tiling, **German Element in Texas**, p. 74.
[8]Biesele, **History of**, p. 80.
[9]German Immigration Contract, Appendix I.
[10]John O. Meusebach, **Answer to Interrogatories**, p. 16.
[11]The wreck of the **Nahant**—from a document in the Verein Collection, University of Texas Archives.
[12]Ship lists, Appendix III.
[13]**Ibid.**
[14]Solms, Prince Carl of, **Texas, 1844-1845**, pp. 80, 81.
[15]Solms, Prince, Sixth Report, p. 45.
[16]Solms, Prince, Eleventh Report, p. 68.
[17]Solms, Prince, Wiesbaden report in Wied Collection, Unviersity of Texas Archives.
[18]Biesele, **History of**, p. 123, note 31, for biography of Meusebach.
[19]**Ibid.**, p. 123.
[20]Don Biggers, **German Pioneers in Texas**, p. 30.
[21]**Ibid.**, p. 30.
[22]Biesele, **History of**, p. 194, note, for list of those who enlisted in Capt. Buechel's company.
[23]Tiling, **German Element**, p. 87.
[24]Tiling, p. 87 estimates the number at more than 1,000 but this is higher than that of Pastor Ervendberg and others.
[25]Ferdinand Roemer, **Texas**, pp. 22, 23.
[26]**Pioneers in God's Hills**, p. XVII.
[27]Tiling, **German Element**, pp. 95-104 gives a complete account of this peace mission to the Comanche Indians.
[28]Biesele, **History of**, p. 146.
[29]**Ibid.**, pp. 145-146.
[30]Tiling, **German Element**, p. 70.
[31]Biggers, **German Pioneers**, 37.
[32]Victor Bracht, **Texas in 1848**, pp. 174-175.
[33]**Ibid.**, p. 195.
[34]Tiling, **German Element**, pp. 112-113.
[35]Sadler, **History of Texas Land**, p. 11.
[36]Tiling, **German Element**, p. 136.
[37]Bracht, **Texas in 1848**, p. 222.

19

Information on
Prince Karl of Solms-Braunfels and the
Eleven Reports written by him to the Directors of the
Adelsverein on the German colonization in Texas, 1844-1847

Prince Karl of Solms-Braunfels, born in 1812, was a descendant of a family of German nobility at Braunfels, Germany. References to this family exist as far back as 946 A.D.

In 1844, at the age of 32, he was chosen by the committee of directors of the Adelsverein as Commissioner-General for the proposed colonial establishment in Texas. Accompanied by Bourgeois d'Orvanne, as Colonial Director, he journeyed to Texas and landed at Galveston on July 1, 1844.

Immediately, he began work on the Verein's project which was to settle several thousand immigrants on a grant of land in Texas. In the process of making arrangements for the prospective colonists, he wrote letters or reports, to the directors in Germany. The eleven reports which he wrote constitute an excellent account of his activities from the time he wrote the first report on July 15, 1844 until the eleventh or last report written on April 30, 1845 at the newly-established town of New Braunfels.

On May 15, 1845, Prince Solms returned to Germany to take a needed rest and to make an oral report to the directors on the progress of the immigration. Prince Solms did not return to Texas; he died in 1875 without seeing again the town he established and named for his family.

The eleven reports of Prince Solms were published in German in the *Neu-Braunfelser Zeitung Jahrbuch* (Yearbook) *für 1916* and in the *100th Anniversary Edition of the New Braunfels Zeitung*. Ten of the reports were translated into English by Oscar Haas, historian of New Braunfels and Comal County. The eighth report was translated by Chester W. Geue of Fort Worth, Texas. In the translation, an endeavor was made to retain as near as possible the structure and descriptive language of the original.

Prince Solms's 1st report dated 15th of July, 1844
at Nassau [Plantation], Texas

I have read the reports of the Colonial Director[1] and am in accord with their entire contents and wording, and can endorse the report. However, based on my own observations, there are certain matters regarding the Plantation[2] and the important work of colonization that were not reported on in sufficient detail, and I feel it my duty to call these to the attention of the directors' committee.[3]

First, with reference to the Nassau Plantation, I agree with the prevailing opinion here that this project which an individual farmer could have established with less money than was actually spent, is not a credit to the Verein.[4] It is very evident from observing the entire operation of the Plantation that the owner must diligently supervise the overseer and laborers. Furthermore, it is important for the success of such a project as this that whoever undertakes it should have a clear conception about farming in this country; at least, he would be wise to follow the experience of local farmers owning similar land, instead of experimenting.

I feel it my duty to the Verein to be frank in my discussion of these matters. I do so without any prejudice or desire to cast reflection on Count Boos[5] whom we all know and esteem as a nobleman and a man of honor. The man employed by him as an overseer became a drunkard. Without any justification he mistreated the negroes of the Plantation so horribly that three ran away. One has been returned and is now working under overseer Denman; he is now a model for other workers. When I arrived, I found this negro sick as a result of overexertion at work, his way of showing appreciation to the overseer for the kind words spoken to him. The other two negroes were shot and killed while attempting a robbery at a settlement near San Antonio. Therewith an investment was lost.

Count Boos appointed Mr. Fortrand[6] as a supervisor of the Plantation at a salary of $250. A comparison of the inventory which the Colonial Director included in his report with the one in the Verein's purchase records will show the overall condition of the inventory.

The manor house is constructed of rough logs, and has windows, but the space between the logs has not been filled in, so that the wind blows through freely and the rain splashes in. As a whole the league is of excellent land and the location of the manor, on a slight hill top, is well chosen. The manor still lacks for its completion the filling in of the space between the logs, a small matter, and a well by the house, a matter of great importance.

As a result of heavy drinking, Overseer Bryan[7] who was appointed by Count Boos became so ill that he had to give up his work on the first of June. This improved conditions on the Plantation since he had brought about endless harm to the undertaking. The cotton which he had planted too deep did not come up so that Denman had to plant a second time in June. Through this loss in time, less than 20 bales can be anticipated this year. The corn crop will be just about sufficient for the negroes with enough seed corn left for planting.

The overseer has asked for more money, as much as double his present salary, which I am not authorized to grant him. In a postscript later I will report on my temporary agreements with him, and I beg for the directors' opinion in the matter.

After I had convinced myself that Mr. Fortrand had faithfully carried out his duties for the best interests of the community, I left matters in his hands temporarily until the arrival of the doctor appointed for Nassau [Plantation]. Mr. Fortrand is the inspector and, as such, he has received full authority from me. He will, upon the arrival of the newcomer, aid him with advice and assistance. The doctor should be provided with the necessary proof of identity and is to be directed to Mr. Fortrand. I have made all arrangements with Mr. Fortrand in this connection.

Wilhelm Etzel,[8] whose contract expires July 1st as manager of the project, has agreed to stay on at the monthly salary of 10 T per Courant[9] as arranged by Count Boos until the arrival of the doctor who has been assigned to Nassau [Plantation]. I have given him the choice of coming to San Antonio after this where, instead of the 50 acres promised him by Count Boos, I would promise him 100 acres because I would like to keep the league [Nassau] intact for sale. He, however, insists on having the 50 acres promised him in the league wherefore I told him that I would have to refer this matter to the directors since I had no authority to give away any land out of the league. This I am doing herewith, and I beg to receive your directions regarding this matter. I personally agree with the Colonial Director's recommendation that this land should not be split up in parcels and sold. (The inventory and costs are enclosed for this reason.)

22

It is impossible to make trips from the west to this place since the distance is great, from 130 to 140 miles. Most of the way is uninhabited and is frequented by Indians and marauders.

And now, finally, to come to the more pleasant and important subject of colonization, on which I can give the directors more pleasant news. Referring again to the Colonial Director's report, it is my pleasant duty to acquaint the Association[10] with the sentiments expressed on all sides to its envoy. On my way to Washington [on-the-Brazos],[11] and in this place, a number of gentlemen sought an introduction, many of them influential in government and Congress. All were pleased with my arrival in this country which they considered to be an indication of considerable German immigration. All who will love their land are welcome and are especially welcome when they come under the auspices of an association such as ours.

The Colonial Director has already reported on our conferences and correspondence with the Secretary of State,[12] Dr. Anson Jones, and I can again but confirm that he [the Secretary] expressed the opinion that by making a personal appearance at the time of the next Congress, we could get anything for which we asked. In the meantime we shall begin our operations near San Antonio.

Unfortunately I have not been able to make the acquaintance of the President.[13] He is at the Trinity River and is not well, and our preparations for the colony cannot suffer any delay at this time.

I have been visited by a number of Germans who settled in Texas. All come with the request to be received into the colony. To all of these I explained the Association's plan, and I told them that I was authorized to give free land only to those settlers coming directly from Germany. However, I also told them that I no doubt could give them good land at a low price with the assurance that they would also have the same privileges as those who came directly from Germany, in the churches, schools, hospitals, etc., that were to be established by the colony.

All unanimously acknowledged the fair and fine purpose of the Association: to fill the long felt need of retaining German character and customs through the church and language. During my visit in Industry, Mr. Ernst[14] proposed this toast, "To the health of the noble and generous German princes who think of the well being of their subjects on the other side of the ocean." Many are happy that through community interests they will be able to have closer ties with the Fatherland.

I will devote my greatest efforts at the next session of Congress[15] to obtain trade advantages which will permit the Association to help the farmer, give German industries a new market, and expand the German maritime industry.

With further reference to the Colonial Director's report, I wish to comment on the appointment of Dr. Meyer[16] who will accompany me to render necessary medical advice in preparation for the colony. I am convinced that he will be of great assistance to the Association in as much as he has lived many years in a hot climate and is therefore familiar with the ailments peculiar to such conditions and the treatment required for these. He will also be able to be an experienced consultant to the doctor to be sent to the colony from Europe.

Before closing my report, I must urgently request the directors to send me fire arms so that I may be in a position to impress the Indians (with whom, however, I expect to have good relations) as well as marauders and other rabble. I would suggest that those members of the Association who have weapons in their arsenals which are no longer suitable for European service, donate these to their emigrating subjects. Since every man here will be on horseback, the most practical weapons would be the short carbine rifle and side arms. Leather straps, leather, also cartridges, or at least gunpowder to make these are also necessary. If another pair of cannon, of the same caliber as the ones I gave to the Association, and a light howitzer could be sent along, it would be a very desirable addition.

Finally, I call attention to the overseer who has agreed to continue the management of the Plantation until the first of December of this year, at a salary of $25 per month. He would make no agreements beyond that. I did not feel that I had the authority to immediately offer him $500 [annually].

I believe that under supervision of the future resident doctor at Nassau it will not be necessary to have a man of as high caliber as Denman[17] to supervise the negroes and their work. However, Denman appears to be an extraordinarily well qualified individual who could well manage a larger farm than ours, and therefore could command a salary of 500 to 600 piaster [Spanish dollars].

Tomorrow I continue my journey to San Antonio and hope that in spite of all the terrible stories about the Indians and marauders, I get there safely. I trust to God's protection for our worthy cause, and upon the advice of our small group.

24

The directors' committee will receive my next report from San Antonio de Bexar.

Nassau   (Signed)   Commissioner General
15th of June,* [July] 1844   Karl Prince zu Solms
*June is in error in the German copy since Solms did not arrive in Texas until July 1, 1844.

Prince Solms's Second Report

dated 20 August, 1844—San Antonio de Bexar

The reason for the delay in sending this report to the directors of the Verein is on account of the lack of communication that exists between Galveston and New Orleans during the summer months. I myself have not had any news from the Verein since the 28th of May, and I am of the opinion that my report from Nassau has not yet crossed the Gulf of Mexico. There is less hope that you would have received the letters that I mailed on the 28th of July from here.

The trip from Nassau [Plantation] to here [San Antonio] was beset with many hardships but this is not the place to describe them. Furthermore, since no one in Europe has the faintest idea of conditions here, it would be impossible for them to visualize what we had to endure.

I arrived here on the 25th of July. Before making a personal inspection, I sought to obtain as much preliminary information about this area as I could from chief surveyor Hays[18] and his deputy, Mr. James. Our position is, as we knew before I left England, that in effect we own no land on which to start colonization. Based on all the information I could get and from personal observation on a short four day tour up the Medina River which I made with the Colonial Director, I feel compelled by my conscience and by the trust placed in me by the Verein, to make the following report.

The grant [Bourgeois-Ducos] consists of good and inferior lands. The good lands lie on the streams and creeks in the "Canon de Uvalde" and in the "Canon del Sabinal," 12 miles west of the former. The inferior rocky lands, suitable for cattle raising only, lie on the edges of the Medina Valley and out toward the hills. These areas are in about equal proportion and extent to those that are suitable for cultivation. The Medina River is not navigable and, on account of the boulders in its bed, cannot be made so. In its valley lie the best and most excellent lands. This is the most favorable location because the valley is heavily forested and healthful throughout. The river has excellent clear water; in fact, it is the only one that has water in its lower course. All the others are entirely dry. At their best during the spring or after a heavy rain, these have an insignificant flow from which no water power is available. At other times they consist of isolated stagnant water holes. So it is with the [reportedly] famous Potranka which is absolutely dry, also of the Quihe which the Colonial Director[19] spoke of as having lakes, thus also the Arroyo Seco (dry brook), another charming product of his imagination. Both of the latter have flowing water in their courses in the hills, where suitable lands for a few farms could be found since no one has settled there so far. Their lower courses are of no use to us since it can readily be seen that they are non-existent. On the Medina River, up to its source, as in the Canon de Uvalde, locations for settlement are not possible, as claimed by the Colonial Director, because from one end to the other all of these are already taken by Americans, Irish, Mexicans, etc.

I therefore consider it fortunate that the government has cancelled the grant, as we would have had to settle the colonists either on the remaining inferior land or up in the hills. The first would not have been up to the Verein's intent, to see the immigrants settled happily; the second would have been impossible. Even if it is admitted that 50 to 100 families living in a group are safe from Indian attacks, there would still be no assurance that their crops in the fields or their herds would be safe. The suitable unappropriated regions on the streams in the hill country can only be settled in safety after towns, villages, and farms have been established along the road to these regions. Only by the forward push of civilization can this be accomplished.

I had difficulty in making this clear to the Colonial Director. He, with the usual French thoughtlessness, could create the most fantastic schemes without any plans on how to settle 30 or 40 families here and there. Against this I argued that the Verein promised the settlers that they would be settled as a group in a community, thereby having the advantages of living together as a unit, keeping the habits of their native land and their nationality instead of living in small groups isolated from each other. For this reason also it is the intended purpose of the Verein to give premium lands, if they can be had, without cost to the settlers. "Pah, nationality is only a word," he said. To this I replied, "Yes, for you perhaps, but not for me and the Verein."

At the moment our problem is to acquire land for starting our operations. This land can be procured by purchase or through agreement [with the owner] to divide a league into sections of which we would get one half, the other to remain in possession of the owner. By such an arrangement our land would be divided by the other man's land and the value of his land would increase. It is a difficult matter to obtain a larger tract of land in this manner since a number of owners would be involved of whom some would and some would not be willing [to participate].

We have been offered land belonging to Mr. Cassiano and others some of whom have agreed to the above plan. It is located at the junction of the Cibolo and San Antonio rivers, 55 miles from here and 50 miles distant from Aransas Bay. This place is good in that it would permit a shorter route for the convoys and later serve as a way station for those intending to go further inland. It is even more important as a merchandise depot since the San Antonio River can be made navigable to this point; it has four or more feet of water all the way. Also, a settlement established here would be halfway between the coast and a settlement to be established on the Medina River and would be on the route from Victoria to Laredo on the Rio Grande River. On account of its proximity to the coast and water transportation, goods could be shipped at less cost to this point than to San Antonio. Merchants from Mexico come to Bexar the year around for merchandise. They would have a shorter route to this point from Laredo. They pay for everything in silver and gold. The land itself is good but only a small portion of it is watered by the San Antonio and Cibolo rivers. Good heavy timber is found in the bottom land and good building stone in a few higher places. Springs are lacking and water would have to be supplied by wells.

Another piece of land that has been offered is the tract of Mr. McMullen.[20] He at first insisted on the division plan but later declared that he wanted to sell all as a whole. This tract embraces sixteen leagues on the Medina River itself. It is a highly fertile land of heavy black soil, well forested with oak. Numerous fresh water springs refresh the travelers and make the land fruitful. I have seldom seen a prettier piece of land than this which I have traversed in length and breadth.

Now, with reference to the proposal that the Colonial Director spoke of while in Europe, namely the above mentioned plan of division in sections: I have already said (1) that not everyone would understand and agree to that, and (2) even if an understanding were reached with the owner, such as Mr. Cassiano, there would not be enough land to settle 100, not even 50, families if each were given a hundred acres. The Verein would have to give up its half of the land which it really should hold for later profitable sale. As an example, let us assume that Mr. Cassiano owns two leagues. The Verein would then get a total of one league in alternate sections of which one half would be given to the settlers. Instead of the Verein acquiring [for itself] two leagues at a nominal price, it would own [by the above method] only one-fourth of the whole or one-half a league with the disadvantage of not having sole disposition of of the land. A league has 4428 acres and one-half, or 2214 acres, would be set aside for the settlers. Were but 100 acres given to a family, only 22 families could be accommodated. I could therefore not even take care of the first contingent of settlers but would have to start at once to establish a settlement at two places which is an absolute impossibility. Also paragraph 8 in the title of the Verein's agreement for colonization states that land would be surveyed for at least 100 families at one place. It therefore is the duty of the Verein to settle 100 families at one location. Estimating the settlement of 22 families (one-half league) did not take into account the land for the village nor for the fort for the protection of the settlement.

Let us now assume that we actually had land available for 50 families (the number on the first transport). It would be impossible to enlarge the settlement because land would have to be purchased in between the sections. The owner could take shameful advantage of the purchaser whether it be the Verein or a private person since it would be in his power to dictate the price of the land. Certainly there is no outlay of money nor any gain by this method; however, serious disadvantages must be anticipated later. I realize full well that any cash outlays must be in accord with the Verein's aims at all times. However, the question resolves itself into this: no outlay, no gain with disadvantages,—or an outlay and a rich reward in three or four years.

The Colonial Director who made all of the estimates is now trying to economize on everything, on food for the workmen and on the scanty wages paid to them. He constantly threatens to employ Frenchmen which I cannot and will not tolerate because there are many unfortunate Germans here seeking employment. I will come back to this later in a separate chapter.

I must now, in order not to break the thread of thought, lay before the directors my ideas about the future of our undertaking. My ideas are based on what I have seen with my own eyes, and on the opinions of men who know this country and who can intelligently evaluate its possibilities.

We must, in order to get started, acquire the land at the junction of the Cibolo and the San Antonio rivers. This land should be acquired under the most advantageous plan and in sufficient quantity to settle all of the families that are coming the first year. It would be impossible for me to make arrangements for a settlement on the Cibolo and then in the same winter at a location 40 miles further west.

In the meantime, steps should be taken to acquire in whole or in part, the McMullen land to serve as a stopover or a base on the Medina River for our next operation, and at which preparations could be made throughout the year for the settlers that are expected to arrive in November, 1845.

The Bourgeois grant in its present state is of no earthly use to us because the small amount of cultivable and unappropriated land could only be settled if there were an established base to protect it or to fall back upon. Considering the small quantity of this land, to try to get this grant reinstated so that Mr. Bourgeois could get his two-fifths of the profits would not be advantageous to the Verein. In the event the government, or rather the Congress, should again bestow the grant to the Verein, it will be because of the Verein and not because of Mr. Bourgeois. I have not had the opportunity to observe his boasted friendship, yes intimacy, with the President and especially with the Vice-President, Mr. Anson Jones; and I question whether Mr. Bourgeois ever inspected the grant, as he said he did. If he had, would he have accepted it? Absolutely not, because he is too shrewd to accept land from the government when the best and largest part of it is already claimed and therefore excluded [from the grant].

What really are grants? All are alike; they are nothing but a farce, a bad jest. They are useful to have if one desires to defraud others. The government grants an enormous extent of remotely situated land in which the grantee receives, under the most stringent stipulations, much unfit and a little good land.

The purpose of the Verein, which is the acquisition of land

for considerable immigration, refutes the idea of constantly buying additional land. This would soon exhaust a fund of millions. However, I am convinced that the purpose can be accomplished without too great an outlay by acquiring the land on the Cibolo and San Antonio rivers, and the McMullen tract, and later probably the Canon de Uvalde which, if bought in time, could probably be obtained at 5¢ an acre. The Canon de Uvalde comprises 30 square miles. It is thirteen miles long and three miles wide.

It is then my plan to obtain from Congress a new grant, with a longer colonization time clause, to include unappropriated cultivable land on the Medina River toward the southwest in order to be closer to the Rio Grande River, and thus attract trade from Chihuahua. The Canon de Uvalde is 65 English miles due west from here. The distance to the Rio Grande is said to be 160 miles, and to Chihuahua 450 miles. Mule caravans make the trip in nineteen days.

In order to make this trade advantageous to our German merchants, I shall endeavor to secure from Congress a reduced import duty on all shipping under the auspices of the Verein. I will wait on this until I receive the grant so that land speculators and unscrupulous persons will not be aware of it. The Verein is entitled to some evidence of appreciation from the Republic for bringing in resources such as man power. I shall also ask that the lands under the grant to us be surveyed so that we will have no expense in that respect when we acquire these for our use.

With this procedure it seems to me that our whole position will be improved, even as it concerns Mr. Bourgeois who became a member because of his grant. His membership should end as soon as his grant expires, and I request the directors to give me the most precise orders and instructions as to what I shall do with him. For this reason I must mention that his own interests are more important to him than the Verein's and much more so than that of the immigrants. To the latter he wants to give the impression that it is through him that the Verein's promises will be fulfilled.

To everything else he is indifferent. It is impossible to place him in any official position with the Germans, and still much less possible to trust him with the well being of the immigrants because just as little as he is gifted to command just as little would anyone obey him.

The same, only to a greater degree, applies to Mr. Ducos[21] whom I brought along at the request of and recommendation of the Colonial Director. Both truly have the typical French arrogance but not the quality to gain for themselves respect, confidence, or obedience in any undertaking, and it taxes all my abilities to maintain respect and order.

Upon my honor, to all that I am reporting here, not one iota has been added or subtracted. I consider it my duty not to becloud any issue. Mr. Bourgeois is more of a hindrance than a help to me because he naturally acts on his own ideas in which I have no confidence. I am therefore on my own, combating all the problems by myself with no one to assist me in my concerns and labors.

It is now high time to start work on the projects. If I should have to be gone for a few days from the first settlement that will be organized, I have no one to leave in charge. Then also I must go to Lamar[22] to make the necessary arrangements, and before Congress convenes I must make an extensive trip into the hill country which will require time (and men for protection) in order to decide definitely for which land I should ask Congress. I do not know yet to whom I shall turn over the command while I am away. I must seek some help.

If this colonization project is to succeed according to the philanthropic ideas of the Verein, as it will with good management, I need the assistance of several reliable men, among them older men who could be entrusted with the command of several settlements, and some younger men who could be used as messengers in emergencies to go inland or to New Orleans. For these purposes I recommend officers, for without such assistance no one can colonize successfully. Since there is no one among the Americans and Mexicans here in Texas that is trustworthy, this request is unavoidably necessary. Also necessary is the establishment of a mounted company of 20 to 50 men for outpost and patrol duty, since the militia of the Republic might do more harm pillaging than they would do good. The Volunteer Company of Captain Hays is fully occupied in watching its own frontier.

It is important that I return to Europe next spring in order that I might report to the Verein about changed conditions here, the prospects for the colony, the prospects for German commerce, and resulting commerce with Mexico which would be an advantage for all of Germany and particularly for the Verein. This all could be brought to the Verein in a clear and concise discussion much better than in a written report. I would also render an accurate accounting of what I have done up to the time of my departure, and I would call attention to the right course to be pursued in the future.

The thought has just occurred to me that it would be advantageous to the Verein to persuade the rulers of the German provinces to take part in the colonization effort. Such an extended colonization effort as we comprehend, which would benefit all of Germany, would not be feasible without their assistance.

I plead with the directors to send to me as soon as possible a number of energetic men and to appoint one of them as my successor. The quicker these, and especially the appointed leader, arrive here, the better it will be for the project.

No ships must arrive here after the month of March, since by that time the season is said to be too far advanced.

I myself shall not be able to depart before March to bring a detailed verbal report of the progress of the colony. I am convinced that the success of the colonization effort, which has been praised in both hemispheres as a great and noble thing, hinges on the above suggestions. I plead for the consideration of these recommendations because I believe that they are absolutely necessary.

I await by return steamer the commands and instructions of the directors on my requests as well as on the question of what I am to declare to the Colonial Director as soon as it is assured that his grant will not be reinstated, and also on reports relating to the men to be sent to me, especially regarding the man to replace me as Commissioner-General. I beg that these [reports] be forwarded to me from New Orleans by special messenger so that they reach me before Congress convenes on the 2nd of December, so that I will have the authority to discuss matters with the Colonial Director and the Congress. I shall leave word in New Orleans about how long I will be in the settlement of the Verein and on what date I shall be in Washington [on-the-Brazos].

When the directors can endorse the confidence placed in me by the Verein, an honor which I appreciate deeply, by agreeing with my proposals, only then can I make a success of the colonization project and bring credit to the Verein.

Only by colonizing rapidly, that is by sending over a large number of colonists annually, can we accomplish our purpose and compete successfully with the English and the French who are establishing their colonies. For that purpose the support of the Government's Customs Authority is required. This is best accomplished by frank statements about the benefits to us of unlimited favorable conditions.

I feel it my duty to mention Mr. Henry Castro[23] who has, for the past two years, had a grant from the [Texas] government. He has solicited through his agents emigrants not only in France and Switzerland but also in Germany, and he has sent them over here with the most glittering promises. They arrived in Galveston where they disembarked and, without a guide and without any news from Castro, were left to their own resources. Finally, at their own expense, they were taken by boat to Port Lavaca where they arrived before Easter absolutely penniless. On the difficult trip to this place they subsisted on unripened fruit found along the wayside, from which 28 died immediately on arrival here. The rest all suffered from fever or were weakened and ailing for the rest of their life. I can vouch that I have never seen such deplorable misery. Mr. Castro pushes his inhumanity to extremes; he does not concern himself with these poor people who have been brought to this unfortunate condition through him. He does not visit them or furnish a doctor or support them. For that reason I entreat the directors to call upon all the German rulers and ask them, in the interest of humanity, to forbid Mr. Castro's emissaries to ply their trade. Another ship for the above named man arrived in Galveston in July and it is reported en route to Port Lavaca. In the first named port it lost a large number of its immigrants through death. Among the unfortunate ones I found here are people from the Rhineland, Pfalz, Baden, and Württemberg. These governments should be notified of these conditions. Those who survive owe their recovery solely to the untiring care of a soldier in Colonel Hays's Company, namely Johann Rahm[24] (Canton Schaffhausen).[25] This gallant, sincere man interested his superior in these unfortunate Germans and fed them with his assistance and with what he, although poor, could secure. After some grew well, he procured employment for them so that they could provide their own scanty needs. He still is providing for the sick. I therefore propose that Colonel Hays's and Johann Rahm's services for these unfortunates be recognized by the Verein and that, as a token of appreciation, a combination rifle-shotgun be sent to the former and a shotgun to the latter.

I am not in a position to answer questions regarding the special instructions of the agreements consummated in Germany.

33

However, as far as I know from hearsay, and here it is generally acknowledged, an agreement signed by a resident of Texas is legal.

With regard to workmen's tools, I deem it practical to let the settlers bring the tools they like and leave only the larger pieces to be supplied by the Verein. An American axe, however, is superior to the German. A reserve of wearing apparel, shoes, etc., is best left to the sponsor, over which he can then maintain control.

In conclusion, I wish to remark that the Colonial Director has let himself be taken in by Mr. Cassiano's method of land acquisition to such an extent that this land cannot be obtained by any other methods. The directors themselves must decide on this when they receive the complete contract.

Since it is of the utmost importance to me to receive answers to my several questions by the end of November, I am sending Dr. Meyer to Galveston expressly for the purpose of securing as quickly as possible any letters that may be waiting for me in New Orleans. The Colonial Director, no doubt sensing what these reports may contain, opposes this and will not assume the responsibility of the expenses of the trip, for which reason I assume all responsibility.

San Antonio de Bexar   (Signed) Commissioner General
the 20th of August, 1844   Karl, Prince of Solms

Prince Solms's 3rd Report
dated
26 August, 1844—San Antonio de Bexar

I have the honor to report to the directors the receipt of two correspondences, as well as those sent expressly through Mr. von Wrede[26] and also those that left Liverpool by boat on June 19. Mr. von Wrede arrived here on the 23rd [of August] and the earlier correspondence on the evening of the 24th [of August]. I had dispatched the packet of letters which you will receive with this by a messenger who met Mr. von Wrede at the Guadalupe River and returned here with him.

From my reports in the packet, the directors will note to their satisfaction that their opinions concerning Mr. Bourgeois' grant coincide with mine. I discussed the matter calmly with Mr. Bourgeois, as one gentleman would discuss a business mat-

34

ter with another. This resulted in the correspondence enclosed herewith.

Mr. B. [Bourgeois] declared that he cannot accept a position as an official [in the Verein]. His own previous suggestion of a 5% commission on the receipts for the officials did not persuade him. He was not interested in the 5% commission on the net income of the sale of the Fisher grant when it is accomplished, even though I explained that this could be a considerable sum, as much as $100,000 on two million acres. He further considers that his contract was violated although I explained to him that the main agreement on his part, namely the grant on which the contract centered, had not been fulfilled, as a result of which the contract was nil. He has made up his mind to return to Europe and lay his grievances before the Verein. In the meantime, he will protest in writing. I have openly expressed my opinions about grants in general and Mr. Bourgeois' grant in particular; therefore it will not be necessary for me to suggest to the Verein not to enter into any agreement on this grant. Should Mr. Bourgeois make a request to Congress, I feel confident that he will not get it; but I feel even as assured that if I request a grant from the government or Congress for the Verein, it would be granted without any further ado.

Now concerning the grant of Mr. Fisher[27]—enclosed is an approximate sketch from descriptions by the surveyor, Colonel Hays, who is familiar with the grant since it lies in Bexar County.[28] The grant starts at the springs of the Llano River, follows the left bank of the same to the Colorado River and extends up on this to a point where a line 45 degrees N.W. from the beginning intersects the Colorado. The land along the Colorado is claimed throughout the grant; other claims are indicated on the sketch. It is hilly, but still choice land with plenty of good soil, well forested and watered; and since large stretches of land are still unclaimed, it is the most superior of all the grants.

Colonel Hays told me that Mr. Fisher, whom he met here in the winter, agrees with the opinion I gave in the previous report which is also shared by Colonel Hays; namely, that it would be impossible to establish the first settlement on the grant because the area is too remote for transporting the immigrants and keeping them supplied with provisions. He also agrees with what I reported that, although the lives of the persons in the settlement might be secure, in no event would their herds or fields be secure. Colonel Hays added that Mr. Fisher had acquired eleven leagues on the Guadalupe River for taxes with the idea of establishing the first settlement there. These [leagues] begin 20 miles above Seguin[2a] and extend 30 miles up to the springs of this magnificent stream. From there to the springs of the Leona[30] [Llano?] (the beginning of the grant) is 15 miles. From there to the San Saba River it is 15 or 20 miles.

I will not venture to make any further decisions until I have seen Mr. Fisher; nevertheless, I am convinced that the first settlement can only be established by this proposed method. The grant of Mr. Fisher, as I said before, is the best of those mentioned, since it has the least amount of appropriated land, and it contains large continuous pieces of good land where a large number of families could be accommodated. Only the northwestern part is composed of lands which, up to now, are the hunting grounds of the Indians. This, of course, is more or less true all over Texas because the Indians are everywhere, but only in large numbers in the uninhabited regions.

With reference to the Indians, these are, namely, the Co-manches who are great in number and brave, and carry on their existence here. I beg, however, not to bother about these people for I shall not wait for them to look me up in the settlement but shall politely pay them the first visit. They will either make peace terms and keep them, or I shall immediately strike them such a blow that they will be rendered harmless for a long time to come, if not forever. However, I cannot do this before winter or spring; by that time I will have sufficient men. In the beginning I must limit myself to a few mounted men for patrolling the surroundings and doing outpost duties. This is a necessary precaution in all new settlements and especially so as one gets closer to the hill country.

In compliance with the orders from the directors, I shall start for Nassau [Texas] next Tuesday, there to await the arrival of Mr. Fisher. The baggage from Lavaca which, because of Mr. Cobb's carelessness, is still en route, will have to be left here when it arrives. From Nassau I shall undertake a trip to Washington [on-the-Brazos] in order to acquaint the President and Secretary of State with the change of affairs. I shall also arrange to have items regarding this in newspapers in Texas as well as in New Orleans and New York, in order to forestall the articles that Mr. Bourgeois will surely publish.

I ask that the directors, on their part, also release items to appear in German, English, and French newspapers similar to those that I shall release here, setting forth the plain facts with the observation that the colonization project is now on a sound footing and its progress is assured.

From President Gen. Houston,[31] as well as Secretary of State, Anson Jones, I continue to receive written assurances of their best wishes and zeal for the Verein's cause.

During my stay in Washington [Texas] I shall also discuss with the government an appointment to appear before Congress. All of this shall be included in my next report which will follow on the heels of this one.

I will remark here that while the grant of Mr. Fisher is very advantageous with respect to agriculture, it is far removed from Mexico and the Rio Grande River for commercial purposes. This is too important a point to overlook and I shall therefore see what steps can be taken. What the attitude of the government would be toward granting commercial advantages to the Verein, I do not know. We have the good will of the people in the West in that they see the benefit to themselves in acquiring better merchandise at lower costs.

Now, once more, to come back to the subject of colonization and Mr. Fisher. As I said before, I will make no decisions until I have personally consulted with Mr. Fisher. I also pointed out that I recognize my duty and I shall carry out closely the commands of the directors. Should Mr. Fisher, however, against all expectations, want to begin [the settlement] on the terrain of his grant at once I shall not stand for the costs which would thereby be created, nor guarantee the success of the venture in that both the difficulties in transporting the settlers and the costs would mount. The location of the grant cannot be reached by ox cart via Austin [Texas]. From here the distance is 80 miles, and to the coast it is 140 miles, a distance of 220 miles to transport settlers and provisions to a tract of land from which the Indians must first be driven. That I shall employ all diligence in carrying out the instructions of the directors for the success of the project, I need not mention.

More than ever do I now consider it absolutely necessary that I return to Europe next spring in order that I may explain verbally to the Verein, sitting in full assembly, its status in the country here, the prospects for colonization and also for commerce, and whether this should be conducted under the name of the firm or the flag. We could thus effectively show the German governments the advantages that would accrue to their

37

subjects, regardless of their skills, if they joined us in the project.

I want to add that, perhaps through carelessness on my part or through constant camping out without a tent, my health is not as sound as it was in Europe. This, however, shall not hinder me one minute in keeping up my duties and interest in the Verein. Nevertheless, it may be set forth that in the coming spring I would be in need of relaxation and I could regain my strength by a rest cure at some mineral springs. For this reason I once more repeat my request to be relieved next spring.

Here it has become a renewed duty for me to implore the directors, in the interest of humanity, to call on the German governments, as well as the Belgian and the Swiss Confederation, to stop Mr. Castro and his accomplices from soliciting colonists. It is horrible and beyond all comprehension with what cruelty he conducts his work. From his last transport, the last wagons arrived here yesterday. All the settlers, with the exception of one, are sick; and two were dead. How many more will die as a result of the fever?

Twenty odd of these settlers who arrived here since May want to come with me, some as laborers, some to enlist in the mounted company to serve as a guard against the Indians. I pointed out to them that I could not be a party to alienate them from Mr. Castro and thus give him cause to complain against the Verein. Since I can get laborers only by paying them high wages and these men can be had for lower wages than can be secured elsewhere, I explained to them that they were not bound by contract. They could go to Castro or not as they wished, but that I would give work to anyone that I could find. The wage of a laborer or ranger is $5 per month with board. The cost of boarding a man is $2.48 per month.

I repeat the request which I made in my first report for weapons of all kinds, especially cavalry arms, carbines, or short rifles, straight but not heavy swords, pistols, etc., since the prairies can only be traversed by horseback. Since the Indians are always mounted too, a company of foot soldiers would be at a disadvantage against them.

The method of combat would probably be similar to that of the dragoons, on horseback and on foot. When Mr. Fisher has arrived and we have established a colony, I will then have to acquire horses to form the nucleus of a mounted troop. I shall, however, approach this in a most economical manner.

I have the honor to announce to the directors that there is

38

an elderly Mexican on one of the nearby ranches who for a remuneration has offered to guide me from here to the nearest silver mine on the San Saba River. It would by all means be necessary, for the purpose of investigating mines that might be found, to send miners over here, and the sooner the better.

The more settlers we can have here by the end of March, the better the outlook will be for success of the undertaking because the larger the number of families and persons there are in a group the greater will be the security. I therefore await ships in November, December, January, February, and March, and I entreat for them; but no ships must arrive here later than the end of March.

(Signed) The Commissioner General
Karl, Prince of Solms

San Antonio de Bexar
the 26th of August, 1844

Prince Solms's 4th Report
dated
20 September, 1844—Nassau [Texas]

After I had received from Mr. von Wrede, on the 23rd of August, the directors' order to go to Nassau [Texas], I left San Antonio on the 27th of the same month and arrived here in Nassau on the 1st of September, having covered 143 miles in five days.

Here I found very little that was satisfactory. The house was still in the same unfinished state as I had left it; the well had not been started, and on the other hand [name omitted] had left the Plantation. Along with him, half of the equipment had vanished, including a part of the china-ware, a gun, saddle and harness, fencing, powder, shot, mattresses, etc., and also a lot of lumber. It is proved that he who was recommended by Count Boos as an honest person, with the help of a few slovenly fellows from the neighborhood, had gradually removed the items. Then, after picking a quarrel with Mr. Fortrand, he left the house to establish himself on land he had purchased two miles from here. Since then he has tried once to start a fire here at night and has made a threat to shoot me. At the attempt to start a fire, he was frustrated by the negro James who chased him off. He is at liberty to shoot me if he doesn't mind running up against obstacles.

Since I left for San Antonio, one negress, Mary, has died and one has run away. The latter, however, has been brought back. The crop looks pitiful. The cotton yield will be about five or six bales which is as good as nothing. The corn may be sufficient for the farm's use.

Since my arrival, the construction of the fireplace is proceeding in a Texas manner; i.e.., the progress is slow. The crevices between the logs still are open to the winds which whistle through merrily at night. When one calls attention to the slow progress of the work and the confusion that exists and asks Mr._____, as manager, for an accounting, he shrugs his shoulders and becomes exceedingly wordy. His lengthy explanation (in short) is that one cannot do anything with these people.

Twenty acres on the farm are fenced to serve as a pasture for cattle and horses, and it is intended to fence another 80 acres for a field.

It would be most advantageous to reach a conclusion regarding the disposition of this project. One way would be to acquire more negroes and operate on a larger scale, as should be done when a league is purchased for farming. An overseer would then be desirable and useful but would have to be paid a higher salary. Another and better solution would be to divide the entire establishment, with all that is on it, into parcels and sell these in Europe at the price suggested in the report made from here by the former Colonial Director.

The doctor intended for this place could then be sent advantageously to one of the settlements of the Verein. This would probably be more agreeable to him since there he could live among his own countrymen, whereas here his only neighbors would be rough, uncultured Americans.

From here I made a trip to Washington [on-the-Brazos] where I again missed seeing the President. However, I had quite a detailed conversation with Dr. Anson Jones.[32] He confirmed my previously expressed suspicions that Mr. Bourgeois would not get his grant re-instated. I could get the grant in the name of the Verein but he—never. Also he found it quite in order that the contract with Mr. Bourgeois was null and void.

In a letter to Dr. Jones, Mr. Fisher writes among other matters regarding the Verein, "They entrusted me with the management of affairs in Texas," which almost leads me to suspect that Mr. Fisher will come with special instructions for overall management. This I will await; and as I hardly expect such to be the case, I will then surely take him somewhat to task for his indiscreet manner of speech.

In July, the ship the *Weser* from Bremen arrived with immigrants sent here by Mr. Fisher. Half of them died immediately; the rest are scattered about this area. They sent a deputation to me to ask whether the land intended for them was lost. I assured them of the opposite, that they were considered equally our settlers. I now ask [the directors] whether they should share equally in the same privileges, such as whether homes should be built for them by cash advances, since they have already used all of their money.

I had planned to start preparations at the beginning of August. Now it is the end of September, and Mr. Fisher has not yet arrived here. I am, therefore, according to the directors' orders, not responsible if no houses are ready by the end of November to receive the settlers. However, the costs will now be much higher.

Concerning the political situation here, the election is over; however, the results are not known as yet. It is said that Dr. Anson Jones[33] has a majority over General Burleson; I cannot give you anything specific.

In closing, I permit myself this observation, that Mr. Fisher has been granted three votes in the Colonial Council. In my opinion this is too many. I therefore beg that in the statutes for colonization, the Commissioner-General be given an additional vote.

Nassau (Texas)   (Signed) The Commissioner General
the 20th of September, 1844   Karl, Prince of Solms

Prince Solms's 5th Report
dated
Galveston—the 25th October, 1844

I have the honor to announce to the directors of the Verein the receipt of all dispatches up to September 12 of this year, and also that Mr. Henry Fisher finally arrived here on the 20th of this month. I had deemed it necessary to come here myself to await his long delayed arrival and, in the event that there were some items yet to be procured from New Orleans, discuss such matters with him and procure them. From here it is an easy matter to get in touch with New Orleans, especially if ships are sailing, whereas from the interior it is more difficult since it is necessary to engage a special messenger.

Mr. Fisher has attended to the purchases assigned to him by the directors, partly in New York and partly in New Orleans. Some items that were not to be had at the latter place will now be ordered from New York from here by Mr. Kaufmann[34] and shipped direct to Matagorda Bay.[35]

I have appointed the firm of Mr. Klaerner [Klaener] in Galveston as agents for the Verein and am confident that they will prove themselves worthy of this trust. The first duty to be performed by this agent will be to see that the settlers are transported to Matagorda Bay. These matters will be simplified if the first ship departing from Bremen will come here first; then it can proceed from here to Matagorda Bay. It will only be necessary to secure permission for this from the Texas government, and I will procure that here.

Mr. Fisher will go with me to Washington [on-the-Brazos] immediately for a consultation with President-Elect Dr. Anson Jones, at present Secretary of State, regarding several agreements to be presented to Congress. From there we will go to Nassau [Plantation] and, after a short stay there, to Matagorda Bay to secure the necessary land and to select a location for harbor facilities. Here we will appoint a harbor superintendent who is to provide the necessary arrangements to receive the settlers. As many persons as necessary will be sent there to assist him. The Germans who arrived on the ship *Weser* belong there, of whom unfortunately only a few families survive since they arrived during the month of July. Also, there will be those Germans who have made up their minds to join us. Some have applied from here and some from Cummings Creek.[36]

I myself, accompanied by Mr. Fisher, will go toward the Guadalupe River over the same route the settlers will have to take. At that river I hope to meet with Major Hays, to whom a messenger will be sent so that he may make his appearance there with part of his troops. We will probably start then on the trip to the grant[37] and inspect part of the same, thereby establishing the eastern boundary and also select the spot for the settlement.

In my previous reports I remarked about the great distance to the hill country from the coast. This now comes alarmingly to the fore; and if it were not for the fulfillment of the terms of the grant, in that 200 families had to be settled on it this

42

year, I would be in favor of the well established principle: to proceed from the coast to the hill country in several stages. I avail myself of this opportunity to remark that Mr. Fisher is in complete accord with my opinion. On the whole, I think that in him I have a calm, thoughtful man, one who is not a schemer.

Matagorda Bay will be the assembling place for the entire expedition, and by New Year I will be there with a part of the men to start the work. It will not be possible to start any earlier because I will need some time to travel over the grant, and I must be in Washington [on-the-Brazos] the early part of December to meet with Congress. My own headquarters will be on Matagorda Bay until I transfer it to the settlement in the interior.

For the present this is Mr. Fisher's and my plan, subject to necessary changes. If the time were not too short, I would be of the unfailing opinion to decide first where to establish the first settlement and then find the shortest route from there to the sea and to a bay where the landing port could be established. Due to the lack of travel facilities between New Orleans and Galveston, the arrival of Mr. Fisher was so delayed that, as I feared, no time will remain to carry out this plan.

One other previously mentioned disadvantage of the Fisher grant which I wish to recall to the directors' minds is, namely, the distance from the Rio Grande and the trade with Mexico. We will have to get the grant extended southward and then acquire a new location on Corpus Christi Bay. For this purpose we will have to enter into negotiations with McLewin[38] for the lands in his possession there. Only then is trade with the Rio Grande assured. This, moreover, is being threatened by the English settlement on Mr. Kennedy's grant which is located on the Nueces River and the Rio Frio. McLewin's lands are better and are closer to the sea than those of the English company; and since we could, at all events, deliver goods to Mexico at a lower cost than the English, we would have nothing to fear from them. Moreover, I am on the best of terms with them. If we should execute these stated ideas, we would possess an excellent fertile tract of land from the Colorado River to the Rio Grande, suitable for any kind of cultivation, cattle industry, rich in minerals of all kinds; and at the same time our holdings would stretch from the San Saba River throughout the rest of the land to the mouth of the Colorado, south from the Canon de Uvalde to the mouth of the Nueces River.

I regret to see from the dispatches of the directors that

rumors of a Mexican invasion have reached Europe through the multi-tongued "Weib Fama" [Lady Gossip] and have frightened some fickle heads. During the summer this rumor was spread around in the west for fourteen days to procure more votes for General Burleson, candidate for the Presidency. Since I was assured by a reliable source that this rumor was without any foundation, I did not deem it worthwhile to mention it at all. Santa Anna is more than ever inclined toward peace since he is too busy with internal affairs and, it is firmly believed, seeks to make himself emperor. According to the latest news, he has freed the Texans who were held prisoners in Perote and in other fortresses, the first step toward peace.

If Texas at this session of Congress successfully avoids annexation, then nothing stands in the way of this country's coming into bloom as, according to my views, peace between Mexico and Texas can be arranged without too much difficulty; and it is not too far off in the future. I am of the firm belief that in Texas few votes would be cast for annexation if it were not for the rapacious politics of the United States which could swing this land to it with all kind of schemes.

With Texas annexed, will the Rio Grande become the boundary for the Yankees, the big "go ahead nation"? Then the United States will be in possession of all commerce along the Gulf of Mexico. What then will become of European commerce? Can the more directly concerned Mexico and England and France put up with it? Then war again will be the only solution, and this land will be overrun with adventurers and villains from the United States. The first step for complete ruin of European commerce is the annexation of Texas.

The great powers of Europe cannot allow this when they see it in the right light. I am of the opinion and firm hope that if the Texas government were counselled wisely, it would do all in its power to prevent the question from ever coming up again. During my presence in Washington [on-the-Brazos] I shall personally present the most urgent objections.

With the greatest vigilance and care, yes even by sacrificing my life if it must be, I will guide the first settlement to success so that the world will know that unquestionably a people can quickly reach a state of well-being here.

I am sorry that such a small number of people are coming this year; and I request the directors, if there still is time, to send as large a number of settlers as possible, the more the

44

better. However, under no circumstances must a ship arrive after the month of March.

By all means ships must depart every month up to January, and no excuse should be tolerated from the Bremen ship owners. In case the total for this year has unfortunately dropped off slightly, preparations must be made for a considerable emigration next year.

I hope that my personal presence in Germany next year will contribute toward an increased emigration. It would be of great help if there were news of a peace settlement with Mexico and recognition of Texas independence by that country.

If it were possible for me to have a part in it, I would not overlook an opportunity to help bring about some favorable action in this matter. This would be to the best interests of the Verein, and especially it might have a favorable reaction toward the Verein's cause.

I cannot state with certainty in which month I can set out on my return journey. At all events, it would be well if the person designated as my successor could be with me for a while, to see how matters are being handled under my guidance. I hope that, if not in the spring then sometime during the summer, I can make my oral report and thus encourage a renewed interest and a renewed challenge.

Galveston   (Signed) The Commissioner General
the 25th of October, 1844   Karl, Prince of Solms

Prince Solms's 6th Report
dated
the 23rd December, 1844—in camp at Port Lavaca

I have the honor to announce to the directors the receipt of all correspondence up to the 30th of October of this year. Consequently, the ship papers of all three ships are in my hands. However, I do not as yet have the duplicate of the contracts.

Since there was nothing to report, a considerable time has elapsed since my last report from Galveston. Toward the end of October, I left Galveston for Nassau [Plantation], by the way of Houston. Mr. Fisher and I had agreed upon a date when he would meet me there. We were detained in Houston by a number of appointments; however, I left for Nassau so that I arrived there on the 5th of November. Mr. Fisher arrived nine days after the agreed date with the result that much time was lost for business matters there. (A special report will be made on the Plantation.)

It was not until the 16th of November that I could depart with the people that I had gathered together to serve as soldiers for the protection of the settlers.

After many hardships and having to make several camps in cold wet weather accompanied by a norther,[39] we arrived in Port Lavaca on the 22nd. We had travelled 150 miles.

On the 23rd, I boarded a small sailing vessel of 13 tons which I had rented in order to explore the entire coast of Lavaca Bay[40] and its bayous. I was looking for a place where the best harbor could be built, and at the same time good healthful land and fresh water could be found. I also was searching for a place from which the route would be shortest for transporting the settlers inland over the bad routes on the low prairies. It is very difficult to obtain this combination. The eastern coast is considered to be very unhealthful and is also furthest from our route to the West. No one in Germany can have the slightest idea of this route; hence, I will not try to describe it to the directors. Furthermore, the water flowing into the Bay from the rivers and brooks is salty or unhealthful. There is no wood, and the water in the upper Bay and in the mouth of the streams has a depth of only two to three feet.

Besides the sand bank of Paso Caballo,[41] there are three other barriers in Lavaca Bay on which most ships run aground. For five days and five nights I navigated all parts of the Bay, and on the 27th of November I met with Mr. Fisher in Port Austin (consisting of only one house) on Tres Palacios Bay. We agreed to keep this spot in mind for the time when making the Colorado River navigable by diverting it over a new bed into Wilson Creek, would not be an idle dream but a reality.

For the present, I decided on Indian Point[42] as the spot which would be most suitable for the West and which fulfilled most of the above mentioned conditions.

At the special request of the Colonial Director, I joined him on the same small vessel to go to Galveston with him where we believed that the first ship of settlers had arrived. I had sent the agent of the Verein, Mr. D. H. Klaerner [Klaener], written orders to hire ships for the voyage to Lavaca Bay, but not to let these depart until either a special messenger from me, or I myself, arrived in Galveston.

On account of a violent norther, our voyage lasted four days and four nights so that we did not enter the above mentioned harbor [Galveston] until the morning of the 2nd of December. To my great amazement, I learned that the settlers' ships had sailed the previous night and passed me in the darkness.

On the 3rd of December, I again put out to sea on board the Texas Revenue Cutter *Alert* with Captain Simpton. Due to contrary winds and high seas, I was forced on the 4th to return again to Galveston. Since a strong norther had arrived in the meantime, I could not set sail again until the 9th. On the 11th, I finally reached Port Lavaca and found that the settlers who had been brought over on the Ship *John Dethart* had encamped two miles from Port Lavaca. (The last boat that brought them from Galveston had arrived shortly before I did.)

A small group of live oak trees provides them protection against the storm and also a source of firewood. A fresh water brook is only 100 steps from the camp. On the morning of the 12th, I rode out and welcomed them in the name of the Verein, and I immediately transferred my headquarters to the encampment. I found all of them in good health. All were satisfied with the treatment and the food except four; these, however, were soon quieted by the others.

On the 14th I rode over to Texana[43] (35 miles) to inspect some land there; however, I found it absolutely poor and unhealthful. On the 16th I made a closer inspection of Indian Point; and on the 17th the owner, Mr. White, came to me. We came to an agreement on terms and as soon as these have been legalized, I shall forward them to the directors. On the 18th I returned to the harbor in his boat, accompanied by Mr. Thielpape.[44]

I have already mentioned the points which were the determining factors and repeat them here briefly:

1. A good harbor for all ships that can pass through Paso Caballo.
2. Good land and a healthful site.
3. Wood for building and firewood.
4. The shortest route to the West and the shortest possible passage through the low prairies.

There is only a superficial knowledge of the whole coast. All investigations must be made in person, since no one can be depended on and every owner considers his own personal interests. Taking all this into consideration, one can see that an already exacting task is made more difficult.

I feel that I may be permitted to flatter myself for having solved this task successfully due to my ceaseless efforts where I did not shun any difficulty or weather on water or on land.

It is out of the question to route the settlers by way of Victoria, Gonzales, and Seguin. Firstly, every town inhabited by wicked rabble of Texas is to be avoided for a number of reasons. Secondly, this route passes through a large number of often-flooded streams over which there are no bridges. These can be crossed by heavy Texas cotton transports, and to them it does not matter if they are delayed a matter of fourteen days or so. Thirdly, none of those towns are our destination.

It is absolutely impossible to make the first settlement on the Llano,[45] as I have thoroughly explained in my previous reports. This year it is only possible to establish a settlement on the southwest edge of the grant on which there are many beautiful spots between the Guadalupe River and the San Antonio River. An excellent and beautiful place where a Senator Smith owns a location of four leagues is at the so-called "fountains" on the route from San Antonio to Austin, 30 miles from the former. This area offers excellent land. It is a beautiful tract with first rate cedar and oak forests and water power. Its proximity to San Antonio and Seguin assures support and help in case of need. Situated at the foot of the hill country, it will be the headquarters for the colonization project, since it is equidistant from the coast and the upper portion of the Verein's land.

The route to there by the way of Victoria,[46] Gonzales,[47] and Seguin is like a bow to the string which would be a route on the water shed between the Guadalupe River on the one side and the San Antonio, Coleto, and Cibolo rivers on the other. For this reason it is evident that the latter route would be the shortest and the best, especially since being on the water shed it is on a plateau.

My next task is to establish this route and I shall endeavor to erect bridges at all the difficult places, such as streams, etc.

The problem now is to find the shortest and best route across the low land prairies to the place where it is best to cross the Guadalupe River. This latter spot will probably be found twelve to fifteen miles below Victoria, and at present there are no intermittent supply stations on the way for ox wagon travel. There is an excellent piece of land twelve miles from Indian Point, belonging to Mr. Hatch, which has sufficient timber for building and for fuel. It also has a very fine spring of abundant good water. From here to the next most favorable place on the Guadalupe

(Mr. Trailor) is about twelve miles. Both of these stretches are over fairly high prairie land with the exception of two swamps on the first twelve miles from Indian Point, which can be by-passed, and one bad place on the last stretch where Mr. Trailor himself has offered to build a temporary bridge.

The entire route through the coastal prairie up to the elevated ridge beyond the Guadalupe is only 24 miles (five to six German miles). Compared to German conditions, this is very little; and here, too, it appears to be very short. Next spring the route can and must be improved by ditches on both sides and made to be the best in Texas. However, I shall come back to this later.

Indian Point meets all of the conditions mentioned before with the exception of building timber which can be brought from the land of Captain Hatch on Chocolate Creek.[48] Since it is the only place where all desirable conditions are met, I have therefore chosen it as the port for the Verein's settlements; and with the agreement of Mr. White have named it "Carlshafen" in consideration that the Christian names of our venerable President, our Director-elect, and mine are Carl.

Several private forwarding and commercial businesses from Port Lavaca have indicated that they will immediately move their establishments to Carlshafen. Everyone recognizes that it is the only important landing place in the West. Ships that can pass Paso Caballo need have no fear of other sand banks and can reach our harbor unhindered. It has a water depth of seven feet at 350 yards from the land. All ships find 14 to 18 feet of water a mile from land which offers safe anchorage for riding out storms.

I therefore will build a storehouse here for the Verein. Also a number of houses will be built. Several families have decided to stay here in this truly delightful place. Good soil, a park created by nature of large and small hardy trees (lignum vitae), and abundant vegetation of yuccas[49] and wild indigo were inducements for staying here.

A trench, with low breastworks on a swampy creek will protect the depot and the first settlements against any possible attack. Mr. Ludwig Willke, former Prussian Lieutenant of the 30th Infantry Regiment, will stay here as commandant of the place.

Next I negotiated with Capt. Hatch for 1100 acres of land which contained quite a large amount of wood. This land (about twelve miles from Indian Point) will be used for our next stopping place. Immediately after Christmas I shall transfer the camp to this place in order to be on our own property where a number of log houses will be built for the purpose of convincing the settlers and giving them employment. I will name this place "Leiningen" in consideration of the many members of the Verein who are named Leiningen.

The third stopping place shall be established at the crossing of the Guadalupe River and will have to be fortified a little later. In honor of our chosen director I will name this place "Castell."

The number of way stations to be established between here and the "fountains" on the land belonging to Mr. Smith, and from there to the San Saba and the main settlement, as well as those necessary to safeguard certain mines, is something I must determine after a personal inspection. It will be impossible to man every way station this year. I must restrict myself to Carlshafen, perhaps Leiningen, and certainly a number of people should be stationed at Castell. The rest must be assigned to the main place.

Furthermore, I shall have the whole road from Carlshafen to the "fountains" made wide enough so that in the coming summer wooden rails (of live oak) can be delivered to the prepared bed. In the following year, a wooden railroad track can be installed similar to the one in a village on the Ruhr in Westphalia, wherein the Verein will be saved considerable costs, time, and trouble. Until we have locomotives, horses can be used to draw cars; and even in this way much can be gained.

Enclosed is a written agreement that was made with the soldiers of the Verein and also the articles of war which were made public.

In camp today, divine services were conducted by the Reverend Ervendberg of the Protestant faith at which people, deeply touched, shed many tears. On the first day of the Christmas holidays, the Lord's Supper will be celebrated. Of the Catholic faith, I have no report as yet on the priest whom I requested from the Superior of the Order of the Holy Redeemer in Baltimore, the Right Reverend Father Alexander. However, Mr. Lanfear reported that he had forwarded the $100 to Baltimore for the priest's traveling expenses.

It is further my duty to remark that the ships' and the Verein's provisions supplied from Bremen are faulty, to put it mildly. The salted meat, as a whole, has a disagreeable odor and is hardly useable; the peas cannot be cooked tender. The barrel of spirits is nothing but the worst kind of potato brandy, and the red wine is of poor quality.

Further, the question was put to Dr. Hill in Bremen by the emigrants whether or not they should procure flour and other food for their children which they were willing to do. Dr. Hill assured them that everything was taken care of. However, none of this was included, and this disappointment had the worst effect and was the cause of many complaints. Dr. Koester[50] had the same experience when in need of medicines on board ship. At all events, it seems desirable if Dr. Hill is to continue to be in charge of the shipping that he will take this assignment more seriously.

A map of Carlshafen and the coast will be ready as soon as possible. Mr. Thielpape is busy with the surveying at this time.

I was advised by letter of the 14th [of December] from Mr. D. H. Klanner [Klaener] of Galveston that the *Herrschel* [sic] on that date had signalled her arrival at the barrier. I therefore expect the immigrants soon.

The things to be done in the coming year: how to take hold of the whole project, and the only way to bring about results— I am reserving for a verbal report to the directors. It is therefore very necessary that I set out on my voyage to Europe as soon as I can get away. Therefore, I urgently request a suitable, highly energetic successor. I will have everything so arranged that he will need only to apply himself with zeal and vigor to see that the arrangements are carried out.

Mr. Fisher whom I left in Galveston on the 9th, from where he was to proceed promptly to Washington [on-the-Brazos] to take up matters with Congress, was still in Galveston on the 14th. I took upon myself all those matters which the Colonial Director should do in order that he attend to matters with the Congress.

I can truthfully say that up to now I have had everything on my own shoulders, a thing which is almost too much for one person. I must also mention that of all the draught oxen, live stock, etc., to be obtained, Mr. Fisher has not secured one head. Wagons are being delivered very sparingly; instead of 50, there are only 15 so far. Thus, everything is moving very slowly; and, as a result, it will be more costly than if Mr. Fisher had hurried here and had attended to everything with zeal and energy. All of the things that are lacking should have been on hand before the arrival of the settlers. The cost of the upkeep would not have been half as high.

Further difficulty arose between Mr. Fisher and me at Galveston. In August of this year I appointed Mr. D. H. Klaerner [Klaener] as agent of the Verein. Against that, Mr. Fisher favors Mr. Kaufmann to whom I personally have no objections. He asserts that the directors verbally authorized him to appoint agents. He has also appointed Mr. Kaufmann to be the agent in Lavaca Bay at Carlshafen, to which I agreed. Mr. Fisher has invested a couple of thousand piaster in Kaufmann's business and therefore wants to appoint Kaufmann the agent in Galveston also. He has requested me several times to dismiss Klaerner [Klaener]. Since I have no cause, I vigorously refused to do this, and I request instructions from the directors on how to resolve this matter.

From all of this, it is indicated that Mr. Fisher should never be entrusted with guidance of the Verein's affairs, even on an interim basis since the best interests of the Verein would suffer. Even if it is only on an interim basis, a reliable and energetic man must be sent here. The earlier such a man arrives the better it will be for the Verein.

With this, I believe I have answered all of those topics referred to in correspondence of the directors of the 9th of October, and I close with the remark that everything therein is in agreement that Capt. Luedering of the ship *John Dethart* in all respects can be considered a praiseworthy man.

In camp at Port Lavaca   (Signed) The Commissioner General
on the 23rd of December, 1844   Karl, Prince of Solms

Post script: On the 24th of this month, all immigrants with the exception of the few who, under the guidance of the treasurer Lt. von Coll are still enroute from Galveston, landed healthy, safe, and sound at Carlshafen. On news of their arrival, I immediately rode over there on horseback and welcomed them. They were all of good cheer and, with diffidence and good manners, presented the same complaints as the first arrivals. Concerning this, I shall make a more detailed report and request the directors that they make Dr. Hill accountable for this, a thing which I feel certain they will not fail to do.

Report about the Nassau Plantation: While awaiting the arrival of Mr. Fisher at Nassau, I immediately proceeded to examine the inventory statement as I was instructed to do. I was greatly astonished as _____, who had constantly spoken

52

of such an existing statement, had to declare that it was not prepared because it was not a custom in America. Mr. Fisher undertook the preparation of the statement, whereby many cows and calves had to be listed as "strayed away" and other objects also had to be listed as "not present." Rumor has it that _____ butchered the cows and calves for his own use; and on closer acquaintanceship, I have no doubt. When I have relieved him of his office, as I am instructed to do in the directors' correspondence of October 9, I shall install Mr. von Wrede, Sr. He will probably have to be offered a small stipend. The overseer "D" is also dismissed, and Mr. Fisher, as Colonial Director, will appoint another man who has good references and in whom he has full confidence. His salary will be between 300 and 400 piasters.

In no case am I in favor of buying slaves but, on the contrary, I stand by my previously established views: the sale of the entire league, including inventory. I must leave the report on the details to Mr. Fisher. From the bottom of my heart, I can only say that this slave mess is an unworthy affair for the Verein. It is truly a stain on human society; and this thing in particular, as well as the whole farm, has caused me more anger, worry, and unpleasantness than all the dangers, privations, and hardships that I have suffered in the interests of the Verein up to now.

At Camp near Lavaca   (Signed) The Commissioner General
23rd Dec., 1844   Karl, Prince of Solms

Prince Solms's 7th Report
dated
1 January, 1845 at Camp near Lavaca
with postscript dated
5 January, 1845 in Camp on Agua Dulce[51]

Most humbly I ask the directors of the Verein to accept my best wishes for the New Year and to pass the same on in my name to the members of the Verein. I beg all of the gentlemen to believe that I have up to this time used all of the energy and means at my disposal for the success of the undertaking and that I shall not rest until I have successfully overcome the endless important tasks for all of Germany.

I may well say that the result for which the Verein strives is a great, fine, nation-wide German objective, and there is not the slightest doubt that, for the present and even more so for the future, this purpose must be worthy of recognition.

With God's help I shall succeed in overcoming the many difficulties that stand in the way here so that I may be in position next summer to make an oral report of what has been done and especially to plan the necessary operations for next fall so that success will not only be made possible but made a certainty.

In encampment at Lavaca, the 1st of January, 1845.

(Signed) The Commissioner General
Karl, Prince of Solms

Postscript: [January 5, 1845]

Since day before yesterday, I have transferred my headquarters to this encampment where today the first divine services were conducted. By this afternoon the remaining two tents with settlers from 'Carlshafen will have arrived here. Mr. von Coll arrived the 29th of December last year in Carlshafen. The people are all well and desire to be brought to the upper land as soon as possible.

Tomorrow I shall convene the first session of the Colonial Council.[52] I have many matters to lay before them. Mr. Fisher, the Colonial Director, whom I left on the 8th of December in Galveston, hastily set out for Washington [on-the-Brazos] to appear before Congress and arrived there on the 21st of December. The things that he was supposed to procure, for which he had instructions and credit, were done sparingly or not at all, and I shall hold him accountable for this. He has until the 30th of January to deliver all of the items that are lacking or bear the consequences because I shall not allow his negligence to contribute to the detriment of the Verein or the immigrants. I want to assure the directors that I will watch this matter with utmost diligence.

As soon as I have completed arrangements for the outer protection and for the orderliness of the inner camp here, I must go to Washington [on-the-Brazos] to prevail upon Congress for incorporation and other necessary matters.

In encampment on the Agua Dulce

the 5th of January, 1845

(Signed)
The Commissioner General
Karl, Prince of Solms

Prince Solms's 8th Report
dated
8th February, 1845 at Galveston, Texas

I dispatched my last report to the directors on the 5th of January this year. Since that time I have completed forming a company of twenty men in the camp, in accordance with "Articles of War" which I am enclosing with the attachment marked No. 1. I myself read these to the men and explained them. I then explained to them the importance of the oath and that a German's handshake is always as good as an oath. After discussing the various serious duties which some individuals are assuming, I received the handshake of each one and observed to my satisfaction, from each one's emotion, that my discussion was thoroughly understood.

I further assembled in front of the camp all of the men capable of bearing arms (with the exception of those in the Company). By count the total was 108. Of these 36 were armed with rifles, 39 with shotguns, and 33 were unarmed. Then I had those step forward who had previously had military experience, and then those who had taken part in campaigns. At the moment I do not have my notes at hand, but I shall include the figures in my next report.

After that I explained to the entire assembly their obligations under the laws of the land. I expected each German to stand ready to defend his hearth.

It is generally said that heads of families and married men are less subject to take up arms. This is a principle to which I do not subscribe since I consider that either here or in the old country those who own homes are more obligated to defend them than the single men. In any event the duties of both are similar. If I should treat the heads of families and married men with more consideration, it will be for good reasons. Such is my wish and I will always do so where circumstances permit.

I must now take all the able bodied men and form a corps which can be used to augment the company in case of an emergency and which can also be used outside of the settlement. From the rest of the men I will organize a reserve company which will get instructions and practice in shooting and other military matters on Sundays. To form the above mentioned reserve company, I called for volunteers who would be ready to serve when the need arose. The men stood in two ranks forming a square, one side of which was left open. I stepped back out of the square and called out "Volunteers forward." At these words the whole group, old and young without exception, came toward me, and I again found myself encircled. Without any intent to praise I said to them, "I was convinced that you would do that. I know my Germans." I then ordered the election of officers and non-commissioned men, subject to my confirmation. I will send the record of this later.

Further, I called the Colonial Council together which, in the absence of the Colonial Director, Mr. Fisher, consisted of five votes. In the attachment No. 2 are copies of the minutes of the first and second meetings. I wish to remark at this time that should the Colonial Director be present at a Council meeting when a disagreement exists, a decision cannot be reached with eight votes (an even number). It is not possible to make changes in the Contract with Mr. Fisher, yet I fear many disadvantages therefrom. The details regarding legal procedures in the encampment which were drawn up by Dr. Lynzee and approved by me will be sent to the directors in due time.

I finally managed to leave here on the 19th of January and arrived at a farm three miles from Washington [on-the-Brazos] in the evening of the 24th after incredible hardships, misery, and vexations. While I was still in the encampment, I had received a letter of the 28th of December of last year from Mr. Fisher. From this I became aware of the most remarkable requests that he was presenting to Congress.

Mr. Fisher, in order to create a favorable impression for himself and Mr. Miller, declared therein that he and Mr. Miller had invested a capital of $60,000 in the colonization project and that five ships had arrived at Galveston, with 500 to 600 immigrants on board. Everyone knows, from the President of Texas down to the smallest negro boy, that if Messrs. Fisher and Miller were put under a cotton press, not $1.00, much less $60,000 could be squeezed out of both of them. The petition made the doubtful Americans even more suspicious since everyone knew that the above mentioned men had transferred their land grant to the Verein under certain known conditions. Thus Mr. Fisher ran into difficulties which he, or I in his place, could have avoided by a frank statement of facts. The American likes frankness and truthfulness, and once he is convinced of this will deal fairly with you. However, should he see that he is being deceived, his distrust cannot be overcome.

Therefore, of all his requests to Congress, Mr. Fisher received only the following:

1. Confirmation of the Contract granted by Gen. Houston.
2. One-twelfth of the intermediate sections to be transferred to us.
3. That the immigrant did not have to cultivate 15 acres and that it was not necessary to settle immigrants on the grant immediately.

These points were still under consideration by the Senate on the morning of the 15th. Mr. Fisher declared that he could do nothing further and asked that I come to Washington [on-the-Brazos], since he would not stay there. His request was so urgent that I could not do otherwise but also travel to Houston and Galveston to permit him no excuse for failure to get his requests approved.

As long as I dealt personally with Americans, I had no complaints about discourtesies toward me, whether in business or my personal affairs. On the contrary, I was impressed when I saw how much my presence was appreciated. Now when it was absolutely necessary that I stay in the encampment, I was compelled to turn business over to Mr. Fisher and immediately things went wrong. I had no one else to rely on for this, and at that time I considered him trustworthy, believing that his interests were inseparable from those of the Verein. Now truly I am better informed, and I will give my frank opinion to the directors, as I did in attachment No. 3 which is a copy of the correspondence with Mr. Fisher since December of last year.

Mr. Fisher spared no pains in raising the necessary funds for a trip to Europe for the purpose of making something out of his contract. Thus he came to Mainz, saw immediately how little the Verein knew about Texas and saw also the possibility of gaining their confidence. As soon as this was accomplished his head swelled, for he was in possession of means (for the first time in his life) and he proceeded to spend them. The minutes of the first Colonial Council meeting show how this money was spent for purchases.

As a typical American or Texan Mr. Fisher thought that through subtle means he could get control of all other matters and he envisioned that he soon would be rid of me. He wanted to appoint all officials and agents and to have his men in every place who could thus line their own pockets, first seeing, however, that Mr. Fisher received his share.

Mr. Fisher soon became aware that I was not pleased that nothing was ever finished. Since he is still trying to take over all authority and thereby to step on the interests of the Verein in order to further his own, he has openly criticized me and found fault with everything that I have ever done. This I have heard from three sources, in Washington [on-the-Brazos], in inns, and in saloons. Yes, he even carries his indiscretions so far that in the stores here in Galveston he accuses me of being unscrupulous in the handling of funds although all purchases, as well as the procurement of building material here for houses which is somewhat expensive for Carlshafen, was handled by Mr. K. [Klaener]. This was done on account of our high regard for him who was originally supposed to have been our agent there. The employment consists of one carpenter, one cabinet maker, one driver of oxen, and one waggoner. The total monthly wages are $205 which is a yearly sum of $2460 or 6150 gulden.[54] Since there is little or no supervision and no attempts at economy, this project will be stopped.

Not much has been done either regarding the incorporation of the Verein whereby the rights of the Verein would be clearly set forth. I had a consultation yesterday with Mr. Rose, a locally recommended lawyer, concerning incorporation and the relationship between the Verein and Messrs. Fisher and Miller. From this I saw that although incorporation was beneficial, it was not necessary since a Commissioner-General of the Verein would always be in the land to act as a trustee of the Verein.

It is now a question of whether I show weakness or at least some forgiveness and thus deliver all authority to Mr. Fisher's hands or else calmly proceed on my way and on the basis of the signed contract, carry out my rightful duties and thus protect the interests of the Verein. The answer to this question does not require any explanation. My course is clear. I will stay on it and not deviate from it since there is yet more to be concerned about in the very serious question: Shall the German basis be maintained in the colony of the Verein or shall it be pressed to earth by the American way which Mr. Fisher through all possible means will seek to bring about so that, if need be, he will have absolute authority in his own hands? This also needs no further clarification, and I will be victorious with the German way or go down in defeat with it.

It was to the interest of Mr. Bourgeois as well as Mr. Fisher to convince the directors that the matter of colonization was an easy task. They were indifferent to whatever might happen later because then the responsibility would be attached to the name of the Verein, and here to me.

I was honored when the Verein entrusted me, as Commissioner General, to establish its first colony in Texas. With that, I was not only entrusted with funds for the administration of the project but I was also held responsible for the life, property, and the very existence of all immigrants of the Verein. Then Mr. Fisher came to Germany and made a superficial estimate of the capital required to defray the expenses of the first settlement. He was allotted $11,000 of which I have as yet to see an accounting. That the account will balance there is no doubt; but how the accounting is made, that is the question on which the Colonial Council must pass judgment. In any case there is very little to show for it, not the quality nor the quantity that the directors commissioned Mr. Fisher to obtain. The little there is, is bad and mostly unuseable.

Furthermore, it is evident from the minutes of the Colonial Council meeting that the designated six months' provisions barely lasted six weeks, particularly bread and salted meat. Vegetables lasted perhaps a little longer. In the budget there is no provision for slaughter cattle of which a considerable number had to be provided, as well as corn for making bread. Due to the negligence of Mr. Fisher nothing has been provided for. Of the purchased wagons, those that were delivered were not useable. The oxen which Mr. Fisher was to have purchased and for which he was given $2300 by me have not been delivered. For this sum I have not received an accounting, only a receipt.

As a result of the original delays, seemingly endless costs have accrued to the Verein and I am afraid that more are yet to come because it is hardly possible that this year's harvest, if there is any, will be adequate. Further, there are the expenses that the Company will entail, and finally the lodging and travel expenses of the Commissioner General in this land from the 1st of July to the present.

I have during this time strived through observation and various activities to learn as much as possible so that I can truthfully say that I know the state of affairs of this land and the character of its people. I have sought to give the Verein a clearer insight into conditions for colonization based on common sense and on local conditions so that they may be better informed and not be forever led astray by speculators. To this end the stay has been worth while in this land that has produced nothing but cotton and corn and where all the necessities of life must be imported and are therefore expensive.

I am transmitting in attachment No. 3 an exact accounting of all expenditures. I will place these before the Colonial Council to get their opinion on whether or not these expenditures were necessary. I will seek this opinion as soon as I return to the encampment and forthwith send it to the directors.

In the meantime, at the third meeting of the Colonial Council it was decided to send Captain v. Wrede to New Orleans to procure those items which Mr. Fisher either did not obtain or which were of such poor quality that they were not useable. Additional costs are thus accruing to the Verein on account of Mr. Fisher's management. The question is: Shall I turn the whole control over to Mr. Fisher and say to him "You said that you could accomplish the mission for $35,000, now show us"? In this case I would be giving him full authority, and I would be placing the interest of the Verein in his hands which he would trod under his feet in order to further his own interests. He would not be able to accomplish it at his own figures. He remarked on his arrival here that if it cost the Verein a little more it would be all the same either way: the interest [in the project] by the Germans would then be lost forever and it was doubtful anyway if the undertaking would succeed.

Or shall I take hold of the reins with a stronger hand and at the same time assume all of the responsibility? The interest of the Verein, the honor of its members, the interest of the German nation dictates the latter course. I have no choice.

And so I beg the directors not only for instructions regarding the $4,000 to be used for repayment of deposits but also for considerable further credit since the Verein very likely must make many advances from its storehouses because the upkeep of so many families is very high. The average cost per person can be assumed to be 2 pounds of meat per day 3¢, per week ½ pound of bacon 5¢, 1 pound of coffee 17¢, 1 pound of sugar 13¢, 1 pound of salt 5¢, 1 bushel of corn 33¢. This adds up to a monthly total of $2.68 per man. From this the directors can readily see how much is required. Up to now we have allowed only one pound of meat and have been as sparing as possible with the bread. But the boundless confusion on the ships and Mr. Fisher's lack of foresight in procuring men for Mr. K. [Klaener] to send to Port Lavaca and Indian Point to start operations there has resulted in much loss of time.

I will hold Mr. Fisher accountable to the Colonial Council: Firstly, for the sum of $13,360 and especially for

1. what he purchased, to be accompanied by receipts.
2. what he has purchased at too high a price.

3. The worthless things which he has purchased that had to be thrown away.
4. what is lacking.

Secondly, on account of his negligence, for all of the faulty vehicles, necessitating a long wait which resulted in large accrued costs.

Thirdly, because of negligence, it is hardly probable that a harvest can be expected by the immigrants.

Fourthly, for his appointments, namely:

1. Mr. Burchhardt Miller as agent of transportation.
2. Mr. Theodor Miller as agent of Mr. Kaufmann to receive the wares at Indian Point.
3. Mr. Eggers in a similar position in Port Lavaca.
4. The unattached Swiss Texan, Mr. Bollinger ($1/a day).
5. The Dane, Morewood.
6. The unattached Texan, Wirths.
7. The carpenter Moser (daily $3)
8. The cabinet maker Schwarz (daily $2)

Fifthly, for the costs of transporting the immigrants of the Ship *Weser* [which arrived in July] under the guidance of Mr. Burchhardt H. Miller.

It must be further noted that some postal arrangement must be made between Galveston and the encampment or settlement, since the Texas Post is dependent on the weather and more or less on the amount of whiskey the mail rider has consumed, and therefore is very uncertain. Also regular communication must be established between Carlshafen, Galveston, and New Orleans. This will entail additional costs.

Finally, it must be mentioned that 200 families and single persons must be brought into the land; otherwise the grant will be lost. We now have about 140 heads of families and single persons. Among these are the Hannoverian Lieutenant D. Claren (artillery) and v. Cloudt (infantry, but a good horseman), both of whom arrived on the Ship *Apollo*. This also includes those who arrived on the Ship *The Weser*. Thus we still lack 60. Our agent, D. H. Klaerner, [Klaener] arrived on the Ship *Neptune* from Bremen, and with him there were ten persons (heads of families and single persons) who will join us. This leaves 50 which the directors will send, namely the miners. The arrival of the Ship *Weser* is being awaited again.

A ship has arrived from New Orleans with 204 immigrants

for Mr. Castro, and these already are in distress. I do not have the means to help them, although without exception all want to join the Verein. I could well use them, especially as settlers beyond the Guadalupe [River] or else in Carlshafen.

Since our costs have increased, this should be chargeable to Mr. Fisher since his preparations or lack of preparations can be blamed for this to a great extent. Neither the Verein nor the immigrants are able to resolve this; it is up to the directors to withhold the $2,000 due Mr. Fisher in September of this year, or else lay claim to an equivalent amount from his one third of the land so that we will thus be indemnified as to capital and interest thereon.

The Congress has already adjourned or will disperse in a few days without having acted on annexation, although many members favored it. The possibility of an extra session should not be discounted, although I doubt if there will be one.

A year lies ahead of us in which to prepare ourselves for protection against the unfriendly elements. That these hazards exist, there is no question. If everything is done well this year, resulting in a great influx of immigrants, then all is won; if this year is a failure, then everything will be unredeemably lost. A great future, a rich reward, an entirely new stimulus to everything in the beloved Germany, may God bless it; a new blossom time, this all for the German fatherland, yes for the entire astonished world, all brought about by the Verein.

Aren't these great and wonderful things worth sacrificing and fighting for? Or should this undertaking take its place with the unsuccessful ventures, common enterprises, and speculations? The eyes of Germany, no the eyes of all of Europe are on us and on our undertaking. German princes, counts, and nobles are at its head. There must be no hesitation in their minds; they must be mindful of honor attached to their names and the historical fame of their ancestors and of the desire to add new laurels to the old honors, at the same time assuring immeasurable riches to their children and grandchildren.

Galveston,   (Sig.) Commissioner General
8th of February, 1845   Carl, Prince of Solms
Postscript, 9th February, 1845

Just now I received the epistle and report from Mr. Fisher which is included as item No. 6 in attachment No. 3. I have found out that he has engaged a lawyer and told him that I was trying to protect the German interests in the colony and therefore would not consider taking in any Americans, that after all I was hostile to the Americans and that I was also opposed to annexation and other matters of a like nature.

In this way he seeks to stir up people against me, and he has been successful to the extent that there has been discussion and criticism in a grog shop. Mr. B. Miller has remarked that he and Mr. Fisher would take the next ship from here to the encampment by way of Port Lavaca where they would take up their complaints with the Colonial Council. After this incident, I will watch out for all, especially underhanded, actions by these two and thus be prepared for them.

I have the honor to include attachment No. 4 with my last report to the directors. It consists of a general summary and details of expenditures of capital funds. This was prepared with the kind help of Mr. Rainer (from the firm of D. H. Klaerner [Klaener]). Since I am not familiar with commercial accounting, I could not do anything but promptly and with painstaking accuracy vouch for every item, and assemble and keep records of every transaction.

At this moment, I am not able to find any suitable accounting form on which to itemize the expenditures under the proper heading as they are on the budget. Closer examination may indicate that some items should have been put under different headings. I beg the directors to excuse my errors.

I wish to remark further that the responsibility of administering the funds and establishing an accounting system, plus the worry that there would always be sufficient funds available so that I would not be left high and dry with so many people, has caused me more anxiety and distress and worry, and has wrung more beads of sweat out of me than the July sun and all the Indian tribes in Texas together.

After deducting purchases being made now in New Orleans and other expenses, there should be about $7,000 left on hand.

Galveston   (Signed)
the 12th of February, 1845   The Commissioner General
                           Carl, Prince of Solms

Prince Solms's 9th Report
dated
5 March, 1845 in encampment at McCoy [Creek][55]

I report most obediently to the directors that I left Galveston February 23rd and arrived at Carlshafen on the 25th at one o'clock at night. I covered the 140 miles in 61 hours, partly by horseback and partly in an open boat. At seven o'clock in the evening I arrived in Victoria where the storehouse is located at present. A portion of the immigrants are encamped two miles beyond that town. I found that at least they were not idle during my absence. Engineer Zink, using the few oxen and wagons procured by Mr. Fisher and hiring wagons as a final resort, had, with the help of the immigrants, moved part of them to Victoria and the rest 42 miles further on.

In the meantime, three field blacksmith shops are at work in the encampment at Victoria; fourteen wagons and carts were produced by their own resourcefulness, a cannon was mounted, and the carriage for the other is in the process of being made. Everything is in readiness so that we can break camp on Monday the tenth and leave here with all the wagons.

Simultaneously with me, yes at the same moment, Mr. Fisher arrived in Victoria after visiting both encampments. There he made unbecoming remarks about the Verein and was especially insulting about its representatives. He has done the same with every individual immigrant he has met in an effort to clear himself of all blame. At the same time he has awakened the spirit of opposition to the Verein and its officials. The ideas of freedom and equality expounded by Mr. Fisher himself serve to loosen all bonds of obedience. He even sought followers for himself among the supervisors by promising them raises in salaries and also by other crude methods, thereby again inciting one against the other. For the time being his typical American game of intrigue has caused no mischief.

In Victoria in the presence of Engineer Zink[56] I had a preliminary conference with Mr. Fisher which was fruitless. From there on March 2, I went to the encampment on McCoy Creek where I heard more details of Mr. Fisher's efforts.

Just as I must praise to the Verein the demonstrated enormous activity and tact of Engineer Zink which no one can appreciate unless he is personally acquainted with conditions here in Texas, so must I also on the other hand mention Mr. von Coll.[57] Despite all possible instigations to rebellion, he has kept up the spirit of those in this encampment, namely the Company, which could only have been accomplished through his fair and tactful conduct. To my regret, it is my duty to report the opposite regarding Dr. C. From many statements on record and from written complaints, I am compelled, on account of his hard and inhuman manner, to suspend his office until I have received orders from the directors about what to do with him. From the records which will be studied more closely, it is apparent that there was a breach of contract. A report will follow in due time. In the meantime I shall permit Dr. Meyer to practice in the colony.

Mr. Fisher arrived in the encampment here the evening before last, and at noon yesterday the session of the Colonial Council was held. The minutes of the meeting are enclosed, as well as the resolution which was the only one that could be drawn because the conviction of the officials collectively, as well as my own, is that Mr. Fisher's presence in the management [of the immigrants] for four weeks would loosen all bonds that tie us together.

To all the complaints with which we confronted him, he answered either, "Yes, that is what you believe (for instance that eight wagons were not enough for the transportation of 400 persons from the bay to the colony) because you do not understand how to do it," or, as shown by the enclosed legal and sworn official document, "That is not so." In the supplement to the contract that was concluded with him, he wanted to recognize that part only which, in his opinion, was not in conflict with the contract itself; in other words, only the portion that suited him. He refused to recognize a Commissioner-General who, at the most, was only a banker to the Colonial Council, for which I thanked him. Furthermore, he wanted Mr. Müller or B. Miller[58] on the Colonial Council with a salary for this title; and so on with other nonsense and absurdities.

I definitely support the Colonial Council's suggestion of a security guarantee or bond, or better yet, purchasing the [Fisher's] third part. I shall endeavor to explain further verbally.

I believe that Mr. Fisher will come to Germany himself where he expects to clear himself of all misunderstanding with a few words to the directors. I suspect that I will be in Germany myself at that time when I can contribute my bit toward clearing up any doubt about the mistakes that Mr. Fisher made. He has not presented any accounting but has promised to do so.

Tomorrow I shall leave via Gonzales and Seguin for San Antonio where I shall take care of details concerning the land belonging to the late Senator Smith. I will expect the immigrant colony at Seguin or on the land itself.

(Signed)
The Commissioner-General
Karl, Prince of Solms

In encampment at McCoy Creek
the 5th of March, 1845

Prince Solms's 10th Report
dated
27 March, 1845 on Comal Creek

I have the honor to advise the directors that after completing the business with Mr. Fisher I inspected the assembled company. I was generally pleased with their horsemanship and marksmanship, as well as their deportment.

I left after that on my trip to San Antonio where I arrived on the 10th. The 11th, 12th, 13th, and 14th were spent in negotiations with Messrs. Veramendi and LaGarza[59] for the purchase of the land which had been erroneously reported as belonging to Senator Smith. Upon my return [to Germany], I shall report in more detail, and I can assure that the transaction can be proven to be advantageous.

The contract was signed on the 15th.[60] On the 16th I rode back to Seguin where on the 17th Messrs. Zink and von Coll arrived with thirteen men of the company. On the same day, I traveled six miles further and made camp at a spring flowing into the Guadalupe River. A furious norther blew up during the night and has been blowing continuously ever since.

On the 18th I crossed the Guadalupe at the ford of the great military[61] road from Nacogdoches[62] to San Antonio. The river is locked in by rocky cliffs and rushes wildly over rocks and boulders. Right here is the beginning of the land which I brought into the Verein's possession. The Comal Creek runs through it. On the right bank of this Creek there is rich prairie land with open terrain which continues toward a dominant elevation. On the left bank of Comal Creek there is well forested bottom land which extends to the cedar, oak, and elm covered cliffs which here already have considerable height. Beyond this there is a high ridge with summits here and there similar to our Black Forest.[63]

The ridge runs from N.W. to S.E. Through this bottom land the Comal Spring [River] flows. It bubbles forth from the cliffs in seven separate springs and immediately attains a width of twenty steps. This stream of crystal clear water of considerable depth steadily widens, winds about like a forest torrent, and rushes on.

From its confluence with the Comal Creek I, with four companions, attempted to reach the head spring. However, having covered only five miles after hours of chopping through underbrush and heavy forest, we had to return without success. On the following day, guided by two Americans who were bear hunting, we reached the spring without any difficulty. [Comal River 3¼ miles, measured by R. S. Jahn, Civil Engineer, 1950.]

Each day, I rode about in the region to familiarize myself with the country. On the 20th of this month, for the first time I ascended the ridge on horseback, forcing a path through the heavy cedar thickets and using the outcropping ledges as steps. The view from the high ridge, behind which there is a plateau several miles wide, is enchanting. I rode three or four miles into this tableland without coming to its end. As soon as time permits, I shall make another tour up there.

All over the country there are signs of large and smaller camps of the Indians who, on account of the good hunting and excellent water, occasionally pitched their nomad tents here. However, as soon as civilization comes near, they withdraw because the sound of the ax in the woods is annoying to them. Should some go astray and wander this way, I believe that the clatter of the mills on the river and the noise of the forges would scare them off. The Comal River is especially adapted for just such installations on account of its ever constant water supply.

Enclosed herewith is a map of the land as attached to the purchase contract. Only the location of the high ridges is omitted.

Field plots have been staked out and the plow is turning the sod. I myself traced the outline of the citadel [fort] yesterday on the dominant height, below which the city is to be laid out in all directions.

Thirty-one wagons have arrived, and I am expecting the last half of the immigrants within a few days. I had an encampment erected on a bluff overlooking Comal Creek. For its protection I think it urgent that three sides be enclosed by palisades, whereas the fourth side is amply protected against attack by the high steep bluff of Comal Creek.

In my next report I hope to be able to announce the layout of the town and its consecration; and I shall then enclose an exact plan of it.

The weather is cool and moist; yes, on the morning of the 19th we had a home-like scene of snow. The health of the immigrants is satisfactory.

(Signed)

Encampment on Comal Creek   The Commissioner-General
the 27th of March, 1845   Karl, Prince of Solms

Prince Solms's 11th Report
dated
30 April, 1845—Sophienburg[61]

I can announce to the directors today that I have transferred to the immigrants half acre city lots and ten acre farm lots located on the land here, and that I have named the new city "New Braunfels." On April 28th, I also laid the cornerstone of the proposed fort for the protection of the city. This will also enclose the Verein headquarters, and I have named the fort "Sophienburg."

The encampment has become less and less occupied whereas the erection of temporary homes on the building sites has begun. It is a cheerful sight to see this beauty spot of nature developing and the land becoming inhabited.

Only the buildings for the Verein and the urgently needed storehouse show very little progress. Engineer Zink's excuse is that there is a scarcity of workers since each one wants first of all to provide for his own.

The three supervisors [of the Verein here] have requested that they be given the greater part of their land allotment here since they would have to reside in the settlement. I discussed this with them; and since it is only fair that they receive a portion here, we came to an agreement that they have one third, that is 100 acres, surveyed for themselves, pending the approval of the directors.

Instead of a storehouse, the subordinate officials erected an inadequate shack in which many goods spoiled during the continuous rains, particularly four wagon loads of maize [corn].

Although Mr. v. Meusebach[65] (from whom I received a letter dated the 6th of April in New Orleans) has not arrived yet, I expect him any day, and I have arranged for my departure on Thursday the 15th of May. I hope to arrive in Boston in a month so that I can depart from America by steam boat on the 15th of June. However, on account of slow traveling conditions here, irregular communication [transportation] between Galveston and New Orleans, and the long trip up the Mississippi, nothing definite can be planned.

I am very anxious to arrive in Germany in due time so that some very important changes can be made in our colonization system. Among these are:

1. That only selected immigrants be sent because only able, upright, and steady people can build up a colony.
2. Immigrants are to be divided into two classes: the first, [class] those paying or making deposits for the overland trip must pay at least five times the present sum required. Furthermore, they must bind themselves, once their credit has been exhausted, to pay for everything they withdraw from the Verein's storehouse.

   The second class to be sent by the Verein must bind themselves to work at least one year for the Verein, for which they are to be boarded by the Verein, and a second year for day wages to be set by the Verein.
3. During a recent visit of Captain Hays, he told me that the eastern boundary of the grant [Fisher-Miller Grant] was probably 70 miles distant from here and that very likely four to six settlements [way stations] would be necessary before reaching the grant with settlers. Therefore, land may be promised to the settlers in the grant; however, temporarily they must be content with ten acres which they would receive in the settlements. It would be necessary to acquire this land beforehand. This applies also to those who are to be settled inland from the Bay [Lavaca] and also upwards from Victoria.

I shall personally discuss these points in detail, and I hope that upon my arrival there will still be time enough to change the contracts accordingly.

That I shall speed my voyage as much as possible, I need not mention. Since this is my last report before my departure, I shall verbally report on all matters which may occur between now and the time of my leaving.

	(Signed)
Sophienburg	The Commissioner-General
the 30th of April, 1845[66]	Karl, Prince of Solms

NOTES ON
THE ELEVEN PRINCE SOLMS'S REPORTS

First Report dated 15th of July, 1884 at Nassau (Farm), Texas

[1]The Colonial director—Bourgeois d'Orvanne, appointed by the directors of the Verein to go to Texas with Prince Solms as Colonial-Director of the Verein's project.

[2]The Plantation—Nassau Plantation or Farm in Fayette County, Texas bought by Count Boos-Waldeck out of the W. H. Jack league of land in 1843.

[3]Directors' Committee—A committee of the Directors of the Adelsverein in Germany.

[4]Verein—A short name for the Adelsverein, the Society for the Protection of German Immigrants to Texas.

[5]Count Boos-Waldeck—Count Joseph Boos-Waldeck who came to Texas in 1843 for the Verein. He bought the W. H. Jack league of land in Fayette County and named it Nassau Farm in honor of the Duke of Nassau, one of the directors of the Verein. Biesele, **Hist. of the German Settlements,** p. 53.

[6]Mr. Fortrand—Charles Fortrand who came to Texas in 1831 with Friedrich Ernst and surveyed Ernst's league of land in Austin County, Texas. Biesele, p. 43.

[7]Overseer Bryan—A man hired to take care of Nassau Farm.

[8]William Etzel—Etzel was placed in charge of Nassau Farm by Charles Fortrand. Biesele, p. 53.

[9]10 T per Courant—possibly 10 dollars in currency.

[10]The Association—The Adelsverein.

[11]Washington (on-the-Brazos)—Capital of Texas in 1843.

[12]Secretary of State—Texas, as a Republic, had its own governmental staff. Dr. Anson Jones was Secretary of State in 1843.

[13]President—In 1843, Sam Houston was President of the Republic of Texas.

[14]Mr. Ernst—Friedrich Ernst who came to Texas in 1831 and founded the town of Industry in Austin County. Biesele, p. 46.

[15]Congress—the legislative body of the Republic of Texas.

[16]Dr. Meyer—Dr. Emil Meyer, appointed by Prince Solms as the Society's physician at Carlshafen.

[17]Denman—?

Second Report dated 20 August, 1844 at San Antonio

[18]Surveyor Hays—Colonel Hays, surveyor, Indian fighter, and scout in the Republic of Texas.

[19]Colonial-Director—Bourgeois d'Orvanne.

[20]McMullen Tract—a land grant south of San Antonio.

[21]Mr. Ducos—partner with Bourgeois d'Orvanne in the Bourgeois-Ducos Grant.

[22]Lamar—A town established in present Aransas County and named for Mirabeau B. Lamar, third president of the Republic of Texas.

[23]Henry Castro—One of the men who had received a grant of land from the Republic of Texas. He established Castroville in 1844. **Handbook of Texas,** Vol. I, page 308.

[24]Johann Rahm—The man who told Prince Solms about the Veramendi land at present New Braunfels.

[25]Canon Schaffhausen—a district in Switzerland.

Third Report dated 26 August, 1844—San Antonio

[26]Mr. von Wrede—Captain von Wrede in February 1845 was sent to New Orleans to procure needed articles. See 8th report.

70

[27]Mr. Fisher—Henry Fisher who with Burchard Miller secured the Fisher-Miller Grant.

[28]Bexar County—Bexar County, Texas in 1844 comprised all land north of San Antonio.

[29]Seguin—a town 14 miles southeast of New Braunfels.

[30]Leona—Leona River, southwest of San Antonio; more likely Llano is meant here.

[31]President Gen. Sam Houston—In 1834, General Sam Houston was serving his second administration as President of the Republic of Texas.

Fourth Report dated 20 September, 1844—Nassau

[32]Dr. Anson Jones—Vice-President of the Republic of Texas in President Sam Houston's second administration.

[33]Dr. Anson Jones succeeded Sam Houston as President of the Republic of Texas on December 9, 1844.

Fifth Report dated Galveston, 25 October, 1844

[34]Mr. Kaufmann—E. Kaufmann & Co., appointed by Prince Solms as agent for the Verein at Carlshafen (Indianola).

[35]Matagorda Bay—a bay southwest of Galveston.

[36]Cummings Creek—Cummings Creek in Colorado County, Texas.

[37]The grant—The Fisher-Miller Grant located between the Colorado and Llano Rivers.

[38]McLewin—Probably misspelled for McGloin who had a grant of land near Corpus Christi Bay. Biesele, page 109.

Sixth Report dated 23rd December, 1844—in camp at Port Lavaca

[39]Norther—a cold north wind in Texas which can cause a sudden drop in temperature.

[40]Lavaca Bay—the upper part of Matagorda Bay.

[41]Paso Caballo—the pass between Matagorda Bay and the Gulf of Mexico.

[42]Indian Point—on Texas maps now called Indianola, formerly Carlshafen.

[43]Texana—in south central Jackson County.

[44]Mr. Thielpape—Surveyor of Lavaca Bay.

[45]Llano—The Llano River, the southern boundary of the Fisher-Miller Grant.

[46]Victoria—About 30 miles northwest of Indianola.

[47]Gonzales—About 60 miles northwest of Victoria.

[48]Chocolate Creek—near Indianola.

[49]Yucca—a desert plant with a large white blossom.

[50]Dr. Koester—The Verein's doctor at Carlshafen and at New Braunfels.

Seventh Report dated 1 January, 1845 at Lavaca

[51]Agua Dulce—17 miles from Carlshafen on road to Victoria.

[52]Colonial Council—In Texas the Colonial Council was the governing body of each settlement and consisted of five people: a physician, a minister, a civil engineer, a bookkeeper, and the agent of the company. Biesele, p. 87.

Eighth Report dated 8th February, 1845—Galveston, Texas

[53]Dr. Lynzee—?

[54]Gulden—about 40 cents.

Ninth Report dated 5 March, 1845—McCoy Creek

[55]McCoy Creek—80 miles north of Carlshafen on the road to Gonzales.

[56]Engineer Zink—Nicolaus Zink, surveyor for the Verein and founder of Sisterdale, Texas.

[57]Mr. von Coll—Jean Jacques von Coll—assisted Prince Solms in moving the immigrants from Carlshafen to New Braunfels.

[58]Mr. Miller—Burchard Miller, partner with Henry Fisher in the Fisher-Miller Grant.

Tenth Report dated 27 March, 1845—on Comal Creek

[59]Messrs. Veramendi—Juan Martin Veramendi, Spanish governor of San Antonio, 1832-1833 and owner, with Garza, of the land at New Braunfels. Garza: Rafael Garza—whose wife was Maria Antonio Veramendi.

[60]The price paid for the Veramendi-Garza tract was $1111.

[61]Military road now known as the Old San Antonio Road.

[62]Nacogdoches—a town in East Texas, founded as a mission in 1716.

[63]Black Forest—in Württemburg, southern Germany.

Eleventh Report dated 30 April, 1845, Sophienburg, New Braunfels.

[64]Sophienburg—the fort erected by the Verein in New Braunfels and named Sophienburg by Prince Solms in honor of Princess Sophie.

[65]Mr. v. Meusebach—Baron Ottfried Hans von Meusebach—successor to Prince Solms as Commissioner-General of the Verein in Texas in May, 1845.

[66]On 15 July, 1845, Prince Solms made a report at Wiesbaden on the Verein's colonization project in Texas. See report, pp. 8, 9, and 10.

Introduction to

INDEXED LIST OF IMMIGRANTS

In order to include all possible information about a given immigrant, data is listed from German Immigration Contracts, land sale contracts, ship lists, and a list of the names of 850 emigrants who left Europe in 1845.

An effort was also made to establish the residences in Texas of the more than four thousand immigrants listed. Information was gathered from every possible source. Among these were deed and naturalization records in county courthouses in Texas, registers in churches, data given in books, and information in United States Census records for Texas counties for the years 1850 and 1860. This information was not found on some names due to the fact that some returned to Europe or went to other states, some died and were buried in unknown places with no record left of their death, and some enlisted in United States Army and no record was found.

In instances where there were several immigrants with a common name, such as Johann Schmidt or Heinrich Meyer or Mayer, and these names were found in more than one county in census lists, it was impossible to establish the correct county in which this person had settled. In these cases no residence in Texas has been named.

No attempt has been made to list the names of children in United States Census reports since these records are available on microfilm in so many libraries in the United States. In instances where the names of wives and children are given, the data is compiled from ship lists which are harder to find.

An attempt has been made to give a clear record of each immigrant so that further research may be made. A list of sources, abbreviations, and key signs follows. A careful study of these will be helpful in interpreting the data.

With regard to the use of umlauts, such as ä, ö, ü, as used in German names, such as *Müller*, the American spelling is used, as *Mueller*.

A form has been used, as far as possible, in presenting the name and information about each immigrant: 1) name; 2) whether single (s) or married (m); 3) age, if known; 4) residence in Europe; 5) name of ship and date of arrival in Texas; 6) maiden name of wife and names of children, when known; 7) other information, such as date of death when known; 8) residence in Texas, if known. For instance:

> Gerhard, Wilh.—m, 43 from Dillenburg, Nassau; **Herschel,** 1845
> w—Cath. nee Straube; ch—Johanna, Elis.; Comal Co.

It is possible that some towns will be hard to locate on maps or may not be found at all. These are usually small towns that 1) may no longer exist; or 2) the spelling has changed; or the spelling on written records was not clear; or 3) because, as Karl Friedrich von Frank has pointed out, there are several towns by that name in Germany; as, for instance, Münster. There are 31 towns in Germany named Münster; therefore, without further information it would be impossible to indicate in which province a town like Münster could be situated.

A list of the immigrants was sent to Karl Friedrich von Frank in order that he might check the spelling and location of towns in Europe as much as possible. Corrections were made according to his suggestons. German gazetteers were also used. Every effort was made in reading Texas records to copy all names as accurately as possible, but former errors made by persons who did not understand German pronunciation caused mistakes in the original records and printed lists in Texas.

A few immigrants, mostly from Baden, Alsace Lorraine, and Switzerland who came to Texas with Henry Castro, joined the Verein Colony at New Braunfels in 1845. These came on the Castro Colony ships: *Ocean, Heinrich, Jean Key,* and perhaps other ships whose passenger lists are not available at present.

Karl Friedrich von Frank has not only corrected the spelling of towns in Europe from which the immigrants came but has also described the geographical location of many. Some of these governmental divisions are mentioned in the index of immigrants.

1) Kreis (Kr.) = district, corresponding to American county.
2) Reg. (ierungs) = Bez. (irk) = governmental district (Rgbz), containing a number of Kreis.
3) Amtsgericht = jurisdictional district. There are several Amtsgerichte (AG) in one Kreis.

Abbreviations and symbols used
in indexed list of German immigrants to Texas

Abbreviation of names:		Abbreviation of places in Germany:	
Ad.	= Adolph	Brnschwg	= Braunschweig = Brunswick
Aug.	= August	Han.	= Hannover
Balth.	= Balthasar	Kurh.	= Kurhessen
Bernh.	= Bernhard	Mecklbg	= Mecklenburg
Caro.	= Caroline	Nass.	= Nassau
Cath.	= Catherine	Wurtt.	= Wurttemberg
Chr.	= Christian	Ff/M	= Frankfurt/Main
Dietr.	= Dietrich	Ff/O	= Frankfurt/Oder
Elis.	= Elisabeth		

Other abbreviations:

Ferd.	= Ferdinand	Co.	= Country
Friedr.	= Friedrich	Ch.	= Church; (NBChR) = New
Gus.	= Gustav		Braunfels Church Record
Hein.	= Heinrich		(FChP) = Fredericksburg
Herm.	= Hermann		Church Record
Jac.	= Jacob	Gal.	= Galveston
Joh.	= Johann	(IC)	= Immigration Contract
Jos.	= Joseph	(SL)	= Ship List
Ludw.	= Ludwig	(VF)	= Verein File = Verein Collection
Marg.	= Margaretha	*	= born, as 2.IV.1845 means born
Nic.	= Nicolaus		2 April, 1845
Ph.	= Philipp	†	= died, as 4.V.1832 means died 4
Theo.	= Theodor		May, 1832
Val.	= Valentine	m or oo	= married
Wilhme	= Wilhelmine	s	= single
Wilh.	= Wilhelm	w	= wife
		dau.	= daughter
		ch	= child or children

In dates, the Roman numeral indicates the month, as: 6.VIII.1846 = 6 August, 1846.

Notes:

The name of the ship on which an immigrant sailed to Texas is listed with his name. Also listed is date of arrival at Galveston, Texas. Other information about the ships may be found in the "List of Ships from Germany and the United States".

The residence of an immigrant in Germany may not necessarily be his birth place. Frequently, a large town may be named while his birthplace may be a smaller town nearby. When a town cannot be located, it is either too small or it may have disappeared in the last 120 years. See also paragraph 2, page 74.

Names of wives and children are given only when found on ship lists. In other cases, these names may be found on Microfilm of the United States Census, beginning with 1850, for counties in Texas. These Microfilms may be found in most large libraries in Texas and perhaps other states.

The name of a home town given on a German Immigration Contract (IC) is considered more reliable than the town named on a ship list (SL) unless the ship list is from the Verein File (VF) in the University of Texas Archives.

The listing "New Braunfels 1845" indicates that the person named was a founder of New Braunfles.

— A —

Aake, Charles—arr. 1.V.1846; died
Abe, Caspar Johann—s, 45; from
Kaltennordheim, Weimar; Nep-
tune, 1845
Aberstug, D.—from Stettin, 1845
Achen (Acher?), Reiner—s; had
Verein land grant
Achler, Hein.—s, 34, from Stock-
hausen, Kurh.; Garonne, 1845
Acker, Hein.—from Orb; 2 persons;
Comal Co.; James Edward, 1846
Acker, Philipp—s, 26, from Orb,
Comal Co.; James Edward, 1846
Acker, R.—from Orb; James Edward,
1846; Comal Co. 1850
Ackermann, Eva Magda., nee
Wieland—from Appenweiler,
Württ; †8.XII.1846,(NBChR)
Ackermann, Johannes—31, and
mother from Stettin; arr. 1846;
Bexar Co. 1850
Ackermann, Jos.—from Auenstein,
Wurtt,; 3 persons; Comal Co.;
Hamilton, 1846
Adam, Joh. and family—from
Thomashardt, arr. 1846; Bexar Co.
Adam, J.—from Niederelbert;
Herschel, 1845
Adams, Jacob—from Rosnowo;
w—Bertha nee Steingut; ch—
Augusta, Aug., Oetribecham,
Emilie, Gustav; Guadalupe Co.;
Johanna, 1846
Adrian, Bernhard, Sr.—from Schön-
enberg; Colchis, 1846
Adrian,Bernhard(son)—fromSchön-
enberg; Colchis, 1846
Adrian,Josef Clemens—from Schön-
enberg; widower and 3 ch; 10 per-
sons; Bexar Co. 1850; Colchis, 1846
Adrian, Josef Hubert (son)—age 22,
from Schonenberg; Bexar Co.;
Colchis, 1846
Agram, Carl—s, Joh. Dethardt, 1846
Ahlert, Friedrich—s, from Havel-
berg; 1846
Ahrens, Albert—32, Neptune, 1845
Ahrens, Conrad—44, from Oberg,
Han.; w—Dorothea nee Witte;
ch—Hein. 16, Conrad 13, Christian
10; Gillespie Co. 1850; Margaretha,
1845
Ahrens, Diedrich—wife and 4 ch;
Apollo, 1844
Ahrens, Friedrich—from Thielbeer,
Prussia; Gillespie Co.; Louise
Friedricke, 1847

Ahrens, Friedrich—s, from Pretzier,
Prussia; Gillespie Co.; B. Bohlen,
1847
Ahrens, Hein.—wife and 4 ch.;
Margaretha, 1845
Ahrens, Joh. Friedr.—s, from Mor-
ingen; Hamilton, 1846
Ahrens, Leonhard— from Oberg;
October 1845
Ahrens, widow—age 40, from Gaden-
stedt, Han.; ch—Caro, 17, Sofia 13;
Hercules, 1845
Ahrens, Wilh. Albert—s, 32, from
Braunschweig; Gillespie Co.;
Neptune, 1845
Albert (Albrecht?), Hein.—s, 19,
from Eitzum, Han.; Weser, 1845
Albachter, Hubertus—s, 19, from
Münster, Westphalia; Harriet,
1845
Albrecht, Blazens—45, from
Dezeln?, Baden; Castro Colonist;
New Braunfels 1845; Jean Key,
1844
Albrecht, Justus Friedr.—age 42,
Fayette Co. Mercur, 1846
Albrecht, Hein.—from Eitzum;
Weser, 1845
Albrecht, Martin—s, Andacia, 1846
Albrecht, Wilhelm—s, from Glessen;
Austin Co.; Mercur, 1846
Algrimm, Carl—Fredericksburg,
1847; Johann Dethardt, 1846
Alldoerfer, Jacob—s, from Rohr-
bach; Talisman, 1846
Al(l)senz, Adam—died, from OberIn-
gelheim; Barbara—widow; 4 per-
sons; Comal Co.; Talisman, 1846
Alsenz, Barbara—widow; Comal Co.
1848; Talisman, 1846
Alsenz, Joh.—s; Comal Co. 1850's;
Talisman, 1846
Albacher, Caspar—19; Harriet, 1845
Althaus, Christian—s, 29, from
Erndtebrück; Gillespie Co.; York,
1846
Althofer, Joh.—from Moscheim; 6
persons; Gillespie Co.; Riga, 1845
Altstaedten, August—s, 30, from
Bonn; Washington, 1845
Altstaedten, Emil—s, from Bonn;
Galveston Co.; James Edward,
1846
Altwein, Edgar—from Leuba Alten-
burg; Comal Co.; Margaretha, 1846
Alves, Friedr.—from Holtensen,
Han.; w—Ernestine neé Schoen;
ch—Friedr., Wilh., Johanna, Aug.,
Conrad †1846; Comal Co.; Gesina,
1846

Alves, Ludwig—s, from Holtensen, Han.; †23.VII.1846; buried at Fredericksburg; Gesina, 1846
Amberg, Anton—s, from Schleusingen; Hamilton, 1846
Amelung, Ernst Otto—s, 20; Bexar Co.; St. Pauli, 1847
Amelung, Otto—s, from Wolfhagen; Comal Co.; Harriet, 1845
Amendt, Friedr.—22, from Darmstadt; Bexar Co.; Andacia, 1846
Amendt, Samuel—s, from Darmstadt; †28.VIII.1846, age 47 (NBChR); Sarah Ann, 1845
Amlebach, John—s, 40; Dyle, 1846
Ammann, Carl—Kendall Co. 1850's; Neptune, 1846
Anderten, Christian—s, 20, from Einbeckhausen, Han.; Gesina, 1846
Anding, Hein.—45, from Weidenbrunn, Kurh.; w—Elisa nee Kresch—†1846, age 32 (NBChR); ch—Rosine 9, Louise 7, John 5, Henry 1; Garonne, 1846
Andreae, Carl Otto—from Petershütte, Han.; w—Wilme nee Bergmann; Elsia and Charlotte, 1846
Andreas, Jost Daniel—from Weidelbach †1855; w and 3 ch; Sarah Ann, 1845
Anschuetz, Andrew—60; Garonne, 1845
Anschuetz, Georg—30, from Meitingen; w—Cath. nee Brautigam; Anna 15; Gillespie Co.; Garonne, 1845
Arhelger, Jacob—49, from Rittershausen, Nassau; w—Elis. nee Mueller 50; ch—Elis. 18. Cath. 16, Henry, killed by Indians in 1863 near Fredericksburg, Wilh. 8, Aug. 2; Gillespie Co.; Herschel, 1845
Arhelger, Jacob—age 27; Herschel, 1845
Arhelger, Wilh.—from Rittershausen; w—Cath. nee Gruen; Herschel, 1845
Arnd, Joh. David—s, 22, from Fulda; Fredericksburg 1847; Neptune, 1845
Arn(h)old, Anna—from Oberscheid and son Heinrich; Arminius, 1845
Arn(h)old, Gottlieb— from Udersleben, Schwarzburg; widower and 3 ch.; Comal Co.; Elisa & Charlotte, 1846
Arnholt, Joh.—s, 27, from Rumbach, Hesse; New Braunfels 1845; Weser, 1844
Arnold, Peter—from Stephanshausen, Nassau; w—Cath. nee Ridel

† 1849, age 52; New Braunfels 1845; Ferdinand, 1844
Arnons, Andre Charles—from Berlin; 2 persons; Apollo, 1846
Arnsberger, Alex—23, from Germany; Star Republic from New York 1845; New York from New Orleans 1845
Aschauer, Friedr.—from Celle, Han.; Anna, 1846
Aschemann, Friedr.—s, from Lochtum, Brnschwg, Comal Co.; Louise, 1847
Aschemann, Gottlieb—Elisa & Charlotte, 1846
Aschenbach, Christian—from Oldenburg; wife and 2 ch; Colorado Co.; Franziska, 1846
Aschoff, J.H.A.—m, had land grant
Assel, Hermann von—s, 25, from Braunschweig; New Braunfels, 1845; Johann Dethardt, 1844
Assmann, Carl—s, from Sontra, Kurhessen; Fayette Co.; Elisa & Charlotte, 1846
Assmann, Ferd.—from Sulz by Sontra, Kurh.; w—Sophie nee Jesinicke; Elisa & Charlotte, 1846
Auberer, Ulrich and family—from Oberbach, Württ., arr. 1846
Aurand, Elisabeth—widow and 2 ch; Arminius, 1845
Aurand, Friedr.—s, from Steinbrücken, Nassau; Arminius, 1845
Aurand, Jacob—from Steinbrücken, Nassau; † 5.VI.1846, age 42 (NBChR); w—Elisa nee Nickel; ch—Jacob, Fried., Fried. Wilh., Christine, Wilhme; Arminius, 1845
Auterer (Anterer?), Conrad Isaac Nic.; Comal Co., New York, 1846

— B —

Bachmann, Ludwig—from Kerstenhausen; 6 persons; w.—Anna nee Stieping; ch.—Georg., Hein.; Galveston Co.; Johann Dethardt, 1845
Backhaus, Heinrich—from Gadenstedt, Han.; w—Dor. nee Dennings † 27.VI.1846, age 33; ch—Hein. age 1; Hercules, 1845
Backhofen, Hein.—s.; St. Pauli, 1847
Bade, Ludwig—from Visselhövede, Han.; w—Elisa nee Bremer; B. Bohlen, 1845
Bader, Gottfried—31; from Ilsfeld; Talisman, 1846
Bader, Jacob—s, from Oberlenningen; Nahant, then Timoleon, 1846; Austin Co.
Bader, Johann—from Oberlenningen; 3 persons; Nahant, 1845

77

wrecked, then **Timoleon**, 1846; Harris Co.

Bader, Joh. Michael—from Oberlenningen; 3 persons; Austin Co.; **Nahant**, 1846 wrecked at sea, then **Timoleon**, 1846

Bader, Karl Gottlieb—from Oberlenningen; Gillespie Co.; **Timoleon**, 1846

Baenfer, Joh.—s, from Dillenburg or Feudinger-Hütte; **York**, 1846

Bahndge, J.—died; from Zellerfeld; widow—Louisa and 2 ch.; **Anna**, 1846

Baldus, Joh.—s, from Hellenhahn, Nassau; New Braunfels, 1845; **Ferdinand**, 1844

Balhorn, Charlotte—widow from Wolfenbüttel, Brnschwg. Balhorn, Hein.—Colorado Co. 1869; **Louise**, 1846

Balmert, Anton—from Oberelbert; 4 persons; Fredericksburg, 1847; **Riga**, 1846

Balmert, Simon—from Oberelbert, Nassau—†4.VI.1846, age 45 (NBCh.R.); widow Elis. and 2 ch.; **Riga**, 1846

Baltuer, Chr.—w. and 2 ch.; **Sarah Ann**, 1845

Balzer, Johannes Schmidt—from Rennerod; arr. 15.IX.1845

Bamberger, Adam Val.—from Schmalkalden, Kurh.; 2 persons; **Everhard**, 1845

Banndt, J.D.—from Steinacker; **Harriet**, 1845

Bante, Georg. Friedr.—s, from Ottenstein, Braunschweig, **Mercur**, 1846

Bardenwerper, Carl—from Braunschweig; Comal Co.; **Arminius**, 1845

Bardenwerper, Joh. Ludwig—from Braunschweig; Bexar Co.; **Arminius**, 1845

Barmann,(=Bormann?), Conrad—from Everode, Han.; **Margaretha**, 1845

Bart(h)els, Aug.—from Harsum, Han.; **Weser**, 1845

Bartels, Bernhard—s, 21; **George Delius**, 1845

Bart(h)els, Cath.—from Stederdorf, Han.; **Hercules**, 1845

Bartels, Christian—†10.IV.1846, age 24 (NBCh.R.)

Bartels, Fried.—s, 21; **George Delius**, 1845

Bart(h)els, Hein.—from Rhoden; w—Henriette nee Keune; ch.—Andrew, Christian, Hein., Friedr.; Comal Co.; **Louise**, 1846

Barthelmes, Hein. Gustav—from Mehlis bei Zella; w—Ernestine nee Weimar; **Flavius**, 1846

Barthelmes, Michael—50; son Friedrich—16; from Kaltennordheim, Weimar; **Neptune**, 1845

Bartholomae, Andreas—from Eisenach (VF) or Creuzburg (IC); mother—Christina Elisa; cousin—August Grimm; sister—Christine Maria; **Johann Dethardt**, 1845

Bartholomae, Charles—s, 24; **Johann Dethardt**, 1845

Basel, Wilh.—s, from Bremen; Comal Co.; **Flavius**, 1846

Basler, Michael—s, from Offenburg; Austin Co., 1850; **Colchis**, 1846

Basse, Pastor Hein. S.W.—from Erndtebrück; w—Fredericke Charl. nee Quintel; ch—Bertha, Emma, Carl, Olga, Oscar; Gillespie Co.; **York**, 1846

Basson (Baston?) Hector—from Ath, Belgium (IC), Einbeck (VF); 3 persons; w.—Caro. nee Luecke; **Franziska**, 1846

Bast, Paul—from Unzenberg; w.—Marg.; ch.—Hanna, Mathias; Gillespie Co.; **James Edward**, 1846

Bauer, Alexis von—s, 32; New Braunfels, 1845; **Weser**, 1845

Bauer, Conrad—from Königstein; **Sarah Ann**, 1845

Bauer, Elis.—from Königstein (See Peter Stock); **Sarah Ann**, 1845

Bauer, Joh.—from Aschhausen; 5 persons; **Nahant** (wrecked) then **Dyle**, 1846

Bauer, Johann—w and 1 child; **Sarah Ann**, 1845

Bauer, Johann Georg.—s, from Dettenhausen; Gillespie Co.; **Element**, 1846

Bauer, Joseph—m, from Königstein; **Sarah Ann**, 1845

Bauer, Melchior—m, from Dettenhausen; w.—Rosina; ch—Jacob, Joh.; Gillespie Co.; **Element**, 1846

Baumann, Abraham—s, 36; from Winterlingen; **Andacia**, 1846

Baumann, Conrad—from Bruchköbel, Kurh.; w—Marg. nee Hosch ch—Cath., Marg., Conrad, Peter, Wilhme; **Louise Friedrike**, 1847

Baumann, Fr.—age 34; from Winterlingen; **Andacia**, 1846

Baumbach, Wilhelm von—s, from Siebertshausen, Kurh; Comal Co.; 1846

Baumeister, Michael—from Bruchkobel, Kurh.; w—Marg. nee Schliepler; **Louise Friedricke**, 1847

Baumgarten, Fr. Ernst—s, from Clausthal, a/Harz; **Karl Ferdinand**, 1846

Baumgartner, Elisa—Orient, 1846
Baeumche, Baeunche, Baumische,
see Baumsche
Baumsche, Peter—buried at
Indianola, age 38; from Mander-
bach, Nassau; †16.VI.1846;
w—Cath. nee Jung, †15.VII.1846
near Gonzales; Elise †1.IX.1846;
dau. Marg. sole heir; Auguste
Meline, 1845
Bauner, Ph.—s, from Waldal-
gesheim; Andacia, 1846
Bautle, Franz—from Strassberg;
Octave (f)—11, Verena 9, Joh. 8,
Georg. 6, Alex 5; Andacia, 1846
Beasley, Heinrich—m, Cincinnatti,
1846
Beatus, Wilh.—s, 19; died in Galves-
ton, 1846
Becheanz (=Berheanz?), Henry—
Dyle. 1946
Becher, Hein.—from Ohr, Han.;
Auguste Meline, 1845
Becher, Johannes—s, from Hausen;
Harris Co.; Hamilton, 1846
Becher, Wilh.—s, from Ohr, Han.;
Austin Co.; Auguste Meline, 1845
Bechtold, Bernhard—from Hoch-
hausen, Baden; Harris Co.;
Sarah Ann, 1845
Bechtold, Conrad—from Hallgar-
ten; †20.X.1846, age 38; Chris-
tine--widow; ch—Conrad †1846,
age 8; Juliane †1846, age 7; Chris-
tian †1846, age 2, (NBCh.R.);
mother—Juliane †3.IX.1846, age
60; Sarah Ann, 1845
Beck, Christian—s, 40, from
Haberschlacht, Württ; Brazoria
Co.; Talisman, 1846
Beck, Johann—from Hartershau-
sen; 1845
Beck, Philipp—44, from Winter-
lingen, Württ; w—Christina M.—
37, ch—Christian 11, Johann 10,
Philipp 8; Gillespie Co.; Andacia,
1846
Beckel, Joh. Georg. Christian—44;
from Wiesbaden; w—Caro. nee
Strauss—43; Joh. Dethardt, 1845
Beckels, Homan—died 1848; arr.
July 1848
Becker, Adam—from Camberg; 7
persons; Bastrop Co., Bohemia,
1846
Becker, Adam—age 29; from
Neudorf; Neptune, 1845
Becker, Caspar—s, 23, from Motzlar,
Kurh.; Garonne, 1845
Becker, Conrad—s, from Glauberg,
Ober-Hesse; James Edward, 1846
Becker, Friedr.—from Ochtrup,
Westphalia; w—Cath. nee Dier-
kens; Colorado Co.; B. Bohlen,
1847

Becker, Friedr.—from Quedlinburg,
Prussia; w—Friedricke Hol-
laender; ch—Chr., Albert, Fried-
ricke, Gustav; Joh. Dethardt, 1846
Becker (Boecker), Fried.—28, from
Schmedenstedt, Han.; Comal Co.;
w—Christine Dannsmann, age 45,
Johanna 2; Hercules, 1845
Becker, George—from Camberg; 2
persons; Colorado Co.; Bohemia,
1846
Becker, Wilhelm—s, from Berlin;
Gillespie Co.; Mathilda, 1846
Becker, Wilh.—s, from Ohr, Han.;
1845; Austin Co.
Beckshoeft, Joh. Simon—from Trib-
sees; w—Johanne nee Classen;
1846
Beebham, Sopha—23; Andacia, 1846
Beelitz, C.F.W.—s, 31 from Spandau;
Franziska, 1846
Beermann, Julius—s, from Claus-
thal; Talisman, 1846
Behne, Ludwig—from Fallersleben,
Han.; w—Louise nee Wense;
ch—Arthur, Charl., Ernst; Karl
Ferdinand, 1846
Behne, Otto—s, from Fallersleben,
Han.; Austin Co; Karl Ferdinand,
1846
Behr, Michael—from Hildesheim;
Creole, 1846
Behr, Ottmar von—m; Kendall Co.;
1848; Comal Co. 1850
Behrend, Friedr.—s, 32, from Kö-
penick, Prussia; Franziska, 1846
Behrends, Carl—from Clausthal;
w—Meta nee Stiffer; Anna, 1846
Behrends, J.—m, had Verein land
grant
Behrendt, Joh.—from Culm; 3 per-
sons; Orient, 1846
Behrendt, Julius—m; Orient, 1846
Behrens, Christoph—from Göt-
tingen, Han.; w—Wilhelmine nee
Ahrens; Friedrich, 1846
Behrens, Conrad—from Gebhards-
hagen, Brnschwg; 8 persons;
w—Sophie nee Hauer; Gillespie
Co.; Gerhard Hermann, 1846
Behrens, Friedrich—s, from Ein-
beck, Han.; Fredericksburg; mur-
dered by Indians in 1866(FChR);
Creole, 1846
Behrens, Peter—from Woltwiesche,
Brnschwg; w—Elisa Fischer;
Gerhard Herman, 1846
Behring,Christian—Fredericksburg,
1847
Behring, Joh.—s, age 35, from Han-
nover; Ferdinand, 1845
Behrmann, L.G.A.—m, †before 1860;
had Verein land grant
Behrns,Joh.—age 21; Herschel, 1845
Behrns, Joh. Hein.— †1846; from

79

Fellerdilln, Nassau; w—Anna Marie nee Kring; ch—Joh., Anna Elis.; **Herschel**, 1845

Beiermann, Joh. Friedr.—s, 56, from Heinebuchenbruch, Lippe; **Everhard**, 1845

Beil,———, from Clausthal; **Talisman**, 1846

Beil, Wilh.—from Thalheim; **Hamilton**, 1846

Beisel, Joh. Arnold—s, from Corneli-Münster; FayetteCo.; **Colchis**,1846

Beissner, Mrs.—with 2 ch.; **Comal Co.; Weser**, 1844

Bellmer, Carl—s, from Hiddissen, by Detmold; New Braunfels, 1845; **Joh. Dethardt**, 1844

Bender, Jacob —and wife, from Babstadt; **Henry**, 1846

Bene, Lieut. Ludwig—age 33, from Wetzlar; **Herschel**, 1845

Benfer, George.—s, 30, from Rüppershausen; oo Cath. **Marquardt** (widow) in 1846; New Braunfels, 1845; **Johann Dethardt**, 1844

Bengener, Hein.—s, 19, from Peine, Han.; Travis Co., 1849; **Hercules**, 1845

Bengener, Joh. Hein. Christoph— from Peine, Hann. age 54 † 7.I.1846, buried at Indianola; w—Friederike nee Pape, 47 †1846 buried 16 mi. below Seguin; Hein.; 19, Friedr. 16, † 5.VI.1846, Theo. 12 †26.VIII.1846, Dorette 10, Wilhelm 5; (NBChR); **Hercules**, 1845

Benner, Adolph—s, from Bergheim, Waldeck; New Braunfels, 1845; **Leontine**, 1844

Benner, Joh.—s, 33, from Fleisbach, Nass.; **Neptune**, 1845

Bennings, Louis—s, 27; **Apollo**, 1844

Berberich, Caspar—56, Caro. 20; from Amorbach; Gonzales Co.; **Washington**, 1845

Berberich, Charles—18, from Amorbach; Gonzales Co.; **Washington**, 1845

Berens, Hein.—from Einbeck, Han.; †.1846, age 28 (NBChR)

Berg, Emil—s, 21; **Apollo**, 1844

Berg, Theo.—s, 30; **Franziska**, 1846

Berge, Hermann zum—from Sülfeld, Han.; w—Sophie nee Sturm and baby; Comal Co.; **Creole**, 1846

Berger, Friedricke— **Flavius**, 1846

Berger, Gottlob Joh.—s, from Meissen; Austin Co.; **Flavius**, 1846

Berghoff, Joh.—from Hachen; **Diamant**, 1846

Berghoff, W.—s, from Hachen; **Diamant**, 1846

Bergmann, Carl—28, from Mardorf, Han.; Jacob—33; Henry; Comal Co., 1850; **Weser**, 1845

Bergold, Carl—s, died; from Fürth, Odenwald, Hesse; **Garonne**, 1845

Bering, Johannes—from Hofgeissner, Kurh.; w—Anna Marg. nee Reipe (Reisse?); ch—Carl Theo., Aug., Wilh., Carl, Theo., Ludw., Julius, Sabine, Adolph, Louise; Harris Co.; **Friedrich**, 1846

Beringer, Georg.—from Celle, Han.; Comal Co.; **Creole**, 1846

Ber(c)k, Jos. M.—m, 65; ch—Martin 8, Marie 6, Cath. 3; DeWitt Co.; **Andacia**, 1846

Berlocher, Lawrenz—s, 18; Galveston Co.; **Franziska**, 1846

Bernhard, Elisa—54, from Herbornseelbach, Nassau; ch—Maria, 4; Gillespie Co.; **Herschel**, 1845

Bernhard, Ernst—from Mark, Prussia; 1845

Berns, Joh. Hein.—40, from Fellerdiln, Nass.; w—Anna Marie nee Weber; ch—John Hein., Joh. Chr., Elis.; **Garonne**, 1845

Bernstein, Jos.—s, Fredericksburg, 1847; **Robert**, 1844

Berthold, Lieutenant Louis—s, from Cöln (Cologne); **Washington**, 1845

Bertling, Chr.—from Gifhorn, Han.; † 2.X.1846, age 22 (NBChR)

Bertling (Berkling?), Hein.—from Platendorf, Han.; w—Maria nee Behl; ch—Maria, Hein., Conrad, Dor. and step-son Christ. Tevers; **Everhard**, 1845

Besch, Ferd.—from Beuthen, Prussia; w—Antonie nee Bick; ch—Angelika, Carl, Alex, Emil; Colorado Co.; **Flavius**, 1846

Besier, Gustav—s, 30; **Sarah Ann**, 1845

Besier, Joh.—s, 29, from Hallgarten; Gillespie Co.; **Sarah Ann**, 1845

Beslar, Franz—s, 18, Beslar, Joh.—wife and 6 ch.; **Riga**, 1846

Besseaux, Ekard(t)—s, 22, from Rittershausen, Nassau; **Auguste Meline**, 1845

Best, Joh.—46; from Montebauer, Nassau; †28.VIII.1846; entire family had died by 16.III.1847 (NBCh.R.)

Best, Joh. Hein.—from Eitelborn, Nassau, w—Cath. nee Saal and 4 ch.; **Auguste Meline**, 1845

Best, Joh. Jos.—21, from Hilscheid; 9 persons; Galveston Co., 1850; **Riga**, 1846

Best, Paul—from Unzenberg; **James Edward**, 1846

Bestenpostell, Fried. von—s, 25 from Markoldendorf, Han.; †11.XI.1846, age 25 (NBCh.R.); **George Delius,** 1845
Betke, Wilhelm—from Schlangen, Detmold; **Neptune,** 1846
Betsch, Johann—See Petsch, Joh.
Betsch, Peter—See Petsch, Peter
Bettsbach, Sophie—**Neptune,** 1846
Beuner, Phil—from Rothweil; **Dyle,** 1846
Bevenroth, Christian—from Celle; 2 persons; **Creole,** 1846
Bevenroth, Hein.—†1849, age 52; from Meitze, Han.; w—Cath. Dor. Marie nee Stetter †19.III.1849, age 45(NBChR); New Braunfels, 1845; **Ferdinand,** 1844
Bibo, Jacob—22, from Rauenthal, Nassau; w—Franzizka—24; **Neptune,** 1845
Bickel, Gottfried—from Oberschönau,(VF); 1845
Bickel, Joh.—44 and Caro. 43; **Johann Dethardt,** 1845
Bickel, Peter—s, 36, from Wiesbaden; Gillespie Co.; **Andacia,** 1846
Bickelmayer, Joh.—32, from Oestrich, Nass.; 3 persons; **Neptune,** 1845
Bickenbach (Bueckenbach), Daniel—from Ruppichteroth; w— Anna Sophie nee Willach; ch— Wilh, Friedricia, Frederic; Gillespie Co.; Mason Co.; **Colchris,** 1846
Bickenbach (Bueckenbach), Peter —24, Cath.—18; Mason Co.; Gillespie Co.; **Colchis,** 1846
Bickenbach, Wilh.—s, Mason Co.; **Colchis,** 1846
Bickhoff—see Rickhoff
Bieberstein, Hermann von—from Görlitz, Silesia; w—Adele Hagedorn; Austin Co.; Mason Co.; **Elisa and Charlotte,** 1846
Bieberstein, Hermann von—from Neisse, Silesia; **Elisa and Charlotte,** 1846
Biehls, Christian—from Willingen; **Garonne,** 1845
Bielstein, August—from Semmenstedt, Braunschweig; w—Magda nee Schickerlein; Comal Co.; **Louise,** 1846
Biere, Bernhard—from Paderborn; w—Johanne nee Jaupen; dau—Louise; **Neptune,** 1846
Bierschwale, Heinrich—s, Mason Co.; **Hercules,** 1845
Billo, Andreas—m, from Seelbach; **Andacia,** 1845 (VF')
Bindewald, Rudolph—s, 29, from Engelrod, Kurh.; **Garonne,** 1845

Bingel, Carl—from Diez; 5 persons; **Harriet,** 1845
Bir(c)k, Peter—s, 29, from Werdorf; Fredericksburg and Mason Co.; **Neptune,** 1845
Bischoff Aug.—New Braunfels, 1845; **Herschel,** 1844
Bischoff, Wm.—37; from Kiedrich; w—Marg. B.—37; ch—Anna—2
Bischoff, Joh.—Brazoria Co., 1850; **Andacia,** 1846
Biton—see Pitton
Bitter, Franz—s; **Arminius,** 1845
Bitter, Hein.—from Dillenburg, Nassau; †25.V.1849, age 53; w—Charl. nee Reeb †2.V.1847, age 38; ch—Phil. 17, Franz 13, Hein. 11, Wilh. 9, Friedr. 6, Caro. 4, Elis. 1, (NBChR); **Arminius,** 1845
Bitter, Phillip—s, 17, from Dillenburg; **Arminius,** 1845
Biver, Johann—s, 30, from Esch; **Sarah Ann,** 1845
Blanc, August—s, from Tirschtiegel, Poland; **Margaretha,** 1846
Blandek, Wilh.—s, from Vaduz, Lichtenstein; **Johanne,** 1847
Blank, Jacob—from Frickhofen; 4 persons; **Harriet,** 1845
Blank, Joh.—s, 27, from Frickhofen; Gillespie Co.; **Harriet,** 1845
Blank, Joh.—from Hadamar; †1846, age 46, (NBCh.R.)
Blau, Christian—s, had Verein land grant
Bleck, August (Edward)—from Michelau, Oberhesse; w—Victorine F., age 22 and male ch.; **Neptune,** 1846
Bleckmann, Engel—s, 51; **Margaretha,** 1845
Bletz, Conrad Joh.—s, from Hennethal; **Riga,** 1846
Blicker, Anton—age 41, from Eibelshausen; w—Elis. 42; Joh. 11, Jacob 9, Cath. 3; **Dyle,** 1846
Bliedorn, Ludolph—from Wöhle, Han.; **Strabo,** 1845
Block, Elisa—from Schleusingen; **Orient,** 1846
Bloedner, Hein.—s; **Mathilda,** 1846
Bloh, Gerhard von—s, 22, from Hannover; **Ferdinand,** 1845
Bloh'm, George—s, 24; **Franziska,** 1846
Blohm, Hein—and wife; **Franziska,** 1846
Blom, Friedr.—s, 36, from Gross Elbe; 1845
Blucher, Felix A. von—Fredericksburg, 1847; **Galveston,** 1846
Blucher, O.—41, w—Elis. 42, ch— Cath. 3, Jacob 9, Joh. 11; **Andacia,** 1846

Blum, Casper Fr., Jr.—38, from Schmalkalden, Kurh.; w—Cath. nee Gesser—35; ch—Elise 14, Caspar 12, Ernest 9, Mathilde ½; Comal Co.; **Garonne**, 1845
Blum, Georg.—s, from Bruchköbel, Kurhessen; Comal Co.; **Louise Friedricke**, 1847
Blum, Hein.—from Einbeck, Han.; 4 persons; w—Johanne nee Schramm; Guadalupe Co.; **Creole**, 1846
Blumberg, Carl—age 48; from Kokocko; w—Cath. nee Ruff (Russ?), 43; Albertine 24, Henriette 14, Friedr. 11, Ernst 9, Hulda 7; Comal Co.; **Neptune**, 1845
Blumberg, Julius—age 23; **Neptune**, 1845
Blume, Hein.—from Einbeck, Han.; w—Johanne nee Schramm; Comal Co.; **Creole**, 1846
Blumenthal, Dr.—from Hannover; 1845
Bluthard, Gotfried—and family; from Schmiden, Württ; 1846
Bock, Christian—s, 24, from Nöttingen, Bock, Wm., Comal Co., 1855; **Gerhard Hermann**, 1845
Bode, Conrad—s, 18, from Mark, Prussia; Galveston Co.; **B. Bohlen**, 1845
Bode, Friedr.—25, from Peine, Han.; Fredericksburg; **Hercules**, 1845
Bode, Hein.—†1846, from Lechstedt, Han.; w—Elisa nee Armgard; ch—Conrad, Christina, Ferdinand; **B. Bohlen**, 1845
Bode, Joh. Hein. Christoph—from Hordorf to Texas 1846
Bodemann, Gustav—s, 27 and Robert --s, 27, from Imsen, Han.; Comal Co.; **Sophie**, 1846
Bodemeyer, Dorothea—from Celle; **Anna**, 1846
Bodenstedt, Fritz—from Peine; 1845
Bodie, Johann—s, from Weiler; **Talisman**, 1846
Bodmer, F.—New Braunfels, 1845
Boeckel, Adam—59, from Mühlhausen; w and ch—Christina 23; Conrad 15, Anna M. 19; **Weser**, 1844
Boeckel, E. Asmus (Erasmus?)—s, 22 from Mühlhausen; **Weser**, 1844
Boecher, Johannes—from Hausen; 1846
Boeddeker, Anton—from Geseke, Westph.; w—Angela nee Roth; **Friedrich**, 1846
Boedecker, Carl—from Celle; sons Louis, Theo.; Colorado Co.; **Creole**, 1846
Boehl, Christoph--s, 24, from Köl-

zow, Mecklenburg; Comal Co.; **Apollo**, 1846
Boehl, Georg—s, 21, from Kölzow, Mecklenberg; Comal Co.; **Apollo**, 1846
Boehringer, Christian—37; from Treschklingen; w—Christine R 33 and baby boy; Elis 9, Jane 5, Justina 3; **Dyle**, 1845
Boelsche, Ernst—s, from Sülfeld, Han.; Austin Co.; **Creole**, 1846
Boetel, Hein.—s, from Küblingen, Brnschwg; arr. 1846; Austin Co.
Boettcher, Aug.—from Pöhlde; 2 persons; **Talisman**, 1846
Boettcher, August—s, 27, from Landenhausen; **Sarah Ann**, 1845
Boettcher, Johannes—from Mingerode, a/Harz; w—Anna nee Rose; **Karl Ferdinand**, 1846
Boewinghausen, Carl von—from Ludwigsburg; 2 persons; **Element**, 1846
Bohls, Heinrich—wife and 3 ch; **Apollo**, 1844
Bohme, Fried.—s, 25, from Saxony; Bexar Co.; **Franziska**, 1846
Bohmerth, Bernard—34, from Münster; wife, sister, mother, and 2 ch.; **Weser**, 1844
Bohrmann, Fr.—from Altenau; **Talisman**, 1846
Bokermann, Hein.—and wife; **Franziska**, 1846
Bokus, Carl—from Osterburg, Prussia; **Joh. Dethardt**, 1846
Bolaender, Andreas—s, from Wehrda; Gillespie Co.; **Colchis**, 1846
Bolde, (Bolte?), F. W.—Fredericksburg, 1847
Boldt, Wilh.—from Rostock, Han.; **Karl Ferdinand**, 1846
Bonn, Jacob—s, from Belg by Zell a/Mosel; **York**, 1846
Bonn, Mathias—from Belg by Zell a/Mosel; Gillespie Co.; **York**, 1846
Bonn, Peter—from Belg by Zell a/Mosel; **York**, 1846
Bonnet, Johann Carl—s, Bexar Co., 1850; Kendall Co., 1860; **Harriet**, 1846
Bonnet, Philipp Daniel—from Charlottenburg; 7 persons; Bexar Co.; **Harriet**, 1846
Bopp, Conrad—27, Bopp, Theresa—19, from Amorbach; **Washington**, 1845
Borchardt, Carl—s, from Tribsees; 1846
Borchers, Christ.—s, 27; Borchers, Friedr.—s, 25; Borchers, Joh.—s, 22; Borchers, Ludw.—m, with 5 persons, from Luttringhausen, Han.; **Gerhard Hermann**, 1845

82

Borel, August—s, from Neufchatel, Switzerland; arr. 1846
Borges, Charlotte—Creole, 1846
Borgmann, Wm.—s, 30; Bastrop Co.; Franziska, 1846
Bormann, Conrad—s, Guadalupe Co.; Margaretha, 1846
Borrmann, Friedr.—s, from Altenau; Austin Co.; Talisman, 1846
Bose, Julius—age 25; from Prussia; Comal Co.; Joh. Dethardt, 1845
Both, Anna Maria (widow)—from Nieder-Bollentin, Prussia; arr. 1846
Bothe, Carl (Ernst) August—from Hannover; w—Sophie nee Schraeder; ch—Carl, Aug., Marie, Ludwig; B. Bohlen, 1845
Bothel, Hein.—s, arr. 1846; died 1848
Bothmer, Hein. Wilh. Anton—wife and 2 ch.; William Bryan, 1845
Botte, Friedr.—from Stederdorf; Bexar Co.; arr. 1845
Botte, Wilhelm—from Brevörde Han.; Bexar Co.; Mercur, 1846
Braach, Martin—from Volkenrath, Brnschwg; † age 37, 6.XII.1846 (NBCh.R.); w—Sophie
Bracht, Martin—from Düsseldorf; Johann Dethardt, 1845
Bracht, Victor—25, from Düsseldorf; Comal Co.; Johann Dethardt, 1845
Brackmann, Carl—from Berlebeck, Han.; arr. 1846 Mason Co.
Braden, Adam—from Büdesheim; w—Marg.; Colorado Co.; Andacia, 1846
Braden, Anton—from Büdesheim; 3 persons; Colorado Co.; Andacia, 1846
Braden, Johann Baptist—s, from Büdesheim; Colorado Co.; Andacia, 1846
Braes, Albert Joh. Hein.—s, from Nienstedt, Han.; Weser, 1845
Braeutigam, Andreas—38, from Frickenhausen, Meiningen; widower with 2 ch.; Garonne, 1845
Braeutigam, Anton—s, 30; Johann Dethardt, 1845
Braeutigam, Edward Carl—34, from Bavaria, Johann Dethardt, 1845
Braeutigam, Val.—from Kaltenlengsfeld, Mein., † 1846; w—Maria nee Pfeiffer; ch—Wolfgang, Anna, Elis; Gillespie Co.; Johann Dethardt, 1845
Braeutigam, Wolfgang—s, 17, from Kaltenlengsfeld; Joh. Dethardt, 1845
Branco, Adalbert—s, from Rudolstadt, Schwarzburg; Margaretha, 1846
Brand, Hermann—s, from bei Ver-

den, Han.; †1847, age 46; Matador, 1845
Brand, Wilh.—Sophie, 1846
Brandes, Carl—from Clausthal; Anna, 1846
Brandes, Carl Fried. Ernst—from Celle; 3 persons; Apollo, 1846
Brandes, Christian—from Peine; Hercules, 1845
Brandes, Christian—28, and wife; from Wolfenbüttel, Han.; B. Bohlen, 1845
Brandes, Christine—from Gross Lafferde, Han; Flavius, 1846
Brandes, Friedr.—from Salzgitter, w—Louise nee Staace; Fayette Co.; Anna, 1846
Brandes, Hein.—s, 22, from Barum, Han.; Everhard, 1845
Brandes, Hein.—and wife, from Wolfenbüttel, Han.; B. Bohlen, 1845
Brandes, Hein.—from Peine, Han.; †26.XI.1846, age 25
Brandes, Hein.—from Siersse, Han.; B. Bohlen, 1845
Brandes, Hein.—s, 47, from Gifhorn, Han.; B. Bohlen, 1845
Brandes, Johann Dietrich—s, from Gifhorn, Han.; †1847, age 27; Bexar Co.; B. Bohlen, 1845
Brandes, Joh. Hein.—s, from Gifhorn, Hannover; †21.VIII.1847, age 27 (NBCh.R.); Matador, 1845
Brandes, Ludwig—from Salzgitter; w—Johanne nee Diester; Anna, 1846
Brandes, Theo. Christian—s, from Peine, Han.; arr. 1845
Brandes, Wilh.—s, died 1846, age 25; from Peine, Hannover, Margaretha, 1845
Brandhorst, Adolph—s, 22, from Herzberg; Franziska, 1846
Brandis, Carl—s, from Hildesheim; arr. 1846; Timoleon, 1846
Brandis, Hermann M., Dr.—wife and one child; from Hildesheim Timoleon, 1846
Brandt, Heinr.—s, had Verein land grant
Brandt, Joh.—from Berlin, 1845
Brandt, Wilh.—from Stadtoldendorf; Comal Co.; Sophie, 1846.
Brasche, Hein.—m, from Wagendorf (Wagenhoff?), Han.; Comal Co.; Everhard, 1845
Braubeck, Wilh.—from Oberfischbach; 3 persons; arr. 1845
Braum, Joh. Fried.—28, from Dillenburg, Nassau; w—Marie nee Re(e)b; sons—Friedr., Ph. Chr.; Comal Co.; Arminius, 1845
Braun, Christian—m, from Derschlag; Fayette Co.; Hamilton, 1846

Braun, George—m, from Hüffenhardt; 3 persons; **Dyle,** 1846
Fraun, Gottfried—m, from Derschlag; Fayette Co.; **Hamilton,** 1846; **Talisman,** 1846
Braun, Joh.—from Eitelborn, Nassau; wife and 2 ch.; **George Delius,** 1845
Braun, Joh. Hein.—from Breitscheid, Nassau; w—Anna nee Petri; **George Delius,** 1845
Brauneck, Florian W. von—from Wierzebaum near Birnbaum, Kr. Schwerin; **Harriet,** 1845
Braunholz, David—from Farnroda, Weimar; w—Johanna; Comal Co.; **Elisa & Charlotte,** 1846
Brauning, Cath.—age 19; **Dyle,** 1846
Brauns, Ferdinand W. F.—m; **Galveston,** 1847
Brebham, Sopha—24; **Andacia,** 1846
Breche, Balthasar—died; from Altendiez; 5 persons; **Andacia,** 1846
Breche, Joh.—s, from Altendiez; **Andacia,** 1846
Brecher, Joh. Jacob—from Bretthausen; w—Elis. nee Schultheiss; † 1845, age 33; ch—Gustav, Rosina † 1845, age 5 (NBCh.R.); New Braunfels, 1845; **Johann Dethardt,** 1844
Brecher, Marianne—New Braunfels, 1845; **Ferdinand,** 1844
Bredenschey, Franz—from Hirschberg; **Hamilton,** 1846
Breier, Gustav—s, 30; **Sarah Ann,** 1845
Breilipper, G. A.—New Braunfels, 1845
Breilipper, Joh. H.—s, 37; New Braunfels, 1845; **Ferdinand,** 1844
Breis, Anton—from Kurhessen; † 1846 (NBCh.R.)
Breitenbauch, Ludwig von—* 1823, in Schloss Brandenstein, Thuringia; †1908 in San Antonio, Texas; 1848 lived in Sisterdale, Texas
Breitenscheid, Franz—from Hirschberg; **Hamilton,** 1846
Breitenstein, Joh.—s, from Bruchköbel; **Louise Friedricke,** 1847
Brelze, Johann von der—s, 23, from Rape (Rapen? or Rehe?); **George Delius,** 1845
Bremer, F. W.—s, Comal Co.; **Franziska,** 1846
Bremer, Fried.—s, from Peine, Han.; Comal Co.; **John Dethardt,** 1844
Bremer, Friedrich Anton—s, **B. Bohlen,** 1845
Bremer, Fritz—son of H. C. Bremer; New Braunfels, 1845; **Johann Dethardt,** 1844
Bremer, Juergen Hein.—from Ot-

tingen, Han.; w—Maria Rinkel; ch—Joh., Marg., Maria, Hein.; **B. Bohlen,** 1845
Bremer, Heinrich Christian (Conrad?)—from Verden, Han.; w—Judith Goldbeck; ch—Henrich 12, Adolph 3, Caroline 9 mo., Theo. Goldbeck, Fried. Goldbeck; New Braunfels, 1845; **Johann Dethardt,** 1844
Bremer, Joh.—s, 18; **B. Bohlen,** 1845
Bremer, Joh. G.—w. and ch.; Comal Co.; **Franziska,** 1846
Bremer, Louis—s, 30; **Franziska,** 1846
Breuer, Wilh. Hein.—s, from Hannover; **B. Bohlen,** 1845
Breustedt, Andreas—s, from Westerode a/Harz; oo Caroline Dauer; Comal Co.; **B. Bohlen,** 1847
Brinkhof, Franz—from Kaschel, Bz Dresden; w—Maria nee Deuslake; ch—Marie, Adam, Gertrude; **Friedrich,** 1846
Brin(c)khoff, Heinrich—39,
Brin(c)khoff, Gertrude—29,
Brin(c)khoff, Bernard—8,
Brin(c)khoff, Gerhard—6,
Brin(c)khoff, Theo.—3 mo.,
Brin(c)khoff, Henry—69,
Brin(c)hoff, Anna—68,
Muncher, Cath.—27; Castro Colonists; **Albertine,** 1845
Brinkrolf (?), Christoph—from Bielefeld or Rietberg, Westpha; 2 persons and 1 baby; w—Cath. nee Becker; ch—H. Ellen; Gillespie Co.; **Apollo,** 1846
Brinkhof, Christoph—m, from Rietberg, Westphalia; 2 persons and 1 baby; **Apollo,** 1846
Britting, Margaretha—New Braunfels, 1845; **Herschel,** 1844
Bro(a)dbeck, George Joh.—s, from Plattenhardt; **Element,** 1846
Broadbeck, Jacob—s, **Element,** 1846
Brockhuisen (Brockheim), Carl—New Braunfels, 1845; a Castro Colonist; **Ocean,** 1844
Brod, Johannes—s, 37, Austin Co.; **James Edward.** 1846
Brodtmann, Cath.—with Catharine, Martin, Marie, and Victor Bracht; **Joh. Dethardt,** 1845
Broegger, Caspar—from Fretter, Prussia; w—Eva nee Guenke; ch—Joh., Franz, Jos., Theresa; **Friedrich,** 1846
Broegger, Johann—from Fretter, Prussia; w—Bernhardine nee Hermes; **Friedrich,** 1846
Bromann, Hein.—s, from Brome, Han.; **B. Bohlen,** 1846
Bruch, Sophia—widow and 2 ch.; See Braach, Martin; **Everhard,** 1845

Bruchard, Adam—from Bargen; Hamilton, 1846
Brueger, Ludwig—from Hildesheim; w—Ernestine nee Sandhorst; ch—Johanna, Aug., Nannette; Gerhard Hermann, 1845
Bruels, Nikolaus—from Malmedy; Henry, 1846
Bruening, Hein.—s, from Zellerfeld; Karl Ferdinand, 1846
Bruening, Ludwig—and wife, from Zellerfeld; Anna, 1846
Brumme, Ludwig—from Göttingen; and bride Doris Albrecht; Comal Co.; Orient, 1846
Brune, Edward—New Braunfels, 1845; New York, 1843
Brune, G.—New Braunfels, 1845
Brunkow, Friedr.—New Braunfels, 1848
Bruns, Christian—from Burgstemmen, Han.; w—Henriette nee Lange; ch—Friedr.; Gesina, 1846
Bruns, Friedrich—s, 30, Comal Co.; Ferdinand, 1844
Brust, Christian—s, 30; New Braunfels, 1845; Ferdinand, 1844
Bub, Peter—s, from Heppenheim; † 21.VIII.1847 (NBChR); St. Pauli, 1847
Bube, Wilh.—s, from Hannover, Creole, 1846
Buch, F. Leonhard—s, from Eisenach; †18.XI.1846, age 28;(NBChR), Sarah Ann, 1845
Buchel, Aug.—s, 18; Sarah Ann, 1845
Buchel, Carl August—from Kreuznach; wife and 5 ch.; Sarah Ann, 1845
Bucher, Hein.—wife and ch; Fayette Co.; Franziska, 1846
Buchholz, Michael—from Dubielno, Prussia; Comal Co.; w—Marg. nee Naber, † 1849; ch—Wilhelmine, Theo., Louise; Johanna, 1846
Buchner, George L.—24; Andacia, 1846
Buchner, Hein.—from Zinnhain; w—Elis. 39; ch—Anton 12, Wilh. 9, Cath. 6, August 4; Andacia, 1846
Buchner, Gerhard—from Stangerode Cath. F.(died); ch—Louisa 12, Auguste 10, Carl 8, Philip 6, Wilhelmine 3, male infant; Andacia, 1846
Buechel, Peter—36; Andacia, 1846
Buechner, Christian Hein.—from Witzenhausen, Han.; ch—Aug., Friedr., Christine, Johanna; Galveston Co.; B. Bohlen, 1845
Buehler, Carl—s, from Dürkheim; Comal Co.; Element, 1846
Buehmann, Herman W.—s, 21, from Dahlhausen; Weser, 1844

Buescher, Hermann—s, from Neustadt a/Harz; Flavius, 1846
Bundorf, Cath.—New Braunfels, 1845
Bunnemann, Joh.—s, 33; Apollo, 1844
Burchard(t), Adam—s, from Bargen; Hamilton, 1846
Burckart, Joh.—from Hasselbach; James Edward, 1846
Burchkart, Martin—s, from Siegelsbach; Diamant, 1846
Burg, Peter—s, 24; New Braunfels, 1845; Ferdinand, 1844
Burgdorf, Cath.—s, 22; Ferdinand, 1844
Burgdorf, Hein. Leopold—s, 19, from Gross Lafferde, Han.; Mason Co.; Hercules, 1845
Burgdorf, Christian Joh. Hein.—25, from Gross Lafferde, Han.; Maria—22, Martha—50; Hercules, 1845
Burgdorf, Maria—22 from Schmedenstedt, Han.; Hercules, 1845
Burkhard, H.—30, w and 2 ch.; New Braunfels, 1845
Burkhardt, Joh.—from Hasselbach; 4 persons; James Edward, 1846
Burkhardt, Joh. Hein.—New Braunfels, 1845; New York, 1844
Burtschell, Franz—s, from Büdesheim; Colorado Co.; Hamilton, 1846
Burtschell, Lucas—m, from Büdesheim; 12 persons; Hamilton, 1846
Busch, Christian—s, Harriet, 1845; Comal Co.
Busch, Heinrich—s, age 19, Comal Co.; Harriet, 1845
Busch, Joh. Hein.—from Steinbrucken; † 1846 at Seguin; w—Wilhelmine nee Koch; ch—Wilhelmine, oo Hein. Staats 1847; Harriet, 1845
Buschel, Aug.—age 30; Star Republic from N.Y.; New York from N. O., 1845
Busing, Heinrich—wife and 1 child; Apollo, 1844
Busser, Alois—s, 37; Ferdinand, 1844
Bussmann, Daniel—39, from Grone, Han.; w—Friedricke nee Otte 43; Comal Co.; Johann Dethardt, 1845
Butte, (Budde?) Fried.—43, from Stederdorf, Han.; w—Sophie, (Cath: Ilse?) nee Ernst; ch—Louis 5, Wilhme. 2, Neptune, 1845

Cabanis, Albert—from Raschdorf, Silesia; w—Auguste nee Wittmann; ch—Herm., Bertha, Agnes, Emma, Max, Casper; **Friedrich**, 1846

Cabron, Peter Franz —with wife and 3 ch.; from Malmedy; Fredericksburg, 1847; **Henry**, 1846

Calmbach, Georg (Johann)—s, from Westhausen, Meiningen; **Elisa & Charlotte**, 1846

Caspar, A.B.C.—from Kaltennnordheim, 1845

Caspary, Anton—s, from Villmar; † 1854; Comal Co.; **James Edward**, 1846

Caspary, Joh.—s, from Oberasbach; Comal Co.; **Washington**, 1845

Christ, Joh.—s, from Offdilln, Nass.; Fayette Co.; **Arminius**, 1845

Christ, Joh. Aug.—from Üdersleben, Schwarzburg; w—Christine nee Suge; Bexar Co.; **Elisa & Charlotte**, 1846

Christ, Joh. Peter—from Gemünden; † 1847; w—Marg. Cath nee Christ (NBChR); Bexar Co.; **Diamant**, 1846

Claas, Conrad—from Uckersdorf; died; widow Elis and 6 ch.; **Harriet**, 1845

Claas, Joh. and Peter—See Klaas

Clages, Fried.—s, 24, from Nettlingen; **Gerhard Hermann**, 1846

Claren, Lieut. Fried von—from Brunswick; **Apollo**, 1844

Claren Lieut. Oscar von—s, 33, from Shöppenstedt, Brunswick; New Braunfels, 1845; †24.X.1845, killed by Indians near Manchaca Springs (NBChR); **Apollo**, 1844

Clarenbach, Hugo—s, from Remscheid; **Element**, 1846

Clear, John—wife and 2 ch; **Republic**, 1845

Closener, Johann—from Bruchhausen; 6 persons; **Diamant**, 1846

Closon, Johann Jakob—48, from Malmedy, Belgium; w and 2 ch; Galveston Co.; **Henry**, 1846

Cloudt, Richard von—s, 26, New Braunfels, 1845; **Apollo**, 1844

Coers, Friedrich—s, 17, from Wöhle, Han.; Comal Co.; **Gesina**, 1846

Coers, Hein.—s, 19, from Wöhle, Han.; oo Caro. Startz; Comal Co.; **Gesina**, 1846

Coers, Joh. Hein.—31, from Wöhle, Han.; 5 persons; w—Elisa nee Hagemann; ch—Elisa, Marianne; Comal Co.; **Gesina**, 1846

Coers, Matthias—60, from Wöhle, Han.; **Gesina**, 1846

Co(e)rssen, Hein. Fried.—s, by land across Red River at Sabine Town, Jan. 1845

Co(e)rssen, Cath.—† 1846 age 33

Coll, Jean von—s, 40, oo Margaretha Scherz, 1849; New Braunfels, 1845; Gillespie Co.; **Ferdinand**, 1844

Conrad, Joh. Theis—from Feudingen Hütte; Comal Co.; **Bohemia**, 1846

Conrads, H.—from N. Breisig; 3 persons; 1845

Copp, Georg W.—22, **Andacia**, 1846

Cordes, Harm—38, from Niendorf, Han.; w—Maria nee Wolf; ch—Herm, Hein.; Comal Co.; Gillespie Co.; **B. Bohlen**, 1845

Cords, Ernst Wilh.—31, **Chas. N. Cooper**, 1847

Cords, Joh. M.—29, from Holstein; **Chas. N. Cooper**, 1847

Coreth zu Corredo, Count Ernst—from Hallein (IC), Hallensheim (VF), Austria; *1803; w—Agnes nee Erler., ch—Agnes, Charles, Rudolph, Emilie, John, Francizka, Mary; Comal Co.; **York**, 1846

Cornelius, Christian—from Dillenburg, Nassau; w—Cath. nee Schraeddor; ch—Jeannette, Cath., Phil.; Austin Co.; **Johann Dethardt**, 1845

Cossmann, Heinrich—and family, from Geroldstein; 1846

Cramer, Ernst—from Rudolstadt; w—Friedricke nee Habfurtes; ch—Rudolph, Emilie, Theo., Carl, Amalie, Friedr., Wilh.; Fredericksburg; **Louise**, 1846

Cramer, Hein.—from Gross Lafferde; Bexar Co.; arr. 1845

Cramer, Hein. Fried.—from Osterode; **Weser**, 1845

Cra(e)mer, Joh. —See Kraemer, Joh.

Cramm, Christian—40, w—Sophia nee Theis—38, ch—Johanne 15, Helene 10, Hein. 8, Joh.3; Victoria Co.; **Hercules**, 1845

Cramm, (Kramm), Christoph—s, 33, from Gross Lafferde, Han.; Comal Co.; **Hercules**, 1845

Cramm, Hein.—s, from Gross Lafferde, Han.; Fredericksburg; **Hercules**, 1845

Cramm, Hermann—from Bockenem, Han.; Gillespie Co.; **Hercules**, 1845

Cramm, Sophia—from Gross Lafferde, Han.; **Hercules**, 1845: see Cramm, Christian

Creydt, Moritz—s, 24, from Dassel Han.; †27.VII.1847 (NBChR); Auguste Meline, 1845
Curth, Georg Friedr.—from Mosbach, Weimar; 4 persons & 1 baby; Fayette Co.; Everhard, 1845
Curth, Joh.—s, 18; Everhard, 1845

— D —

Dahlem, Fr.—from Diersheim,arr. 1845
Dahlem, Joh.-from Diersheim, arr. 1845
Dahlhaus, Joseph—43, from Braunsdorf; w and ch to follow; Weser, 1844
Dahlmann,Carl—s,40;fromRondorf; DeWitt Co.; Hamilton, 1846
Dahm, F.-Special Contract with, Texas Immigration and Land Co. 1846; New Orleans to Bonham, Texas; Fayette Co., 1848
Dahme, Hein.-s, 23; from Riede, Han.; Auguste Meline, 1845
Dahme, Joh. Dietr.—s, 27, from Riede, Han.; Auguste Meline, 1845
Dalwigk, Georg. von-s, from Fulda, Kurh.; George Delius, 1845
Dalwigk, Hermann-Bexar Co., 1885
Dambach, Jean F.—m, 58, from Büdesheim; w—Christine W. 50, ch—Magda 10, Louis 8; Andacia, 1846
Damm, Dittmar—from Nieder Vellmar at Cassel; w—Anna nee Siebert, ch—Gertrude, Joh., Christoph, Adam, Anna; Galveston Co; Friedrich, 1846
Damm, Jos.—m, from Nieder-Vellmar; Friedrich, 1846; Gonzales Co., 1847
Dammann,Carl—fromGeorginenau, Strelitz; w—Friedke nee Botte, ch—Friedke, Caro, Carl, Wilhme; Guadalupe Co.; Neptune, 1846
Dammann, Christian-s, 19; Hercules, 1845
Daneke, Carl—wife and 2 ch., Friedrich—s, 18, Hermann—s, 25, John—s, 40; Franziska, 1846
Dangers, Burchard Pastor—32, from Langenhagen, Han.; w—Mathilda nee Max, son—Theo; Gillespie Co.; Joh. Dethardt, 1845
Dann,Carl Wilh.—from Cassel; 4 persons and 1 baby; Galveston Co.; Austin Co.; Franziska, 1846
Dannheim, Ernst. Fried—from Walle, Han.; w—Juliana nee Kalberlein; ch—Julian, Otto, Johanne, Ernest.; Mason Co.; Everhard, 1845
Danz, Casper—26, from Wahles, Kurh.; w—Elis. nee Salzmann 26, Friedr.—¼ yr.; Fredericksburg; Garonne, 1845

Danz, Jacob-from Trusen, Kurh.; with 4 persons
Danz, Reinhard-37, from Wahles, Kurh.; Garonne, 1845
Dapprich, Hein. Peter—38, from Waigandshain; w—Cath. † 1846, age 32 (NBChR); ch—Leonore 12, Henriette 9, Agnes 6; Comal Co.; Washington, 1845
Darmstaedter, Philipp—s, 28; from Eberstadt; Gillespie Co.; Andacia, 1846
Dattner, Joh. Chr.—from Dornholzhausen Nassau; †1.VIII.1846 at Indianola (NBChR); Sarah Ann 1845
Dattner, Maria Elisa—widow and 2 ch—Elisa, Aug.; Sarah Ann, 1845
Dauer, Christian—from Dölme;w—Louise nee Jaco, ch—Aug., Caro., Wilhme; Comal Co.; Mercur, 1846
Daum, Anton—53; w—Cath. 58; Calhoun Co.; Herschel, 1845
Daum, Charlotte—from Rehe, Nassau; sons: Leonhardt, Adolf; George Delius, 1845
Daum,Christian and wife; Franziska, 1846
Daum,Joh.—38,from Holler,Nassau; w—Marie nee Stauder 35; ch—Joh. 10, Adam 6, Marie 3; Comal Co. Herschel, 1845
Daumast, Joh.-from Thalheim; Harriet, 1845
Debour, Diedrich Harms—Jean Key; a Castro colonist, 1844
Decker, John Hein—43; from Roth Nassau; w—Cath nee Peter 30; Jost Hein. 11, Elis. 9, Joh. 6, Phil 1; Arminius, 1845
Dechert,Hein.—from Wabern,Kurh.; ch—Joh., Cath., Conrad, Anna; w—Elisa nee Nussbaum; Johann Dethardt, 1845
Dechert, Hry—s, 20; Joh.—s, 22; Johann Dethardt, 1845
Decker, Hein.Joh.-s, 21; from Hirschberg, Nassau; Neptune, 1845
Dedeke,Joh. Hein.—from Werneborstel?(=Berenbostel?); w—Maria nee Bartels; ch—2 boys and 1 girl; Comal Co.; Nat. record-Austin Co.; George Delius, 1845
Degener, Eduard—Sisterdale, Kendall Co.; 1848
Degener, F.—25; from Germany; Star Republic from N.Y.; New York from New Orleans, 1845
Deichert, Adam--s, St. Pauli, 1847
Delf, Friedr.-Kerr. Co.
Demmer, Martin-from Eisenach, 4 persons; Nahant, 1846 (wrecked); then Timoleon, 1846
Denker,Mathias—31;fromAlpenrod;

87

w—Cath. S. 24 and male infant; Fayette Co.; **Andacia**, 1846
Deppe, Aug.—s, 54; Carl—s, 18, Ludwig s, 25; from Einbeck, Han.; **Franziska**, 1846
Deppe, Carl Philipp—from Einbeck, Han.; 10 persons; w—Christine nee Keese; **Franziska**, 1846
Deppermann,Ernst—s,19;fromSalzgitter, Han.; Harris Co.; **Franziska**, 1846
Deppermann, E. H. Gustav—26,from Salzgitter, Han.; 5 persons; w—Sophie nee Guttermann; Harris Co.; **Franziska**, 1846
Dermstyne, F. B.—35; **Andacia**, 1846
Dernt,Joseph—from Arzbach, Nassau; w—Marg. nee Fuellbach; ch—Maria, Adam, Peter; **Auguste Meline**, 1845
Dettmer, Caro.—18; from Gross Lafferde; Dettmer, Conradina—20; **Hercules**, 1845
Dettmer, Conrad—32; from Gadenstedt, Han.; w—Marie nee Trappe; ch—Elise, Hein., Sophie, Ilse; Austin Co.; **Apollo**, 1846
Dettmer, Leonard and wife—from Gadenstedt, Han.; **Apollo**, 1846
Deubach, Nickolaus—s; from Göppingen; 1846
Deubner, Ernest—s, 33; **Johann Dethardt**, 1846
Deutsch, Carl-s.; from Büdesheim; or Aspisheim; **Andacia**, 1846
Dickhut, Wilh.—from Ebergötzen, Brschwg;w—Cath.nee Aul;Austin Co.; **Margaretha**, 1846
Dickmann, W.-s, 21; **Weser**, 1844
Diedrich, Christian—from Rhens; wife and 5 ch; **Henry**, 1846
Diedrich,Hein.—s,34;from Einbeck, Nassau; Colorado Co. 1860; **George Delius**, 1845
Dieffenbach, Carl—‡20.VIII.1846, age 26, from Kunzel, Hesse-Nassau; w—Auguste nee Bindewald; **Garonne**, 1845
Dieffenbach, Georg—s, 22; from Künzel (IC) or Stockhausen (VF) **Garonne**, 1845
Diehl, Christian—56, died; from Bretthausen; widow—Christine nee Brandenberger, 8 persons and 1 baby; **Garonne**, 1845
Diehl, Martin-s, from Camberg; **Bohemia**, 1846
Dierks, Christian—from Ottingen, Han.; † before 1860; 7 persons, ch—Hein., Herm., Wilh., Comal Co.; **B. Bohlen**, 1845
Dierks, Elisa-from Ottingen, Han.; **B.Bohlen**, 1845
Dierks, Friedr.-s, 18; **Franziska**, 1846
Dierks, Joh Hein.Fried.-s, 47; from

Ottingen; Herm.-19; **B.Bohlen**, 1845
Dietrich, Hein.—from Nassau; † 26.XII.1849, age 29; (NBChR); **George Delius**, 1845
Dietz, Andreas—widower from Becheln, Nassau; †10.VII.1846, age 56 (NBChR); 4 persons; **Talisman**, 1846
Dietz, Hein.-s, from Arolsen; Comal Co.; **Colchis**, 1846
Dietz, Joh.--s, from Appenhofen; **James Edward**, 1846
Dietz,Joh. Georg—32; from Becheln, Nass.;w and2ch; Comal Co.; **James Edward**, 1846
Dietz, Joh. Hein.—from Appenhofen; 8 persons; Comal Co.; **James Edward**, 1846
Dietz, Ph.Hein.—from Becheln; 3 persons; **Talisman**, 1846
Dietz, Phil.Jacob-s; from Becheln; Comal Co.; **Talisman**, 1846
Dietzel, Joh.—from Rosa, Meiningen; w—Anna nee Seifert, ch—Anna, Christianna, Georg, Elis.; Calhoun Co.; **Everhard**, 1845
Dietzel, Ottilie-from Zillbach, Weimar; **Everhard**, 1845
Dikkop, Matthias-from Wallmerod; **Sarah Ann**, 1845
Dillenger, Daniel-s; from Lorsch; **Talisman**, 1846
Dish, Peter-s, 22; **George Delius**, 1845
Dittmann, Friedr. Aug.—s, 28; from Grieben, Prussia; Colorado Co.; arr. 1846
Dittmar, Georg Caspar-from Kalten Nordheim; 6 persons; Guadalupe Co.; **Harriet**, 1845
Dittmer, Joh.—s, 27; from Gerstungen, Weimar; **Everhard**, 1845
Dittmar, Martin-died 1846, age 48; from Weidebrunn, Kurh.; w-Cath. nee Oschweiler 43, ch-Cath. 19, Anna 8, Martin 6, Joh. 5, Anna Elise 1½; **Garonne**, 1845
Doebbler, Ferd. Fried.—from Berlin; w—Auguste nee Matheus; son—Theo.; Gillespie Co.; **Elisa and Charlotte**, 1846
Doebner, Joh. Christ.-from Ohrdruff; 7 persons; Gillespie Co.; **Harriet**, 1845
Doebner, John-s. 63; from Ohrdruff; **Harriet**, 1845
Doell, Georg Adam-34; from Rosa, Meiningen; w-Anna Cath. nee Seifferth 26; **Garonne**, 1845
Doell, Joh. Adam, Jr.-died; from Rosa Meiningen; w-Anna Marg. nee Craemer; ch-Georg 6, Henry 3; **Garonne**, 1845

88

Doerflinger, Georg–s; from Frankfurt a/M; **Talisman,** 1846
Doering, Ferdinand von–s, **Fyen,** 1846
Doernemann, Christoph—34; †14.VI.1846, from Lauterbach, Hesse; w—Cath. nee Durlan 23; **Neptune,** 1845
Dohm, Theo.–and wife; **Franziska,** 1846
Donop, Ludwig von—s, 28; from Detmold; Kendall Co.; **George Delius,** 1845
Dorries, Franz–s; from Mackensen; Montgomery Co; **Sophie,** 1846
Dotter, Friedr.–s; from Fulda, Kurh.; **Sarah Ann,** 1845
Draft, Martin—from Siegelsbach; **Talisman,** 1846
Dralle, Friedrich—from Imsen, 1845
Draub, Daniel–s; from Schweidnitz, Silesia; Austin Co.; **Creole,** 1846
Draub, Ferd.–s; from Schweidnitz, Silesia; **Creole,** 1846
Drawe, Ludwig—s, from Berlebek, Detmold; Fayette Co.; **Neptune,** 1846
Drechsler, Wilh.–s; from Clausthal, a/Harz; **Flavius,** 1846
Dreier, Friedr.—s, 18; De Witt Co.; **Franziska,** 1846
Dreier, Hein.—s, from Glentorf; w— Johanna nee Every, ch—Marie, Dorothea, Sophie, Johanna; Colorado Co.; **Karl Ferdinand,** 1846
Dreier, Joh. Hein. Ernst–s; from Emmerstedt; born in Glentorf; **Karl Ferdinand,** 1846
Dreiss, Gustav—s; from Calw, (IC); Comal Co.; **Sarah Ann,** 1845
Dreiss, Valentin—s, †5.XI.1846, age 25; from Lorch/Rüdesheim, Nassau, (NBChR); **Johann Dethardt,** 1845
Dresel, Emil, Julius, Rudolph— Kendall Co.
Dresel, Gustav—New Braunfels 1845; born in Geisenheim 26.I.1818; came to Texas in August 1838; wrote *Houston Journal*; Agent for German Emigration Co.
Dreser, Aug.–s, from Fronhofen; **Riga,** 1846
Dreste, Anton—m; from Königstein; Colorado Co.; **Sarah Ann,** 1845
Dreste, Joh. and wife; Peter—s, 35; **Sarah Ann,** 1845
Dreste, Peter–s, 35; **Sarah Ann,** 1845
Dreyer, Anton with wife and 3 ch; **Franziska,** 1846
Dreyer, B.–30; from Prussia; **Johann Dethardt,** 1845
Driver, Edward–and bride Elisabeth nee Holz; from Schwerin, Mecklenburg; **Neptune,** 1846

Droege, Fried.—died; from Netze, Waldeck; w—Dorothea nee Woechter; **Margaretha,** 1845
Drost, Bernhard–s, 18; from Mark, Prussia; **B. Bohlen,** 1845
Duerks, J.–from Culm; arr. 1845
Duerwang, George and Hein.–from Rappenau; **Dyle,** 1846
Duffy, Peter—from Fachbach; 9 persons; **Harriet,** 1845
Duncker, Adolph–m; from Cassel; **Friedrich,** 1846
Dunker, Mathias–**Andacia,** 1846
Durand—wagonmaster for Verein; New Braunfels, 1845
Durst, Christian–s, 25; from Dettenhausen; Gillespie Co.; **Element,** 1846
Durst, Joh.–47; from Dettenhausen; w–Marg.; ch–John, Cath., Jacob, Bernard Frederica; **Element,** 1846
Durst, Joh.–s, 21; from Dettenhausen; Gillespie Co. 1850; Mason Co. 1859; **Element,** 1846
Durst, Melchior—from Dettenhausen; **Element,** 1846

— E —

Ebeling, Ernst–s, 35; from Elze; Austin Co.; **Weser,** 1844
Ebeling, Friedr.–s, 20; **Franziska,** 1846
Eberland, Aug.–from Muskau; arr. 1845 (VF)
Eberle, Gottlieb—s; from Bonfeld or Fürfeld; **Dyle,** 1846
Eberlein, Caspar—and wife, from Hannover; **B. Bohlen,** 1845
Eberling, Carl—†23.VIII.1846, age 52; from Dillenburg, Nassau; w—Cath. †20.IX.1846, age 49; ch—Carl 22, Henry 19, Martin 17, Christian, Wilh., Caro., Marianne; **Johann Dethardt,** 1845
Eberling, Carl—s, 22; from Dillenburg; Brazoria Co.; **Johann Dethardt,** 1845
Eberling, Christian–wife and 2 ch.; **Johann Dethardt,** 1845
Eberling, Fried.–s, 20; from Dillenburg; **Johann Dethardt,** 1845
Eberling, Hein.–s, 19; from Dillenburg; **Johann Dethardt,** 1845
Eberling, Martin—s, 17; **Johann Dethardt,** 1845
Ebers, Christian–38; from Greene, Brnschwg; w–Johanna nee Ficht-—34; Aug. 13, Caro. 11, Fried Hein 8, Carl—l; Gillespie Co., **Neptune,** 1845
Ebert, Anton—m; from Niederheimbach; died 1846 at Indianola; **Andacia,** 1846

Ebert, August–from Mainz; **James Edward**, 1846
Ebert, August–from Ottenstein, Han.; w–Justine nee Hansemann; Comal Co.: **Mercur**, 1846
Ebert, John—m; from Büdesheim; **Dyle**, 1846
Ebert(h).Joh.–45; from Callies, Prussia; w–Wilhme–38; ch–Pauline 10, Auguste 2; Gillespie Co.; **Joh Dethardt**, 1846
Eberth, Martin–m; from Callies; Comal Co.; **Johann Dethardt**, 1846
Eberts, Joh.–died; from Manderbach, Nassau; w–Cath. nee Dietrich; ch–Joh., Elis., Hein. died 1847 age 7; **Auguste Meline**, 1845
Ebstein, Ludwig–s, 25; from Breslau; **Franziska**, 1846
Eckers, Jacob–60; from Mittelsdorf; **Neptune**. 1845
Eckers, Joh.–33; from Mittelsdorf; **Neptune**, 1845
Eckert Ludwig—from Huffenhardt; w—Christiana, ch—Adolph, Christine; Gillespie Co.; **Dyle**, 1846
Eckhardt, Hein.—24; from Steinbrücken; Gillespie Co.; **Arminius**, 1845
Eckartsberg, Paul von—s, 23; from Glogau; †23.VII.1846, age 24 in Fredericksburg (NBChR); **Johann Dethardt**, 1846
Eggeling, Friedr.—from Wolfenbüttel; w—Sophie nee Hess; Comal Co., **Louise**, 1846
Eggeling, Hein. Juluis—from Salzgitter; w—Caro. nee Ettling; 3 persons; Comal Co.; **Anna**, 1846
Eggert, Friedr.–s, from Lenzen, a/Elbe; **Orient**, 1846
Eglinger, Frau Helena–widow; from Kreuznach; **Sarah Ann**, 1845
Ehlers, Conrad—from Mardorf; arr. 1845
Ehrenpfort, Georg–s; from Berlebeck Detmold; **Neptune**, 1846
Ehrhardt, Moritz—from Rollsdorf; wife and child; **Apollo**, 1846
Ehrler, Franz–from Zaisenhausen; 2 persons; **Nahant**, 1846 wrecked at sea; then **Timoleon**, 1846
Eich, Christian—43; from Niederheimbach; **Andacia**, 1846
Eichhorn, Peter with 4 ch.–**Leo**, 1846
Eichmann, Christian–s, 21; from Heilberscheidt; **Riga**, 1846
Eickel, Andreas and wife—from Prussia; New Braunfels 1845; **Weser**, 1844
Eickenroht, Friedr.—from Wolfenbüttel; w—Auguste nee Mueller and 4 ch; Guadalupe Co.; **Louise**, 1846
Eichler, Wilh.—from Osterode; w—

Dor. nee Stubberg (Strubberg?); ch—Marie, Carl, Ludwig, Wilh., Aug.; **Anna**, 1846
Eidelbach, Joh.—from Fachbach; 6 persons; **Harriet**, 1845
Eifes, Paul–s, from Beaufort; **Henry**, 1846
Eike, Carl–s, 37; from Wehrstedt; **Margaretha**, 1845
Eilers, Friedr.–s; from Stadtoldendorf; Comal Co.; **Sophie**, 1846
Eilers, Joh.–s, 25; **Franziska**, 1846
Eimcke, Hein.—from Semmenstedt, Brnschwg; w—Sophie nee Behrends;ch—Johanna,Maria;Louise, 1845
Eisenbach, Anton—s, 40; from Villmar; Bastrop Co.; **James Edward**, 1846
Eisenbach, Christian—s, from Villmar; Bastrop Co.; **James Edward**, 1846
Eisenbach, Wilh.—s, 31; from Villmar; Bastrop Co.; **James Edward**, 1846
Eisentrager, Bernhard–m; from Cassel; Harris Co.; **Diamant**, 1846
Elbers, Joh.–from Clausthal, Han.; **Karl Ferdinand**, 1846
Elbert, August—s; from Mainz; Gillespie Co.; Calhoun Co.; **James Edward**, 1846
Elbert, Emil–s, 27; **Sarah Ann**, 1845
Elbert, Joh.–30, and wife; Galveston Co.; **Sarah Ann**, 1845
Elbert, Ludwig–s; from Mainz; **Sarah Ann**, 1845
Ellebracht, Fried. Albrecht—from Zersen, Kurhessen; 7 persons; w—Dor. nee Stemener; Gillespie Co.; **B. Bohlen**, 1845
Ellermann, Hein.—s, 24; from Abbesbüttel, Han.; **Everhard**, 1845
Elmendorf, Carl—from Düsseldorf; w—Wilhelmine nee Kuemmel and son Carl; Bexar Co.; **New Braunfels**, 1845; **Joh. Dethardt**, 1844
Elze, David—from Graste, Han.; w—Elisa nee Warnecke; ch—Johanna, Johann; Comal Co.; **Margaretha**, 1845
Embach, Conrad—45; from Rauenthal, Nassau; w—Kunigunde 49; **Neptune**, 1845
Emmel, Joh.—m; from Bruchköbel; arr. 1847
Emmerich, Philipp Anton–m; from Geisig; died in Fredericksburg.; **Andacia**, 1846; Joh. Hein. soleheir.
Emmert, Jacob—m; from Rappenau; **Timoleon**, 1846
Ender, Joseph Jacob—m; from Rosnowo, Poland; Jefferson Co.; arr. 1847

Enders, Caro.—**Auguste Meline**, 1845
Endres, Joh.–s, 22; from Oestrich, Nassau; **Neptune**, 1845
Engel, Aug.–27, 4 persons; from Ebingen; Austin Co.; **Andacia**, 1846
Engel, Christian—s, 21; from Wilsenroth, Nassau; New Braunfels 1845; Austin Co.; **Johann Dethardt**, 1844
Engel, Gottlieb–from Brotterode, Kurh.; **Friedrich**, 1846
Engel, Peter–from Rauenthal; arr. 1845
Engelbert, Joh.-42 †1854 (NBChR); w-Cath. 28; ch-Gustav 10, Ferd 6, Wilh. 3, Rud. ½; **Garonne**, 1845
Engelbert, Joh.—42 w—Cath. 28; ch—Gustav 10, Ferd. 6, Wilh. 3, Rud. ½; from Willingen; **Garonne**, 1845
Engelhardt, Hein. Fried. Christian —s, 22; Fayette Co.; **George Delius**, 1845
Engelke, Conrad—s, 34; from Stelingen, Han.; Cath. Depke—m, 1848; Comal Co.; **George Delius**, 1845
Engelmann, Martin—s, 27; from Hallgarten; m—Caro. Rothe 1847; Comal Co.; **Sarah Ann**, 1845
Engelmann, Peter–s; from Neudorf, Nassau; **Neptune**, 1845
Ennert, Joh.—39; from Oberndorf, Nassau; †1.III.1847, age 39. (NBChR)
Epple, Gottlieb Joh.–from Waldenbuch; 3 persons; **Element**, 1846
Epple M.(Max) Gottlieb–from Waldenbuch; **Element**, 1846
Erbe, Hein—s; from Schmalkalden; †29.VI.1846, age 48 (NBChR); **Garonne**, 1845
Erben, Conrad—s, 24; from Horchheim; Guadalupe Co.; **Strabo**, 1845
Erbs, Wilh.–37; from Kemel; w-Cath, 37, George, 5; **Strabo**, 1845
Er(c)k, Joh. Georg.—from Oberkatz, Meiningen; w—Anna Barbara nee Fink; ch—Chr., Ludw.; **B. Bohlen**, 1845
Erdmann, Carl-s, from Halle; Colorado Co.; **Elisa & Charlotte**, 1846
Erlenmaier, Adolph–s; from Monsheim; Gillespie Co.; **Nahant**, wrecked—1846; later **Timoleon**, 1846
Erneste, Wilh.—s, 18; **George Delius**, 1845
Ernst, Adam—s, 20; from Petershütte; Guadalupe Co.; **Everhard**, 1845
Ernst, Aug.—from Herborn-Seelbach; ch—Ernst, Aug., Wilh., Hein., Friedr., Elise; **Herschel**, 1845

Ernst, Carl Ludwig–s; from Havelberg; arr. 1846
Ernst, Conrad—from Reppner, Brnschwg; w—Sophie nee Rothacker; ch—Sophie, Hein., Hein., Aug.; Gillespie Co.; **Gerhard Hermann**, 1846
Ernst, E.–New Braunfels 1845
Ernest, Friedr. Ferd. W.—s, 31; from Petershutte, Han.; **Franziska**, 1846
Ernst, Georg Adam–s; from Kaltennordheim; **Everhard**, 1845
Ernst, Ludwig Nic.–m; from Limburg(IC), or Helmeren(VF) Bohemia, 1846
Ervendberg, L. C., Pastor; Protestant pastor at Frelsburg 1842; pastor at New Braunfels 1845; w—Luise Muench (Monch); ch— Auguste
Eschelbach, Philipp–s, 21; from Hochhausen; **Sarah Ann** 1845
Eschenbrenner, Wilh.–w and 3 ch; from Braubach/Rhein; **Henry**, 1846
Eufinger, Nicolaus–from Villmar; Bastrop Co.; **James Edward**, 1846
Evelt, Georg—from Münster; 2 persons; Galveston Co.; **Diamant**, 1846
Evers, (Ewers), Bernhard-from Sohlde, Han; 6 persons, w-Tina nee Eberling; ch-Tina, Chr., Ferd.; **B. Bohlen**, 1845
Evers, Joh.–**Herschel**, 1845
Ewald, Conrad–from Zennern, Kurh; w—Elisa nee Riemenschneider; Fredericksburg; **Johann Dethardt**, 1845
Ewald, Joh.–s; from Zennern, Kurh.; Maria nee Klemm; from Wabern, Hesse †1846, age 21 (NBChR); **Joh. Dethardt**, 1845

— F —

Faber, Anton–32; from Ketten, Weimar; 7 persons, w–Anna Maria nee Danburg–44; **Garonne**, 1845
Faerber, Martin–from Hallgarten; 5 persons
Fahlbusch, Christian–s; from Wachenhausen, Han.; **Talisman**, 1846
Fahrenhorst (Vahrenhorst), Christian—s, 32; from Hohenbuchen, Han.; **Gerhard Hermann**, 1846
Fahrenkamp, Diedrich—from Hannover; **Ferdinand**, 1845
Fahrenkamp, Joh. Georg—s, 21; from Hannover; Colorado Co.; **Ferdinand**, 1845
Fahrholz, Hein.–s; from Jeeben, Prussia; **B. Bohlen**, 1847
Falter, Joh. Friedr.—with mother

and family; from Haberschlacht, Württ; arr. 1846

Falter, Johann Heinrich and family —from Haberschlacht Württ; 1846

Falter, Mrs. Salamo, (Maria) and her family—from Haberschlacht; arr. 1846

Fartscher, Joseph—from Rückers, Silesia; arr. 1845

Faver, Ludwig–s; **B. Bohlen**, 1845

Faxel, Joh.–from Villmar; 6 persons; Bastrop Co.; **James Edward**, 1846

Fehlis, Wilh.–s; from Dohnsen, Han.; Comal Co.; **Sophie**, 1846

Fehn, Kunogunde–**Flavius**, 1846

Fehrmann, Otto–s; from Birkholz, Prussia; arr. 1846

Feick, Caspar—from Hesse; New Braunfels 1845; **Ferdinand**, 1844

Feick, Marg.–17; New Braunfels 1845; **Ferdinand**, 1844

Fein, Joh. Peter–s; from Niederahr; Comal Co.; **Strabo**, 1845

Feldmeier, Joh. Hein.–s; from Hofgeismar, Kurh.; **Friedrich**, 1846

Feller, Carl—Gillespie Co.; **Arminius** 1845

Feller, Philipp—died; from Dillenburg, Nassau; w—Maria; sons—Carl, Wilh.; **Arminius**, 1845

Feller, Wilh.—son of Philipp Feller; Gillespie Co. 1848

Fend(t), Wm.—from Camberg; Bohemia, 1846

Fenner, Henry–34; **Johann Dethardt**, 1845

Fenski, Wilh.—from Sobbowitz by Danzig; w—Amalie nee Lange; **Mercur**, 1846

Ferguson, James–age 24, s; from Scotland; Comal Co.; arr. from U. S. 1846

Ferking, Heinr.–s, 18; from Langenhagen, Han.; **Johann Dethardt**, 1845

Ferris, Joh. W. and wife—from Befart (=Befart?); **Anna**, 1846

Feuerriegel, Christ.–s; from Clausthal; **Talisman**, 1846

Feuge, Christoph—from Heiningen, Han.; Gillespie Co; **Mathilde**, 1846

Feuge, Hein.–s; from Heiningen, Han.; Gillespie Co.; **Mathilda**, 1846

Fey, Valentin–31; from Rumbach, Hesse; New Braunfels 1845; **Weser**, 1844

Fibiger, Friedrich—s; from Fürstenwerder, Prussia; **Neptune**, 1846

Fiedler, Adam Jacob–34; from Oestrich, Nassau; w–Francisca 34; Fayette Co.; **Neptune**, 1845

Fietsam, Friedr.—s; from Oestrich; † before 1860; **Diamant**, 1846

Fietsam, Georg Jos.–s; from Oestrich; **Diamant**, 1846

Fietsam, Joh. Jos.–s; from Oestrich; Fayette Co.; **Diamant**, 1846

Fietsam, Michael–s; from Oestrich; **Diamant**, 1846

Fietsam, Wilh.—s; from Oestrich; † before 1860; **Diamant**, 1846

Find, Daniel–s, 32; from Werdorf, Prussia; Austin Co.; arr. 1846

Fink, Anton—from Erbach or Kiedrich; 6 persons; **Nahant** 1846, wrecked at sea; then **Timoleon**, 1846

Fink, Bernhard-from Kiedrich; **Andacia**, 1846

Fink, Franz-from Kiedrich; **Andacia**, 1846

Fink, Sebastian—from Kiedrich; 10 persons; **Nahant**, 1846—wrecked at sea; then **Timoleon**, 1846

Finke, Christian–s, 19; Galveston Co.; **Apollo**, 1844

Finkenstein, Hein.–s, 32; from Barum, Han.; **Everhard**, 1845

Fircks, Baron Hein. von—from Breslau; 2 persons; **Arminius**, 1845

Fischer, Anna–from Fuhrberg; **George Delius**, 1845

Fischer, Christoph–s; from Kiedrich; **Nahant**, 1846–wrecked at sea; then **Timoleon**, 1846

Fischer, Conrad–s, 23; **Margaretha**, 1845

Fischer, Edw.—s, 22; **Fischer, Friedr.**—s, 24; **Franziska**, 1846

Fischer, F. Joh.–s, 28; from Pottum Ff/M, New Braunfels 1845; **Weser**, 1844

Fischer, Gottlieb—s, New Braunfels 1845; **Weser**, 1844

Fischer, Gustav—from Frücht; 8 persons; **Talisman**, 1846

Fischer, Hein.–from Netze, Han.; † 1846, age 29; w–Caro. nee Droege; ch-Wilhelmine, Friedrich, and baby; **Margaretha**, 1845

Fisher, Hein.—from Rietberg; 7 persons and 1 baby; **Apollo**, 1846

Fisher, Henry–from Cassel; † 1867 in Wiesbaden; partner with Burchard Miller in Fisher-Miller Contract.

Fischer, Henry–s, 22; **Franziska**, 1846

Fischer, Joh.—s; from Fulda, Kurh.; **Margaretha**, 1845

Fischer, Joh. Hein. Conrad—from Wehrstedt, Saxony; **Margaretha**, 1845

Fischer, Joseph–s; from Kiedrich; **Nahant** 1846–wrecked at sea, then **Timoleon** 1846

Fischer, Martin—s, 20; **George Delius**, 1845

Fissler Joh. Leonhard–from Haberschlacht; arr. 1846

Fissler, Severus—from Haber-schlacht; arr. 1846
Fix, Michael—66; from Bonfeld; w—Marie 60; Anne 31; Dyle, 1846
Flach, Christoph—m, from Hesse Darmstadt; Kerr Co.; St. Pauli, 1847
Flagge, Andreas–s; from Markoldendorf; Comal Co.; Hamilton, 1846
Flagge, F. W.—from Markoldendorf; †23.V.1847(NBChR); Comal Co.; Hamilton, 1846
Fleischhack, Wilh.—from Arnstadt, Schwarzburg; †3.XI.1846, age 60, (NBChR); Mathilde, 1846
Fleischmann, Hein.–24; from Silbach, Weimar; Garonne, 1845
Flick, Adolph Wilh.—36; from Emmerichenhain; Marg—36, Henrietta–8, Herm.–6, Louise–4, Pauline–1;see Caspar Danz in Gillespie Co. 1850 census; Washington, 1845
Flick, Franz–s, 25; from Homberg; Washington, 1845
Floeck, M.—from Mühlheim by Coblenz; 7 persons; arr. 1845
Floege, Carl—from Hildesheim; Comal Co.; Creole, 1846
Foerster, Edward—37; from Roetgen; w—Emily nee Spatz 35; ch—Friedr. 9, Gustav 5, Louise 3; and baby boy; Comal Co.; Dyle, 1846
Foerster, Emelia Charl.—sister of Edw. Foerster and only heir of Hein. Spatz; Dyle, 1846
Foerster, J. W.—m; from Rötgen; Dyle, 1846
Foerster, Regina—widow, age 32; ch—Bertha 12, Edward 7; Dyle, 1846
Folte, Jacob–s, 26; Apollo, 1844
Ford, Aug. and wife—Franziska,1845
Forke, Aug. F. and Henriette–from Hildesheim, Han.; Comal Co.; Creole, 1846
Forke, Friedr.–from Hildesheim, Han.; 4 persons; Creole, 1846
Fortemps, Carl–s; from Cologne; New Braunfels 1845; Herschel, 1844
Foth, Jacob–Neptune, 1846
Fraenkel, Robert–s, from Leipzig; Mathilde, 1846
Fran(c)k, Gustav—s, 18; from Witzenhausen; B. Bohlen, 1845
Frank, Andreas–s; from Tennstedt; near Cappel; arr. 1846
Frank, Carl—from Witzenhausen Kurh.; w—Elis. nee Hayne; Fayette Co.; Friedrich, 1846
Frank, Joh.–from Leinefelde; York, 1846

Frank, Joh.–m; from Leinefelde by Erfurt; York, 1846
Frank, Joh. George—from Herrnhof by Ohrdruff; w—Elisa nee Fischer; ch—Eva, Joh., Friedr., Johanna, Marie; Elisa and Charlotte, 1846
Frank, Martin–from OberWalluf; 6 persons; 1845
Franke, Ernst–from Goslar, Han.; 3 persons; arr. 1846; Fayette Co.
Franke, F. W.–from Wriezen; Elisa & Charlotte, 1846
Franke, Joh.–s, 67; Franziska, 1846
Franke, Joh. Ludw.–from Barigau, Schwzbg; w–Marie nee Mueller; Fayette Co.; Margaretha, 1846
Franke, Ludwig—s, 27; from Güstrow, Mecklbg.; Fayette Co.; Gerhard Hermann, 1846
Franz, Carl—from Kleingeschwende, Schwzbg; w—Christine nee Starke; son—Ludw.; Weser, 1845
Franz, Conrad–s, 38; Talisman, 1846
Franz, Edward–s, 40; from Wissenbach, Nassau; Fayette Co.; George Delius, 1845
Franz, F. Carl–m, died; Talisman, 1846
Franz, George–from Windecken; 3 persons; James Edward, 1846
Franz, Hein.–Neptune, 1846
Franz, Jacob–from Kirchberg; James Edward, 1846
Franz, Joh.–from Solms-Laubach; 7 persons; Talisman, 1846
Franz, Joh.-w-Cath. Stock 2.IV.1845; †3.VIII.1846, age 34; from Leerbach, Darmstadt. (NBChR); George Delius, 1845
Franz, Joh. Conrad–38; from Wissenbach, Nassau; w–Elisa nee Strackbein; ch–Elisa, Wilh., Wilhme, Cath., Joh., Aug.; George Delius, 1845
Franz, Julius Moritz–s, 20; from Eisleben; Bexar Co.; Franziska, 1846
Franzen, Erasmus–m, from U. S.; Gillespie Co.; Sam Ingham, 1845 from New Orleans
Free, Roolf Janszen–s; Orient, 1846
Freibig, Nicolaus–from Veilsdorf; 6 persons; Austin Co.; Nahant 1846 (wrecked); then Timoleon, 1846
Freitag, Fr.–s; 28; from Kolenfeld; Weser, 1845
Frels, Friedr. and wife—Franziska, 1846
Frels, Hein.—s, 25; Franziska, 1846
Frels, Gerhard–s, 23; Frels, Wilh.–s, 23; Apollo, 1844
Fremdling, Carl Ferd–s, 35; from Einbeck, Han; Franziska, 1846
Frensch, Martin J.—39; from Schönberg,Nassau;†14.VI.1847(NBChR),

age 42; widow—Marie 34; ch—
Christian 10, Georg. 7, Maria 4,
Dor. 2; **Strabo,** 1845
Frentge, Wilh.–30; **Johann Dethardt,**
1845
Frerichs, Tenculo and wife—Fre-
richs, Herm.—s, 24; Colorado
Co.; **Franziska,** 1846
Freudenthal, Friedr., Aug.—from
Barlage, Osnabruck; w—Elisa
nee Huebner; ch—Dor., George; **B.
Bohlen,** 1845
Frey, Conrad—from Baden;
†19.V.1847, age 23 (NBChR)
Frey, Friedr.–s, 19; Sarah Ann, 1845
Frey, Joh.—s, from Budesheim; Co-
mal Co.; **Andacia,** 1846
Frey, Julius–s, 22; Frey, Martin–s,
17; **Sarah Ann,** 1845
Frey, Paul—from Büdesheim;
Andacia, 1846
Frey, Peter (widower)—from Hoch-
hausen, Baden; †12.VIII.1846,
age 54(NBChR); **Sarah Ann,** 1845
Frey, Phil. Jos.—from Büdesheim, 5
persons; **Andacia,** 1846
Frick, Anton—from Ueckersdorf
(Nebendorf?); 6 persons; Colorado
Co.; **Riga,** 1846
Frick, Joseph—w and 3 ch; from
Ueckersdorf; **Riga,** 1846
Frick, Julius—from Brenkenhof; ch
—Christian,Albert,Gustav,Friedr.,
Ida, Tobert, Franziska; **Johann
Dethardt,** 1846
Fricke, Georg–24, from Hannover; 3
persons, Austin Co.; **Gerhard
Hermann,** 1845
Friedhoff, Hein.–s, 20; from Netze,
Waldeck; **Margaretha,** 1846
Friedrich, Aug.–New Braunfels 1845
Friedrich, Carl—s; from Gross Vahl-
berg, Brnschwg; **Louise,** 1846
Friedrich, Heinr.—from Fallers-
leben; **Karl Ferdinand,** 1846
Friedrich, Lorenz–s; from Grossgar-
tach; **Diamant,** 1846
Friedrich, Marg.—from Kaltennord-
heim; **Neptune,** 1845
Friedrich, Wilh.—s; Mason Co.; **St.
Pauli,** 1847
Friedrichs, Joachim Hein.–s; from
Mieste; **B. Bohlen,** 1847
Friess, Adam—s, 27; from Nassau;
Gillespie Co.; **Riga,** 1846
Friess, Joh.–from Kadenbach; 6 per-
sons; died 1847; sole heirs-
—Marianne, Joseph; Gillespie
Co.; **Riga,** 1846
Fries II, Peter–died; from Kaden-
bach, Nassau; w–Maria nee
Eberts 32; ch–Jos. 6, Peter Jos. 4,
Joh. ½; **Herschel,** 1845
Friesenhahn, Anton—39; from
Dahlheim, Nassau; w—Maria 35;

ch—Jacob 13, Anna Maria 11;
Anton 9, Andreas 5, Nicolas 9 mo.;
Comal Co.; **Strabo,** 1845
Frinn, Christoph–from Schmalkal-
den; arr. 1845
Frist, Anton—from Kieslegg (=
Kieslau? Kiesling?); **Riga,** 1846
Fritsch, Fried. Christ.–s; from Stras-
burg; **Herschel,** 1844
Fritz, Christian–24; **Andacia,** 1846
Fritz, Jacob—from Seinscheider-(
mühle; 5 persons; wife and son
† New Braunfels VII.1846; Har-
riet, 1845,
Fritz, Phillip–from Waldalgesheim;
Dyle, 1846
Fritze, Ferd.–s; **Johann Dethardt,**
1845
Fritze, Georg–40; from Dillenburg,
Nassau; w–Cath. Caro. Becker, 40;
ch–Dan. Bernh. 10, Caro. Louise
5, Joh. Hein., Wilh. Dan; Comal
Co.; **Johann Dethardt,** 1845
Fritze,Jacob—from Hadamar,Nass.;
†18.III.1847 age 40; wife †1846,
age 33; 1 orphan left behind;
(NBChR)
Fritzsche, Carl A.—from Brome,
Han.; w—Friedricka nee Radeke;
Harris Co.; **B. Bohlen,** 1847
Fritze, Ludw. Friedr.–s, 25; from
Dillenburg; Comal Co.; **Johann
Dethardt,** 1845
Froeba, Andreas—m; from Buch-
bach, Mein.; **Flavius,** 1846
Froelich, Elisa.–from Ellar; widow of
Georg Froelich; **Henry,** 1846
Froelich, Joh. Jost.—26; w—Cath.
Wilhme nee Nickel, 23; ch—
Wilh. Fried. ½; from Bicken, Nas-
sau; Comal Co.; **Herschel,** 1845
Fromme,Georg—m;fromUnterrohn,
†1847 age 41; from Oberzella,
(NBChR); w—Elis. nee Heise; ch
—Daniel; **Orient,** 1846
Fuchs, Adam—from Kolzow; **Ger-
hard Hermann,** 1846
Fuchs, Adolph and 8 persons—from
Kolzow, Mcklbg; w—Louise nee
Ruencker and 6 children; Austin
Co.; **Gerhard Hermann,** 1846
Fuchs, Arnold—s; from Nieder-
lückerath; **Colchis,** 1846
Fuchs, Georg—42; from Fambach;
w—Barbara nee Reinhard; ch—
Elis. 10, Conrad 6, Joh. 8, Caspar
3; Austin Co.; **Gerhard Hermann,**
1846
Fuchs, Hein.—s, 36; from Köl-
zow, Mcklbg; Austin Co.; **Gerhard-
Hermann,** 1846
Fuchs, Joh.–s, 20; **Gerhard Hermann,**
1846
Fuchs, Peter—from Neuhäusel;
died 1846; wife and 5 ch; Marg.
and Anna sole heirs; **Riga,** 1846

Fugel, Sopha–24; **Andacia, 1846**
Fuhrhop, Jürgen—from Niendorf,
Han.; 5 persons; 1845
Fuhrmann,Aug.—fromBaumgarten
Silesia
Fuhrmann, Joh.–s; from Gartow;
Fredericksburg; **Orient, 1846**
Fullmann, John—s, 39; Steamer
Galveston, 1846
Funk, Christian—s; from Fürfeld;
Dyle, 1846
Funk, Christoph—34; Anna S.—
36, and 1 female ch; Jacob 5;
Dyle, 1846
Funk, Friedr. Werner and wife; from
Wriezen a/Oder; **Elisa and Char-
lotte, 1846**
Funk, Jacob—from Fürfeld, Württ.;
wife—Cath. †1.VII.1846, age 37;
Comal Co.; Calhoun Co.; **Dyle,
1846**
Funk, Wilh.—from Hohenhameln; w
—Louise nee Fricke; **Anna, 1846**

— G —

Gabel, Joseph—†6.IX.1846, age 48
(NBChR); **Washington, 1845**
Gadt(Gatt), Hein.–from Lechstedt,
Han.; w–Dor; ch–Hein., Christian,
Aug.; Gillespie Co.; **Everhard, 1845**
Gaertner, Christian–from Eisenach
(IC), or Aschhausen (VF); 3 per-
sons; Gillespie Co.; **Nahant**
(wrecked 1846), then **Timoleon,
1846**
Gaertner, Eva(widow)–from Lim-
burg a/Lahn; **Bohemia, 1846**
Gaeschel, Aug.–s; **Mathilde, 1846**
Gais IV., Joh.–s; from Villmar; **James
Edward, 1846**
Garken, Fried.–s, 44; **Gesina, 1846**
Garthe, Jost Curth–from Franken-
berg; **Element, 1846**
Gatho, (Jatho?), Joh.—see Jatho,
Joh.
Gauer, Carl Ludwig–s, 23; from
Abbensen, Han.; **B. Bohlen, 1845**
Gaugler, Joh. Martin—s, 25; from
Bonfeld; **Dyle, 1846**
Gebhardt,Andreas—s;fromSchlüch-
tern; **Diamant, 1846**
Gebhardt, Joh. Jac.–s, 45; from
Erlenbach; **Washington, 1845**
Geffers, Wilh.–from Neudorf, Han.;
w–Elisa nee Jahr; ch–Wilh., Hein.,
Elis.; Dor., Joh.; **Everhard, 1845**
Gehring, Friedr.–m; had Verein land
grant;
Gehrke, Daniel–from Leistrup, Det-
mold; w–Christina nee Grethe and
one ch.; **Gesina, 1846**
Gehrke, Hein.–s, 22; from Platen-
dorf, Han.; **Everhard, 1845**

Gehrke, Leonhard–s, 20; from Leistrup, Detmold; **Gesina, 1846**
Gehsdorf, Carl—from Köpenick
by Berlin; †26.VIII.1846, age 47,
w—Anne 38 from Linz, Austria;
ch—Josephine †1846, age 9, Caro.
†1846, age 7, one male child
(NBChR); **Dyle, 1846**
Geier, (Geyer) Andreas—from Rem-
lingen or Hedeper, Brnschwg; w
—Anne Dor. Sophie Vahldick;
ch–Regine Wilhmne, Dor. Chris-
tiane; **Louise, 1846**
Geissendoerfer, Kath.—**Ferdinand,
1844**
Geissler, C. W.–m; from Hoheneiche;
arr. 1845; Kendall Co.
Geit, Margaret–from Holler, Nas-
sau; **Hercules, 1845**
Gellermann, Ferd.—from Weibeck,
Hesse; 2 persons; Gillespie Co.;
Apollo, 1846
Gellermann, Hein.–from Weibeck;
Apollo, 1846
Gellhorn, Roderich von–2 persons;
from Schweidnitz; Gonzales Co.;
arr. 1846
Gengerbach, Elis.—from Ebers-
bach; arr. 1845
Georg. Joh. Georg—see Goerg, Joh.
Goerg
Georg, Joh. Carl—from Altensteig;
Comal Co.; **Element, 1846**
Gerbert, Wilh.–from Eselbach,
Altenburg; w–Charl. nee Lemm;
Margaretha, 1846
Gerhadt, (=Gerhardt?), Peter—from
Eberfeld; **Henry, 1846**
Gerhard, Joh. Christian—70; from
Dillenburg; Comal Co.; **Herschel,
1845**
Gerhard, Wilh.—19, from Dillen-
burg; w—Cath. nee Straube; ch—
Johanna, Elis.; father—Joh. Chris-
tian, age 70; Comal Co.; **Herschel,
1845**
Gerhardt, Georg—24; from Winter-
lingen; **Andacia, 1846**
Gerharts, Robert—m, 36; from
Waldbröl; w and 1 ch; Harris Co.;
Timoleon, 1846
Gerharz, Joh.–s, from Arzbach, Nas-
sau; **Auguste Meline, 1845**
Gerlach, Franz—from Mark, West-
phalia, 1845
Gerloff, Carl—from Berlin; w—
Charlotte nee Hehlne; ch—Carl,
Emil; **Franziska, 1846**
Germain, Maurice—New Braunfels,
1845
Germann, Friedr.–49; w–Anna 41;
ch–Aug 12, Adolph 5, Gustav 2;
Neptune, 1845
Germann, Philipp–from Driedorf,
Nassau; w–Anna Marie nee

Lauer; ch–Joh., Adolph, Phil., Jacob, Gustav; **Neptune**, 1845
Gerner, Joh.–s, 30; from Flinsbach; New Braunfels; **Sarah Ann**, 1845
Gerner, Philipp–from Flinsbach; **Sarah Ann**, 1845
Gerrmann, Jacob—m; from Mangelsbach by Erbach; **Bohemia**, 1846
Gerstenberg, Otto–s; from Garmissen, Han.; **Margaretha**, 1845
Geyer, Edward and w—Marg. nee Schmidt; ch—Theresa, Herm., Aug., Albertine; Bexar Co.; **Margaretha**, 1846
Geyer, Georg—s; from Bingen **Hamilton**, 1846
Giehl, Christian–s, 31; from Langenbach; **Harriet**, 1845
Giese, Wilh.–s; from Lenzen; **Orient**, 1846
Giesecke, Adolph—s; from Clausthal a/Harz; **Karl Ferdinand**, 1846
Giesecke, Albert–s; from Clausthal, a/Harz; **Karl Ferdinand**, 1846
Giesecke, Carl Friedr.–from Clausthal, 11 persons; Washington Co.; **Talisman**, 1846
Giesecke, Christian—from Clausthal; w—Friedricke nee Stahrenberg; ch—Bertha, Pauline, Gustav, Minna, Julius; Fayette Co.; **Karl Ferdinand**, 1846
Giesecke, Joh. Wilh.—from Clausthal a/Harz; w—Ernestine nee Spangenberg; ch—Johanne, Auguste, Otto, Sophie; **Karl Ferdinand**, 1846
Giesecke, Wilh.—s; from Clausthal a/Harz; Washington Co.; **Karl Ferdinand**, 1846
Gieseler, Carl—s, 39; from Bärenklau, Prussia; **Franziska**, 1846
Giesler, Wilh.–s, 40; (torn contract), Galveston Co.
Girke, Erdmann–s, 40; from Niederdorf, Silesia; **Louise**, 1846
Glab, Conrad–from Wehrda; 7 persons and 1 baby; **Colchis**, 1846
Glaeser, Joh.–from Amecke; Colorado Co.; **Talisman**, 1846
Glaesner, Joh.–†13.VII.1846, age 49; from Bruchhausen, bei Arnsberg; **Talisman**, 1846
Glaum, Joh–from Oberkleen, Prussia; 5 persons; Austin Co.; arr. 1846
Gleissner, Anton—s; August—s; Carl —s; Wilh.—s, Ludw.—s, Wilh—m; 10 persons; from Arolsen; Harris Co.; **Colchis**, 1846
Glockner, Phillip–s, 20; Bastrop Co.; **Harriet**, 1845
Godeke, Juergen–from Peine; arr. 1845
Goebel, Joh. Jost–m; from Driedorf, Nassau; ch–Elisa, Jost Henry; Comal Co.; **Arminius**, 1845

Goebel, Jr., Jost Hein.—from Breitscheid, Nassau; w—Anna Maria nee Kolb; ch—Marianne, Emma, Friedr., and baby; Gillespie Co.; **Auguste Meline**, 1845
Goebel, Wilh.–s, 20; **Auguste Meline**, 1845
Goehmann, George–s, from Kirchbrak; Gillespie Co.; **Sophie**, 1846
Goerg, Joh. Goerg—from Breitscheid, Nassau; w—Christine nee Hoffmann; ch—Aug., Ferd.; Gillespie Co.; **George Delius**, 1845
Goers, (Gorries?) Christian–s, 25; from Klein Mahner, Han.; **Everhard**, 1845
Goertz, Hein. Mack—27; w—Elis. 40; from Rennerod; see also Mack, Hein.; **Strabo**, 1845
Goette, Franz–s, had Verein land grant.
Goldammer, Hein.–s, 25; **Franziska**, 1846
Goldbeck, Friedr. and family—from Verden, Han.; New Braunfels 1845 Kendall Co. later; **Johann Dethardt**, 1844
Goldbeck, Theodor—*Oct. 12, 1826 in Verden, Han.; m—Miss Nohl; had 4 ch; †Feb. 11, 1890 in San Antonio; New Braunfels 1845; **Ferdinand**. 1844
Gollmer, Christian—m; from Oberlenningen, Württ.; w—Friedricke nee Fischass; Austin Co.; **Timoleon**, 1846
Gollmer, Joh.—s; from Oberlenningen; † in Galveston 1846; **Timoleon**, 1846
Gombel, Friedr.–s, 19; from Werdorf, Nassau; **Neptune**, 1845
Gombel, Josephe.–38; **Neptune**, 1845
Gorries–see Goers
Gottbehut, Georg–s, 72; from Oberwied; **Harriet**, 1845
Gottesleben, Herm.–from Hildesheim; arr. 1845
Gotthardt, Ernest—s, 19; **Johann Dethardt**, 1845
Gotthardt, Gustav–s, 25; Comal Co.; **Johann Dethardt**, 1845
Gotthardt, Jacob Wilh.—from Liebenscheid, Nassau; w—Elisa nee Fasch; ch—Gustav, Ernst., Wilh., Rudolf, Wilhme, Caro., Friedr.; Comal Co.; **Johann Dethardt**, 1845
Graf, Theo.–from Gadenstedt; arr. 1845
Graf, Wilh.–from Laaslich; w–Caro. nee Schrader; Fayette Co.; **Orient**, 1846
Grahn, H. Ludw.–26, from Norden; w–Louise 22; **Dyle**, 1846

Gramme, Conrad—from Gross Lafferde, Han.; w—Theresa nee Luedecke; ch—Mina, Cath., Dor.; **Bexar Co.; Flavius, 1846**
Graudt, A.—Fredericksburg, 1847
Graumann (Greumann?), Hein.—and wife, from Rossing, Han.; **Everhard, 1845**
Gravert, Claus-s; from Rendsburg; **Emily, 1847**
Grebel, Dor.–from Frankenhausen, Prussia; **Elisa & Charlotte, 1846**
Grenwelge, Georg Fr.—32; Grenwelge, M.E.—58; from Bruchweiler; Gillespie Co.; **Dyle, 1846**
Grewe, Fr. Jurgen, Jac.—from Glückstadt; **Natchez, 1847**
Grewe, Ida Rosa Anna–from Itzehoe, Schleswig-Holstein; 1847
Grimm, Aug.—s, 30; **Johann Dethardt, 1845**
Grimm, Carl—25; from Möhrendorf, Nassau; **Garonne, 1845**
Grimm, Friedr-s; from Zegartowith, Poland; Comal Co.; **Johanne, 1846**
Grimm, Hein.-s; from Camberg; **Bohemia, 1846**
Grimm, Joseph–from Herbolzheim; **Margaretha, 1846**
Grobe, Christ. Conrad-†20.III.1847, age 18; from Oberg, Han.; **Hercules, 1845**
Grobe, Hein.—42; from Oberg, Han.; w—Marie Cath. nee Wolbers, age 41, died at Indianola; ch—Cath.; † 9.IV.1847, age 15, Henry 9, Ferd. ½; m—Caro. Hennings in 1846; Comal Co.; **Hercules, 1845**
Grobecker, Berthold—from Hottorf, Han.; w—Regina nee Beusshausen; ch—Aug., Jacob, Conrad, Daniel, Georg., Regina; **Elisa & Charlotte, 1846**
Groos, Joh.-24; **Herschel, 1845**
Groos, Joh. Jacob—23; from Offenbach, Nassau; w—Cath. nee Blieder, 23; Comal Co.; **Herschel, 1845**
Grosch, Franz–from Offenburg; 10 persons; **Colchis, 1846**
Gross, Adam Val.—43; from Näherstille, Kurh.; w—Anna nee Weiher 50; **Garonne, 1845**
Gross, Christina—17 from Kleinschneen, Carl 14, Mathias 12; lived with Franz Grosch in New Braunfels, step-children of J.H. Metz (q.v.); **Johann Dethardt, 1845**
Gross, Franz-s; from Ehrenbreitstein; Gillespie Co.; **Riga, 1846**
Grossmann, Jacob–from Bischoffen; **Element, 1846**
Grote, August-arr. Gal. 20.XII.1845
Grote, Rev. Charles A.-arr. Gal.20.XII.1845; with nephew Aug. Grote

Grote, Hein.—from Warbsen, Brnschwg; w—Johanna nee Hundertmark;ch—Caro.,FriedrickeWilhme Louise; Comal Co.; **Elisa & Charlotte, 1846**
Grote, Wm.-† before 1860; had Verein land grant.
Grotjaehe, Wilh.–from Adenstedt; arr. 1845
Grube, Diedrich and wife–**Franziska, 1846**
Gruen, Franz—from Altendiez; 4 persons; **Andacia, 1845**
Gruen, Hein.-s, 22; **George Delius, 1845**
Gruen, Jost Hein.—from Rabenscheid, Nassau; w—Cath. nee Theiss; son Fried; Gillespie Co.; **George Delius, 1845**
Gruene, Engel-from Netze; mother of Ernst Gruene; **Margaretha, 1845**
Gruene, Ernst-from Netze, Waldeck; w—Antonette nee Kloepper; Comal Co.; **Margaretha, 1845**
Grundgrieper, Marie–from Lenzen, Prussia; **Orient, 1846**
Grussendorf, Friedr.-from Gifhorn, Han; 3 persons; Bastrop Co.; **Everhard, 1845**
Grussendorf, Hein.—m; from Gifhorn, Han.; **Everhard, 1845**
Grussendorf, Ludwig-s; from Fallersleben, Han.; **Karl Ferdinand, 1846**
Gscheidle, Christoph—s; from Auenstein, Württ.; **Talisman, 1846**
Guenther, Carl-s, 26; from Wiesbaden; Bexar Co.; **Washington, 1845**
Guenther, Conrad-s, 17; **Everhard, 1845**
Guenther, Friedr.—s; from Schöppenstedt, Brnschwg.; **Sophie, 1846**
Guenther, Georg Adam—widow from Diedorf, Weimar; and 3 ch.; **Everhard, 1845**
Guenther, Jacob—from Diedorf, Weimar; †22.VIII.1847, age 35; w—Sophie nee Hoessel (died); ch —Kath., Anna, Marie, Christian; 2 orphans left behind (NBChR); **Everhard, 1845**
Guenther, Mrs. M.-early New Braunfels settler
Guenzel, Christian F. and family —from Beilstein, Württ., arr. 1846
Guenzel, Georg-from Veilsdorf; 4 persons; Austin Co.; **Nahant** (wrecked) 1846, then **Timoleon, 1846**
Gun(c)kel, Carl Friedr.-s, 19; from Herzberg, Hesse; or Rosenthal; **Franziska, 1846**
Gunst, Louis—s, from Bingen; **Hamilton, 1846**

Guse, Carl—m, from Zegartowith, arr. 1846
Gus(s)mus, Joh.—s, 46; from Winzenburg, Han.; Bexar Co.; **Margaretha,** 1845
Gutbrod, Carl–s, from Dillenburg; **Element,** 1846
Gutbrod, Friedr.–m; from Dillenburg; 4 persons; **Element,** 1846
Gut(h)brod, Wilhelm–from Dillenburg; **Element,** 1846
Guth, Carl Theo.–from Rehe; arr. 1845

— H —

Haab, Joh. Georg.—s; from Waldenbuch, Württ.; **Element,** 1846
Haab, Rudolph–m; from Waldenbuch; 6 persons; **Element,** 1846
Haag, Jacob Friedr.–from Frankenbach; 5 persons; Comal Co.; **Talisman,** 1846
Haarnagel, Louis–s, 28; from Holtensen, Han.; **Gesina,** 1846
Haas(s), Christian–s, 30; from Niederhofen; Comal Co.; arr. 1847
Haas, Friedr. Aug.—s, 25; **Washington,** 1845
Haas, Jacob–George Delius, 1845
Haas, Johann Jost.–34; from Gusternhain; Wilhelmina–25; Carl 6, Reinhard 4, Adolph ¼; Comal Co.; **Washington,** 1845
Habenicht, Hein.—from Betheln, Han.; †24.XII.1845 (NBChR); w —Amalie nee Hillner; ch—Joh. Hein. Ludolph 21, only heir; Gillespie Co.; **Everhard,** 1845
Habich, F. A.–from Sachsenhagen; 9 persons; **Neptune,** 1845
Habich, Julius Mart–33, from Cassel; w–Charl. nee Schalm 18; **Neptune,** 1845
Hackbarth, Mrs. Charlotte–from Czychen, East Prussia; **Johanna,** 1846
Hackbarth, Friedr.–46; from Czychen; w–Christina nee Kaupitz; ch–Gustav, Albert; Austin Co.; **Johanna,** 1846
Haddenbrock, Franz Arnold–s; from Remscheid; 2 persons; Kendall Co.; **Element,** 1846
Haeberle, Adam—s, from Haberschlacht; Medina Co.; arr. 1846
Haerter, Adam—Kendall Co.; **Timoleon,** 1846
Haerter, Constantin–Kendall Co.; **Timoleon** 1846
Haerter, Jacob.–Kendall Co.; **Timoleon,** 1846
Haertig, Adam–from Aschhausen; 2 persons; **Nahant** 1846 (wrecked); then **Timoleon** 1846

Haeseler, Wilh.–from Rennerod, 1845
Hafert, Gottlieb—s; from Wiesenbach; 1846
Haffelder, Phil.–24; w–Cath. 30, Caro. 10, Gustav 5, Adam 3; Comal Co.; **Washington,** 1845
Hafner, Christ. and wife—from Oberschönau; **Everhard,** 1845
Hafner, Leonhard—s, from Ebersbach; **Element,** 1846
Hagedorn, Hein. Conrad—from Wolfshagen; w—Marie Caro. nee Heine; ch—Hein. Fr. Julius 5, Johanne Henrietta 2; arr. 1846
Hagelmann, Carl Wilh.–arr. 1846
Hagemann, Bernhard and wife —from Dingelbe, Han.; Kendall Co.; **Gesina,** 1846
Hagemann, Christian—s, 24; from Barwedel, Han.; **Gerhard Hermann,** 1845
Hagemann, Christoph—from Woltwiesche, Brnschwg.; arr. 1845
Hagemann, Ch. Wilh.—†5.X.1846, age 40 (NBChR); from Weibeck, Han.; w—Sophie nee Steinbring and 2 ch; **Apollo,** 1845
Hagemann, Elisa (widow)–from Dingelbe, Han.; 3 persons; **Gesina,** 1846
Hagemann, Friedr.—s, 37; from Münstedt, Han.; Austin Co.; arr. 1846
Hagemann, John–s, 50; Hagemann, John–38, and wife; Galveston Co.; **Gesina,** 1846
Hagemann, Sophie—from Münstedt, Han.; arr. 1845
Hagemann, Wilh.–s, 54; from Weibeck, Nassau; **Apollo,** 1846
Hagenbruch, Aug.–from Hersberg, Han.; 2 persons and 1 baby; arr. 1845
Hager, Christoph–44, w–Augusta S. 48; ch–Anton 19, Joh. 17, Christine 14, Marie 1; **Andacia,** 1846
Hahn, Adolph—from Darmstadt; † 17.X.1847 (NBChR), age 20 or 22; **St. Pauli,** 1847
Hahn, Christian–s; from Thalheim; **Harriet,** 1845
Hahn, Christian Aug.—from Stein, Nassau; w—Anna nee Reeh; ch—Dan, Justine, Alwine, Ludwig; **Johann Dethardt,** 1845
Hahn, Conrad—from Appenhofen; w—Elisa; Gillespie Co.; **James Edward,** 1846
Hahn, Jonas–m; died 1846; **Auguste Meline,** 1845
Hahn, Wilh.–**Bohemia,** 1846
Hahne, Christoph–m; **Margaretha,** 1846
Hahne, Hein.–from Almstedt, Han.; w—Caro. nee Heinemann; ch—

Hein., Johanne, Conrad, Christian; **Margaretha**, 1845
Hahne, Hein.–from Amecke; 4 persons; **Diamant**, 1846
Halbe, Christ.–**Dyle**, 1846
Halberstadt, Hein. Gustav—from Herzberg, Han.; **Elisa & Charlotte**, 1846
Halm, Joh.—from Mengerskirchen, Nassau; w—Marg. nee Mack; ch— Carl, Wilh., Joseph; Guadalupe Co.; **Auguste Meline**, 1845
Halm, Joseph—s, 18; from Rennerod, Nassau; Guadalupe Co.; **Auguste Meline**, 1845
Halm, Wilh.—s; from Mengerskirchen, Nassau; **Auguste Meline**, 1845
Halm, Wilh.–from Mengerskirchen, w–Cath. nee Bolzer; ch–Wilh. 22, Cath. 21; Galveston Co.; **Auguste Meline**, 1845
Ham, Christian–58; Calhoun Co.; **Andacia** 1846
Ham, Hein.—from Emmerichenhain, †26.X.1846, age 46; (NBChR)
Hamers, Edward–from Uerdingen; **Element**, 1846
Hammel, Michael—s, 22; from Württemberg; **Weser**, 1844
Hanebuth, Friedr.—s; from Horst, Han.; †30.VI.1846, age 29 (NBChR); **Weser**, 1845
Hanewacker, Heinr.—from Pöhlde, 2 persons; **Talisman**, 1846
Hankamer, G.W.–m; from Neesbach, †14.X.1846, age 45, NBChR); w— Anna C. 41; ch—Maria 9, Carl 6, Philippine 5, Henriette 1; **Washington**, 1845
Hannel, Stephan–Galveston Co.; **Louise Friedricke**, 1847
Hans, Albert–from Herborn; 6 persons and 1 baby; **Element**, 1846
Hansen, Fritz Hein.–s; from Peine, Han.; Galveston Co.; **Margaretha**, 1845
Hantke, Gottlob—from Wellersdorf, Prussia; w—Christina; ch—Carl, Caro., Aug., Christine; Galveston Co.; **Joh. Dethardt**, 1846
Hanz, Christian—s, 32; from Oettingen, New Braunfels 1845; **Ferdinand**, 1844
Harbs, G. Ph.–from Dachsenhausen; **Talisman**, 1846
Hardt, Aug. Herm.–from Hannover; New Braunfels 1845; †6.V.1847 (NBChR), age 26
Hardt, Henry–47; **Strabo**, 1845
Hardt, Jac.—s; from Büdesheim; **Andacia**, 1846
Hardt, Jacob–s; from NiederIngelheim; **Hamilton**, 1846
Hardt, Wilh.—s, 18; from Ernsthausen; **Strabo**, 1845

Harland, Hein. Conrad–from Herkendorf, 1845
Harlos, G.Ph.—from Dachsenhausen, 4 persons; Comal Co.; **Talisman**, 1846
Harlos, Philipp. Wilh.—s, from Frücht; **Talisman**, 1846
Harmel, Stephan—s; from Josephowo, Poland; **Louise Friedricke**, 1846
Harms, Joh. Hein.–s, 24; Washington Co.; **Franziska**, 1845
Harms, Julius—Comal Co.; **Ferdinand**, 1844
Harmuth, August—s; from Benau, Ff/O; Comal Co.; arr. 1846
Harrien, M. F.—s; from Böckingen; **Talisman**, 1846
Harter, Joh.–22; from Hannover; **Joh. Dethardt**, 1845
Hartmann, Adolph—s, 40; from Clausthal, a/Harz; Austin Co.; **Karl Ferdinand**, 1846
Hartmann, Clemens and wife–from Hildesheim, Han.; ch–Hermann 17, Marie; Comal Co., DeWitt Co. later; **Margaretha**, 1845
Hartscher, Joseph—from Rückers, Silesia; w—Theresa nee Lask; **Joh. Dethardt**, 1845
Hartung, Hein.–from Celle; 2 persons; arr. 1845
Hartung, Joh. Christian—from Schallenburg, Prussia; w—Frederica nee Schroeder; ch—Joh. Zach, Joh. Ludw., Fr. Ludw., Marie Christiane; New Braunfels 1845; **Johanne Dethardt**, 1844
Hartung, Joh. Ludw.—s, 18; **Joh. Dethardt**, 1844
Hartwig, Ludw.–s, 40; New Braunfels 1845; **Ferdinand**, 1844
Hartz, Eduard von—from Göttingen, Han.; New Braunfels 1845; Comal Co.; **Herschel**, 1844
Hasenkamp, Christoph–m; from Rohrberg, Prussia; Kendall Co.; **Mathilde**, 1846
Hasenkamp, Friedr. and Hein.—from Rohrberg; Kendall Co.; arr. 1846
Hasper, Wilh.–s; from Stadtoldendorf; Gillespie Co.; **Sophie** 1846
Hasse, Hein.–from Nienstedt, Han.; 6 persons; Gillespie Co., Fayette Co. later; **B. Bohlen**, 1845
Hasseroth, George—from Herzburg a/Harz; **Elisa & Charlotte**, 1846
Hasseroth, Hein.—m; Hasseroth, Gustav—**Elisa and Charlotte**, 1846; **Fredericksburg**, 1846
Hassler, Frau Christine—from Oberndorf; 3 persons; **York**, 1846
Hassler, Joh.—m, from Oberndorf; †7.X.1846, age 29 (NBChR); New Braunfels 1845; **Joh. Dethardt**, 1844

Hassler, Joh. Jost–from Oberndorf; 2 persons, Austin Co.; **York**, 1846
Hattermann, Diedrich–s, 24; from Oldenburg; Fayette Co.; **Franziska** 1846
Hauer, Chr.-from Gebhardshagen; w-Louise nee Biedenbrink; **Gerhard Hermann**, 1845
Haun, Adolph–s; from Teichroda, Schwarzburg; **Margaretha**, 1846
Haun, Christian—from Winterlingen; **Dyle**, 1846
Haup, Chr.—s, from Ebingen; **Andacia**, 1846
Hausdoerfer, Ernst–s; from Warmbrunn, Silesia; **Mathilde**, 1846
Hausler, Rudolph–s, 23; **Galveston**, 1846
Hausmann, Friedr.—from Bösingfeld; w—Charlotte nee Dreyer; De Witt Co.; **Creole**, 1846
Haussmann, Wilh.–s; from Cassel; Victoria Co.; **Herschel**, 1845
Heberer, Georg—s, 33; from Fürth in Odenwald, Hesse; **Garonne**, 1845
Hebgen, Georg—from Fulda, Kurh.; w—Josephine nee Meyer; **Neptune**, 1845
Heck, Hein.—from Burg, by Herborn; 3 persons; **York**, 1846
Heckel, Nic.—s, 29; from Schmalkalden, Kurh.; **Everhard**, 1845
Heckmann, Jac.—from Baden; † 21.X.1846, age 25 NBChR) Heckmann, Joh. Leopold—s; from Rappenau; **Talisman**, 1846
Heffter, Hermann—s; from Merseburg; Comal Co.; **Elisa & Charlotte**, 1846
Hegar, Otto—s, from Darmstadt; **Colchis**, 1846
Hehl, Sebastian—†1846; from Niederelbert; wife and 4 ch; Gillespie Co.; **Riga**, 1846
Heidelberg, Jost. Heinr.—from Pöhlde; 5 persons; **Talisman**, 1846
Heidemeyer, Friedr.—m, 24; New Braunfels 1845, **New York**, 1843
Heidemueller, Conrad—from Völksen; 1845
Heidenreich, Bernhard—s, from Buchhausen or Bonhausen; **Element**, 1846
Heid(e)rich, Franz—s, from Dölitz; 2 persons; **Talisman**, 1846
Heiderich, Jacob—from Steinbrücken; wife and 1 ch; Comal Co.; **Harriet**, 1845
Heidrich, Christian—m, from Queckenberg; **Timoleon**, 1846
Heidrich (Heydrich), F. G.—s, from Schleusingen; **Hamilton**, 1846
Heil, August—from Hallgarten; 5 persons; **Colchis**, 1845

Heil, Jacob—from Hallgarten; 5 persons; 1845
Heil (Heyl), Joh.—s, from Schlitz; **Colchis**, 1846
Heim, Friedr.—s, 35; from Berlin; **Franziska**, 1845
Heim (Hein.?), F. W.—s, from Olürer (=Oeleroth?); **Franziska**, 1846
Heim, Jacob—from Orb, (=Ort?) Bavaria; w—Anna Maria nee Praehler † 3.VII.1845, age 49 (NBChR) and 3 ch; New Braunfels 1845; **Herschel**, 1844
Heimann (Heymann), Gottfried—42, from Manderbach, Nassau; w—Maria nee Walter 34; ch—Aug. 11, Wilh. 9, Hein. 5, Elisa 2; Gillespie Co.; **Auguste Meline**, 1845
Heimann, Hein. Aug.—widower; from Manderbach, Nassau; 5 persons; Gillespie Co.; **Herschel**, 1845
Heimann, Val.—55; w—Cath. 50; Martin 14; Gillespie Co.; 1850
Heimel, Sophie—17; from Fulda; **Neptune**, 1845
Heimstedt, Carl—wife and child; **Franziska**, 1846
Heindorf, August—s; from Zellerfeld, Han.; **Johann Dethardt**, 1846
Heine (Heyne), Diedrich—s, 25; **George Delius**, 1845
Heine, Edward—s, 28; **George Delius**, 1845
Heine, Friedr.—s, 18; from Fallersleben, Han.; Galveston Co.; **Karl Ferdinand**, 1846
Heine, H.—s, age 25; from Hannover; **Ferdinand**, 1845
Heine, Hein.—w—Cath. nee Voges; dau.—Sophie; Austin Co.; **George Delius**, 1845
Heine, Joh. Hein.—from Peine, Han.; w—Dor. nee Brandes, ch—Elisa, Joh., Wilhme; Austin Co.; **B Bohlen**, 1845
Heineken, H.—s, 20; Austin Co.; **Franziska**, 1846
Heinemann, Friedr.—s, 30; from Berlin; **Apollo**, 1846
Heinemann, Fried.—from Platendorf, Han.; w—Dor. nee Goll; ch—Doris, Hein.; Austin Co.; **Everhard**, 1845
Heinemann, H.—s, 30; **Neptune**, 1845
Heinemann, Joseph Werner—from Wehrstedt, Han.; 3 persons; **Margaretha**, 1845
Heinemann, Valentin—46; from Heuthen, Prussia; w—Cath. 42; ch—Cath. 11, Martin 8, Maria 3; **Joh. Dethardt**, 1845
Heinemeier, Conrad—m; from Warmse; **Sophie**, 1846
Heinemeier, Ludwig—s; from Lüerdissen; Comal Co.; **Sophie**, 1846

100

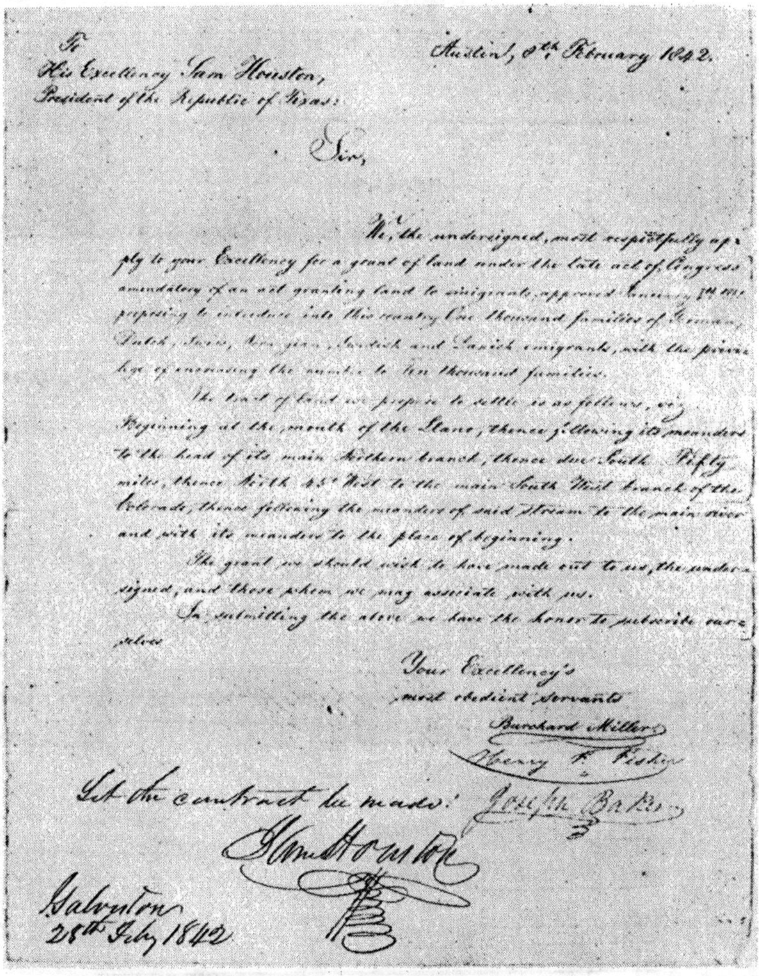
To
His Excellency Sam Houston,
President of the Republic of Texas:

Austin, 8th February 1842.

Sir,

We, the undersigned, most respectfully apply to your Excellency for a grant of land under the late act of Congress amendatory of an act granting land to emigrants, approved January 4th 1841 proposing to introduce into this country One thousand families of German, Dutch, Swiss, Norwegian, Swedish and Danish emigrants, with the privilege of increasing the number to Ten thousand families.

The tract of land we propose to settle is as follows, viz
Beginning at the mouth of the Llano, thence following its meanders to the head of its main Northern branch, thence due South Fifty miles, thence North 45° West to the main South West branch of the Colorado, thence following the meanders of said Stream to the main river and with its meanders to the place of beginning.

The grant we should wish to have made out to us, the undersigned, and those whom we may associate with us.

In submitting the above we have the honor to subscribe ourselves

Your Excellency's
most obedient servants
Burchard Miller
Henry F. Fisher
Joseph Baker

Let the contract be made.
Sam Houston

Galveston
28th Feby 1842

Application of Fisher and Miller
for a grant of land in the Republic of Texas

Plate No. 1

Schiffs-Listen

Bremen, Monat 1846

1846	Name of Ship	Captain	Passengers for Galveston	New Braunfels	Total
1. August	Mathilde	D. Bosse	Galvest. 38	Braunfels 76	Tot. 114
13.	Frederick	Raiher	„ 87	42	12?
21.	Margaretha	Lubben	„ 17	73	9.
23.	Sophie	Cloeke	„ 17	63	8.
27.	Mexica	Ruschen	7	59	6.
7. September	Elise Charlotte	Wendt	„ 29	„ 91	„ 12?
8.	Louise	Miller	6	112	11?
18.	Joh. Dettharel	Fisching	34	67	10.
30.	Orient	Sitorius	10	75	8.
1. October	Carl Ferdinand	Cochta	122	-0-	12
2.	Flavius	Davis	„ 116	„ 2	11
12.	Johannis	Sachens	„ 77	48	„ 12?
4. Novemb.	Nöhlen / B. Behten	Monke	„ 133		„ 13
„	Louise Friderike				

From Verein Collection, University of Texas Archives.

Plate No. 2

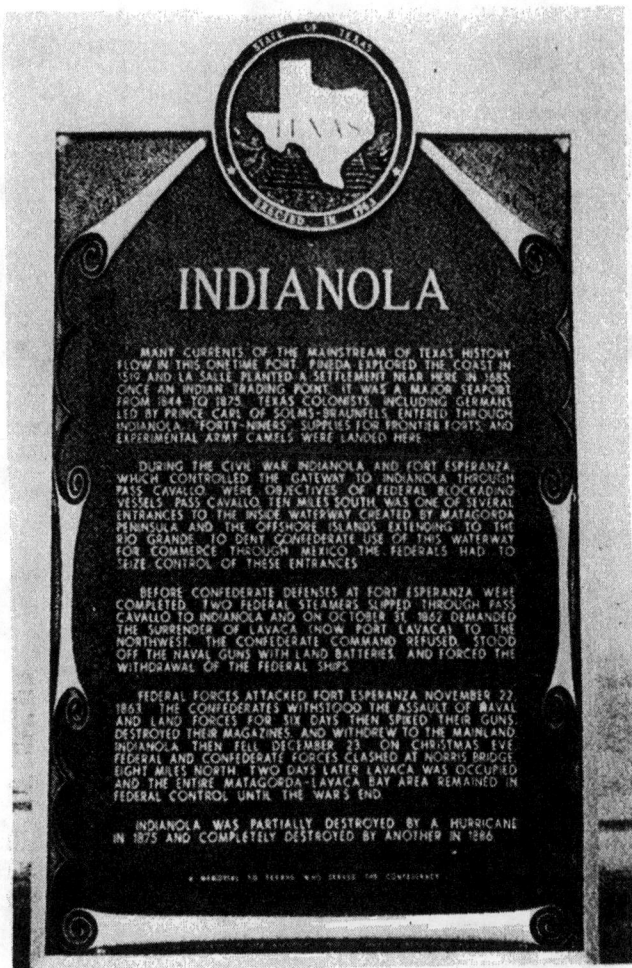

Texas Historical Survey Marker
for Indianola, Texas

Plate No. 3

FISHER-MILLER GRANT
STRETCHES BETWEEN LLANO AND
COLORADO RIVERS WESTWARD ALMOST
TO THE PECOS. AN 1842 GRANT OF
3,800,000 ACRES FROM THE TEXAS
REPUBLIC, PURCHASED IN 1844 BY
THE GERMAN EMIGRATION COMPANY

COMMISSIONER GENERAL JOHN O.
MEUSEBACH FOUNDED FREDERICKS-
BURG IN 1846 AS WAY-STATION TO
THE GRANT. NEGOTIATED PEACE
WITH COMANCHES, TO PROVIDE FOR
UNMOLESTED SETTLEMENT FOUNDED
3 TOWNS IN GRANT. IN 1854 WAS
APPOINTED TO ISSUE HEADRIGHTS.

COUNTIES FORMED FROM GRANT:
CONCHO, KIMBLE, LLANO, McCULLOCH,
MASON, MENARD, SCHLEICHER, SAN
SABA, SUTTON AND TOM GREEN.
(1968)

Texas Historical Survey Marker
for Fisher-Miller Grant

Plate No. 4

Prince Carl of Solms-Braunfels
First Commissioner-General of the Adelsverein
and Founder of New Braunfels

John O. Meusebach
Second Commissioner-General
of the Adelsverein
and Founder of Fredericksburg

New Braunfels in 1848 from a Lithograph
by Carl von Iwonski

Plate No. 7

Map of Texas showing location of Indianola, New Braunfels, Fredericksburg; Immigration route, Fisher-Miller Grant, and the seven counties carved from the Grant.

Plate No. 8

The Sophienburg with early settlers, about 1886

Plate No. 9

German Immigration Contract of
Christian Gollmer
See Appendix I

Plate No. 10

TRANSLATION of part of

EINWANDERUNGS-VERTRAEG or IMMIGRATION CONTRACT

of CHRISTIAN GOLLMER

from OBERLENNINGEN in WURTTEMBERG

Between the Society for the Protection of German Immigrants
to Texas, represented by Mr. Gustav Merz, authorized to make
contracts, of the first part and

Christ. Gollmer from Oberlenningen

party of the second part, the following agreement has been concluded.

Paragraph 1.

The Society for the Protection of German Immigrants to Texas
grants to *Chr. Gollmer* , presently of married status, *320
acres* of land, who accepts the same for himself, his family, and
his heirs, and assigns *three hundred and twenty acres* to be taken from
its lands located in the present county of San Antonio, Republic
of Texas, in the present condition of the grant and to be designated to the immigrant by an agent of the Society.

Paragraph 2.

The immigrant will use the tract assigned to him as owner,
fully protected in all rights of property from the day of taking
possession, without, however, being allowed to alienate the
tract, in whole or in part, during the next three years following.

. . . .
The present agreement is to be dutifully and faithfully observed in all respects by the contracting parties, as their own
signature witnesseth.

Done at Antwerp, the *22 Novbr* 1845
                                    The authorized agent.
                                    Gustav Merz
                                    Christian Gollmer
Consulate of the Republic of Texas for the port of Antwerp.

These are to certify, that appeared before me Mr. *Christ Gollmer*
and made oath, that the whole content of the aforegoing agreement
was well comprehended and consented by him, and both parties
signed the same in my presence.

Done in Antwerp, this *25* of *November* 1845

                    Max Vandenberg
                    Texian Consul

Plate No. 11

German Emigration Company land sale contract

See Appendix II

1844 · 1847

German Immigrants

TO TEXAS

CAME MOSTLY FROM
THESE AREAS

AREA BETWEEN DOTTED LINES
IS NOW DDR OR EAST GERMANY

Plate No. 13

BALTIC SEA

FORMERLY POMERANIA

FORMERLY SILESIA

POLAND

ODER RIVER

NEISSE RIVER

BERLIN

BRANDENBURG

SAXONY

MECKLENBURG

SCHLESWIG HOLSTEIN

HANNOVER

BRAUN–SCHWEIG

THURINGIA

BAVARIA

MUNICH

BREMEN

HANNOVER

WÜRTTEMBERG

NORTH SEA

OLDENBURG

WESTPHALIA

NASSAU

B A D E N — H E S S E

SWITZERLAND

NETHERLANDS

RHINE LAND

RHINE RIVER

FRANCE

BELGIUM

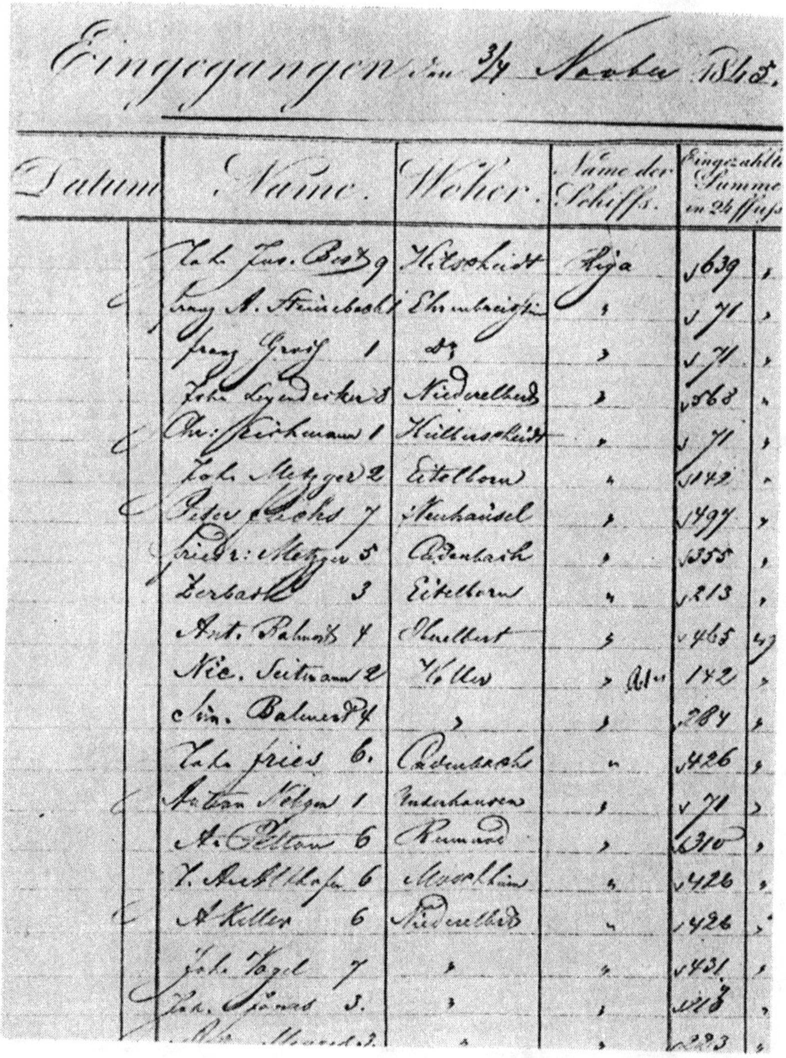

German list of passengers on ship *Riga* from Antwerp*
See Appendix III

*From Verein Collection in the University of Texas Archives.

Plate No. 14

List of Passengers who sailed here pr. Ship Riga Mason Mr. from Antwerpen, for the German Emigration Company and who are hereby entered at the State Department of Texas as settlers on the Grant, ceed to Messrs Hry f Fischer & B. Miller under date Washington Oct 4th 1843 transferred to said Company as pr. Contract, of 28th of June 1844, 9th Congress of 29th Jany 1845.

	Names	Native Country	Occupation	whether family or single men	Age
1	John Lyendecker	Germany	School Master	wife and 4 children	
2	John Lyendecker	do	farmer	single	18
3	Mathias Lyendecker	do	do	do	71
4	Peter Fuchs	do	Schoemaker	wife & 5 Children	
5	John Vogel	do	Smith	wife & 4 do	
6	Christian Vogel	do	do	single	20
7	Fridk Metzger	do	farmer	wife & 1 child	
8	Jacob Metzger	do	do	single	24
9	Anton Metzger	do	do	do	25
10	Adam Althoren	do	do	wife & 4 children	
11	Anton Pilton	do	do	& wife	
12	Widow Pilton	do	do	& 3 children	
13	Peter Maurer	do	do	wife & 3 do	
14	John Thies	do	do	wife & 4 do	
15	Joseph Sing	do	do	wife & 3 do	
16	Simon Balmuth	do	do	wife & 2 do	
17	John Lyendecker	do	do	wife & 2 do	
18	John Jonas	do	do	& wife	
19	Peter Jonas	do	do	single	26
20	Nicolas Seideman	do	do	& wife	
21	Anton Balmith	do	do	wife & child	
22	Anton Menger	do	do	wife & child	
22	carrd over				

Republic of Texas list of passengers
on ship *Riga* from Antwerp.*

See Appendix III

*From Fisher-Miller Papers in the Texas State Archives

Plate No. 15

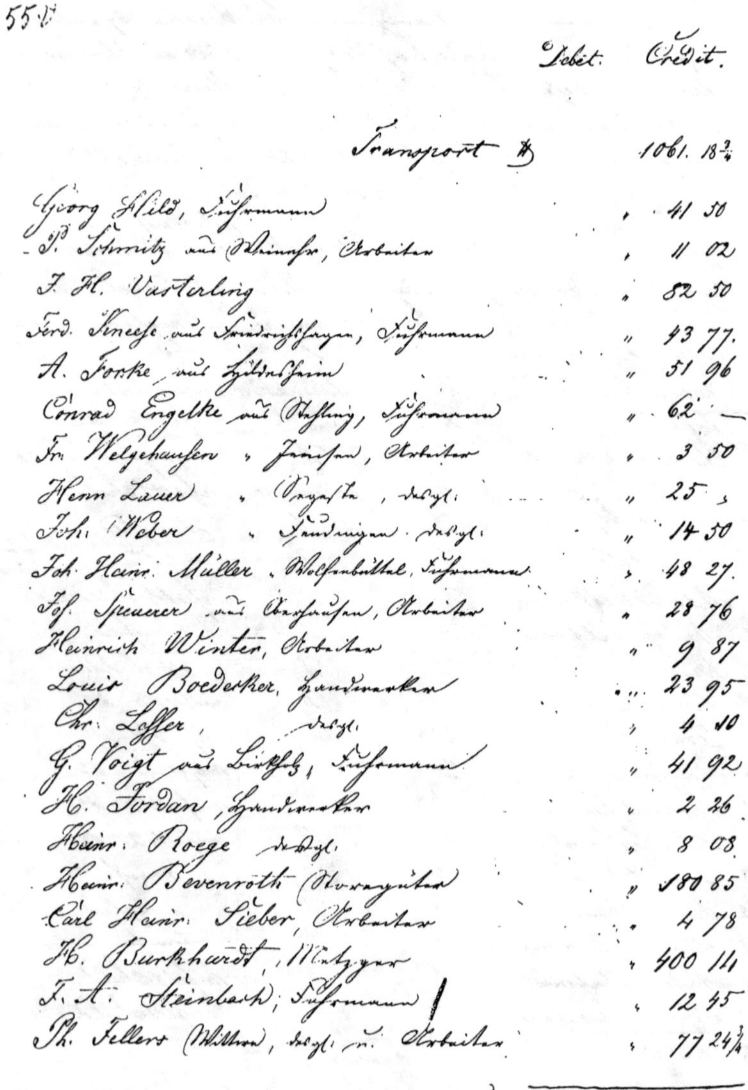

Debit. Credit.

Transport ℳ 1061. 18¾

Georg Hild, *Fuhrmann* . 41 50
J. Schmitz aus Rheinfr., *Arbeiter* , 11 02
F. H. Vasterling . 82 50
Ferd. Kneese aus Friedrichsfeyn, *Fuhrmann* „ 43 77.
A. Fonke aus Hildesheim „ 51 96
Conrad Engelke aus Pakling, *Fuhrmann* . 62 —
Fr. Welgehausen , *Jünisen, Arbeiter* . 3 50
Henn Lauer , *Ongesta , dsgl.* „ 25 ,
Joh. Weber , *Sandnigen. dsgl.* „ 14 50
Joh. Heinr. Müller . *Wolfenbüttel, Fuhrmann* . 48 27.
Jos. Spenner aus Osnabrück, *Arbeiter* . 28 76
Heinrich Winter, *Arbeiter* „ 9 87
Louis Boederker, *Handwerker* .„ 23 95
Chr. Löffer , *dsgl.* , 4 50
G. Voigt aus Lirtfch, *Fuhrmann* „ 41 92
H. Jordan , *Handwerker* . 2 26
Heinr. Roege *dsgl.* „ 8 03
Heinr. Bevenroth (*Hausgenossen*) „ 180 85
Carl Heinr. Sieber, *Arbeiter* .. 4 78
H. Burkhardt , *Metzger* . 400 14
F. A. Steinbach; *Fuhrmann* . 12 45
Ph. Fellers (*Witthon*), *dsgl. u. Arbeiter* . 77 24½

Transport 2,239. 60½

Accounting Record of Immigrants at New Braunfels.
From Verein Collection, University of Texas Archives.

Plate No. 16

Heinemeier, Wilh.—s; from Heiligendorf; arr. 1846
Heinrich, Christian—from Hedeper; w—Marie Dor. nee Lueders, ch—Anne Marie Regina; Ship? date?
Heinrich, Christoph—from Gross Lafferde, Han.; **Hercules,** 1845
Heinrich, H.—s, 30; **Ferdinand,**1844
Heinrich, Joh.—from Bruchköbel, Kurh.; w—Anna nee Basemann, ch—Joh., Jacob, Philipp, Conrad, Marie; **Louise Friedricke,** 1847
Heinrich, Joseph—s, from Siegelsbach; Fayette Co.; **Talisman,** 1846
Heins, Otto—s; from Harburg; **Johann Dethardt,** 1845
Heinsohn, Diederich—s, age 25; from Hannover; Colorado Co.; **Ferdinand,** 1845
Heinsohn, Joh.—23; from Hannover; Austin Co.; **Ferdinand,** 1845
Heintz, Kath. and son Joh.—from Holler, Nass.; **Hercules,** 1845
Heinz, August—s; from Oellingen; **Timoleon,** 1846
Heinz, Gottfried—s; from Oellingen; **Timoleon,** 1846
Heinz, Joh.—s; from Oellingen; **Timoleon,** 1846
Heise, Christian—m; from Guntersberg, a/Harz; arr. 1846; **Heiser, Christian;** Guadulupe Co.
Heise, Hein.—from Everode, Han.; **Margaretha,** 1845
Heiss, Bernhard—from Bargen, Baden; †8.VIII.1849, age 46 (NBChR); 5 persons; **Hamilton,** 1846
Heissner, Conrad—s, 27; from Munich, Bavaria; **Joh. Dethardt,** 1845
Heitkamp, Carl Friedr.—s; from Hochhausen, Prussia; Comal Co.; **Herschel,** 1844
Heitkamp, H.—**New Braunfels,** 1845
Helbe, Christ.—from Rothweil; Fayette Co.; **Dyle,** 1845
Held, Louis—from Wiesbaden; 2 persons; Galveston Co.; **Bohemia,** 1846
Heldberg, Gottlieb—s, 29; from Isenbüttel, Han.; oo Magda. Reinlander 1847; Comal Co.; **B. Bohlen,** 1845
Helfenberger, Mathias—from Herdwangen; 6 persons; **Bohemia,** 1846
Helfrich, Joh.—s, from Fürth; **Colchis,** 1846
Helke, Chr.—s, 30; **Alabama,** 1845
Hellermann, Eugen—s, from Mainz; **Bohemia,** 1846
Hellmann, A.—s, had Verein land grant
Hellmann, Friedr.—s, 30; **Auguste Meline,** 1845

Hellmann, Peter—s, 25; **Apollo,** 1844
Hellmuth, Martin—s, 27; from Riede, Hesse; New Braunfels 1845; Gillespie Co. later; **Ferdinand** 1844
Helmes, Joh.—s, from Unglinghausen, by Siegen; **Element,** 1846
Hemme, Dietr. H.—from Bissendorf, w—Amelia nee Betsch; **George Delius,** 1845
Hemme, Friedr. Jurgen Hein.—from Gailhof, Han.; w—Sophie nee Dobke; son—Joh.; **Weser,** 1845
Hemmerle, Franz—from Hattersheim, Nassau, w—Marg. nee Becker and 2 ch; New Braunfels 1845; **Joh. Dethardt,** 1844
Hempler, Heinrich—s, from Berlin; **Johann Dethardt,** 1846
Henck, Hein.—s, from Laasphe; **Element,** 1846
Henck, Joh.—from Laasphe, 11 persons and 1 baby; **Element,** 1846
Henendorf, Joh. N.—28; **Andacia,** 1846
Henke, Hein.—from Hohe, Brnschwg; w—Wilhme nee Hohmeier; ch—Caro., Wilhme, Johanne; **Mercur,** 1846
Henkel, Count Arnold von Donnersmark—s, from Eisleben; † 16.XI.1850, age 30, (NBChR); New Braunfels 1845, **Johann Dethardt,** 1844
Henne, Hein.—s, from Gestorf, Han.; **1845**
Henne, Joh. Ludw.—32, from Peine, Han.; w—Henriette nee Deppe, 35; ch—Louise 10, Amalie 7, Aug. 3, Wilh. 1; Comal Co.; **Hercules,** 1845
Hennecke, Ilse Dor.—*Wendeburg 13.I.1822, To Texas 1846
Hennerich, Joh.—s, from Nentershausen; **Dyle,** 1846
Henniger, Hein.—52, from Gadenstedt, Han.; w—Cath. nee Bierschwale 50, ch—Dorette 20, Hein. 17, Maria 10; **Hercules,** 1845
Hennigs, Hein.—s, from Pretzier, Saxony; arr. 1846
Hennigs, Joh.—m, from Pretzier, Saxony; arr. 1846
Hennils, Carl and wife—**Margaretha** 1845
Henning, Joh.—s, from Göringen; **Timoleon,** 1846
Henninger, Franz Josef—s, from Herbolzheim; **York,** 1846
Henninger, Hein. Jos.—from Herbolzheim, or Gadenstedt; 5 persons and 1 baby; **York,** 1846
Henninger, Mathias—s, from Herbolzheim, **York,** 1846
Henrich, Joh.—s, 31; from Nentershausen; **Harriet,** 1845

Henrich, Jon.—from Nassau; †
12.X.1846, age 27, (NBChR)
Henrich, Joh.—23; Dyle, 1846
Henrich, Jost—s, 23; from Hel-
lenhahn; **Harriet**, 1845
Hennings, Caro.—from Heersum,
Han.; **Margaretha**, 1845
Henrich, Erasmus—from Erdbach
Nass.; w—Anna nee Conrad;
ch—Conrad, Moritz; **Johann Det-
hardt**, 1845
Hense, Christ.—from Einbeck, 1845
Hentze, Wilh.—New Braunfels, 1845
Henzel, W. F.—from Hameln, 1845
Herber, Caspar—38, from Schwal-
bach, Nassau; w—Theresa 38;
ch—Caro. 5; Bexar Co.; **Joh.
Dethardt**, 1845
Herber, Joh.—w—Dor. nee Pack-
busche, ch—Elisa, Sophie; Vic-
toria Co., **Louise Friedricke**, 1847
Herber, Justus—35, from Schwal-
bach, Nassau; w—Marg. nee
Eicher—28; ch—Hein. 2, Maria 1;
New Braunfels 1845, Gillespie Co.
1848; **Johann Dethardt**, 1845
Herber, Theo.—s, 18; **Johann Det-
hardt**, 1845
Herberer, Georg—from Fürth; arr.
1845
Herbst, Andreas—from Rottweil,
†25.VIII.1846, age 48; w—
Ottilie nee Vollmer † 4.VIII.
1846, age 35; ch—Maximilian †
1846, age 16, Hein. Wilh. from Hil-
desheim † 1846, age 23, Englebert
from Hildesheim † 1846, age 14,
(NBChR); **Dyle**, 1846
Herbst, Andreas—s, Kendall Co.;
Dyle, 1846
Herbst, Carl—Kendall Co.; **Dyle**,
1845
Herbst, Christoph—s, from Hinden-
burg, Prussia; **Joh. Dethardt**, 1846
Herbst, Hein.—s, 20; New Braunfels
1845; **Apollo**, 1844
Herburg, Conrad—s, 17; from Jein-
sen, Han.; Gillespie Co.; **Gesina**,
1846
Herburg, Friedr.—from Jeinsen,
Han.; 5 persons; w—Theresa nee
Freitag; **Gesina**, 1846
Herburg, Hein—s, 23; from Jeinsen,
Han.; **Gesina**, 1846
Herburg, Joh—s, 19; from Jeinsen,
Han.; **Gesina**, 1846
Herdejuergen, Anton—m, from
Schlangen, Detmold; arr. 1846
Herff, Ferdinand von—s, 39, doctor
from Darmstadt; Bexar Co.;
Galveston, 1847
Hering, Jacob—m, from Mühlbach;
5 persons; **Hamilton**, 1846
Hermann, Adolph—s, 30; from
Clausthal; Gillespie Co.; **Andacia**,
1846

Hermann, Peter—s, 21; from Loren,
near Rüdesheim, Nassau; Fayette
Co.; **Joh. Dethardt**, 1845
Hermes, Dr. Wilhelm—**Element**,
1846
Hernani, Peter—36; **Johann Det-
hardt**, 1845
Herold, Joh. Conrad—from
Hoheneiche, Kurh.; † 17.X.1846,
age 21 (NBChR); **Sarah Ann**, 1846
Herrmann, Carl—from Schweidnitz,
Silesia; 2 persons; Bastrop Co.;
arr. 1845
Herrmann, Christian Ludw.—41;
from Hillingsfeld, Han.;
w—Wilhme nee Schwiegendeck;
Comal Co.; **Everhard**, 1845
Herrmann, Friedr.—s, 20; from Hill-
ingsfeld; Comal Co.; **Everhard**,
1845
Herrmann, J. C.—from Schweidnitz;
arr. 1845
Herrmann, Phil. O.—s, 23; **Andacia**,
1846
Hertes, Sophie—**Orient**, 1846
Herting, Wilh.—from Geseke, Detmold; w—Theresa nee Brockhoff;
ch—Theresa, Conrad; **Friedrich**,
1846
Herzog, Joh.—s, from Weiler; **Talisman**, 1846
Hesse, Aug. Wilh.—from Clausthal
a/Harz; w—Johanna nee Just;
Flavius, 1846
Hesse, Christian von—from Darm-
stadt; Kendall Co.; **Neptune**, 1845
Hesse, Joh. Friedr.—s, 21; from Ga-
denstedt; **Nahant** (wrecked) 1846;
then **Timoleon**, 1846
Hessig, Albert—s, from Michelstadt;
arr. 1846
Hessler, Henry—s, 23; from Stutt-
gart; arr. 1846
Hetzel, George—from Wiesbaden; 6
persons; Gillespie Co.; **Bohemia**,
1846
Hetzel, Hein.—s, from Wiesbaden:
Bohemia, 1846
Hetzer, Carl—from Adelebsen,
Han.; 3 persons; **Elisa & Char-
lotte**, 1846
Hetzer, Hein.—from Adelebsen,
Han., w—Henrietta nee Pflug;
Elisa and Charlotte, 1846
Heuer, Sophie—30, from Oberg;
Hercules, 1845
Heuner, Hein.—s, 27; from Gestorf;
Gerhard Hermann, 1845
Heuschel, Theresa—from Salzdet-
furt, Han.; **Everhard**, 1845
Heusinger, Gustav von Waldegg—s;
from Schwalbach; Comal Co.;
Bohemia, 1846
Heusinger, Julius von Waldegg—s,
from Schwalbach; **Bohemia**, 1846

102

Heusinger, Otto Jans von Waldegg;
Bohemia, 1846
Hevekerdei, Friedr.—from Quarnebek, w—Maria nee Schulz; B.
Bohlen, 1847
Hick, Hein.—m, from Hadamar; arr.
346; Hick, Friedr., Gillespie Co.
Hickmann, Joh. Georg.; from Trennfurt; Talisman, 1846
Hild, David and family of 8 persons;
from Niederneisen; Bohemia, 1846
Hild, Georg-s, from Niederneisen;
Guadalupe Co.; Bohemia, 1846
Hild, Joh. Peter-36; from
Oberscheld, Nassau; w-Cath. nee
Sommer 36; ch-Hein. 11, Wilh.
Christian 9, Joh. Hein. 6, Georgine
Elis. 4; Arminius, 1845
Hildebrand, F.—s, 21; Franziska, 1846
Hilde(n)brand, Reinhard-from Hartershausen; Fayette Co.; Colchis,
1846
Hilfers, Herm.-s, 31; Franziska, 1846
Hilge, Anton—s, 17; Gerhard Hermann, 1846
Hilge, Gottfried—27; from Langscheid; Harris Co.; Strabo, 1845
Hilge, Herm.-s, 19; Hilge, Joh.-s, 22;
from Patersberg, Nassau;
Colorado Co.; Gerhard Hermann,
1846
Hilge, Justus David—from Patersberg; w—Cath. nee Zimmermann;
ch—Cath., Maria, Anne, Johanne:
Gerhard Hermann, 1846
Hilge, Moritz—s, 19; from Patersburg, Nass.; Gerhard Hermann,
1846
Hillebrandt, Georgine—from Sulserd
(=Sulzern?), Creole, 1846
Hillemann, Charlotte—from Kleinschneen; Timoleon, 1846
Hillmann, Anton—s, 34; from Waldorf, Silesia; † before 1854; Johann
Dethardt, 1845
Hillmann, Fried.—s, 22; Georg.—s,
24; Herm.—s, 18; Herm. and wife;
Fayette Co.; Franziska, 1846
Hinz, Wilhelmine-Johanna, 1846
Hirschhauser, Conrad—45; from
Offdilln, Nassau; w—Marg. nee
Schmidt 45; ch-Elise 17, Fried 14,
Anna Marg. 11, Cath. 5; Herschel,
1845
Hirschhauser, Job-18; w-Louise 48;
from Offdilln; Herschel, 1845
Hirth. Friedr.—s; from Affaltrach;
oo Julian Fey 1849 (NBChR); Talisman, 1846
Hirth, Martin-m; from Zegartowith,
Poland; arr. 1846
Hitzfeld, Herm.—47 and Henriette,
Gillespie Co.; Karl Ferdinand, 1846
Hobart, Elis.—New Braunfels, 1845
Hoch, Valentin—from Oberschonau,

Kurh.; w—Elisa nee Pabst; ch—
Maria, Aug., Amanda; DeWitt Co.;
Everhard, 1845
Hochkirch, Joh.—s; from Dürkheim;
Element, 1846
Hochkirch, Joh.—from Dürkheim, 2
persons; Comal Co.; Element, 1846
Hoecker, R.—m; had Verein land
grant
Hoehn, Nicolaus-s, 18; from Ketten,
Weimar; Garonne, 1845
Hoepfner, Carl-s, 20; from Cassel;
Neptune, 1845
Hoermann, Christian Ludw.-from
Herkendorf, Han.; 5 persons; arr.
1845
Hoerner, Joh.—s; St. Pauli, 1847
Hoerster, Hein.—from Pirzenthal;
w—Mary C.; ch—Friedr., Daniel,
Anton; Gillespie Co.; James Edward, 1846
Hoertling, Hein. Friedr.—s; from
Fürfeld; Dyle, 1846
Hoesch, Andreas and wife—from
Mohrenbach near Arnstadt;
Mathilde, 1846
Hoesch, Casper—s; from Möhrenbach; Mathilda, 1846
Hof, Christian—s, 25; from Wallmerod, Nass.; New Braunfels,
1845; from Langenbach, †3.IX.1846
(NBChR); Johann Dethardt, 1844
Hof, Joh. Jost—from Langenaubach,
Nassau; w—Elisa nee Clas; ch—
Christine, Elisa, Caro., Theo.
†26.IX.1846, age 15; Elisa, Caro.,
Ernestine, (NBChR); Comal Co.;
Auguste Meline, 1845
Hofacker, Alois-s; from Orb; James
Edward, 1846
Hofacker, Georg Philipp-from Orb;
6 persons and 1 baby; Comal Co.;
James Edward, 1846
Hoffmann, Aug.-from Dubielno, Kr.
Kulm; w-Caro. nee Leissner; Gillespie Co.; Johanna, 1846
Hoffmann, Carl-from Hildesheim;
Creole, 1846
Hoffmann, Carl Fried. Ludw.-s;
from Bockenem, Han.; DeWitt Co.;
Hercules, 1845
Hoffmann, Edward—32; from Bavaria; Comal Co.; Johann Det
hardt, 1845
Hoffmann, Elisa-B. Bohlen, 1846
Hoffmann, Friedr.—from Braunschw., w—Maria nee Salari; ch—
Amalia, Wilh., Carl, Maria;
Austin Co.; B. Bohlen, 1847
Hoffmann, Friedr.-from Culm,
Gerhard Hermann, 1846
Hoffmann, Gustav-s, 24; from
Stuhm, Prussia; New Braunfels
1845; Joh. Dethardt, 1844
Hoffmann, H.-s, 28; Herschel, 1844

Hoffmann, H.L.—23; from Wedel-heine, Han; **Garonne,** 1845

Hoffmann, Joh.—23; from Bel-lersdorf, Nassau; **Herschel,** 1845

Hoffmann, Joh.—from Fellerdilln, Nassau; **Garonne,** 1845

Hoffmann, Joh. Georg.—29; from Weidhausen; †.8.VIII.1846, age 31 (NBChR); **Andacia,** 1846

Hoffmann V, Joh. Peter—m, 33; from Niederscheld, Nass.; w— Cath. nee Ebert 31; ch—Char., Fried., Chris. Ludw., Georg.; **Garonne,** 1845

Hoffmann, Jos.—s, from Bayreuth, Bavaria, New Braunfels 1845; **Herschel,** 1844

Hoffmann, Leonhard Hein.—s; from Offdilln, Nassau; **Garonne,** 1845

Hoffmann, Val.—from Gleimenhain, Hesse; w–Cath. nee Stump; Washington Co.; **Mathilde,** 1846

Hofhaintz, Joh.—s; from Bruck-enheim (=Bruchheim?); † 1852, age 38 (NBChR); Comal Co.; arr. 1846

Hofmann. Hein-from Offdilln; arr. 1845

Hofmann, Jacob Hein.-s, 25; from Rabenscheid, Nassau; **George Del-ius,** 1845

Hofmann, Mathias and 2 sons—from Büdesheim; **Henry,** 1846

Hofmeister, Carl—Fredericksburg, 1847

Hohlbach, Jacob—from Mühlbach; **Hamilton,** 1846

Hohlfeld, Fried.—s, 18, **George Delius,** 1845

Hohlefeld, Philipp–from Wabern, Kurh.; w–Martha nee Dittmar.; **Joh. Dethardt,** 1846

Hohmann, Eliz.–from Kalten-nordheim; **Neptune,** 1845

Hohmann, Hein.–48; from Kalten-nordheim; w–Cath. nee Schleger 40; ch–Dor. 11, Anna 8, Christian 6; Comal Co.; **Neptune,** 1845

Hohmann, Val.–18; **Neptune,** 1845

Hohmann, Valentin—40; from Kal-tennordheim; w—Ottilie nee Diet-zel; †.1858 ?(FChB); ch—Elisa 13, Ursula 11, Maria 9, Anna 7, Elis. 22; Gillespie Co.; **Neptune,** 1845

Hohmann, Val.—from Mittelstille, Kurh.; w–Eva nee Erdmann; ch —Maria,Carl,Emma;GillespieCo.; **Everhard,** 1845

Hohmann, Valentin–45; from Kal-tennordheim; w–Maria nee Diet-zel 42; ch–Maria 20, Jos. 11, Kath. 8, Wilh. 3; Gillespie Co.; **Neptune,** 1845

Holekamp, Georg. Friedr.–from

Hannover, Han.; w–Betty nee Abbenthern; New Braunfels 1845; **Johann Dethardt,** 1844

Hollien, George and wife–Austin Co.; **Apollo,** 1844

Hollien, J.–Austin Co. 1847; **Apollo,** 1844

Hollingshausen, Joh–s, from Erbach; Calhoun Co.; **Bohemia,** 1846

Hollingshausen, Jos.–from Erbach; 7 persons; Calhoun Co.; **Bohemia,** 1846

Holl(e)mann, Joh.–s, 30; Fayette Co.; **Franziska,** 1846

Holmann, Henry–s; **B. Bohlen,** 1845

Holtermann, Juergen Hein.–from Ottingen, Han.; †.30.VIII.1850, age 60 (NBChR); w–Dor. nee Lot-tman; **B. Bohlen,** 1845

Holzapfel, Joh.—from Münchhaus-en, Kurh.; w—Martha Schmidt; New Braunfels 1845; **Herschel,** 1846

Holzfuss, Jurgen—w and 2 ch; **B. Bohlen,** 1845

Holzgrefe, Conrad–from Eldagsen, Han; w–Johanna nee Kuenicke; ch–Anna, Wilhme, Sophie; Comal Co.; **Gerhard Hermann,** 1846

Holzgrefe, Henry–s, 20; Holzgrefe, John–s, 22; Comal Co.; **Gerhard Hermann,** 1846

Holzhauser,Christian—fromPaters-burg, Nassau; w—Anna nee Liss; ch—Hein.; Peter, Joh. Fr., Philipp; **Gerhard Hermann,** 1846

Holzhausen, Georg.—from Alferde, Han.; w—Sophie nee Dismer, ch— Friedr., Chr., Hein., Ludwig, Adolph; **Gesina,** 1846

Holzhauser, Peter–s, 23; from Ret-tert; Nass. †9.VI.1847, age 25 (NBChR); **Neptune,** 1845

Holzmann, Wilh.—49; from Schwal-bach, Nassau; w—Martha nee Haerter 52; Phillipine 18; **Joh. Dethardt,** 1845

Homann, Wilh.—from Fallersleben; 1845

Hombach, Bernhard–from Hallgar-ten; †1.VI.1847, age 54(NBChR); and wife; **Sarah Ann,** 1845

Hombach, Eva–from Oestrich, Nas-sau; **Neptune,** 1845

Homburg, H.—Galveston Co.; **Fran-ziska,** 1846

Homburg, Joh.–s, 25; from Siersse, Braunschw.; **B. Bohlen,** 1845

Honig, Hermann—s, from Steinbach near Erndtebrück; Gillespie Co.; **York,** 1846

Honig, Peter–s, 29; from Steinbach; Gillespie Co.; **York,** 1846

Hopf. Caspar—from Kaltennord-heim; Gillespie Co.; **Joh. Det-hardt,** 1845

104

Hopf, Val.—s, 27; from Kaltenlengsfeld or Diedorf; Gillespie Co.; **Joh. Dethardt**, 1845

Hopf, Val.—m; from Kaltenlengsfeld; **Joh. Dethardt**, 1845

Hoppe,Franz—s,30;from Mahlerten, near Elze,Han.; **Gerhard Hermann**, 1846

Horlen, Peter and wife–from Beerfelden; Gillespie Co.; **Sarah Ann**, 1845

Horlen, Peter—s, 29; from Königstein; Fredericksburg 1847; **Sarah Ann**, 1845

Horlen, Peter—from Hammelbach; †.23.VIII.1846, age 60; (NBChR)

Horlen, Wilh.—and wife; Horlen, **Wilh.**—s, 18; Fredericksburg 1847; **Sarah Ann**, 1845

Horn,Balthasar—s;from Weidmanngesees, Bavaria; arr. 1846

Horn, Hein.—s, **Andacia**, 1846

Horn, Val.—m; **Dyle**, 1846

Hornburg, Christoph–from Platendorf. Han.; w–Dor. nee Harmme; ch–**Maria**, Sophie, Henriette, Christoph, Joh.; Victoria Co.; **Everhard**, 1845

Hornburg, Hein.—33; from Platendorf, Han.; w–Dor. nee Wiethers; ch–**Hein.**, Christine, Friedr.; Galveston Co.; **Everhard**, 1845

Hornburg, Joh.–s, 30; Martin–s, 18; from Mosbach, Weimar; **Everhard**, 1845

Horne, Peter—from Niedernhausen near Jostein, Nassau; w—**Anna Maria Reininger**, †3.VIII.1846, age 38 (NBChR); 1 ch; New Braunfels 1845; **Ferdinand**, 1844

Horne, Valentin—33; from Hattenheim; 2 persons; Comal Co.; **Dyle**, 1846

Horsek, Christian von—from Lewe, Han.; **Friedrich**, 1846

Horste, Anna, widow–New Braunfels 1845; **Apollo**, 1844

Horth, Fr.—from Affaltrach, near Heilbronn; **Talisman**, 1846

Hotzfeld, Adam—Fredericksburg, 1847

Houy, Ernst.—28; w—Dor. 28; **Andacia**, 1846

Hoyer, Julius—s, from Clausthal a/Harz; Bexar Co.; **Karl Ferdinand**, 1846

Hubertus, Joh.—from Schönberg, †17.X.1846, age 39, w—Anna †29.IX.1846, age 45; ch—Elisa †17.XI.1846, age 18 (NBChR), Wilh. 16, Eva 12; **Strabo**, 1845

Huebinger, Bernbard - s, 32, from Bavaria; **Weser**, 1844

Huebler, Joh.—s, from Breslau; arr. 1845

Huebner, Aug. – 31, Comal Co. 1850

Huebner, Carl – from Flinsbach; 4 persons, York,1846

Huebner, Hein.—from Horssum, Braunschw.; w—Sophie nee Glindemann; ch—Wilh., Andreas; Austin Co.; **Mathilde**, 1846

Huebsch, Friedr. - s, from Rudolstadt, Schwarzburg; **Margaretha**, 1846

Huker, Christian – from Geseke, arr. 1845

Humar, Georg, New Braunfels, 1845

Hummel,Joh. and family—from Canfeld; Bexar Co.; arr. 1846

Hundhausen, Joh. Peter—s; **Colchis**, 1846

Hundhausen, Christian—from Rosbach; 6 persons, Gillespie Co., **Colchis**, 1846

Huntebush, Friedr.—s, 28; **Weser**, 1845

Hutschmann,Hein.—from Sechshelden by Dillenburg, †2.VIII.1846, age 51(NBChR); ch—Jacob,Anna; **Auguste Meline**, 1845

Hutschmann, Jacob - s, 19; from Ohr, Han.; **Auguste Meline**, 1845

Hutt, W – from Culm; 1845

Hutz, A.—m; had Verein land grant

Hutzfeld (=Hitzfeld?), Adam—from Kleinern, Ff/M, arr. 1846

— I —

Idel, Christian—s, 24; from Kurtsiefen,/Koln; **Hamilton**, 1846

Idstein, H.–from Oestrich; 2 persons; 1845

Ilfrich, Christian Joh–from Leutenberg, Saalfeld; 1846

Illian, Joh.–s, 37; from: Arolsen; Galveston Co.; 1846

Imbeer, Jos.—from Rothweil; 10 persons; **Andacia**, 1846

Imhoff, A.—40 and Imhoff, B.—18; **Joh. Dethardt**, 1844

Imhoff, Hein.—from Felsberg, Bz. Cassel; w–Barbara nee Selig; New Braunfels, 1845; **Joh. Dethardt**, 1844

Imhoff, Peter—New Braunfels 1845 **Joh. Dethardt**, 1844

Immel, Aug.—from Rehe, Nassau; †.IX.1846, age 29; Carl †29.VIII. 1846, age 26; Charlotte †1846, 16; Leonard †1846, 16; Phillip †1846, 16; Phillip †1846, 22; (NBChR)

Immel, Christian–†29.VII.1846, age 54; w—Cath. Elis nee Diehl, †24.

VllI.1846, age 56; (NBChR); from
Rehe, Nassau; **Harriet**, 1845
Immel, Christian–s, 24; from Rehe,
Nassau; **Harriet**, 1845
Immel, Joh.—from Rehe, Nass.;w
—Marie nee Schaefer; ch—Elis.,
Peter; **Louise Friedricke**, 1847
Irgahn, Leopold–s; from Schweid-
nitz; 1845
Isenhard, Fried. Wilh.—s, from
Waldbröhl; 1846
lsenhard, J(?) Fried—25; from
Waldbröhl; **Timoleon**, 1846
I(h)sensee, Carl—† Jan. 1847; Chris-
tina Elis.—widow and 2 ch; Chris-
toph only son; **Louise**, 1846 .
Isensee, Hennig and w–Elis. from
Wittmar, Brnshwg.; Comal Co.;
Louise, 1846
Iwonsky, Carl von—s, from Rückers
Silesia; Comal Co.; **Arminius**, 1845
Iwonsky, Leopold von—died; widow
—Marie nee Kalinowska; sons—
Carl, Adolph; Comal Co.; **Joh.
Dethardt**, 1846

— J —

Jacob, J. G.—from Berlin, w and 3
ch.; **Franziska**, 1846
Jacobi, Ann Maria—19, from Ketten,
Weimar; **Garonne**, 1845
Jacobi, Friedr. – s, 40; Gillespie Co.,
Apollo, 1844
Jacobi, Nic. – from Oberkostenz,
Rhine Pfalz; w –Mary; ch–Peter,
Dor.: Gillespie Co.; **York**, 1846
Jaeger, (Joh.?) Christian—s, 29;
from Creuzburg; **Andacia**, 1846
Jaeger, Philipp – from Camberg;
Bohemia, 1846
Jaentschke, Franz—s, from Studein,
Oestreich; Fayette Co.; **Neptune**,
1846
Jahn, Herrm.—from Zellerfeld
a/Harz; w—Emma nee Giesecke;
Karl Ferdinand, 1846
Jahn, Joh. Michael—s; from Bath,
Pomerania; New Braunfels 1845;
Herschel, 1844
Jahn, Wm.—w and 3 ch; Jahn, Wm.
s, 18; **Harriet**, 1845
Jahns, Christian—from Platendorf,
1845
Jansing, Hein. – s, 35, **Apollo** 1846
Jatho, Joh.—from Cassel; w—Elisa
nee Mueller; ch—Sophie, Jo-
hanne, Adam, Amalie, Marie;
Everhard, 1845
Jauer, Ludwig—s, **B. Bohlen**, 1845
Jockel, Anna – New Braunfels, 1845
Joehn. (Jehn), Jacob—s, 29; from
Lorch, Rüdesheim, Nass.; **Joh.
Dethardt**, 1845

Joerns (Joerdens), Christof—from
Vöhrum, Han.; w—Anna Elisa nee
Koerner; **Louise**, 1846
Johannes, Joh. Michael—26, w—
Henriette nee Stolzer 28; from
Schmalkalden; Calhoun Co.;
Garonne, 1845
Johr, Ludwig – from Dubielno,
Poland; w – Caroline nee Zarberg;
ch – Ottilie; **Louise Friedrike** 1847
Jonas, Joh. – from Niederelbert, 3
persons; Comal Co. **Riga** 1846
Jonas, Peter – s, 26, **Riga** 1846
Jord, Aug. and wife, **Franziska** 1846
Jordan, Ernst Christian Franz-
from Wehrstedt; w-Wilhmine nee
Uflaker; dau.-Johanne †5.XI.1846
age 6 (NBChR); Gillespie Co.
1850, Mason Co. 1856; **Margar-
etha**, 1845
Jordan, (Johann) George – s; from
Zwergen, Kurh. **Friedrich** 1846
Jordan, Hein. –, from Zwergen,
Kurh.; Gillespie Co., **Friedrich**
1846
Jordan, Joh. George—s, 33; from
Heersum or Hörsum, Han.; **Mar-
garetha**, 1845
Jost, Joh. George and wife—**Auguste
Meline**, 1845
Juencke, Joh. Hein. Ludw.—from
Einbeck, Han.; w—Regina nee
Meyer; Fredericksburg 1847. **Joh.
Dethardt**, 1846
Juenke, Wilh. –from Wolfshagen,
Brnschwg; w – Henriette nee
Tilly, ch – Dor., Caro., Wilh., Hein.;
Gillespie Co.; **Mathilde** 1846
Juerden, Joh.—arr. 1846
Juergens, Friedr. – s- 24; **Apollo** 1844
Juerges, Christoph – s, from Bandau,
Prussia; **B. Bohlen** 1847
Juffrig, Christian –from Leuten-
berg, Schwarzb.; w–Gertrude nee
Mener; ch –August, Carl, Caro.,
Wilh.; **Johanna** 1846
Jung, Anton – s, 19, **George Delius**
1845
Jung, Conrad—from Sinkershausen,
by Gladenbach; 8 persons; **Bo-
hemia**, 1846
Jung, Gustav—s, 19; Fredericksburg
1847; **Harriet**, 1845
Jung, Hein. –wife and 3 ch., Jung,
Hein. –s, 30; **George Delius** 1845
Jung, Jacob—from Rehe; †20.XI.1849
(FCB); 4 persons; Gillespie Co.;
Harriet, 1845
Jung I, Jacob—from Liebenscheid,
Nass; w—Elise nee Fasch; ch—Ma-
thilda, Helene, Sabine; Fredericks-
burg 1847; **Joh. Dethardt**, 1845
Jung, Joh. –**Ferdinand** 1844
Jung, Joh.—s, 50; †2.VI.1849 age
51, (NBChR) Jung, Joh.—single,
age 21, **Harriet**, 184£

106

Jung, Joh. Jost –24, from Hesselbach, Nass, Bexar Co. 1850 **Arminius 1845**

Jung I, Joh. Martin—from Niederrossbach, Nass.; †1846, age 54 (NBChR); w—Marie nee Betz; ch —Franz, Hein., Aug., Ludw., Eleanore, Caro., Sophie, Emilie; **Comal Co.; George Delius, 1845**

Jung. Joseph – s, 27; from Irmtraut, Rhine Pfalz; **Joh. Dethardt** 1845

Jung, Peter – Comal Co., **Washington 1845**

Jung, Philipp – 49, from Frickhofen: w–Cath, 39; ch–Wilh. 15, Peter 14, Jacob 10, Joh. 8, Joseph 6, Anton 4; Comal Co.; **Washington** 1845

Jung, Philipp,—from Seelbach?; 5 persons; **Element, 1846**

Jung, Wilh. –**Washington** 1845

Jung, Widow—York's Creek 1860 Comal Co.

Junginger, Joh.—s; from Gerstetten. Württ.; 1846

Junker, Carl –, 2 persons, from Grumbach; **Colchis** 1846

Junker, Philipp –from Grumbach; 8 persons, **Colchis** 1846

Junker, Wilh. – from Grumbach; 4 persons; **Colchis** 1846

Jurgens, Joh. & wife, and Peter – s, 20; **Franziska** 1846

Just, Georg – s from Zellerfeld, Han. **Flavius** 1846

Just, Herm. – from Zellerfeld; **Flavius, 1846**

— K —

Kaderle, Jacob–21 and Joh. 18–from Champaux, Switz; New Braunfels 1845; Castro Colonists; **Ocean, 1844**

Kaetelhodt, Wilh.—s; from Sobbowitz, bei Danzig; **Mercur, 1846**

Kage, Ludwig–from Reppner, Brnschwg.; w–Friedricke nee Jacobi; ch–Ludwig, Hein., Christian; Anderson Co; **Flavius, 1846**

Kahlden, Fr.—s; † before 1860; had Verein land grant.

Kahle, Carl–s, from Ebergötzen, Han; **Margaretha, 1846**

Kahler, Edward–33; from Fulda, near Rinteln; 2 persons; **Neptune, 1845**

Kahn, Gottlob–s, 30; arr. 1846

Kahr, Charles–s, 22; **Harriet, 1845**

Kaincke, Georg–from Born at Berlin; **Mathilde, 1846**

Kaiser, Carl–s, 22; **Harriet, 1845**

Kaiser, Carl–s, 20; from Sontheim; Comal Co.; **Sarah Ann, 1845**

Kaiser, Christian–from Schönberg, Nass.; w–Christina Philippina nee Weber; New Braunfels 1845; **Ferdinand, 1844**

Kaiser, Elias–from Farnrode, Weimar; **Elisa & Charlotte, 1846**

Kaiser, G. F. W.–s; had Verein land grant.

Kaiser (Kayser, Keyser), Martin— from Schonberg; †29.VIII.1846, age 63; widow—Cath. age 56; ch Anna Maria (Fey) 24, and Christian; **Strabo, 1845**

Kalb, Carl–and son Alexander, from Zwickau, Saxony; **Margaretha, 1846**

Kalb(e), Fried.–**Margaretha, 1846**

Kalnke, Wilh.–**Neptune, 1846**

Kamecke, Georg von–s; from Borna at Berlin; **Mathilda, 1846**

Kamman, Hein.–from Dungelbeck by Peine, Han.; †22.VIII.1846 age 48; sister Ilse Cath. †7.VII.1846 age 44; (NBChR); **Weser, 1845**

Kammlah, Hein. Theo.—from Kochin gen, Brnschwg.; w—Augustee nee Bockelmann; ch—Hein., Wilh.; Gillespie Co.; **Gerhard Hermann, 1845**

Kampe, Christ.–died 1846; from Platendorf, Han.; w–Sophie nee Klause; ch–Marie, Christian Hein., Sophie, Friedr. & baby; **Everhard, 1845**

Kanngieser,Fried.—s,33;fromFrankenhausen or Eisleben; **Franziska, 1846**

Kanow, Adolph–s, from Lagnitz, Prussia; **Mathilde, 1846**

Kanz, Christian—from Volkstedt bei Rudolstadt; †1847; w—Marie; ch— Marg.,Anton,Mathilda;ComalCo.; **Margaretha, 1846**

Kanz,Joh.Adam—m; SarahAnn,1845

Kapp, Dr. Ernst–38, arr. 1846; w–Ida nee Kappell; ch–Antonie, Alfred, Julia, Hedwig, Wolfgang; Comal Co.; 1850; **Kendall Co.** 1860

Kappel, Joseph–s, 18; **Apollo, 1844**

Kappmann, Hein.; from Elberfeld; **Henry, 1846**

Karbach, Carl–s, 17; died at Victoria; **Joh. Dethardt, 1846**

Karbach, Fried. David–from Sieden Bollentin; w–Marie Caro. nee Mewe; Comal Co.; **Joh. Dethardt, 1846**

Kattmann, Hein.—s, Dr. Juris from Frankfurt; Guadalupe Co. 1850 age 23; **St. Pauli, 1847**

Kauf, Joh. T.—from Nieder Ingelheim; **Talisman, 1846**

Kaufholt, Lorenz.–s, 28; from Diedorf; Harris Co.; **Weser, 1844**

Kaufmann, Carl Bergold—from Fürth, Hesse; †16.VII.1846 (NBChR)

Kaufmann, Fr.-s, 28; from Hannover; Ferdinand, 1845
Kaufmann, Georg.—s, from Reihen; Nahant, wrecked 1846; then Timoleon, 1846
Kaulvers, Gottlieb—from Linderode or Sorau; w—Johanne Christine nee Schulz; dau.—Pauline; Creole, 1846
Kavelmacher, Joachim-s, from Richtenberg, Prussia; arr. 1846; oo Sophie nee Kramm; Comal Co.
Kayser, Joh. Christoph—from Eisenach; died age 53; widow —Louise 45; ch—Harriet 14, Christian 12, Louise 10; Gillespie Co.; Andacia, 1846
Kehrer, A.-s, had Verein land grant
Keidel, Dr. Wm.-s, from Hildesheim; Gillespie Co.; Margaretha, 1845
Keil, George-s; from Frankenberg; Element, 1846
Keinegar, Henry and wife-arr. 1844
Keller, Anton-from Niederelbert; wife and 5 ch; Calhoun Co.; Riga, 1846
Keller, Hein.-s, from Rohrberg Prussia; Comal Co.; B. Bohlen 1847
Keller, Henry J.—s; Gillespie Co., Neptune, 1845
Keller, Joh.—30, from Niederelbert w—Cath. 30, Maria 50, Helena 6, Anna 3, Adam 1; Fredericksburg 1847; Strabo, 1845
Keller, Joh. Adam—s, 18; from Niederelbert; Gillespie Co.; Strabo, 1845
Keller, Peter-43, from Bingen by Braunfels; w-Anna Maria nee Mohr 30, ch-Joh. 16, Hein. 11, Wilh. 10, Cath. 6; Gillespie Co.; Neptune 1845
Kellner, Justus—s, 23; from Braunschweig; † 1851; Arminius, 1845
Kempenich, Joh.—47, from Hattenheim; w—Marg. nee Uberech; † 1846, age 41 (NBChR); ch—Marg. 14, Cath. 14; Comal Co.; Washington, 1845
Kensing, Adam—s, 19, Carl—s, 20, Friedr.—s, 25, Hein.—s, 23; from Hamelspringe, Han.; Gillespie Co.; Gerhard Hermann, 1845
Kensing, David-from Hamelspringe, Han.; w—Henriette nee Brehmeyer; 7 persons; Gerhard Hermann, 1845
Kerner, Christ.—from Oberlenningen; Timoleon, 1846
Kessler, George and wife-from Klings, Weimar; Bexar Co.; Everhard, 1845
Kessler, Gustav-57; Strabo, 1845
Kessler, H. Carl-s, from Michelstadt; Colorado Co.; Colchis, 1846

Kessler, Joh.-from Wiesbaden; Riga, 1846
Kessler, Joh.-30; Dyle, 1846
Kessler, Joh.-from Hochheim; Washington, 1845
Kessler, Ludw.-31; from Willingen; w-Julia 28; ch-Louis 9; Comal Co.; Strabo, 1845
Kessler, Peter Ludwig and son John—from Wiesbaden; Comal Co.; Gesina, 1846
Keune, Andreas—s, from Rhoden, Prussia (Waldeck?); Louise, 1846
Keuter, Wilh.-s; Joh. Dethardt, 1844
Keyser (Kaiser) Martin-60, from Schönberg; †22.VIII.1846 (NBChR); w-Cath. 56; Anna 24; heirs: Christian, Anna Fey; Strabo, 1845
Kiefer, Joseph—s, from Mühlheim; Hamilton, 1846
Kiehne, Friedr.—from Everode, Han.; w—Johanne nee Kreinsen; ch—Friedrich, Wilh., Minna; Margaretha, 1845
Kiesewetter, Ernst—37, from Langwiese; w—Johanne nee Siebels, ch —Friedke, Friedr., Emil; Mathilda, 1846
Kiessler, W.-from Holzhausen; Sarah Ann, 1845
Kimbel, Fried.-s, 33; from Oberkatz, Meiningen; B. Bohlen, 1845
Kimpel, Chrs.-23; Gerhard Hermann, 1845
Kimbel, Carl Philipp—from Patersberg, Nass.; 4 persons; Gerhard Hermann, 1846
Kimbel, Hein.-s, 21; Gerhard Hermann, 1846
Kimbel, Hein. Georg-s, 20; Gerhard Hermann, 1846
Kimbel, Joh. Georg—from Lierscheid, Nass.; w—Maria nee Tauss; ch —Cath., Maria, Peter.; Gerhard Hermann, 1846
Kimpel, Philip A-s, 25; † before 1860; Gerhard Hermann, 1846
Kimmel, Georg—from Bruchköbel; w—Elisa nee Loos; Louise Friedricke, 1847
Kind, Carl-s, 25; from Fulda, Kurh.; Garonne, 1845
Kinger, Michael—from Gemünden; Talisman, 1846
Kinkler, Fried. Jacob-from Wetzlar; 6 persons; arr. 1846; Austin Co.
Kirchner, Christian-s, 25; Travis Co.; Mathilde, 1846
Kirchner, (Hein.) Christian-from Hedeper, Brnschwg.; w-Marie Dor. nee Gold; Gillespie Co. Louise, 1847
Kirchner, Joh. E-†.3.VI.1849 (NBChR); widow-Cath. nee Bernhard and 4 ch; Mathilde, 1846

Kirchner, Joh. George–from Bieb-
rich, Nass.; † 27.I.1846, age 34
(NBChR); w–Marg. Kirchner and
2 ch; New Braunfels 1845; Johann
Dethardt, 1844
Kirchner, Ludwig–from Gehren bei
Arnstadt; w–Bernardine nee
Streber from Doren, Schwarzburg
† 7.V.1847, age 47 (NBChR); ch
.. –Mathilde, Christian, Wilh.;
Liebrech, Minna; Mathilda, 1846
Kirchner, Wilh.–s; Mathilde, 1846
Kirchstein, Carl Ferd. and Hein.
Ludw.—Mary, 1847
Klaas–see also Claas
Klaas, Joh.–from Sinn; w–Marie nee
Hinz; ch–Louise, Ernestine,
Caro.; Bastrop Co.; Louise
Friedricke, 1846
Klaas, Joh. and wife—from Paters-
berg, Nass.; 4 persons; Fredericks-
burg, 1847; Gerhard Hermann, 1846
Klaas, Peter and wife—from Paters-
berg, Nass.; 4 persons; Fredericks-
burg, 1847; Gerhard Hermann, 1846
Klaehn, Ludwig–s, from Glogau;
Franziska, 1846
Klaener, D. H.—Agent for Adels-
verein at Galveston
Klaerner, Adam Anton–35; from
Nauroth; w–Cath. 31; Magda 10,
Christiana 7, Christian 5, Adam 1;
Washington, 1845
Klaerner, Philipp—from Nauroth; w
—Elis; ch—Wilhme, Cath., Philipp,
Marg.; Gillespie Co.; Strabo, 1845
Klamberg, Fried. and family–from
Wiesbaden; Bohemia, 1846
Klappenbach, George—† 1868; from
Anklam, near Stettin; Comal Co.;
Weser, 1846
Klappenbach, Louis—Comal Co.;
Weser, 1846
Klar, Ernst—s, 18; Klar. Joseph and
wife; 4 persons from Ebingen;
Riga, 1846
Klasing, Hein.–from Hildesheim,
Han.; w–Cath. nee Guenther; ch–
—Sophie, Antoinette; Guada-
lupe Co.; Creole, 1846
Kleck, Joh.–33, Victorine–22, and
male child; from Harthausen; Gil-
lespie Co., 1860; Andacia, 1846
Kleiker, Thomas—Galveston Co.;
Timolean, 1846
Klein, Anna—27; from Stephanshau-
sen; Washington, 1845
Klein, Casper–Element, 1847
Klein, Christian–from Frickhofen;
†July 1850, age 40; 3 persons;
Element, 1846
Klein, Daniel—from Hallschied;
James Edward, 1846
Klein, Eberhard—s, from Allenbach
by Erndtebrück; Comal Co.;
Element, 1846

Klein, Franz—from Dünebusch; 4
persons; Bastrop Co.; James
Edward, 1846
Klein, Georg Joh.–s, from Altensteig;
Element, 1846
Klein, Hein, Christian—from Dune-
busch; 5 persons; James Edward,
1846
Klein, Jacob–† 28.VII.1846, age 23
(NBChR); from Hattenheim, Amt
Elfeld; Herschel, 1844
Klein, Joh.–from Niederelbert,
Nass.; w–Anna Marie nee
Spritzhorn 40; ch–Christian 15,
Joh. 15, Adam 12, Joh. Adam 10,
Mary Anna 8, Helene 10, Gertrude
2; Gillespie Co.; Herschel, 1845
Klein, Joseph–s, 31; New Braunfels
1845; Herschel, 1844
Klein, N.–New Braunfels 1845
Klein, Peter—from Dünebusch; 3
persons; Bastrop Co.; James Ed-
ward, 1846
Klein, Stephan–from Hattenheim,
Nass.; w–Marg. nee Hoffmann;
New Braunfels 1845; Herschel,
1844
Klein, Valentin–s, 18; New Braun-
fels 1845; Herschel, 1844
Klein, Wilh.–s, 55; from Haiger,
Nass; Auguste Meline, 1845
Kleinecke, Carl Aug.—from Grund
a/Harz; w—Johanna nee Munn;
Flavius, 1846
Kleinecke, Ludwig–s; from Grund
a/Harz; Galveston Co.; Flavius,
1846
Kleineden, Aug.—s, 43 and Kleine-
den, Aug.—s, 18; from Osterode,
Han.; Gesina, 1845
Kleineden, Hein.–s, 20; from
Osterode, Han.; Gesina, 1845
Kleinhaus, Joh.–s, 35; from Tet-
tenhausen, Bavaria; Comal Co.;
Friedrich, 1846
Klemm, Anton—s, 22; from Stuttgart;
Joh. Dethardt, 1845
Klemm, Chs.—s, 18; John Dethardt,
1845
Klemm, Joh.—from Wabern, Kurh.;
† 1850, age 58; w—Helene nee
Hausmann; Comal Co.; Joh. Det-
hardt, 1845
Klemm, Martin–s, 24; Joh. Dethardt,
1845
Klenner, Adam–from Naurad,
Nass.; † 10.X.1846, age 36
(NBChR)
Kliewer, Peter–from Gruppe, Prus-
sia; w–Eva nee Bartel; Neptune,
1846
Klimarz, Inas–s, from Lemberg;
Orient, 1846
Klinge, C. von–s, from Gefell; Orient,
1846

Klinge, Carl—s 18; Ernst—s, 25; Fried.—s, 20; **Franziska, 1846**
Klinge, Friedr.—from Wolfenbüttel, Brnschwg.; w—Caro. nee Gochig;; ch—Ernst, Carl, Fritz, Mina, Elisa, Theo., and 1 baby; **Franziska, 1846**
Klingelhoefer, Joh. Jost–44, from Eibelshausen; w–Elisa nee Heiland 39; ch–Aug., Louise, Henriette, Elisa., Wilhelmine; Gillespie Co.; **Joh. Dethardt, 1845**
Klingemann, Diedrich–s, 18; **Weser, 1845**
Klingemann, Joh. Hein.–from Negenborn, Han; w–Cath. nee Moeller; ch–Cath., Henriette, Dorette, Hein. Ferd. and baby; Colorado Co.; **Weser, 1845**
Klinger, Christian–s, from Gefell; **Comal Co.; Orient, 1846**
Klinger, Wilh.–s, from Steinsfurt; **Diamant, 1846**
Kloes, Adam–s, from Langscheid, **Talisman, 1846**
Kloes, Cath.–age 20, from Merkelbach, Nassau; **Arminius, 1845**
Kloes, Christoph–from Langscheid; 5 persons; **Diamant, 1846**
Kloes, Justus Adam–s, from Langscheid; **Diamant, 1846**
Kloes, Peter–s, from Langscheid; **Diamant, 1846**
Knauer, Gottlieb—m, from Frankenhausen; Bexar Co.; **Elisa & Charlotte, 1846**
Knebel, Carl Philipp–from Patersberg; **1845**
Knebel, Joh. Georg.—from Lierscheid; **1845**
Kneese, Chr. Ludw.–s, 22; Gillespie Co.; **Hercules, 1845**
Kneese, Hein. Ferd.–from Friedrichshagen, Kurh.; w–Marie nee Schirmer; ch–Fried., Ludw; Louise; Gillespie Co.; **Hercules, 1845**
Kneese, Joh. Fr.–s, 24; from Friedrichshagen; **Hercules, 1845**
Kneiber, Cath.—widow and 2 ch; **Arminius, 1845**
Kneiber, Jacob—s, 17; from Uckersdorf, Nassau; **Arminius, 1845**
Kneiber, Joh.–39, from Uckersdorf, Nass.; w–Cath. nee Glas 44; Jacob 17, Carl 14, Franz 12, Marie 7; **Arminius , 1845**
Knepper (Kneupper?), Hein.–and wife; **Franziska, 1846**
Knetsch, Joh.—35, from Seilhofen, Nass.; w—Sophie nee Nickel; † 1.VIII.1846, age 29 (NBChR); ch—Caro. 10, Wilhme 8, Henriette 6, Louise 3; Comal Co.; **Herschel, 1845**
Knetsch, Wilh.—25, from Seilhofen;

w—Wilhelmine nee Triesch 24; ch—Elisa. Wilhme 3, Anna. Wilh. † age 7; **Herschel, 1845**
Knibbe, Hans Diet.—w—Sophie nee Regenberg; †13.XII.1846, age 21 (NBChR); Comal Co.; **George Delius, 1845**
Knibbe, Jürgen Hein.—s, 30; from Bissendorf, Han.; **George Delius, 1845**
Knigge, Juergen–from Platendorf, Han.; †Oct. 1850, age 39 (NBChR); Comal Co.; w—Dor. nee Mueller; ch—Ludwig, Dor., Henriette, Sophie; **Everhard, 1845**
Knipscheer, Adolph–s, from Elberfeld; **Louise Friedricke, 1847**
Knolle, Christoph–from Adensen, Han.; w–Elisa nee Bost; son–Aug.; **Gesina, 1845**
Knopf, (Knopp), Jacob—from Arzbach; w—Cath. nee Vogt; ch—Joseph, Peter, Joh., Maria; **Auguste Meline, 1845**
Knopf (Knopp), Peter—from Eitelborn, Nass.; w—Marie nee Segner; ch—Gertrude, Elisa, Marg.; **Auguste Meline, 1845**
Knopp, Christian–w–Marg. nee Muller; **Auguste Meline, 1845**
Knopp, H.–from Eitelborn; arr. 1845
Knopp, Jacob–from Eitelborn; 5 persons; **Dyle, 1846**
Knopp, Jacob—s, 22; from Coblenz; †15.X.1846, age 23, (NBChR); **Andacia, 1846**
Knopp, Joh.—1815-1909; from Eitelborn; w—Gertrude nee Segner; ch—Joh. Jos., Peter, Marie, Joh.; **Auguste Meline, 1845**
Knopp, Peter Anton–28, from Fulda, Kurh.; **Garonne, 1845**
Koch, Albert—s, from Rudolstadt; Colorado Co.; **Johanna 1846**
Koch, Anna—from Cassel; and Barbara—17; **Neptune, 1845**
Koch, E. M.—from Hörsum; arr. 1845
Koch, F. H.—38, from Prussia; **Weser, 1844**
Koch, Friedr.—from Hirschhausen; **Weser, 1845**
Koch, Friedr.—from Oestrich; ch—Elisa, Rosina, Hein., Cath., Barbara, Bernh., Maria; Colorado Co.; **Neptune, 1845**
Koch, Friedr. and wife; Koch, Friedrich.—s, 18; from Hannover; **Margaretha, 1845**
Koch, Joachim—Karl Ferdinand, 1846
Koch, J. Andreas—s, from Eisleben; New Braunfels, 1845; **Weser, 1844**
Koch, Joh. Andreas—w—Wilhelmine nee Cordes; from Nienburg; †11.VI.1847; **Weser, 1844**

110

Koch, Joh. H.—w and 1 ch; **Franziska,** 1846
Koch, Joh. Peter—s, from Nauroth; **Timoleon,** 1846
Koch, Karl and wife—from Irmelshausen; Intend to emigrate to Texas, 16.XII.1845; Koch, Carl—36, w—Elis. 36; ch—Wilh., Sophie, Friedr., Louise; Comal Co.; 1850
Koch, Marie and Sophie—from Frankenhausen, Prussia; **Elisa & Charlotte,** 1846
Koch, W.—New Braunfels, 1845
Koch, Wilh.—from Burkardrodt (Burkardroth?), Weimar; w—Anna nee Baumgaertner; ch—Louise, Kath., Kaspar; **Orient,** 1846
Koedinger, Elis and 3 ch—from Athus, Luxemburg; **Henry,** 1846
Koehler, Christian—s, 18; **B. Bohlen,** 1845
Koehler, Conrad—21, from Schmalkalden; **Washington,** 1845
Koehler, Georg—29, from Rosa, Mein.; **Garonne,** 1845
Koehler, Hein.—s; **B. Bohlen,** 1845
Koehler, Hein.—from Ottingen, Han.; w—Anna nee Dierks; **B. Bohlen,** 1845
Koehler, Hein. Friedr.—50, from Ottingen, Han.; 5 persons; w—Cath. Marg. †24.VIII.1846, age 55 (NBChR); Cameron Co.; **B. Bohlen,** 1845
Koehler, Joh.—s, 33; from Fulda, Kurh.; **George Delius,** 1845
Koehler, Joh. Conrad—s, from Schmalkalden; **Washington,** 1845
Koehler, Johanna—widow and son Ernst; from Volpriehausen; **Orient,** 1846
Koehler, Joh. Friedr.—from Ottingen; **B. Bohlen,** 1845
Koehler, Ludw.—from Creuzburg, Weimar; w—Charlotte nee Jaeger; ch—Carl, Charlotte, Edward; **Joh. Dethardt,** 1845
Koelsch, Peter Joseph—s, from Kiedrich; **Nahant** 1846, wrecked, then **Timoleon,** 1846
Koenecke, Conrad—s, from Bodenwerder; Comal Co.; **Sophie,** 1846
Koenemann, Friedr.—40, from Stederdorf, Han.; w—Dorothea nee Kobbe 40; ch—Sophie 14, Hein. 7, Herm. 11 mo.; Gillespie Co.; **Everhard,** 1845
Koenemann, Hein,—from Vöhrum, 1845
Koenig, Friedr.—and son Christian Carl; from Marlow, Mecklbg.; Gillespie Co.; **Joh. Dethardt,** 1846
Koenig, Gebhard—s, died; **Joh. Dethardt,** 1845

Koenig, Georg.—from Mehlis, Gotha; w—Dor. nee Munk; Gonzales Co.; **Orient** 1846
Koeppel, Adam—s, Gonzales Co.; **St. Pauli,** 1847
Koepsel, Carl—m, **Johanne,** 1846
Koepsel, Daniel—from Rynarzewo; w—Anna nee Krause; Comal Co.; **Johanne,** 1846
Koepsel, Fried. Wilh.—s; Comal Co.; **Johanne,** 1846
Koepsel, Gottfried—from Rynarzewo; w—Caro. nee Geruker; **Johanne,** 1846
Koerner, Joh. Michael—from Hof.; 1845
Koerner, Valentin—38, from Rauenthal, Nass.; w—Josephe nee Schlosser; ch—Josephe 9, Aug. 7, Clara 5, Caro. 3, Christoph ¼; **Neptune,** 1845
Koerper, Hein.—32, from Ueberhof (Ueberhöfe?); w—Elis. 31; ch—Elis. 1½; **Strabo,** 1845
Koester, Dr. Theodor—and Mrs. Sophie Koester; New Braunfels, 1845; **Joh. Dethardt,** 1844
Koether, Christian—died; from Stederdorf, Han.; w—Anna nee Fricke; ch—Wilhme 12, John 10; Comal Co.; **Neptune,** 1845
Kohl, Henry—s, 25; from Lauenstadt, Han.; **Gesina,** 1846
Kohler, Magda.—from Herbolzheim; **York,** 1846
Kohlmann, Fried—and wife; **Everhard,** 1845
Kohlmann, Joh. Peter—s; **Neptune,** 1845
Kohs, Hein. and wife—from Stadtoldendorf; **Sophie,** 1846
Kolbe, Bernhard—s, from Gotha; **Hamilton,** 1846
Kolbe, Carl Julius—s, from Gotha; Colorado Co.; Harris Co.; **Hamilton,** 1846
Koller, Christoph—45, from Oestrich, Nass.; w—Marg. nee Hombach 33; ch—John 12, Franz 9, George 6, Jos. 5, Appolonia 2½; **Neptune,** 1845
Koller, Fried.—s, 18; **Sarah Ann,** 1845
Kollmer, Peter—from Boppard; **Bohemia,** 1846
Kollmer, Wilh.—m, from Mangelsbach by Erbach; 2 persons; **Bohemia,** 1846
Kolmeyer, Conrad—from Alverdissen; w—Amalia nee Hitker; 3 persons; **Orient,** 1846
Kolmeyer, Friedr.—from Wolfenbüttel or Hesslingen, Han.; **Everhard,** 1845
Kolmeyer, Wm—from Alverdissen; **Orient,** 1846

Kolshorn, Ernst—from Adensen; 1845
Koock, Friedr. Ludw. Wilh.—46, from Hörsum, Han.; w—Cath. nee Bartels; ch—Louise, Wilh., Johanne †1846, age 6½, Aug, Theo. †1846, age 2½ (NBChR); Margaretha, 1845
Kopp, Georg. W.—22, from Bendorf; Andacia, 1846
Koppel, Jos.—s, 18; Apollo, 1844
Koppelten, Caro.—from Gera; Louise Fredricke, 1846
Korn, Carl—s, Bexar Co.; 1846
Korn, Henry von—s, 27; Gerhard Hermann, 1846
Korn, Louis Jacob—s, Bexar Co.; New York, 1845
Korn, Val.—s, 35; from Schwalbach, Nass.; Fayette Co.; Joh. Dethardt, 1845
Korn, Wilh.—s, from Ehrenbreitstein; Element, 1846
Kortenacker,Joh.—from Wallmerod; Sarah Ann, 1845
Kortzenacker, Peter—from Staudt, Nass.; † 7.VII.1847, age 25 (NBChR); Harriet, 1845
Koss, Hein.—m, from Stadtoldendorf; Guadalupe Co.; Sophie, 1846
Kossenberger, Anton—m, from Roth; w—Anna, ch—Christian, Jacob; Washington, 1845
Kothe, Wilhelm and w—Johanna, from Immendorf, Brnschwg; Gillespie Co.; Elisa & Charlotte, 1846
Kothmann, Carl Dietr.—from Wedelheine, Han.; w—Ilse Cath. nee Ahlmann; B. Bohlen, 1845
Kothmann, Hein. Conrad—from Wedelheine, Han.; w—Cath. nee Fohlmann; ch—Cath., Dietr., Friedr., Caro., Dor.; Mason Co.; B. Bohlen, 1845
Kott, Aug.—s, 27; Gillespie Co.; Elisa & Charlotte, 1846
Kott, Friedr. Wilh.—from Ohrdruff, Gotha; † 3.XII.1846, age 60; w—Auguste nee Weymann, † 23.XI.1846, age 52; both buried at Indianola (NBChR); Elisa & Charlotte, 1846
Kracke, Wilh.—s, 25; † 1850, age 29 (NBChR); from Verden, Han.; New Braunfels 1845; Joh. Dethardt, 1844
Kraemer, Caspar—s, from Mittelsinn; Talisman, 1846
Kraemer, Charles—s, 24; Comal Co.; Weser, 1845
Kraemer, Edward—s, Gillespie Co. 1850; Weser, 1845
Kraemer, Friedr.—from Darmstadt; Llano Co.

Kraemer, Hein. Friedr.—from Osterode, Han.; son—Theo. Friedr., Weser, 1845
Kraemer, Joh.—from Ulfen, near Erfurt; 4 persons; Comal Co.; Talisman, 1846
Kraemer, Peter—with wife and 5 ch; from Weidenbach; Henry, 1846
Kraemer, Wilh.—26, from Osterode, Han.; Gillespie Co.; Weser, 1845
Kraeter, Joh.—s, from Grabenstetten; Timoleon, 1846
Kraft, Joh.—age 29, from Steinbrücken, Nassau; Arminius, 1845
Kraft, Hein.—s, 29; from Wehrda, Hesse; New Braunfels 1845; Herschel, 1844
Kraft, Lisbeth—s, 20; New Braunfels 1845; Herschel, 1844
Kraft, Martin—s, from Eschenau; Diamont, 1846
Kraft, Melchior—s, 29; from Neuhausen; 1846
Krakau, Wilh. Hein.—s, 21; from Abbesbüttel, Han.; †18.VII.1846, age 22; buried 3 miles from San Marcos on road from Seguin (NBChR); Everhard, 1845
Kramm, Conrad—from Gross Lafferde; arr. 1846; Orient, 1846
Kraus, Wilh.—s, 21; Franziska, 1846
Krause, Caspar—from Netra; arr. 1846
Krause, Christoph—from Zegartowith; w—Caro. nee Kilper; ch—Enuk?(Enoch), Amalia, Anna, Rud., Wilh., Comal Co.; Johanna, 1846
Krause, Hein.—from Hanelde (Hanefeld?) Han.; w—Johanna nee Mueller; ch—Christian, Johanna; Harris Co.; Karl Ferdinand, 1846
Krause, Joh.—from Steimke, Prussia; arr. 1846; Colorado Co.
Krause, Joh.—from Brome, Han.; B. Bohlen, 1845
Kraushaar, Conrad—s, from Niedraula, Hesse; New Braunfels 1845; Herschel, 1844
Krauskopf, Engelbert—s, from Bendorf; *1820, †1881; gunsmith in Gillespie Co.; oo Rosa nee Herbst 1849; Andacia, 1846
Kraut, Friedrich—s, from Hungen; Colchis, 1846
Krebs, Michael—48; from Sindringen; w—Rosina 48; Gillespie Co.; Andacia, 1846
Krechel, Peter—55, from Rauenthal, Nass.; Neptune, 1845
Krehrens, Joh.—from Culm; 3 persons; Orient, 1846
Kreibaum, Christoph; from Klein Ilsede, Braunschw.; w—Dor. nee

Fricke from Bettmar, Brnschwg.; †24.VIII.1846, age 45 (NBChR); ch—Dor, Ludw., Friedr.; **Everhard, 1845**

Kreibaum, Conrad—from Everode, Han.; †24.XII.1846, age 31; and bride Dorothea Heise, †9.X.1846, age 28 (NBChR); **Margaretha, 1845**

Kreibaum, Henry Conrad—wife and 1 ch; from Everode, Han.; **Margaretha, 1845**

Kreibaum, Hein—s, 20; Theo—s, 21; Wm.—s, 36; **Everhard, 1845**

Kreibaum, Sophia—from Klein Ilsede by Peine; † 18.VII.1846, age 57; Kreibaum, Hein.—from Klein Ilsede, † 4.VIII.1846, age 16, (NBChR)

Kreiber, Joh.—from Ueckersdorf; **Arminius, 1845**

Kreiber, Cath.—widow and 2 ch; **Arminius, 1845**

Kreid, Georg—from Klein Ilsede; Brazoria Co.; arr. **1845**

Kreid, Jakob—from Burkhardtroda, Weimar; w—Anna nee Kehr; ch—Georg, Christine; Brazoria Co.; **Orient, 1846**

Kreikenbaum, Christ.—died 1846; son—Heinrich; **Sophie, 1846**

Kreikenbohm, Hein.—s, from Stadtoldendorf; Guadalupe Co.; **Sophie, 1846**

Kreikenbohm, Ludwig—s, from Stadtoldendorf; Guadalupe Co.; **Sophie, 1846**

Kreiker, Thomas—from Laubach; 9 persons; **Element, 1846**

Kreinsen; Conrad—and family of 2 persons; from Everode, Han.; **Margaretha, 1845**

Kreinsen, David and wife—**Margaretha, 1845**

Kreis, Michael—s, 32; from Stephanshausen; **Strabo, 1845**

Kreische, Carl Emanuel—s; Hein. Ludw.—s; Fayette Co.; **Albatross, 1847**

Kreisle, Joh.—44, from Winterlingen; w—Maria 40 and baby girl; ch—Joh. 18, Mathias 14, Cath. 12, Sophie 11, Wilh. 8; Kreisle, Mathias 77; **Andacia, 1846**

Kreith, Moritz—s, 24; from Cassel, Han.; See Creydt, Moritz; **Auguste Meline, 1845**

Kreitz—see also Kreuz

Kreitz, Carl Friedr—New Braunfels, **1845**

Kreitz (Kreutz?) Joh. Mathias—from Rotgen; w—Marie Elise nee Rodscheid; New Braunfels 1845; **Johann Dethardt, 1844**

Kreitz, Joh. Peter—from Rötgen; 3 persons; **Element, 1846**

Krending, Anton—s, 25; from Wipperode, Han.; **Gerhard Hermann, 1846**

Kretzer, Hein.—44, from Offdilln; w—Marg. nee Moos † 29.XI.1846, age 41; ch—Joh. H. †3.XI.1846, age 14, Anna Elis. †3.XI.1846, age 6; Aug. † 5.VII.1846, age 11 mo.; other ch—Cath. 10, Wilh. 8, (NBChR); **Neptune, 1845**

Kretzer, Fr.—† 28.VIII.1846, age 53, (NBChR); from Offdilln; **Neptune, 1845**

Kretzmeier, Friedr. Aug.—from Luttmersen, Han.; w—Marie nee Steinkel; ch—Hein., Dor., Aug.; Comal Co. 1850; **Weser, 1845**

Kretzmeier, Hein.—s, 18; Comal Co.; **Weser, 1845**

Kretzmeier, Joh.—from Metel, Han.; w—Sophie nee Vogeler; **Weser, 1845**

Kreudler, Christian Friedr.—from Efringen; **1846**

Kreusler, Georg Christian—s; Comal Co.; **Talisman, 1846**

Kreussler, Geo. Joh. Wilh.—from Arolsen, Waldeck; † 14.II.1847, age 43; (NBChR); **Diamant, 1846**

Kreutzer, Caspar F.—s, 25; **Ferdinand, 1844**

Kreutzer, Conrad—**Ferdinand, 1844**

Kreuz, (Kreutz), Conrad—New Braunfels, 1845; **Joh. Dethardt, 1844**

Kreuz, Fried.—New Braunfels, 1845

Kreuz, Hein.—s, 30; 1846

Kreuz, Joh. Mathias—from Rötgen bei Aachen; † 24.II.1846, age 65 (NBChR); w—Maria Elis. and ch—Conrad, Friedr. Helene, Maria Elis., Anna; New Braunfels 1845; **Johann Dethardt, 1844**

Krieger, Adam—45 and Eve 47; from Bingen; 6 persons came later. Gillespie Co.; **Andacia, 1846**

Krieger, Francis—Gillespie Co.; **Andacia, 1846**

Kriegner, Edward—s, from Merseburg, Saxony; Comal Co.

Kriewitz, Emil—s, 24; from Zinna near Jüterbog; guided immigrants to Fisher-Miller grant; **Franziska, 1846**

Kring, Carl—m; from Salzburg, Amt Rennerod; † 15.X.1846; Kring, Johannette nee Schneider, † 26.X.1846; Kring, child † 16.X.1846; all 3 buried in Fredericksburg; **Garonne, 1845**

Kring, Joh. Henry—43, from Herbornseelbach, Nass.; w—Elis. nee Mueller, 38; ch—Aug. 14, Wilh. 11, Hein. 8, Friedr. 4, Lisa ½;; **Herschel, 1845**

113

Kring, Joh. Jacob—32, from Herborn-seelbach, Nass.; w—Anna Maria nee Cullmann 32; ch—Jacob Wilh. 9; Carl Hein. 4; **Herschel, 1845**
Kripp, Friedrich Philipp—from Frankfurt a/ Main; 5 persons and 1 baby; **Element, 1846**
Kropp, Engel—s, 23; from Netze, Han.; **Margaretha, 1845**
Kropp, Hein.—s, 17; from Hainchen; **Sarah Ann, 1845**
Krueger, Franz Wilh—s, from Frankenhausen; Comal Co.; **Elisa & Charlotte, 1846**
Krueger, Hein and wife—Comal Co.; **Margaretha, 1845**
Krueger, Ludwig—from Hildesheim, Han.; 4 persons and 1 baby; Comal Co.; **Gerhard Hermann, 1846**
Krueger, Maria—**Louise Friedricke, 1847**
Kruse, Hein.—m, from Klein Steimke, Han.; Fayette Co.; arr. **1846**
Kruse, Hugo—s, 21; from Dessau; **Franziska, 1846**
Kuckuck, Joh. Hein.—from Wehrstedt, Han.; w—Christine nee Jordan, ch—Johanne; **Margaretha, 1845**
Kuebler, Ferd.—from Ilsfeld.; **Talisman, 1846**
Kuebler, Friedr.—s, from Heilbronn; **Talisman, 1846**
Kuechler, Carl—s, from Berlin; 1845
Kuechler, Jacob—s, *1823 in Hesse-Darmstadt; Gillespie Co.; **St. Pauli, 1847**
Kueffler, Ludw. Christian—s, from Diez; **Harriet, 1845**
Kuehn, Adolph—m, from Freistadt, Silesia; 1846
Kuehn, Carl—from Rehe, Nassau; 3 persons and 1 baby; New Braunfels; **George Delius, 1845**
Kuehn, Christian—from Rennerod; w—Maria, ch—Joh., Phil., Marg., Cath., Christian; Bexar Co.; **Strabo, 1845**
Kuehn, Emil—s, from Freistadt, Silesia; **Neptune, 1846**
Kuehn, Ludwig—s, 22; from Schmalkalden, Kurh.; **Garonne, 1845**
Kuehn, Theo. Wilh.—s, 29; **Ferdinand, 1844**
Kuehne, J.—New Braunfels 1845
Kuehnert, Edw.—s, from Berlin; **Creole, 1846**
Kuenzel, Christian,—from Rappenau; 3 persons; **Nahant 1846** wrecked at sea; then **Timoleon, 1846**
Kuern, Joh. Georg—from Altensteig, **Element, 1846**
Kuester, J. C. C.—s, from Frankfurt a/M; **Talisman, 1846**

Kuhfuss, Carl Hein.—†2.IX.1847, age 39; from Zellerfeld Han.; (NBChR); w—Johanna nee Richter, ch—Wilh., Elis., Otto, Emma; **Sophie, 1846**
Kuhl, Joh—s, from Wetterburg; **Sarah Ann, 1845**
Kuhlmann, Friedr. Wilh.—s, 33; from Bargen, Han.; **Gerhard Hermann, 1846**
Kuhlmann, Joh. Peter—21, from Giesenthal, Prussia; w—Marg. nee Sauer; Harris Co.; **Neptune, 1845**
Kuhlmann, Wilh.—s, 17; from Gadenstedt, Han; **Apollo, 1846**
Kuhn, Gottlob—from Freistadt, Silesia; **Neptune, 1846**
Kuhn, Marianne—New Braunfels 1845
Kuntze, Friedr.—s, 31; **Everhard, 1845**
Kunz, G. Friedr.—s, 27; from Johannesberg/Rhine; Comal Co.; **Washington, 1845**
Kunz, Jacob—from Rheinböllen, 2 persons; **York, 1846**
Kunz, Joh. Adam—s, 39; from Bergebersbach; Comal Co.; **Sarah Ann, 1845**
Kurre, Ludw.—s, from Hardegsen, Han.; Comal Co.; **Orient, 1846**
Kurzenacher, Philip—s, 32, from Staudt; 2 persons; **Harriet, 1845**
Kurzenacher, Wilh.—s, 25; **Harriet, 1845**
Kurzleben, Joh.—wife and 3 ch.; **Franziska, 1846**
Kussenberger, Christian—s, 19; and Joh.—s, 17; **Washington, 1845**
Kutscher, Fried.—† 1851 (F ChB); Gillespie Co.
Kutscher, Ludwig—from Zellerfeld, w—Doris nee Behrens; dau—Mina; **Anna, 1846**

— L —

Laade, Christian—from Hildesheim; w—Louise nee Weber; 4 persons; **Creole, 1846**
Laas, Fried.—from Lübz, Mcklbg.; 9 persons; Joh.—s, 21; Simon Carl —s, 19; Christian—s, 17; Austin Co.; **Apollo, 1846**
Laecheln, Ad. Fried—s, from Sobbowitz near Danzig; Comal Co.; **Mercur, 1846**
Laesecke, Caro.—from Luttmersen, Han.; **Weser, 1845**
Laesecke, Joh. Hein.—from Metel, Han.; w—Charlotte nee Kretzmeier; Fried—s, 18; Hein.—s, 24; **Weser, 1845**

114

Lafferre, Jacob—from Lauterecken; 2 persons; Colorado Co.; **Colchis, 1846**

Lager, Hein.—s, from Nieder Ingelheim; **Hamilton**, 1846

Lager, Herm.—from Nieder Ingelheim; **Hamilton**, 1846

Lamborg, Joh.—from Westernohe; arr. 1845

Lambrecht, Friedr.—from Salzdetfurth, w—Elisa nee Schickedanz; Guadalupe Co.; **Everhard**, 1845

Lander,---, from Berlin; arr. 1845

Lander, Katharina—widow with 2 ch.; arr. October 1843

Landgraf, Hein.—s, 21; from Oberkatz, Meiningen; **B. Bohlen**, 1845

Landrum, Larkin—s, from Alabama; Medina Co.; Steamer **Galveston** from N. O., 1846

Lang, Andreas—s, from Rappenau; **Nahant** (wrecked) 1846; then **Timoleon**, 1846

Lang, David—from Wiesbaden; 1845

Lang, Hein.—s, **Sarah Ann**, 1845

Lange, Adam—s, from Katzenstein; Grimes Co.; **Talisman**, 1846

Lange, Carl Friedr.—s, from Raderhorst, Prussia; **Creole**, 1846

Lange, Christian—from Brüggen, Han.; 3 persons; w—Cath. nee Klingelbe; Comal Co.; **Gesina**, 1846

Lange, Christian—from Fallersleben, Han.; Comal Co.; **Karl Ferdinand**, 1846

Lange, Fried.—from near Preuss Minden; † 17.VII.1846, age 46, (NBChR); w and 4 ch in Germany

Lange, Gottfried—from Wellersdorf, Prussia; w—Marie nee Kirchner; ch—Marie, Carl, Ernestine; **Joh. Dethardt**, 1846

Lange, Hein. Edw.—s, from Clausthal a/Harz; **Karl Ferdinand**, 1846

Lange, Wilh. G.—from Brome, Han.; w—Dorette nee Fritsche; **B. Bohlen**, 1847

Langeluedecke, Christian—s, from Fallersleben, Han.; arr. 1846

Langer, Georg—from Biebrich; **Neptune**, 1845

Langer, Joh.—48, from Biebrich; w—Marg. nee Bolz † 14.XI.1846, age 39; from Rod am Berg, Nassau; ch—Louis † 1846, age 12; Charles † 1846, age 3 (NBChR); other ch—Francisca 10, Louise 8 and Wilh.; **Neptune**, 1845

Langgraf, (Landgraf?) Hein.—from Oberkatz; 1845

Langguth, Cath.—New Braunfels 1845

Langkopf, Carl Hein.—from Klein Henstedt, Han.; † 27.XI.1846, age 36 (NBChR); widow—Johanna nee Voges; **B. Bohlen**, 1845

Langkopf, Jacob—from Remlingen, Brnschwg; Comal Co.; **Elisa & Charlotte**, 1846

Langkopf, Joh.—s; Comal Co; **Elisa & Charlotte**, 1846

Langwell, H. Aug.—from Clausthal; 5 persons; Bexar Co.; **Talisman**, 1846

Lankenau, Vincent—s, 18; Cameron Co.; **Neptune**, 1845

Laub, Adam—from Ebersberg; 4 persons; **Nahant** (wrecked); then **Dyle**, 1846

Laubenstein, Philipp—s, from Wiesbaden; **Diamant**, 1846

Laue, Bertram—from Hachenhausen; **Friedrich**, 1846

Laue, Carl—s, from Radegast, Prussia; **Margaretha**, 1846

Laue, Herm.—s, 41; from Segeste, Han.; † in 1847, age 43; (NBChR); **Margaretha**, 1845

Laue, Wilh.—from Radegast, Prussia; w—Julie nee Behr; ch—Emma; **Margaretha**, 1846

Lauer, Joh.—with wife and child; Fayette Co.; **Franziska**, 1846

Laux, Jacob—29, from Nastätten, Hesse; w—Wilhelmine †29.XI.1846, age 33; ch—Ludwig †1846, age 7; ch—Cath. 4; oo Christine nee Ackermann in 1848 (NBChR); **Washington**, 1845

Laux, Peter—40, from Elz; w—Rosina 47; ch—Marg. 20, Cath. 15- Joh. 8, Anna 3; Fayette Co.; **Strabo**, 1845

Lehmann, Daniel—from Friedersdorf, Lausitz; w—Johanna nee Erdmuth; ch—Ernst, Pauline, Carl., Augustine; **Louise**, 1846

Lehmann, Friedr. Aug.—s, from Friedersdorf, Lausitz; Fredericksburg 1847; **Louise**, 1846

Lehmann, Gottfried.—from Friedersdorf, Lausitz; w—Anna Lehmann; ch—August, Mortiz, Ernestine, Wilh.; **Louise**, 1846

Lehmann, Gottlieb—from Friedersdorf, Lausitz; w—Ernestine nee Abecke; Gillespie Co.; **Louise**, 1846

Lehmann, (Loehmann), Hein.—Travis Co.; **Louise**, 1846

Lehmann, Samuel—s, from Friedersdorf, Lausitz; **Louise**, 1846

Lehr, Fr.—from Württemberg, † 1.IX.1846, age 36, (NBChR)

Lehrke, Daniel—from Listringen, Han.; 4 persons; arr. 1845

Leifermann, Conrad—m, from Neustadt, Han.; arr. 1846

Leifeste, Friedr.—s, 35; Hein.—s, 27; from Reppner, Brnschwg; Gillespie Co.; **Gerhard Hermann**, 1846

Leih(e)ner, Wilh.—from Stein, Nass. (IC), Emmerichenhain (NBChR); 8 persons; w—Marie Gotthardt, widow of Joh. Wolf; ch—Jeanette Wolf, Sophie Leihener, Theodore Leihener; **Joh. Dethardt,** 1845

Leih(e)ner, Wolf—s, 21; **Joh. Dethardt,** 1845

Leilich, Wilh.—s, 33; from Neu-Ruppin, Prussia; Gillespie Co.; **Garonne,** 1845

Leinuller, Joseph—from Degmann; 3 persons; **Diamant,** 1846

Leissner, Joh.—from Dubielno, Prussia; w—Elise nee Rodemann; ch—Amalia, Johanna, Ferd., Pauline; **Johanna,** 1846

Leissner, Joh. Aug.—s, Guadalupe Co.; **Johanne,** 1846

Leissring, Carl—s, from Halle Saale; **B. Bohlen,** 1847

Leissring, Otto—s, from Halle; **Elisa & Charlotte,** 1846

Leith, Hein.—from Hesse; **Weser,** 1844

Leitzmann, Andreas—s, from Lündersbühl(?), Bavaria; arr. 1846

Leitzmann, Carl—m; Schooner **Mary,** 1847; arr. Carlshaven

Lejoly, Joh. Nic.—from Breverce, **Henry,** 1846

Lemme, Carl—s, 31; from Berlin; **Apollo,** 1846

Lemons, James Aug. and family—from Germany; New Braunfels, 1845

Lentz, Hein. Werner—s, 21; from Braunschweig; Bastrop Co.; **Everhard,** 1845

Lenz, Andreas—23, from Offenbach, Nassau; w—Susanne nee Selzer; ch—Elis. 5, Jacob 2; **Herschel,** 1845

Lenz, Anton—s, 30, from Offenbach, Nassau; **Arminius,** 1845

Lens, August—from Driedorf, Nassau and wife; son—Joh. Hein. † 13.III.1846, age 3 weeks; (NBChR); dau.—Louise; **Arminius,** 1845

Lenz, Joh.—from Culm; arr. 1845

Lenz, Joseph—from Cologne; **Anna,** 1846

Leonhard, Joh. Jacob—from Bottenhorn, Kr. Biedenkopf; 3 persons, Medina Co.; **York,** 1846

Lerch, Aug.—s, St. Pauli, 1847

Lesser, Christian—m, from Brotterode, Kurh.; Guadalupe Co.; **Friedrich,** 1846

Lessmann, Heinrich—from Stadtoldendorf; w—Wilhme nee Meier; ch—Wilhme, Johanne; Guadalupe Co.; **Sophie,** 1846

Letsch, Daniel—from Herzberg, Han; w—Augusta Caro. nee Bischoff; New Braunfels 1845; **Herschel,** 1844

Levi, Johanna—from Netze, Waldeck; **Margaretha,** 1845

Leyendecker, Joh.—from Kadenbach; w—Myrina; ch—John, Anna Marie, Francis, Jacob; Gillespie Co.; **Riga,** 1846

Leyendecker, Joh.—s, 18; from Kadenbach; Gillespie Co.; **Riga,** 1846

Leyendecker II, Joh.—w and 2 ch; Bexar Co.; **Richard,** 1846

Leyendecker Mathias—71; from Kadenbach; **Riga,** 1846

Lichen, Carl—from Hildesheim; **Creole,** 1846

Lichtenberg, Ernst von—from Darmstadt, †28.XII.1849 (NBChR); Lichtenberg, Ludwig von—from Darmstadt; Comal Co.

Liebermann, Aug.—from Rottweil; **Dyle,** 1846

Liebermann, Jacob—from Ebersberg (Ebersbach?); **Dyle,** 1846

Liebscher, Hugo—from Halle, Prussia; **Creole,** 1846

Liehfeld, Hein.—from Westfeld, Han.; **Margaretha,** 1845

Linck, Dr. Christ.—from Darmstadt; **Colchis,** 1846

Lincke, Albrecht—s, Gillespie Co.; **Strabo,** 1845

Lincke, G.—s, 17; from Germany; **Star Republic** from N.Y.; **New York** from N.O., 1845

Lincke, N.—39, from Germany; **Star Republic** from N.Y.; **New York,** from N.O., 1845

Lind, Daniel—arr. 1846

Lindemann, Hein.—from Moringen; **Creole,** 1846

Lindemann, Joh.—from Konczenitz (=Konczyce?), Silesia; w—Eva nee Ockner; ch—David, Hein. Carl, Marie, Anna, Friedricke, Hermine; Guadalupe Co.; **Johanna,** 1846

Lindemann, Joh. Andreas—m, from Nälenz ? (=Nehlitz?), Prussia; **Johanna,** 1846

Lindenberg, Friedr.—from Hamburg; w—Anna nee Pascut, dau—Leontine; **Johanna,** 1846

Lindenberg, Joh. Hein. Mathias—**Neptune,** 1846

Lindheimer, Ferdinand—from Frankfurt; New Braunfels 1845; Great naturalist and editor of *New Braunfels Zeitung*

Lindig, Casper—s, 54; from Eisenach; **Dyle,** 1846

Lindmueller, J. W. C.—s, from Eisenach(IC) or Abbesbüttel(VF); **Everhard,** 1845

Lindmueller, Wilh. Christian—† 5.III.1847, age 53; w—Christine nee Schader; family of 9 persons; from Abbesbüttel, Han.; **Everhard**, 1845

Link, Michael—s, from Heiligenstadt; **Timoleon**, 1846

Linnartz, Peter—35; from Düsseldorf; 4 persons and 1 baby; Comal Co.; **York**, 1846

Linz, Hein. Jos.—from Braunstein Amt Wiesbaden; † 21.VIII.1846, age 38 (NBChR)

Lippel, Georg—see Sippel, Georg

Lobenstein, Caspar—s, from Ichtershausen; Galveston Co.; **Mercur**, 1846

Lobenstein,Gotthelf—GalvestonCo.; **Mercur**, 1846

Lobenstein, Julius—s, from Ichtershausen; Galveston Co.; **Mercur**, 1846

Lochte, Andreas—from Gadenstedt; **Hercules**, 1845

Lochte, Conrad—from Gadenstedt; and Friedr.; **Hercules**, 1845

Lochte, Friedr.—36, from Gadenstedt, Han.; w—Dor.(Cath.) nee Moellring 30; ch—Friedr. 9, Caro. 6, Hein. 2; Gillespie Co.; **Hercules**, 1845

Lochtelbach, Joh.—from Rappach; **Harriet**, 1846

Lock, Fried.—w—Marie nee Jaeger; ch—Joh., Friedke, Dor., Henriette; **Karl Ferdinand**, 1846

Lockhausen, Edward von—s, 25; New Braunfels 1845; came by land from Louisiana; DeWitt Co.; Feb. 1845; Lockhausen, H.—m, **Louise**, 1846

Lockmann, Conrad—died; ch—Hein. and Sophie, sole heirs; **Louise**, 1846

Lockstedt, Friedr.—from Warbsen, Brschwg; w—Wilhme nee Jaeger; Comal Co.; **Elisa & Charlotte**, 1846

Loebich, Friedr. and family—from Haberschlacht; arr. 1846

Loeffler, Andreas—**Flavius**, 1846

Loeffler, Christian—from Württemberg; wife and 1 child; New Braunfels 1845; **Johann Dethardt**, 1844

Loeffner, Christine—from Haberschlacht; **Hamilton**, 1846

Loehmann, Conrad—**Louise**, 1845

Loehmann(Lehmann), Hein.—from Hoppenstedt, Prussia; w—Sophie nee Resslingen; Travis Co.; **Louise**, 1846

Loehmann, Hein. Christoph and mother Sophie Dor. from Semmenstedt; **Louise**, 1846

Loehr, Ludwig—s, from Langenbach; **Washington**, 1845

Loehrberg, H. F.—2 persons; from Altenau; Comal Co.; **Hamilton**, 1845

Loew, Franz—from Camberg, 3 persons; **Bohemia**, 1846

Loew, Joh.—s, from Camberg; **Bohemia**, 1846

Lohman, Hry—and wife; **Neptune**, 1845

Loo(c)k, Friedrich—m, 52; from Tappenbeck, Han.; arr. 1846

Loos, Elis.—21; New Braunfels 1845; **Ferdinand**, 1844

Lorenz, Joh. Hein.—died before 1847, from Verden, Han.; w—Anna (Cath. M) Reinken; ch—Cath., Herm., Friedr.; **Apollo**, 1846

Lorsch, Michael—from Schatthausen; **Talisman**, 1846

Louis, Fried.—s, Kendall Co. 1850's; **St. Pauli**, 1847

Luck, Christoph Phil—s, 25; from Schweinfurt, Bavaria; New Braunfels 1845; **Johann Dethardt**, 1844

Luck, Edward—s, 21; from Emmerichenhain; **Washington**, 1845

Luck, Ludw. Christian—s, 40; from Emmerichenhain; New Braunfels; **Washington**, 1845

Luck, Philipp—from Gemünden, Nassau; w—Cath. nee Scheidler, † 15.X.1846, age 36 (NBChR); ch—Philip Carl, Ludw.; New Braunfels 1845; **Johann Dethardt**, 1844

Luckenbach, Jacon—from Stein, Nassau; w—Justina nee Ruebsamen; ch—Amalie, Paul., Henrietta, Mathilde; Gillespie Co.; **Joh. Dethardt**, 1845

Luckenbach, Wilh. and wife—from Stein, Nassau; Gillespie Co.; **Joh. Dethardt**, 1845

Ludewig, Joh. Justus—from Lutterberg, Ff/M; w—Maria nee Froelich; ch—Louise, Lenore, Hein.; Comal Co.; **Everhard**, 1845

Ludwig, Christoph—m, from Kiedrich; Calhoun Co.; **Diamant**, 1846

Ludwig, Jacob and Elisa—with 2 children; **Herschel**, 1845

Ludwig, Joh. Wilh.—s, from Hannover; Comal Co.; **New York**, from N.O. 1846

Luebky, Chr.—from Triebsees, Pomerania; w—Lenora nee Lueders and baby; **Apollo**, 1846

Luecke, Carl—s, 20; **Margaretha**, 1845

Luecke, Hein. Wilh.—from Westfeld, Han.; w—Wilhme nee Rabe; ch—Wilh., Joh., Aug., Auguste, Friedr.; Fayette Co.; **Margaretha**, 1845

Lued(t)ke, Aug.—s, from Rynarzewo, Prussia; **Johanna**, 1846

Luedke, Peter—from Rynarzewo;

w—Henriette nee Krause; **Flavius**, 1846
Luehrig, Ludwig—m, from Dassensen; **Hamilton**, 1846
Luehrs, Hein.—from Speckenholz; w—Anna nee Mensching; Comal Co.; **Auguste Meline**, 1845
Luenert, Aug.—from Clausthal, Han.; w—Auguste nee Molle; ch—Richard, Albert, Anna, Agnes; **Karl Ferdinand**, 1846
Luentzel, Christoph—s, New Braunfels 1845; **Johann Delhardt**, 1844
Luentzel, Friedr.—from Abbensen; arr. 1845
Luentzel, Max—from Hildesheim, Han; Comal Co.; **Matador**, 1845
Luer, Friedr.—s, from Dorste, Brnschwg; **Talisman**, 1846
Luer, Fried.—from Abbensen; 1845
Luer, Wilh.—s, arr. 1846; died 1846
Luering, Christoph—s, arr. by land, 1844
Luerse, Hein.—from Celle, 1845
Luersen, Louis and wife—**Franziska**, 1846
Luessmann, Georg Hein.—from Essel, Han.; w—Marie nee Debke † 26.II.1847, age 32 (NBChR); ch—Hein., Anna, and baby; **Weser**, 1845
Luetze, Hein.—from Fallersleben, Han.; w—Henriette nee Koenecke, **Karl Ferdinand**, 1846
Lundgraf, Hein.—s, 20; from Oberkatz, Meiningen; **B. Bohlen**, 1845
Lungkwitz, Herman—famous Texas painter, from Halle; w—Elisa nee Petri; Gillespie Co.
Lutterbrodt, Wilh. and sister Wilhelmine—from Hillingsfeld, Han.; **Everhard**, 1845
Luther, Engelbert—s, from Steinbeck; **Diamant**, 1846
Lutz, Christian, Friedr.—s, from Haberschlacht; arr. 1846
Lutz, Jacob—s, from Reihen; Comal Co.; **Diamant**, 1846
Lux, Christian Ph.—from Hambach, Prussia; and Lux, Joh. Hubert; New Braunfels 1845; Castro Colonists; **Ocean**, 1844

— M —

Mack, Heinrich—died; Elis. widow, sole heir; See also Goertz, Hein. Mack; **Strabo**, 1845
Madgen, F. J.—age 42 and wife; Milam Co.; **Neptune**, 1845
Maehl, Carl Gustav—Schooner **Mary**, 1847
Maemecke, Wilhelm—s, from Friedrichsbrunn; **Flavius**, 1846

Maerz, Joh. and wife—New Braunfels 1845
Magdeburg, August—from Gossmar, Ff/M; with sons Hermann and Guido; **Louise**, 1847
Mahr, Andreas—s, 20; and Mahr, Joh—s, 20; **Strabo**, 1845
Mahr, Martin—age 58, from Nauroth; w—Elis. 52; Cath. 12; **Strabo**, 1845
Mahr, Phillip—s, 23; **Strabo**, 1845
Maier, Anton—s, 30; from Fulda, Kurh.; Gillespie Co.; **Garone**, 1845
Maier, Franz Andreas—from Fulda; ch—Anton, Josephine; arr. 1845; Edward (came in 1854)
Maier, Wilh.—from Rohrburg, w—Johanna nee Hofmann; ch—Caro., and Carl; **B. Bohlen**, 1846
Maierhoefer, Joseph—37, from Helmhof; w—Eva 37; ch—Valentine 16, Cath. 15, Jos. 12, Christine 10, Anton 8, Adam 1½; **Washington**, 1845
Malsch, Ullrich—from Brotterode, Kurh.; w—Anna nee Voigt; Harris Co.; **Friedrich**, 1846
Mander, Hein.—44; from Dillenburg, Nass.; **Arminius**, 1845
Mangold, Alois—s, from Röhlingen; **Timoleon**, 1846
Mann, Christian—s, from Derschlag; Grimes Co.; **Talisman**, 1846
Mann, Joh. Peter—from Heiligenroth; **Strabo**, 1845
Marburger, Hein.—from Erndtebrück; 7 persons; Austin Co.; **York**, 1846
Marburger, Jacob—from Lützel, near Erndtebrück; 2 persons; Fayette Co.; **York**, 1846
Marheinicke, Franz—s, 24; New Braunfels 1845; **Ferdinand**, 1844
Mark, Balthasar—s, 35; from Acholshausen, Bavaria; **Joh. Dethardt**, 1845
Marklof, Conrad—from Niederneisen; 5 persons; **Bohemia**, 1846
Marguard, Joh. Martin—36, died; w—Wilhelmina 35, died; ch—Caro. 11, Henrietta 6, Gustav 4, Adolph 3, Ferdinand 1, died; Comal Co.; **Arminius**, 1845
Marschall, Caspar—32, from Kaltennordheim, Weimar; w—Eva nee Braeutigam 31; ch—Aug., Andrew, Pauline; Gillespie Co.; **Everhard**, 1845
Marschner, Gottlieb—s, from Freistadt, Prussia; arr. 1846
Martens, Fried. Wilh.—† 1846, age 35; from Boitzum, Han.; w—Wilhme nee Moeller; ch—Minna † 1846, age 9; Johanne

118

† 1846, age 12, (NBChR); Austin Co.; **Gerhard Hermann**, 1846

Martens, Joh.—died; from Boitzum, Han.; **Gerhard Hermann**, 1846

Martens, Wilh.—s, 27; **Apollo**, 1844

Martin, Christian—from Lemke, Han.; w—Wilhelmine nee Sauder; son—Hein. 21; Austin Co.; **Everhard**, 1845

Martin, Conrad—from Wendershausen, Kurh.; w—Martha nee Reise; Galveston Co. **Friedrich**, 1845

Martin, Henry—s, 21; Marie; Henry and wife; **Everhard**, 1845

Martin, Jacob—s, 53; from Klein Schmalkalden, Kurh.; Galveston Co.; **Everhard**, 1845

Martin, Joh.—s, 42; **B. Bohlen**, 1845

Martin, Joh. G. Jacob—from Kleinschneen; ch—Cath. Elis., Joh. **Fried, Marcus Anton; Timoleon**, 1846

Martin, Ludwig—s, 25; from Erndtebruck; New Braunfels 1845; **Johann Dethardt**, 1844

Martz, Edward and wife—**Ferdinand**, 1846

Maser, Joh.—s, 24; **Sarah Ann**, 1845

Mathee, Joh. Wilh.—from Rötgen; 3 persons and 1 baby; **Element**, 1846

Mattern, Andreas—s, 25; from Dertingen, Baden; New Braunfels 1845; **Joh. Dethardt**, 1844

Mattern, Carl Andreas—m, New Braunfels 1845; **Johann Dethardt**, 1844

Mattfeld, Joh.—from Armsen, † 15.V.1847 (NBChR); Catherine—widow; ch—Sophie, Friedr., Alfred; **Matador**, 1845

Matthaei, Dr. Christian H.—44, from Rodenberg; wife and children to follow; **Weser**, 1844

Matzke, Christian—from Kleintahse (Kleintauscha?); w—-Klein; **Mathilda**, 1846

Maul, Anton—26, from Niesig, Kurh.; **Garonne**, 1845

Maul, Joh. Adam—s, from Niesig, Kurh.; **Garonne**, 1845

Maurer, Christoph—from Zegartowith; w—Eva nee Grimm; ch—Caro., Cath., Wilh.; Galveston Co.; **Johanna**, 1846

Maurer, Peter—from Eitelborn; wife and 3 ch; **Riga**, 1846

Mavers, Wilh. and wife—from Salzgitter; **Franziska**, 1846

Mawicke, Franz—from Ossenzhausen; 3 persons and 1 baby; **Colchis**, 1846

Max, Mathilda—from Langenhagen, Han.; **Johann Dethardt**, 1845

May, Edward—28; Cath. 66, Ida 24, Elnora 21; **Dyle**, 1846

Mayer, Barth—s, from Siegelsbach; **Diamant**, 1846

Mayer (Meyer), Hein.—s, from Berwangen; **James Edward**, 1846

Mayer, Joh.—s, **Andacia**, 1846

Mayer(Meyer), Martin—s, from Berwangen; Austin Co.; **James Edward**, 1846

Mebus, Michael—m, from Eberbach, Württ.; arr. 1846

Mechels, Christian—m, from Hildesheim, Han.; **Weser**, 1845

Mechels, Jos.—m, 3 persons; from Hildesheim; **Weser**, 1845

Meckel, Carl—18; **Herschel**, 1845

Meckel, Cath.—† 4.III.1846, age 30; from Bicken, Nass.

Meckel, Cath. Elisa—18; **Herschel**, 1845

Meckel, Daniel—Kendall Co. 1850's; **Herschel**, 1845

Meckel, Fritz—24, Kendall Co.; **Herschel**, 1845

Meckel, Hugo—from Halle; 2 persons; **Creole**, 1845

Meckel, Joh. George—41, from Bicken, Nass.; w—Cath. nee Graf 29; Cath 23, Anna Elis. 21, Phil D. 11, Cath. 9; Comal Co.; **Herschel**, 1845

Meckel, Joh. Hein.—53, from Dillenberg; w—Frederica 51; ch—Sophie 21, Cath 15, Daniel 12; Comal Co.; **Hercules**, 1845

Meckel, John Philipp—from Bicken, Nass., † 4.VIII.1848 age 32; w—Cath. †4.III.1846 age 30 (NBChR); ch—Wilh Fr. 7, Pauline 5, Frjedr. 3; **Herschel**, 1845

Meckel; Phillip Hein.—25, Comal Co.; **Herschel**, 1845

Meder, Christoph—m, Osterburg, Prussia; arr. 1846

Meder, Jos.—s, 23; from Ehrenbreitstein; **Riga**, 1846

Mehmark, Friedr.—from Breslau; **Creole**, 1846

Mehrmann, Friedr.—from Schöppenstedt, Brnschwg; w—Caro. nee, Bormann; dau.—Emilie; **Louise**, 1846

Meier, Car., sister Elisa and brother Wilh.—from Rohrberg; **B. Bohlen**, 1846

Meier, (Meyer), Hein.—from Lutterberg, Han.; Austin Co.; **Everhard**, 1845

Meier, Joh.—w—nee Dettmar and ch.; Gillespie Co.; **Ferdinand**, 1844

Meilsch, M.—from Berlin; 7 persons; **Hamilton**, 1846

Meimann, Hein.—37, and wife from Münster; ch—Joh. 18, Jos. 9, Lisette 5, Wilhme 1; **Weser**, 1844

119

Meine, Friedr.—s, from Einbeck, Han.; Comal Co.; **Creole**, 1846
Meine, Hein. Conrad, Friedr.—from Bäsche, Han.; 4 persons; Comal Co.; **George Delius**, 1845
Meineke, Albert—from Schöppenstedt; w—Elisa nee Karsten; **Sophie**, 1846
Meine(c)ke, Hein.—s, from Brome, Han.; **B. Bohlen**, 1847
Meineke, Ludw. and wife—from Schöppenstedt; ch—Christian, Aug., Caro., Wilhme., Leopold, Charlotte; Austin Co.; **Sophie**, 1846
Meinert, C. A.—m, 39; from Hartenstein; 2 persons; Fayette Co.; **Talisman**, 1846
Meinhardt, Edm. A.—from Arnstadt; Gillespie Co.; **Hamilton**, 1846
Meinold, Theo. and Albert—**Anthony**, 1846
Meisel, Henriette—Anna, 1846
Meismer, Balthasar—44; from Celle; ch—Barbara Josepha 14, Johann Adam 9; Colorado Co.; **Weser**, 1844
Meissbach, G. Aug.—from Osterode a/Harz; 1846
Meissbach, Hein.—s, from Osterode, a/Harz; 1846
Meissner, Conrad—27 from Bavaria; **Johann Dethardt**, 1845
Meissner, Joh.—s, from Herzhausen, Kreis Siegen; Calhoun Co.; **Element**, 1846
Meissner, Joh.—m; died 1849; from Altwildungen; arr. 1846
Meister, Michael H. G.—s, from Uffhofen; **Talisman**, 1846
Meixner, Andreas—from Forchheim, Bavaria; w—Marianna nee Pöhlert and 3 ch; New Braunfels 1845; **Herschel**, 1844
Menger, Gustav—s, from Böhlen Thüringia; Kerr Co. 1857; **Sophie**, 1846
Menger, Joh. Simon Nicholaus—from Stadtilm, Thüringia; w—Aususte nee Schoniger; **Sophie**, 1846
Menges, Anton—from Niederelbert; w—Cath; ch—Cath., Adam; Gillespie Co.; **Riga**, 1846
Menk, Joh. Anton—from Salzburg, Nass.; † 20 VII.1846, age 55 (NBChR)
Menn, Joh.—s, from Erndtebrück; Austin Co.; **York**, 1846
Menz, Christian—from Oberschönau, Kurh.; **Everhard**, 1845
Menz, George—from Oberschönau, Kurh.; w—Anna nee Sondergold; ch—Benjamen, Louise, Thielmann; **Everhard**, 1845

Menzing, Hein—† 14.VII.1851 in New Braunfels, age 41
Menzler, Peter—s, 55; from Grebenau, Hesse; † 1.VIII.1846, age 55(NBChR); **Herschel**, 1845
Mergele, E. and J.—New Braunfels 1845; Castro colonists; **Jean Key**, 1844
Mergele, (Pierre) Peter—age 23, from Rüdesheim; w—Barbe 30; ch—Jacques 7, Emilie 5, Charles 1; Castro colonist; New Braunfels 1845; **Jean Key**, 1844
Merk, Michael and 2 sons—from Effringen; arr. 1846
Merkel, Christoph Friedr.—s, 48; from Schmalkalden, Kurh.; **Garonne**, 1845
Merkel, Joh.—from Coblenz, 8 persons; Austin Co.; **James Edward**, 1846
Merkel, Wilh.—26; **Arminius**, 1845
Merrem, Edgar—s, 18; from Witzenhausen, Kurh.; **B. Bohlen**, 1845
Merten, Lorenz—s, 28; from Seeburg, Brnschwg; Austin Co.; **Margaretha**, 1846
Mertens, Franz Joseph—s, from Hildesheim, Han.; Fayette Co.; **Weser**, 1845
Mertens, Joh.—from Lohne, Prussia; w—Anna nee Schulze; **Louise Friedricke**, 1847
Mertz, Carl Conrad—from Wiesbaden; w—Marie nee Burkhard; ch—Geo. Ludwig, Hein., Caro., Elise; Calhoun Co.; **Joh. Dethardt**, 1845
Mertz, J.—New Braunfels 1845
Merwark, Friedr.—s, from Breslau; arr. 1846
Merz, Anna(widow)—from Holler, Nass.; ch—Joh., Anna, Anna Marie, Magda; Comal Co.; **Auguste Meline**, 1845
Merz, Joh.—from Gräfenburg, Bavaria; w—Marg. nee Britting, † 22.XI 1846 (NBChR); New Braunfels 1845; **Herschel**, 1844
Merz, Joh.—s, from Holler, Nassau; **Auguste Meline**, 1845
Merz, Peter—s, 26; **Riga**, 1846
Meseck, Aug.—from Schöneck near Danzig; w—Auguste; **Mathilde**, 1846
Messerschmitt, Michael—s, from Zeil, Bavaria; **Alabama** from New Orleans, 1846
Metz, Cath., widow with 2 ch.—**Andacia**, 1846
Metz, Conrad zu—died, Johann Georg Metz—son and sole heir; **Herschel**, 1845
Metz, Joh. M.(P?)—29; w—Caro. H. 30; Henriette—3; and male infant; **Andacia**, 1846

120

Metz, Peter—from Hohenroth, Nass.; † 30.X.1846 age 38; w—Magda nee Dienemann; from Oder by Heiligenstadt; † 10.VIII.1846 age 35 (NBChR); 4 persons; Dyle, 1846

Metz, Phil. Hein.—28, from Patersburg, Nass.; w—Marie nee Meyer; 5 persons; Joh. Dethardt, 1845

Metze, Christoph—40, from Lenterode, Prussia; widower—2 ch: Joseph and Maria; Comal Co.; B. Bohlen, 1845

Metzger, Anton—s, 25; from Hattenheim; Dyle, 1846

Metzger, Franz—21, (son of Peter); Dyle, 1846

Metzger, Friedr.—1779-1871; from Kadenbach, Nassau; w—Cath nee Leyendecker; ch—Anne, Marie, Jacob, John, Anna; Gillespie Co.; Riga, 1846

Metzger, Friedr.—m, Colchis, 1846

Metzger, Friedr.—s, 19; Dyle, 1846

Metzger, Hry—s, 25; James Edward, 1846

Metzger, Jacob—s, 27; from Kadenbach, Nassau; Riga, 1846

Metzger, Jacob—m; Colchis, 1846

Metzger, John—s, from Kadenbach, Nassau; Riga, 1846

Metzger, Joh.—s, Colchis, 1846

Metzger, Joh. and wife—from Eitelborn; Riga, 1846

Metzger, Martin—with family and 2 babies; arr. 1846

Metzger, Peter—54, from Hattenheim; with Ann Marie 23, Jacob 15, Friedr. 11; Dyle, 1846

Metzger, Philip C.—25, (son of Peter); Dyle, 1846

Metzing, Christ. and wife—from Klein Ilsede; Everhard, 1845

Metzing, Friedr.—s, 25; from Klein Ilsede; Everhard, 1845

Metzing, Hein.—† 14.VII.1851, age 41; from Klein Ilsede, Han.; (NBChR); w—Dorothea nee Pape; ch—Dor., Mina; Comal Co.; Everhard, 1845

Metzler, C. M.—6 persons; from Leipzig; James Edward, 1846

Metzler, Hein.—s, from Orb; James Edward, 1846

Metzler, Hein.—from Obernhof; arr. 1846

Metzler, Joh.—38, from Orb; Gillespie Co.; James Edward, 1846

Metzler, Joh.—56, from Orb; 6 persons; Comal Co.; James Edward, 1846

Metzmann, Joh. Peter—from Heiligenroth; Strabo, 1845

Meuerer, Hubert—from Würges; 4 persons and 1 baby; Bohemia, 1846

Meuer, Joh.—46, from Heiligenroth, w—Barbara 45; ch—Marg. 21, Cath. 19, Maria 18, Jacob 16, Susanne 14, Joseph 12, Peter 10, Adam 6; Strabo, 1845

Meurer, Theo.—from Leutenberg; w—Johanna Elisa nee Petsch; Weser, 1846

Meusebach, Heinrich—from Dillenburg, Nassau; Arminius, 1845

Meusebach, John O.(Baron Ottfried Hans von); *1812 in Dillenburg, Nassau; † 27.V.1897 in Loyal Valley, Texas; oo Agnes Coreth in 1852; was second Commissioner General for Adelsverein; founded Fredericksburg; came on steamer from New York, 1845

Meussner, Wilh.—s, 27; Apollo, 1845

Meuster, Peter—from Grebenau; 1845

Meuth, Andreas—s, from Würges, Nassau; Bastrop Co.; James Edward, 1846

Meuth, Franz—s, from Würges; Bastrop Co.; James Edward, 1846

Meutz, Peter—s, 26; from Oberelbert; Riga, 1846

Meuz, Joh.—from Mosbach, Weimar; Everhard, 1845

Meyenberg, Julius—from Hannover; arr. 1845; Fayette Co.

Meyer, Albert Henry—Augusta Meline, 1845

Meyer, Aug.—22, from Friedrichsbruch, Prussia; w—Elisa nee Karge (Kage?); Austin Co.; Johanna, 1846

Meyer, Carl—s, from Markoldendorf; Hamilton, 1846

Meyer, Christian—s, † 13.VI.1846, age 37 (NBChR); Everhard, 1845

Meyer, Conrad—from Gross Mahner, Han.; w—Christine nee Seehaus; Comal Co.; Everhard, 1845

Meyer, Conrad—43 and wife; ch—Wilh. 14, Hein. 12, Ludw. 7, Christian 3; Weser, 1844

Meyer, David—from Störy, Han.; 2 persons and 1 baby; B. Bohlen, 1845

Meyer, Dr. Emil—New Braunfels 1845

Meyer, Franz—from Friedrichsbrüch, Prussia, w—Eva nee Briel; Austin Co.; Johanna, 1846

Meyer, Friedr.—s, 32; Gillespie Co.; Weser, 1844

Meyer, Friedr.—from Dombrowken; w—Rosina nee Gebuchs; ch—Eva, Augusta; Johanna, 1846

Meyer, Friedricke—from Sulserd, Han.; Creole, 1846

Meyer, Georg L.—24; Andacia, 1846

Meyer, Hein.—s, 32; from Eschenhausen, Han.; **Auguste Meline,** 1845
Meyer, Hein.—from Friedrichsbrüch; w—Wilhme nee Brandenburg; ch—Alex, Julius; **Johanna,** 1846
Meyer, Hein.—s, from Berwangen; **James Edward,** 1846
Meyer, Johannes—arr. 1847; died Oct. 1848; Christine Meyer only heir
Meyer, Hein.—m, from Hildesheim, Han.; 4 persons; Fayette Co.; **Creole,** 1846
Meyer, Joh. Hein. Adolph—from Friedrichshagen, Kurh.; sisters —Juliane 22 and Marianne 28; DeWitt Co.; **Hercules,** 1845
Meyer, Ludolph—s, 42; from Gross Lafferde, Han.; Gillespie Co.; **Apollo,** 1846
Meyer, Martin—from Berwangen; Austin Co.; **James Edward,** 1846
Meyer, Mehn—w and 2 ch; **Franziska,** 1846
Meyer, Philipp—s, from Einbeck; **Hamilton,** 1846
Meyer, Wilh.—from Brome, Han.; w—Johanne nee Hoffmann; ch—Carl, Hein., Caro.; **B. Bohlen.** 1846
Meyer(Meier), Wilh.—s, 50; from Celle, Han.; **Franziska,** 1846
Meyer, Wilh.—s, 26; from Hannover; **Weser,** 1844
Meyer, Xavier—m, from New Orleans; **New York,** 1846
Michaeli, Edward—s, from Arolsen; **Colchis,** 1846
Michael, Adam—s, from Harlos (=Harloth?); **Talisman,** 1846
Michel, Conrad—from Braubach; † 2.IX.1846, age 26(NBChR)
Michel, Friedr.—s, **St. Pauli,** 1847
Michel, Joh. Ph.—s, 33; from Dachsenhausen; Comal Co.; **Talisman,** 1846
Michel, Mathias—s, 22; **Gesina,** 1845
Michel, Peter—s, 27; from Niederwald; **Sarah Ann,** 1845
Michel, Ph.—from Nassau; † 1846, age 26(NBChR)
Michelmann, Louise—from Klein-Schneen; **Timoleon,** 1846
Middledorf, Clemens Michael Hein.—s, 28; from Breslau; **Arminius,** 1845
Middelege, Conrad—from Bösingfeld; 7 persons; w—Louise nee Helmhold; **Creole,** 1846
Milde, Edward—from Culm, Poland; family of 2 persons and 1 baby; Goliad Co.; **Apollo,** 1846
Miller, Burchard—from Germany;

partner in Fisher-Miller Contract; Harris Co.
Mirring, Gottfried—s, from Kannedorf (=Karndorf?); **B. Bohlen,** 1847
Mittel, Wendel(in)—s, from Weiler; Gillespie Co.; **Hamilton,** 1846
Mittelege, Ernst—s, 20; from Fuhlen, Kurh.; **Neptune,** 1845
Mittendorf, Erhard—s, Gustav—s, Hermann—s, Ludwig—m; from Stadtoldendorf; Comal Co.; **Sophie,** 1846
Mittmann, Henriette—**Friedrich,** 1846
Mockler, Philipp—s, from Frankenbach; **Diamant,** 1846
Moehle, Conrad—from Auenstein, near Heilbronn; w—Christine nee Bader † 30.X.1846, age 30; Elis. † 1846, age 8½, Friedrike † 1846, age 1½ (NBChR); **Talisman,** 1846
Moeller, Miller—also see Mueller
Moeller, Christian—died 1846; from Boitzum, Han.; w—Johanna nee Blum; dau—Dor. and Wilhme; **Gerhard Hermann,** 1846
Moeller, David—s, 31; **Gerhard Hermann,** 1846
Moeller, Sr., Hein.—from Roth; Austin Co.; arr. 1845
Moeller, Wilh.—s, from Uelzen, Han.; Colorado Co.; **Herschel,** 1844
Moellring, Andreas—35, from Gadenstedt; w—Gesina(Caro.) nee Feldmann 30; ch—Karl 6, Hein. 2, Caro. ½; Gillespie Co.; **Hercules,** 1845
Moeschen, Sebastian Hein. Christof—38, from Menteroda, Thüringia; New Braunfels 1845; **Weser,** 1844
Moeschen, J. Christoph—w—Johanna; dau—Friedricke; New Braunfels 1845
Moetter, Albert—s, from Ketten, Weimar; **Garonne,** 1845
Mohlfeld, Hein.—s, from Grosswedel, Han.; Guadlupe Co.; arr. 1845
Mohr, Adam—from Cappel; 4 persons and 1 baby; Gillespie Co.; **James Edward,** 1846
Mohr, Christian—from Cappel; **James Edward,** 1846
Mohr. Friedr.—s, from Volkstedt, Schwarzbg; **Margaretha,** 1846
Mohr, Joh.—from Rennerod, Nass.; Cath. nee Schmidt; ch—Christian, Cath.; **Augusta Meline,** 1845
Mohrmann, Christoph—s, from Tappenbeck, Han.; **Karl Ferdinand,** 1846
Molitor, Jacob—s, from Weiler; **Diamant,** 1846

Molitor, Jos.—from Weiler; **Talis-mann,** 1846
Mollen, Wilh.—from Peine, Han.; arr. 1845
Molsburger, Anton—from Thalheim; 4 persons; **Element,** 1846
Molzburger, Joh.—s, from Thalheim; **Talisman,** 1846
Molzburger, Oscar—s, 19; **Harriet,** 1845
Molzburger, Peter's widow—from Zehnhausen; ch—Albert, Sabina, Philippine, Justine; **Harriet,** 1845
Mone, Friedbrant—from Karlsruhe; **James Edward,** 1846
Monken, Friedr.—46, from Oestrich am Rhine, w—Christine nee Sauer † VIII.1846, age 46; ch—Hein. † IX.1846, age 18, near Seguin; Rosina † IX.1846, age 20, near Gonzales; Barbara † IX.1846, age 14, in New Braunfels; other ch—Bernard 10, Maria 6; (NBChR); **Neptune,** 1845
Monter, Philip—widower, 63; from Berod; **Strabo,** 1845
Moos, Edward—s, 22; **Arminius,** 1845
Moos, Herman—20, from Offdilln, Nass.; **Arminius,** 1845
Moos, Hubert—s, 20; **Sarah Ann,** 1845
Moos, Jacob—s, from Offdilln; † 3.XII.1846, age 22 (NBChR); **Sarah Ann,** 1845
Moos, Joh.—57, † 15.IX.1846, age 58; from Offdilln; w—Elisa nee Goling 45; ch—Chs. 12, Charlotte 10, Minna 7; **Arminius,** 1845
Moos, Joh.—from Offdilln, Nass.; sons—Joh. H. C., Jacob Leonard, Joh. Christ.; **Arminius,** 1845
Moos, Michael—from Hallgarten; † 10.VII.1846, age 34; ch—Jacob † 1846, age 12; Maria † 1846, age 8; Anton † 1846, age 3; **Sarah Ann,** 1845
Moos, Michael—s, 29; from Kiedrich; Guadalupe Co.; **Washington,** 1845
Moris, Aug.—s, 33; from Fulda; 3 persons, w—Adelheid nee Stumpf 24; DeWitt Co.; **Neptune** 1845
Moritz, Germain—s, New Braunfels 1845; a Castro colonist; **Ocean,** 1844
Morzinski, Franz—s, 24; **Harriet,** 1845
Mosar, Arnold—s; from Berlin; **Mercur,** 1846
Mosel, Nic.—from Niedersohren; w—Elisa; ch—Nic., Peter, Mary C.; Gillespie Co.; **James Edward,** 1846
Mosel, Nic. (son)—from Niedersohren; **James Edward,** 1846
Moser, Hein.—s, † 21.IX.1846, age 25 (NBChR); **Sarah Ann,** 1845

Mottle, Richard—s, from Effringen; arr. 1846
Moye, Albert—26; from Asbach, Kurh.; w—Mathilde nee Braun; ch—Otto, Wilhme; Bexar Co.; **Neptune,** 1845
Muecke, Hein.—from Lenzen, a/Elbe; w—Friedricke nee Grundgrieper; ch—Hein.; Marie, Joh.; Austin Co.; **Orient,** 1846
Muehlbrecht(Muehlenbrecht), Geo. Hein.—from Wildemann a/Harz, † VI.1846, age 38; w—Marie Cath. nee Ohse † 21.X.1846, age 38; from Wetteborn, Han.; ch—Friedke Magda † 1846, age 2(NBChR); **Talisman,** 1846
Muehle, Hein.—from Nettlingen, Han.; arr. 1845
Muehlfeld, Hein.—s, 25; from Gross Burgwedel; **George Delius,** 1845
Mueller, A.—from Antwerp; **Talisman,** 1846
Mueller, A.—from Heiligendorf, Han.; w—Anna nee Tendler; son—Johannes; **Flavius,** 1846
Mueller, Alex—from Elz, Nassau; 7 persons; w—Anna nee Schenck; **B. Bohlen,** 1845
Mueller, Andreas—from Heiligendorf, Han.; w—Johanne nee Albers; ch—Sophie; **Karl Ferdinand,** 1846
Mueller, Anton Carl—s, from Lehesten, Meiningen; Galveston Co.; **Flavius,** 1846
Mueller, Carl—s, 21; from Heilbronn; **Sarah Ann,** 1845
Mueller, Christian—s, 27; from Oberschönau, Kurh.; **Everhard,** 1845
Mueller, Christoph—s, 25; from Tappenbeck, Han.; Gillespie Co.; **Everhard,** 1845
Mueller, Conrad—from Breslau; **Mathilde,** 1846
Mueller, Dr. J(?)—s, from Frankfurt a/Main; **Talisman,** 1846
Mueller, Edward—m; **St. Pauli,** 1847
Mueller, Ernst—from Wülfinghausen; arr. 1845
Mueller, Franz Jos.—s, 27; from Rupertshofen; **Riga,** 1846
Mueller, Fried.—from Hohenhameln, Han.; **Anna,** 1846
Mueller, Friedr.—s, from Wangelnstedt; **Sophie,** 1846
Mueller, Friedr.—s, 22; from Jeinsen, Han.,; **Gesina,** 1846
Mueller, Friedr.—from Louisenthal; 2 persons; **Colchis,** 1846
Mueller, Friedr.—s, 28; **Apollo,** 1844
Mueller, Friedr.—**St. Pauli,** 1847
Mueller, Georg—m, from Bingen; **Hamilton,** 1846

Mueller, Georg—s, 25; from Hesse, **Weser**, 1844
Mueller, Georg Friedr.—s, died; from Haberschlacht; Caro. Rückle—dau. and heir; arr. 1846
Mueller, Gerhard—s, 18; **Franziska**, 1846
Mueller. H.—and son Johannes; **Flavius**, 1846
Mueller, (Miller), Haver—from Kisslegg, Württ.; 4 persons; ¯**Riga**, 1845
Mueller, Hein.—from Jeinsen, Han.; w—Dorette nee Schuetten; 5 persons; **Gesina**, 1846
Mueller, Hein. Conrad—from Dillenburg; 6 persons and 1 baby; **York**, 1846
Mueller, Jacob—s, 36; New Braunfels 1845; **Ferdinand**, 1844
Mueller, Jacob—s, from Ilsfeld; **Talisman**, 1846
Mueller, Jacob—30; from Gmund; **Joh. Dethardt**, 1845
Mueller, Joachim—s, from Breitenfelde; **B. Bohlen**, 1846
Mueller, Joh.—from Feudinger-Hütte; 3 persons; **York**, 1846
Mueller, Joh.—s, 31; from Welschneudorf; **Auguste Meline**, 1845
Mueller, Joh. Christian—from Tappenbeck; **Everhard**, 1845
Mueller, Joh. Friedr.,—from Wolfenbuttel; **Louise**, 1846
Mueller, Joh. Georg—s, †1846; from Thomashardt; Comal Co.; **Hamilton**, 1846
Mueller, Joh. Georg—from Ober Heinriet; **Hamilton**, 1846
Mueller, Joh. Hein.—m, from Wolfenbuttel; **Louise**, 1846
Mueller, Joh. Jos.—from Lenterode, wife and ch—Aug., Wilh., Nic., Christ.; Victoria Co.; **B. Bohlen**, 1845
Mueller, Jos.—s, 18; **B. Bohlen**, 1845
Mueller, Josef—m, from Elz; Austin Co.; arr. 1846
Mueller, Lorenz—33 and wife, from Goppertsofen; Austin Co.; **Riga**, 1846
Mueller, Ludwig—†8.VIII.1846, age 28, from Darmstadt; **Andacia**, 1846
Mueller, M. J.—from Bremen; **Riga**, 1846
Mueller, Marg. Louise—from Mainz; **Talisman**, 1846
Mueller, Martin—s, from Gemmingen; **Talisman**, 1846
Mueller, Martin—s, 18; from Jeinsen, Han.; **Gesina**, 1846
Mueller, Matt.—from Goppertshofen, 9 persons; **Riga**, 1846
Mueller (Moeller?), Michael—from Cardobang,Schwarzburg;w—Elis. nee Eisenkraut; Washington Co.; **Margaretha**, 1846
Mueller, Peter—w and 3 ch; from Goppertshofen; **Riga**, 1846
Mueller, Peter—from Bullau; w and 3 ch; **Nahant** (wrecked); then **Timoleon**, 1846
Mueller, Peter and family—from Elberfeld; Gillespie Co.; **Henry**, 1846
Mueller, Peter Jos.—from Cadenbach, Nassau; w—Cath. nee Zerbach; ch—Marg., Joh., Jacob; **Auguste Meline**, 1845
Mueller, Philipp—from Zwergen, Kurh.; w—Maria nee Jordan; ch—Caro.; Hein; **Mercur**, 1846
Mueller, Philipp David—s, 18; from Rettert, Nass.; **Neptune**, 1845
Mueller, Val. Sebastian—from Oberschonau; wife and 1 ch; Goliad Co.; **Everhard**, 1845
Mueller, Wendlin—s, from Mainz; **Harriet**, 1845
Mueller, Wilh.—s, 31; **Harriet**, 1845
Mueller, Wilh.—from Heiligendorf, Han.; **Flavius**, 1846
Mueller, Wilh.—from Lehesten, Meiningen; w—Caro. nee Walforth; ch—Gustav, Ida, Caro., Otto, Emelie; **Flavius**, 1846
Mueller, Wilh.—25, from Burgdorf, Han.; **Hercules**, 1845
Mueller, Wilh.—s, from Peine, Han.; arr. 1845
Muench, Adam—s, from Sprendlingen; Gillespie Co.; **Andacia**, 1846
Muenckel, Georg Friedr.—s, from Clausthal a/Harz; Gillespie Co.; **Karl Ferdinand**, 1846
Muenker, Friedr.—s, from Herborn; **York**, 1846
Muenzler, Friedr.—s, 32; from Olnhausen, Württ.; New Braunfels 1845; Comal Co. 1850's; **Johann Dethardt**, 1844
Muenzler, Georg Andreas—from Olnhausen; 6 persons; Austin Co.; **Nahant** 1846, wrecked at sea; then **Timoleon**, 1846
Muenzler, G. Chr—from Olnhausen; 6 persons; **Nahant** 1846 wrecked at sea, then **Timoleon**, 1846
Muessel, Christian—s, from Bodenwerder; **Sophie**, 1846
Mundt, Conrad Chr.—s, 18; from Barwedel; **Gerhard Hermann**, 1846
Munk, Christoph—s, from Dungelbeck by Peine, Han.; **Weser**, 1845
Munk, Friedr.—s, from Dungelbeck, Han.; **Weser**, 1845
Murthens, Franz—s, 42; from Hildesheim, Han.; **Weser**, 1845

124

Muth, Christian—s, † 26.VIII.1849;
from Haberschlacht; **Diamant**,
1846
Mylius, Dr. Adolph—from Ho-
henhamelin; w—Emilie nee
Stieren; **Anna**, 1846
Mylius, Fredelin—s, 30; from Bernard—Hütte; **Andacia**, 1846

— N —

Naegele(Negele) David and
family—from Kaub; 1846
Nanz, David H.—s, 23, from Gablen-
berg; **Andacia**, 1846
Napp, Johann D.—m, 44, from Katz-
enelnbogen; w—Maria M. 42; ch—
Maria 10, Frederika 14; Calhoun
Co.; **Andacia**, 1846
Narten, Christian—m, from Lem-
go (Lemke?), Han; died 1849; w—
Wilhme nee Sauder; son—Hein;
Everhard, 1845
Nauch, Joh. Fr.—from Sülfeld; arr.
1845
Naurath, Wilh.—s, from Diez;
Guadalupe Co.; **Bohemia**, 1846
Nebgen, Anton—s, 23; from
Unterhausen; Travis Co.; **Riga**,
1846
Neeb, Ludwig—s,24; from Stein;
Washington, 1845
Neffendorf, Jacob—from Rettert,
Nass.; Gillespie Co.; **Neptune**, 1845
Negedank, Louis—s, 28; arr. 1844;
New Braunfels 1845
Neher, Fried.—m, from Winter-
lingen; died 1846; heirs—Hans
Jurgen and Maria; **Andacia**, 1846
Nehrlich, Friedr.—from Tackau,
Prussia; w—Friedricke nee Schir-
mer; **Elisa & Charlotte**, 1846
Neitsch, Edward—s, from Berlin;
arr. 1845; Fayette Co.
Neitsch, N.—m; from Berlin;
Fayette Co.; arr. 1845
Nette, Dr. August—s, 21; New
Braunfels, 1845; **Ferdinand**, 1844
Netz, Emmerich, and w—Marie;
Gerhard Hermann, 1846
Neuber, Adolph—s, from Kassel;
Kendall Co.; **Friedrich**, 1846
Neuber, Otto—s, from Kassel; Ken-
dall Co.; **Friedrich**, 1846
Neuendorf, Anton—s, 26; Fayette
Co.; **Apollo**, 1844
Neurath, Joh—30, from Horbach;
died 1846; age 31; w—Elis. 21;
ch—Louis 9 mo.; **Fredericks-
burg; Strabo**, 1845
Neuse, Adam—from Katzenstein; 5
persons; Guadalupe Co.; **Talisman**,
1846

Neuse, Carl Ernst—s, Comal Co.;
Talisman, 1846
Neuse, Widow—Comal Co. 1855
Neuser, Martin—from Netphen by
Siegen; 3 persons; **Element**, 1846
Newig, Christet—from Gadenstedt;
1845
Newig, Hein.—35, from Gadenstedt,
Han.; w—Sophie(Marie) nee
Moellring 30; ch—Sophie 16, Caro.
4; **Hercules**, 1845
Nickel, Christian Friedr. Wilh.;
from Mademühlen, Nass. †
11.VI.1846 age 27 (NBChR); sis-
ter—Elis. 40; ch—Ludw. 14, Louise
18; Comal Co.; **Herschel**, 1845
Nickel, Joh. Jost—37. from Bicken,
Nass.; w—Anna Cath.—35; Comal
Co.; **Herschel**, 1845
Nicolay, F.—Fredericksburg
Niebeling, J. C. A.—from Berlin;
w—Johanna nee Pertis(c)h and 1
ch; **Franziska**, 1846
Niebuhr, II, Christoph—from
Brome, Han.; 1846
Niebuhr I, Friedrich Wilhelm—from
Brome, Han.; Austin Co.; 1846
Niedmann, Aug—s, 40; from Ein-
beck; **Franziska**, 1846
Niemann, Anton—36, from Prussia;
wife and Maria Agnes 5, Joseph
1; **Weser**, 1844
Niemann, Elisa—from Alfeld, Han.;
Galveston Co.; **Margaretha**, 1845
Niemann, Friederike—from Hil-
desheim, Han.; Galveston Co.;
Margaretha, 1845
Niemann, Hein.—from Hannover;
Galveston Co.; **Gerhard Hermann**,
1846
Niemann, Hein.—40, and John;
Fayette Co. 1848; **Agnes**, from
New Orleans
Niemeier, Friedr.—s, from
Waldbruch; **Mercur**, 1846
Niemitz, Carl Hein.—s, steamer
Galveston from New Orleans, 1846
Nimitz, Charles H.—Gillespie Co.
1850
Nieper, Joh.—from Jembke, Han.;
Karl Ferdinand, 1846
Nink, Mathias—from Erbach; 5 per-
sons and 1 baby; Bastrop Co.;
Bohemia, 1846
Nittweber, Wilh.—from Peine; 1845
Nix, Hein. Ludw.—34, from Dil-
lenburg, Nass; †7.VII.1850 age 38
(NBChR); w—Johanna (Rosa
Elis.) nee Breitenstein; ch—Maria
Louise; **Joh. Dethardt**, 1845
Nocker, Ph.—from Hallgarten; 4
persons; 1845
Noelke, Theodor—from Hachen; 3
persons; **Diamant**, 1846

Noll, Joh.—from Molsberg, Nass.; †
15.VII.1846, age 46; w—Anna
Maria nee Jung † 12.VII.1846, age
49; Joh. Adam †1846, age 16, Marg.
†1846, age 16, Philipp †1846, age
15, Peter †1846, age 11, Joh. †1845,
age 6 (died at sea), Sophie †1846,
age 4½ (NBChR); B. Bohlen, 1845
Noll, Martin and wife—B. Bohlen,
1845
Noll, Val.—8 persons, from Eltville;
arr. 1845
Nolte, Ferd—s, from Erlinghausen;
Comal Co.; Hamilton, 1846
Nolte, Hein.—37, from Waldeck;
w—Cath.; ch—Justine Auguste 10,
Anna Maria 3; Comal Co.; Weser,
1844
Nonn, W.—from Bröhl; 2 persons;
1845
Norbach, William—20; Dyle, 1846
Nordhausen, Ludw. and family—
from Naumburg, Prussia; Fayette
Co.; Friedrich, 1846
Nordhoff, Anton and Carl—from
Salzheiersum, Han.; 3 persons;
Margaretha, 1845
Norstein, Conrad—from Mardorf;
1845
Nuettelmann, Chr.—24, and Hein. s,
18; from Patersberg, Nassau;
Gerhard Hermann, 1846
Nuettelmann, Joh. Hein.—†1846;
from Dahlskamp, Han.; w—Maria
nee Krek; ch—Elisa, Maria, Wilh.;
Gerhard Hermann, 1846
Nugetter, Joh.—from Behringen,
Thüringia; w—Margarete nee
Stede; Sophie, 1846
Nunn, W.—from Brol.; 2 persons;
1845
Nusser, Felix—s, 23; from Ebingen;
Dyle, 1846

— O —

Obenhaus, widow with 4 ch.—Apollo,
1844
Obert, Jacob—m, Comal Co.; St.
Pauli, 1847
Odenhass, Joh.—s, 26; Franziska,
1846
Oehring, Joh.—from Mehlis bei Zel-
la; w—Sibilla nee Dier; ch—
Robert, Auguste, Aug.; Flavius,
1846
Oelkers, Hein.—s, 17; from Segeste,
Han.; Guadalupe Co.; Margaretha,
1845
Oelkers, Hein.—from Segeste, Han.;
w—Louise nee Rodemann; ch—
Hein., Wilh., Conrad, Christian,
Friedr., Ernst, Christoph, Julius;
Guadalupe Co.; Margaretha, 1845
Oelkers, Joh. Hein. Ch. Ph.—s,
Margaretha, 1845

Oelkers, W. H.—m, had Verein land
grant
Oertling, H.—s, from Görslow;
Talisman, 1846
Oetermann, Emilie—from Helm-
scherode, Brnschwg; Mar-
garetha, 1845
Ohlendorf, Carl—from Heiningen; 2
persons; Austin Co.; B. Bohlen,
1845
Ohlendorf, Ludw.—s, 21; from
Wolfelade (=Wolferode?), Han.;
Weser, 1845
Oldenhausen, Wilh.—from Hörsum;
1845
Oltmann, Joh.—s, 29, and Oltmann,
Joh. Hein.—s, 26; from Hannover;
Austin Co.; Ferdinand, 1845
Onken, Herm.—s, 20; Fayette Co.;
Franziska, 1846
Oppermann, Andreas—s, from
Burgdorf, Han.; Galveston Co.;
Friedrich, 1846
Oppermann, Friedr.—s, from Döl-
me; Bexar Co.; or Victoria Co.;
Mercur, 1846
Oppermann, Gottfried—from Hil-
desheim, Han.; w—Sabine nee
Waldmann; ch—Marie, Theresa,
Herm., Friedr., Antoinette; Gill-
espie Co.; Creole, 1846
Oppermann, Martin—s, from Burg-
dorf, Han.; Friedrich, 1846
Orphans at Waisenfarm (or-
phanage) in 1850 with Pastor
Ervendberg in New Braunfels:
Bitter, Augustine
Fromme, Daniel
Guenther, Christian
Koether, Wilhelmine
Kretzer, Wilhelm
Kreikenbaum, Hein.
Lange, Franziska
Lange, Louise
Schmidt, Lisette
Schmidt, Natalie
Schuessler, Caroline
Stendebach, Marie
Walter, Friedrich
Walter, George
Walter, Peter
Weber, Friedrich
Weber, Heinrich
Wessinger, Joh.
(Copied from HISTORY OF NEW
BRAUNFELS AND COMAL CO.
by Oscar Haas, page 248)
Orth, Anna M. nee Geibel—from Ort,
Bavaria, † 21.IV.1847, age 67
(NBChR)
Orth, Joh.—from Welgesheim;
Comal Co.; Hamilton, 1846
Ortlepp, Henry W.—from Ohrdruff;
w—Elisa B.; ch—Dor., Aug.,
Friedr.; Galveston Co.; Dyle, 1846
Osse, Pius—arr. 1845

Osterhausen, Moritz von—s, from Herzfeld; **Franziska**, 1846
Osthaus, Hein.—from Hildesheim, Han.; **Anna**, 1846
Othmer, Friedr.—s, from Gestorf, Han.; † 8.VIII.1846, age 26 (NBChR); **Gesina**, 1846
Otte, Friedr. Joh.—from Lohne, Prussia; w—Dor. nee Harmsen; **Louise Friedrike**. 1847
Otte, Hein. Friedr.—from Bissendorf; ch—Dor. nee Walken; ch—Sophie, Charlotte, Friedr., Joh., Dor., Wilhme; Gillespie Co.; **Weser**, 1845
Ottenhausen, Wilh.—from Harsum, Han.; w—Christina nee Ochsewk(?); ch—Hein., Louise; **Gerhard Hermann**, 1846
Ottens, Joh. and wife—Marie nee Koehler; **B. Bohlen**, 1845
Ottens, Jürgen Hinrich—from Ottingen, Han.; 7 persons; w—Ilse nee Engel; ch—Joh., Friedr., Cath. †1846, age 24; Comal Co.; **B. Bohlen**, 1845
Otto, Adolph—s, from Nordheim; Harris Co.; **Andacia**, 1846
Otto, Chr.—s, 23; **Andacia**, 1846
Otto, Ludwig—from Zellerfeld, Han.; son—August; **Johann Dethardt**, 1846

— P —

Padderatz(Padelratz), Hein.—from Marlow, Mklbg; **Mathilde**, 1846
Palm, Barbara—23; **Andacia**, 1846
Palm, Joachim—from Laaslich; died; w—Wilhme nee Kuhn; ch—Friedr., Joh., Joachim, Marie Caro., Rudolph; Widow Palm; Austin Co. 1850; **Orient**, 1846
Palm, Wilh.—s, 26; from Bruchweiler; **Dyle**, 1846
Palmer, Joseph—s, 31; from Rothemühl; **Weser**, 1844
Panthel, Christian—from Drinhausen; w and 2 ch; **Henry**, 1846
Panthel, Wilh.—50, from Mannheim; **Andacia**, 1846
Pape, Andreas—35, from Gadenstedt, Han.; w—Cath. 30; ch—Andreas II, Conrad 9, Dorette 3, Louise 2; Comal Co.; **Hercules**, 1845
Pape, Anton—s, 45; **B. Bohlen**, 1845
Pape, Carl—s, from Stadtoldendorf; Gillespie Co.; **Sophie**, 1846
Pape, Christian—s, 24; from Sossmar, Han.; Comal Co.; **Gerhard Hermann**, 1846
Pape, Conrad—40, from Gadenstedt, Han.; w—Dor.(Meta) nee Badenstadt 39; ch—Hein. 15, Dor. 12, Christian 10, Conrad W. 8, Wilh. 2, Caro. ½; Comal Co.; **Hercules**, 1845
Pape, Friedr.—28, from Gadenstedt, Han.; w—Frederike (Cath.) nee Voges 29; ch—Dorette 6, Johanne 4, Caro.; Friedr. ½; Gillespie Co.; **Hercules**, 1845
Pape, Joh. Hein.—37, from Gadenstedt, Han.; w—Ernestine nee Hasper 30; ch—Hein., 8, Carl 5, Wilh. 3; **Hercules**, 1845
Pape, Sophie—28; **Hercules**, 1845
Pape, Wilh.—s, from Wenz(Wenze?, Winz?), Prussia; **B. Bohlen**, 1847
Pasquier, Eugen du—from Neuchatel; 1845
Pauli, Peter—m, from Würges; 4 persons and 1 baby; Comal Co.; **Bohemia**, 1846
Pauling, Friedr.—s, **Weser**, 1845
Pauling, Hein.—s, 18; **Weser**, 1845
Pauling, Joh. Jurgen. Fried.—died; from Abbensen, Han.; w—Marie nee Debke; ch—Hein, Anna; **Weser**, 1845
Paulmann, Christian—m, from Handeloh; arr. 1846
Paulsick, T.—s, 25; **Franziska**, 1846
Pawski, Matthias—from Gorszyn, Poland; w—Anna nee Kobiuska; ch—Georg, Marie, Jos., Peter, Menzel, Franziska; **Flavius**, 1846
Peetz, Friedr. Wilh.—s, from Clausthal a/Harz; arr. 1846
Pehl, Joh. Adam—35, from Holler. Nass.; w—Anna Maria nee Lenz; ch—Elis. 12, Peter 9, Helena 7; Gillespie Co.; **Hercules**, 1845
Pehl, Peter—45, from Holler, Nassau; w—Gesina, 33; Adam 11, Sophia 9, Mathias 7, Joh. ½ yr.; Gillespie Co.; **Hercules**, 1845
Pehl, widow—38; Marg. 17; **Hercules**, 1845
Pelzer, Adam—from NiederElbert; w—Anna Marg. nee Marx † 9.VIII.1846, age 35; 4 children; New Braunfels 1845; **Herschel**, 1844
Pelzer, Michael—s, from Beaufort; **Henry**, 1846
Penshorn, Joh. Hein.—from Essel, Han.; w—Maria nee Meine; ch—Hein., Friedrike; Friedr., Elis., Edward; Comal Co.; **George Delius**, 1845
Peper, Christian—from Brotterode, Kurh.; w—Maria nee Muench; **Friedrich**, 1846
Pepper, Edward—s, 18; **George Delius**, 1845
Pepper, Friedr.—from Isenbüttel, Han.; w—Dor. nee Woltern;

127

ch—Ernst. s, 20; Friedr. s, 20; Hein.
†21.II.1847, age 18 (NBChR); Wilh,
Carl, Christ., Dor., Comal Co.;
Everhard, 1845
Pepper, Hein.—from Gifhorn, †
21.II.1847, age 17; (NBChR)
Perings, George—from Celle; arr.
1845; see Beringer, Georg
Perris, M. F.—† before 1860; had
land grant
Peter, Anna—from Rabenscheid,
Nass; **George Delius,** 1845
Peter, Gerlach—† 8.VII.1845 age 51,
from Bretthausen, Nass.; w—El-
ise Cath. nee Reh † 23.VI.1845, age
50; (NBChR); Wilhme Peter heir,
Johann Dethardt, 1844
Peter, Hein.—from Wattenbach; arr.
1845
Peter, Joh.—from Merkenbach,
Nass.; † 3.VI.1846, age 19; oo Cath.
Kloes 26.II.1846 in San Antonio;
(NBChR)
Peter, Joh. Conrad—from Merken-
bach, Nassau; †22.V.1847, age 53;
son—Joh. †3.VI.1846, age 19 son—
Joh. Hein. only heir; **Arminius,**
1845
Peter, Joh. Hein.—s, from Ober-
scheld; **York,** 1846
Peter, Mathias and daughter—from
Holler, Nass.; **Hercules,** 1845
Peter, Peter—from Holler, Nass.;
w—Marg. nee Stein; ch—Adam,
Sophie; **Hercules,** 1845
Peter, Wilh.—from Ebergötzen;
w—Henriette nee Webner; **Mar-
garetha,** 1846
Petermann, Franz—s, Gillespie Co.;
Andacia, 1846
Peters, Christian—s, 30; from Lich-
tenberg, Brnschwg.; **Gerhard Her-
mann,** 1846
Peters, Friedr.—s, 23; Galveston Co.;
Everhard, 1845
Peters, Joseph—New Braunfels
1845; **Ocean,** 1844
Petersdorf, Friedr.—s, 44; from
Berenbostel, Han.; **George Delius,**
1845
Petmecky, Joseph Gottfried—38,
from Schönau; w—Anna nee
Huebner; from Stadthofen, Nass.;
†19.III.1847, age 35; ch—Franz 11,
Marie 10, Theresa 6, Jos. 4, Lisette
½; **Strabo,** 1845
Petri, Joh.—s, 34; from Lorch, Rü-
desheim; Gillespie Co.; **Auguste
Meline,** 1845, or **Joh. Dethardt,** 1845
Petri, Joh. Hein.—from Breitscheid,
Nass.; w—Elisa nee Aht; ch—Ja-
cob Hein. †1846, age 14; Cath. †
1846, age 10; Marg., Joh.;
(NBChR); Comal Co.; **Aususte
Meline,** 1845

Petri, (Petry), Ludwig—s, 18; **George
Delius,** 1846
Petri, Nicolaus—s, 23; from
Stephanshausen; **Washington,**
1845
Petri, Philipp—23; from Ballers-
bach, Nass.; died; w—Cath. nee
Petri 36, ch—Maria 10, Henrietta
8, Cath. 5; **Neptune,** 1845
Petsch—see Poetsch
Peyke, John—s, 30; from Germany;
Galveston, 1846
Pfaff, Albert—from Anklam, **Apollo,**
1846
Pfaff, Edward—s, 26; from Anklam;
Apollo, 1846
Pfaff, Joh. Wilh.—3 persons; from
Anklam; **Apollo,** 1846
Pfanne, Gottfried—s, from Ummen-
dorf, Prussia; **Sophie,** 1846
Pfannenschmid(t), Georg—from
Einbeck, Han.; w—Elenore nee
Bause; **Creole,** 1846
Pfannstiel, Fried. Wilh.—s, 19;
Guadalupe Co.; **Garonne,** 1845
Pfannstiehl, Justus David—41; from
Trusen, Kurh.; w—Maria Elisa
nee Erbelein 43; ch—Friedr. 19,
Anna Marie 17, Joh. G. 15, Maria
12, Caspar 8, Fried Aug. 2; **Ga-
ronne,** 1845
Pfannstiel, Ludwig—s, 19; from
Osterode a/Harz; Guadalupe Co.;
Flavius, 1846
Pfefferkorn, Christian—s, from
Kreuzburg; **Andacia,** 1846
Pfefferkorn, Friedr. Aug.—s, 24;
from Kreuzburg; 5 persons;
Andacia, 1846
Pfeiffer, Eberhard—s, from Bischoff-
en; **Element,** 1846
Pfeiffer, J.—s, 20; **Neptune,** 1845
Pfeiffer, Joh.—s, from Erbach; Gal-
veston Co.; **Bohemia,** 1846
Pfeiffer(=Pfeuffer?), Sabine—age
38; **Washington,** 1845
Pfeister, Carl Aug.—from Ber-
lebeck, Detmold; **Neptune,** 1846
Pfetzing, Anna Elis.—from Ster-
kelshausen; Galveston Co.;
Everhard, 1845
Pfeuffer, Georg—s, from Obernbreit;
Comal Co.; **Washington,** 1845
Pfeuffer, Georg—45, from
Obernbreit,; w—Barbara 38;
ch—Joh. 15, Val. 13, Christ. 11,
Dan. 7, Barbara 4, Anna 1½;
Comal Co.; **Washington,** 1845
Phillip,---, and w—Anna Marg.;
ch—Anna Elisa, Ph. Hein., Cath.;
Herschel, 1845
Philippi, Friedr.—s, from Boppard;
York, 1846
Philippus, Joh.—w and 2 ch; **George
Delius,** 1845

Philippus, Jost Heinr.—† 1847; from Rabenscheid, Nassau; w—Cath. nee Peter; ch—Ferd., Juliana, Justine; George Delius, 1845
Phillipsen, E.—s, 30; from Germany; arr. 1846
Picker, Christian—s, 28; from Neudorf, Han.; Everhard, 1845
Piel, Wilh.—from Westfeld, Han.; w and 5 ch; Galveston Co.; B. Bohlen, 1845
Pieper, Aug. Anton—s, 22; Bastrop Co.; George Delius, 1845
Pilger, Martin—s, from Bruchköbel; Colorado Co.; Louise Friedrike, 1847
Pinkel, Chr.—† 16.VIII.1846, age 38; w—Johanna † 12.IV.1846, age 32; Carolina † 1846, age 14, Johanna † 1846, age 12, Hermann † 1847, age 5 (NBChR); Wilhelmina; from Berzahn, Nassau; Washington, 1845
Pipo,(Piepho), Christ.—from Nienstedt, Han. † 1846 age 40,(NBChR); w—Dor. nee Gerkens; ch—Hein., Fried., Christine, Carolina; Gesina, 1846
Pitton, Anton and wife—from Rennerod; Riga, 1846
Pitton, Widow and 3 ch—from Rennerod; Riga, 1846
Pitton, Georg—from Rennerod, w—Maria nee Halm from Winkel, Nass.; † 15.X.1846, age 34 (NBChR); Auguste Meline, 1845
Plehve, C. von—had lot in Fredericksburg, 1847
Pletz, Joh. Peter—50, from Breitscheid, Nass.; w—Anna Maria 48; ch—Georg, Wilhme, Ernestine, Hein., Cath.; Gillespie Co.; Auguste Meline, 1845
Pletz, Wilh.—s, 18; from Breitscheid, Nass.; Auguste Meline, 1845
Pleuss, Diedrich—w and 3 ch; Apollo, 1844
Pluecker, Emil—s, from Bilk by Düsseldorf; Strabo, 1845
Pluenneke, Conrad—from Klein Lafferde; w and 2 ch; Conrad and w; Charles and w; Herman—s, 18; 10 persons; Gillespie Co.; Apollo, 1846
Poetel, Hein.—had lot in Fredericksburg, 1847
P(o)etsch, Johann—47, from Frickhofen; w—Elisa 40; ch—(Joh.) Jacob † 1846, age 13, Joh. Juerg (Georg) † 1846 age 12, Elisa † 1847, age 10, Jacob † 1846, age 9, Christian 5, Cath. 2; Gillespie Co.; Washington, 1845
P(o)etsch, Joh.—s, 17; from Frickhofen; Washington, 1845
P(o)etsch, Peter—s, 20; from Frickhofen; Gillespie Co.; Washington, 1845
P(o)etsch, Wilh.—from Clausthal; Karl Ferdinand, 1846
Pohlmann, Adolph—s, 23; from Lanau bei Elze, Han.; † 26.IX.1846 age 23,(NBChR); Apollo, 1844
Pohlmann, Hein. Christoph Conrad—s, 51; from Horst, Han.; Weser, 1845
Polendz, Joh.—s, from Potsdam; Louise Friedrike, 1847
Polster, Joh.—s, from Schleifhäusle, Württ.; Flavius, 1846
Pook, Ludwig—from Dohrenburg (=Dohrens?); near Grohnde, Han.; New Braunfels 1845; Johann Dethardt, 1844
Poppitz, Carl—s, from Hermsdorf, Prussia; Joh. Dethardt, 1846
Post III, Joh. Peter—from Roth, Nass.; w—Maria nee Goebel 39; ch—Christina, Cath., Ludwig, Friedr. Hein., †1.V.1846 age 9 (NBChR); Arminius, 1845
Potthof, Wilh—s, from Enkhausen; † in 1900 in Galveston storm; Diamant, 1846
Prahm, Christian—from Villmar; 6 persons; Austin Co.; James Edward, 1846
Prehn, Otto—from Mikitzsch (Militzsch?); near Breslau, arr. 1845
Preilipper, Joh. Hein.—s, from Unterhasel, Rudolstadt; Joh. Dethardt, 1844
Preiss, Anton—25, and Cath.; from Oberschönau, Kurh.; Cath. † 1.IX.1846, age 22 (NBChR); Everhard, 1845
Preiss, Joh.—from Bodenwerder, Brnschwg; Mercur, 1846
Preiss, Joh. Christian—from Oberschonau, Kurh.; w—Cath. nee Scherschmidt; ch—Marie,Auguste,Aug.; Gillespie Co.; Everhard, 1845
Preiss, Joh. Friedr.—from Oberschönau, Kurh.; Everhard, 1845
Preiss, Joh. Theo.—from Langwiesen near Ilmenau, w—Maria nee Schumm; Mathilda, 1846
Pressler, Carl—from Eisleben; surveyor for de Cordova; worked in state of Texas Land Office 1850-1899; Franziska, 1846
Preuss, Albert—s, 25; Weser, 1845
Preusser, Gottfried—46; from Neesbach; w—Louise 44; ch—Phillipine 17, Phillip 14, Dorothea 11, Theresa 7, Christiane † 1846, age 7 (NBChR), Joseph 3, Christian 1; Comal Co.; Washington, 1845
Preusser, Joh. Georg—s, 21; from Neesbach; Comal Co.; Washington, 1845

129

Priess, Joh.—from Damgarten, Gillespie Co.; **Mercur**, 1846
Priester, Carl August—from Berlebeck, Detmold; arr. 1846; **Harris Co.**
Prinke, Friedr.—s, from Fallersleben, Han.; **Karl Ferdinand**, 1846
Probst, Fried. and sister—from Helmscherode, Brnschwg; **Margaretha**, 1846
Pueschel, Aug.—from Spremberg; **Mathilde**, 1846

— Q —

Quantz, Conrad—s, **Colchis**, 1846
Querin, Joh.—s, from Coblenz; **James Edward**, 1846
Quindel, Christian—from Schulenburg, Han.; w—Elisa; ch—Dor., Caro., Adolph; Gillespie Co.; **Gerhard Hermann**, 1846
Quitzow, Albert von—s, **Alabama**, from N. O. 1845

— R —

Rabe, Aug.—s, 34; from Carlshütte; Fayette Co.; **Margaretha, 1845**
Rabe, Caro. and Wilhme—from Westfeld, Han.; **Margaretha**, 1845
Rabe, Hein.—44, from Waldeck; has family, but wife and children to follow, **Weser**, 1844
Rabe, Peter—s, from Friedrichsbruch, Prussia; **Johanna**, 1846
Rabke, Aug. Ludw. Conrad—from Hohnsen, Han.; w—Friedricke nee Regali; **Everhard**, 1845
Rachermann, Friedricke—from Hohe, Brnschwg; **Mercur**, 1846
Radensleben, F.—s, 30; from Stolzenau; Washington Co.; **Weser, 1844**
Rahm, Joh. Jacob—from Schaffhausen, † 12.X.1845, age 39; **New Braunfels, 1845**
Rain, A. E.—m, from Steinburg; arr. **1846**
Ram (Ramm), A.—New Braunfels **1845**
Ramdohr, Adolph—m, from Veckenstedt; **B. Bohlen, 1847**
Ramm, Friedr. and wife—Washington Co.; **Apollo, 1844**
Ransleben, Julius Joh. Ludw.—from Leipzig; I w—Maria nee Spannagel; II w—Josephine nee Klier; Gillespie Co.; **Mathilde**, 1846
Ranzau, Ludwig—from Vöhrum, Han.; † 15.VIII.1846, age 55; w—Marie nee Ernst †13.VII.1846,

age 43; ch—Caro. †1846, age 10½, Dorette † 1846, age 3 (NBChR); other ch—Mina, Ludwig; **Everhard**, 1845
Rass, Christian Witte—**Louise**, 1846
Rassing, Henriette—from Schöppenstedt; **Louise**, 1846
Rau, Val.—s, 24; from Hattenheim; **Harriet**, 1845
Rauch, Joh. Carl—from Sülfeld, Han.; **Creole**, 1846
Rauch, Joh. Friedr.—from Sülfeld, Han.; w—Henriette nee Meyer; ch—Friedr., Friedricke, Hein.; Comal Co.; **Creole**, 1846
Rauhe, G.—from Berlin, arr. 1845
Real, Casper—came to Texas 1847; * in Düsseldorf; w—Mathilde nee Schreiner; ch—Emma, Mathilde; **Kendall Co.**
Real, Julius—* in Düsseldorf, came to Texas in 1847; **Kendall Co.**
Rechsen, Conrad—arr. 1845; died 1846; Carl, Johanna—ch and heirs
Reckels, Herm.—s, from Ochtrup; **B. Bohlen**, 1847
Re(e)b, Aug.—s, 34; from Dillenburg, Nassau; **Arminius**, 1845
Reede, Friedrich von—32, from Dillenburg; w—Elis. nee Martin; **Arminius**, 1845
Reeh, Christian—57, and Rudolph 15; from Bretthausen; **Washington**, 1845
Reeh, Friedr.—s, 20; Fredericksburg; **Strabo**, 1845
Reeh, Joh. Gerlach—from Bretthausen; w—Charl.; ch—Dor. †1845, age 2; (NBChR) New Braunfels 1845; **Johann Dethardt**, 1844
Reeh, Sebastian—46, from Nister-Möhrendorf; w—Cath. 41;ch— Frederica 18, Ernst 14; Wilhme 11, Arnold 8; **Strabo**, 1845
Reese, Conrad—from Sibbesse, Han.; w—Johanna nee Knoessel; ch—Hein., Ernst, Karl, Johanne, Mina; **Weser**, 1845
Reese, Fried. Wilh.—s, from Holzminden, Brnschwg; New Braunfels 1845; **Ferdinand**, 1844
Regenhardt, Aug.—from Green, Brnschwg.; **Neptune**, 1845
Reher, Calon—m, from Senden bei Ulm, Bavaria; **Element**, 1846
Reher, Joh. Hein.—from Senden, bei Ulm, Bavaria; 7 persons; **Element, 1846**
Rehker, Fried.—s, 19 and Sophie, from Hildesheim; **Weser**, 1845
Rehmann, Gottfried—Gillespie Co.; **Orient**, 1846
Rehner, Lorenz F.—s, 19; from Mainz; **Sarah Ann**, 1845
Rehner, S. Benedict—s, 30; from

Mainz; Calhoun Co.; **Sarah Ann,**
1845
Reibenstein, Carl—from Celle; Austin Co.; **Apollo,** 1846
Reibenstein, H.A.—from Pattershofen; 1845
Reiche, Gottlieb—from Berlin,
w—Auguste nee Stiebler; ch—
Marie, Pauline, Anna Marie; **Creole,** 1846
Reiche, Hein. Friedr. Theo.—s, 25;
from Göttingen, Han.; Comal Co.;
Joh. Dethardt, 1845
Reidel, Helena—18, from Kiedrich;
Washington, 1845
Reider, Daniel—s, and Hein.—s,
from Lenscheid; **Colchis,** 1846
Reiermann, Joh. Friedr.—from
Heinebüchenbruch, Lippe; arr.
1845
Reiman, Balthasar—s, 20; and
John—s, 19; from Ruppach; **Harriet,** 1845
Reimann, Peter and wife—from
Ruppach; **Harriet,** 1845
Rein, Jacob—from Rappenau; 5 persons; **Nahant** (wrecked 1846), then
Timoleon, 1846
Rein, Frau Anna Elise (widow)—5
persons, from Steinberg; **Colchis,**
1846
Reinarz, Eleanore—s, 20; New
Braunfels 1845; **Joh. Dethardt,**
1845
Reinarz, Joh. Math.—65; † before
1860; from Rötgen; ch—Friedr.
10, **Regina** 13; **Dyle,** 1846
Reinarz, Joh. Wilh.—from Rötgen;
w—Friedrike nee Offermann;
ch—Caro., Eleanore, Elise,
Friedr.; Wilme Anna † 1846, age
1½ (NBChR); New Braunfels 1845;
Joh. Dethardt, 1844
Reine, Fried.—from Gronau; 1845
Reinhard, Fr. and Georg—from
Kinhard (Kühnhard, Württ.?);
New Braunfels 1845; Castro Colonists; **Henrich,** 1844
Reinhard, Friedr.—s, 43; from
Horchheim; Guadalupe Co.;
Strabo, 1845
Reinhard, Joh. Adam—from Orb,
Kendall Co.; **James Edward,** 1846
Reinhard, Georg—from Obergladbach,Nassau;w—Anna nee Rodenbach, ch—Marg † 1846, age 4
(NBChR); **Joh. Dethardt,** 1845
Reinhard, Ludwig—s, 22; DeWitt
Co.; **St. Pauli,** 1847
Reininger, Anna Maria—from
Niedenhausen, near Jostein, Nassau; **Ferdinand,** 1844
Reininger, Hein. and wife—New
Braunfels 1845; **Ferdinand,** 1844
Reininger, Joh.—s, 32; **Sarah Ann,**
1845

Reininger, Joh.—from Niedernhausen; wife and 3 ch.; Comal Co.;
Sarah Ann, 1845
Reininger, Joh. Georg—s, 32; from
Niedernhausen; **Sarah Ann,** 1845
Reis, Gustav Adloph—m, **Arminius,**
1845
Reis, Joh. Christian—from Willingen, w—Cath. (widow), ch—Ferd.
20, Gustav 17, Christian 10,
Julius 7, Henriette Wilhme 3,
† 1846, age 4 (NBChR); **Arminius,**
1845
Reis, Joh. Peter—from Stein,
w—Cath. nee Schorn; † 30.V.1846,
age 28 years, 11 mo.; ch—Wilh. †
1846, age 8½, (NBChR); Edward
2; **Washington,** 1845
Reiss, Peter—50, from Rumbach,
Hesse; **Weser,** 1844
Reiss, Valentin—from Wipperode,
Kurh., w—Sybilla nee Klingstein;
ch—Theo, Anna, Elise, Conrad;
Friedrich, 1846
Reissig, Moritz—2 persons; from
Ebingen; Austin Co.; **Andacia,**
1846
Reith, Hein.—s, 19; from Hesse;
Weser, 1844
Reitsch, Nic.—from Berlin, 2 persons; **Hamilton,** 1846
Reitz, Lorenz—from Hausen, 3 persons; Comal Co.; **Hamilton,** 1846
Rekker, (Rehker), M.—from Hildesheim; **Weser,** 1845
Remald(Reinald?), Aug.—from
Stederdorf; arr. 1845
Remer, Dr. Wilh.—s, 28; New Braunfels 1845; Comal Co.; arr. 1844
Remmler, Gabriel—from Berlichingen; Württ., New Braunfels
1845; **Joh. Dethardt,** 1844
Remschuessel, Gottlieb—s, 30; from
Schmalkalden, Kurh.; **Everhard,**
1845
Rennert, Julius—s, New Braunfels
1845; **Ferdinand,** 1844
Rennwitsky,—from Berlin, arr. 1845
Reppien, Carl—from Rostock,
Meckl.; w—Caro. nee Heuris;
ch—Mathilde, Pauline, Marie,
Emma, Friedricke; **Creole,** 1846
Ressmann, Caspar—s, 20; from
Heiligenroth; Gillespie Co.;
Strabo, 1845
Ressmann, Joh. Peter—53, from
Heiligenroth; w—Marg. 55;
ch—Susanne 17, Clara 13, Christ.
10; **Strabo,** 1845
Rether, Maria—from Weidebrunn,
Kurh.; **Garonne,** 1845
Reudenbach, Balthasar—from
Trier, **Colchis,** 1846
Reuss, Anton—from Berlin **Franziska,** 1846

131

Reuss, Jos.—s, 22; from Münnerstadt, Bavaria; **Neptune**, 1845
Reuter, Hein.—s, **Johann Dethardt**, 1845
Reuter, Wilh.—s, from Schweinfurt, Bavaria; New Braunfels 1845; **Johann Dethardt**, 1844
Reuz, Konrad—s, from Effringen; arr. 1846
Rewoldt, Joh. and wife, Maria nee Goldbeck; ch—Joh.—s, 23, from Dammersbach; Charles—s, 21; Adam—s, 19; Theo.—s, 17; Sophie and Marie; **Apollo**, 1846
Rheinlander, Martin—s, 18; from Lenterode; **B. Bohlen**, 1845
Rhodius, Christoph—s, 23; from Sinzig, Kendall Co.; **Dyle**, 1846
Rhodius, Otto—24, from Sinzig; Guadalupe Co.; **Dyle**, 1846
Rhomberg, J. A.—s, from Ravensburg; Fayette Co.; **James Edward**, 1846
Riake, John—45; **Dyle**, 1846
Richard, Anna—from Bandau; **B. Bohlen**, 1846
Richardt, Conrad—32, from Mühlhausen; wife and ch—Marg.; **Weser**, 1844
Richter, Carl—s, from Ballenstedt, Bernburg; arr. 1846
Richter, Carl Ernst—s, from Zellerfeld, Han.; **Sophie**, 1846
Richter, Friedr.—from Calbe a/Saale; w—Friedricke nee Spandau; ch—Carl, Friedke, Hein., Elis.; Austin Co.; **Neptune**, 1846
Richter, Friedr.—s, from Bodenwerder; Fayette Co.; **Sophie**, 1846
Richter, Gottfried—from Breslau; **Mathilde**, 1846
Richter, Hein.—from Breitenfelde; w—Elis. nee Mueller; Comal Co.; **B. Bohlen**, 1847
Richter, Wilh.—s, from Senftenberg, Prussia; **Mathilde**, 1846
Rickel, Angelica—23, **Neptune**, 1845
Rickes, Edward—s, 18; from Stein, Nassau; **Joh. Dethardt**, 1845
Riechers, A.—m, had Verein land grant
Rickhoff, Jacob—s, 26, Joh.—s, 24, Martin and wife, Martin—s, 22, Theo.—s, 18; **Sarah Ann**, 1845
Rieck (Rieg), Joh.—from Wörth, Ellwangen, Württ.; w—Christina nee Kraemer and 5 ch; New Braunfels 1845; **Joh. Dethardt**, 1844
Riedel, Anton—50, from Stephanshausen, Nass.; w—Franziska nee Hombach; New Braunfels 1845; **Herschel**, 1844
Riedel, Helena—19, from Kiedrich; **Washington**, 1845
Riedel, Nicolaus—† 3.VI.1845, age

34, from Stephanshausen; w—Magda nee Hombach, from Hallgarten, Nass., † 28.VI.1845, age 34 (NBChR); 2 children-orphans; New Braunfels 1845; **Herschel**, 1844
Riel, Hein.—s, 21; from Münster; **Weser**, 1844
Riemenschneider, Elis.—from Werkel; **Johann Dethardt**, 1845
Riewitz,(Kriewitz?), Emil—and wife; **Franziska**, 1846
Ringeling, Andreas Friedr.—from Altenau, 4 persons; **Talisman**, 1846
Rinkel, Joachim—from Westerbüttel, Schleswig-Holstein; w— Anna nee Verleben, ch—Joh., Joachim; **B. Bohlen**, 1847
Ritter, Moritz—25, from Moritzberg, Han.; 2 persons; Bexar Co.; **Gerhard Hermann**, 1846
Rochette, A.—Fredericksburg 1847
Rode, Carl Fr., Sr.—8 persons; from Kolzow, Mcklbg.; Mason Co.; **Apollo**, 1846
Ro(h)de, Carl—s, 28; **Apollo**, 1846
Rode, Diederich—s, 20; **Friedrich**—s, 20; Joachim—s, 23; Michael and wife; from Peine, Han.; DeWitt Co.; **Apollo**, 1846
Rodenbach, Hein. Jos.—from Obergladbach, Nassau; 3 persons and 1 baby; **Joh. Dethardt**, 1845
Rodenkirch, Cath.—from Weidenbach; **Henry**, 1846
Rodenkirch, Joh. Peter—from Weidenbach; wife and 4 ch; **Henry**, 1846
Rodenkirch, Wilh.—from Weidenbach; w and 3 ch; **Henry**, 1846
Rodewald, Albert—s, 33; from Adensen, Han.; **Gesina**, 1846
Roebbelen, Hein.—from Hildesheim, Han.; 3 persons; w—Johanna nee Brockenfeld; **Creole**, 1846
Roeder, Jacob—33, from Berod; w—Marg. 34; ch—Anna 11, Caspar 10, Jacob 7; Gillespie Co.; **Strabo**, 1845
Roeder, H.—Fredericksburg, 1847; Roeder, Wilh.; DeWitt Co.; 1849
Roedig, Adam—s, 23; **Strabo**, 1845
Roege, Hein.—from Verden, Han.; w—Marg. (Gesche) nee Brüns; 4 ch; New Braunfels 1845; **Herschel**, 1844
Roehle, Georg—s, from Obernitz, Meiningen; **Margaretha**, 1846
Roehrer, Wilhme. nee Buchholz, † 21.V.1847, age 21; (NBChR)
Roemer, Dr. Ferdinand—geologist, in Hildesheim; arr. in Texas 1845; returned to Germany in 1847; wrote book *Texas*
Roemer, Joh.—s, lawyer from Frankfurt; **Herschel**, 1845

Roe(h)rig, Joh. Gerhard—m, from Ruhresberg; 3 persons; Mason Co.; **Colchis**, 1846
Roerig, Joh. G.—from Beerfelden, Hesse; †30.X.1846, age 19 (NBChR); **Washington**, 1845
Roesch, Adam—from Büdesheim; 5 persons; **Hamilton**, 1846
Roeser, Hein.—s, from Nürnberg, Bavaria; New Braunfels 1845; **Herschel**, 1844; ooTheresa von Kreusser on 16.I.1845 at Aqua Dulce; died before Oct. 1854 (NBChR)
Roesig, Hiob—widower from Beerfelden; ch—Maria 12, Elis. †1846, age 22 (NBChR); **Washington**, 1845
Roetke, C. L.—from Berlin; arr. 1845
Roetzel, Friedr.—s, from Fürthen; arr. 1846
Roghe, Arnold—s, 25; **Mary**, 1845
Rohier, Johanna—from Wuprichhann (=Volpriehausen?); or (Wulfringhausen?); 3 persons; **Orient**, 1846
Rohleder, Val. and wife-from Trennfurt; 3 persons; Galveston Co.; **Diamant**, 1846
Rohrdorff,---, —Fredericksburg, 1847
Rohrweber, H.A.R.—m, from Herzberg; **Hamilton**, 1846
Rolle, Fried. Ludwig—from Hildesheim, Han.; w—Johanna nee Gramm; ch—Charl., Louise, Marie, Sophie, Julia, Carl; **Margaretha**, 1845
Rolle, Leonard—s, 20; Louis—wife and 4 ch; Martin—s, 17; from Hildesheim; **Margaretha**, 1845
Rollwing, Friz—Fredericksburg
Rompel, Joh.—from Tennstedt by Erfurt; w—Caro. nee Herzog; ch—Wilhme, Ernst, Victor, Julius, Edward, Henriette; Comal Co.; **Orient**, 1846
Rompf, Christ. Hein.—42, from Rehe, Nassau; w—Ernestine nee Haustein 38; ch—Edward 16, Susanna 11, Johanna 8, Emilie 4; Aug. †1846, age 17 (NBChR); **Arminius**, 1845
Rontger, Hein.—from Offdilln; arr. 1845
Roos, Anton—s, from Ebersbach; **Element**, 1846
Roos, David and family—from Thomashardt, Württ.; arr. 1846
Roos, Georg Herm.—from Meiningen; **Garonne**, 1845
Roos, Jacob—s, from Ebersbach; Comal Co.; **Element**, 1846
Rosenthal, Hein.—from Ebergötzen, Han.; w—Friedrike nee Kahle; **Margaretha**, 1846

Rossbach, Anton—s, from Villmar; **James Edward**, 1846
Rossner, Anton and wife—from Berlin; **Franziska**, 1846
Rossner, Hein.—s, from Rödelwitz, Meiningen; **Margaretha**, 1846
Roth, Anna Marie (widow)—from Brenkenhof, Prussia; **Joh. Dethardt**, 1846
Roth, Hein.—from Wohnbach; w and 3 ch; Austin Co.; **Sarah Ann**, 1845
Roth, Joh.—from Wehrda; 4 persons; **Element**, 1846
Roth, Manuel—s, 20; from Wohnbach; **Sarah Ann**, 1845
Rothe, Charles—s, 20; and Catharine; **Joh. Dethardt**, 1845
Rothemer, Caspar—from Büdesheim; 7 persons; **Andacia**, 1846
Rothemer, Jacob—from Büdesheim; 2 persons; **Andacia**, 1846
Rothscheid, Elise—widow, nee Kreiz, from Roetgen; †25.VII.1847, age 62 (NBChR)
Rotsch, Franz Wenzel—40; from Berlin; w—Charlotte nee Paul 36; ch—Franz 14, Adolf 13, Reinhardt 11, Theresa 9, Karl 6 Gustav 3; **Neptune**, 1845
Rotsmann, Baron von—from Darmstadt; Comal Co.
Rubach, Joh—from Glentorf, Brnschwg.; **Karl Ferdinand**, 1846
Ruccius, Ferd.—m, from Berlin; 6 persons; **Franziska**, 1846
Ruck, Joh.—New Braunfels 1845
Ruderdorf, Joh.—from Dieblich; 3 persons and 1 baby; **James Edward**, 1846
Rudloff, Caro.—from Kleinschneen; **Timoleon**, 1846
Rudloff, Christian—s, from Marksuhl; Austin Co.; **Nahant** 1846 (wrecked at sea); then **Timoleon**, 1846
Rudloff, Friedr.—s, from Quedlingburg, Prussia; Guadalupe Co.; **Margaretha**, 1846
Rudolph, Friedr. Ludwig—s, 29; from Schierstein; **Washington**, 1845
Ruebsamen, Christ.—from Reh; w and 3 ch; **Harriet**, 1845
Ruebsamen, Friedr.—from Reh; w—Louisa; ch—Fried., Adolph, Ludw.; **Harriet**, 1845
Ruehl, Joh.—from Nieder Ingelheim; 6 persons and 1 baby; **Bohemia**, 1846
Ruekle, Joh. Chr. and family—from Haberschlacht, Württ.; arr. 1846; Rue(c)kle, Christoph † 1851, age 24 (NBChR)
Ruesch, Adam—from Büdesheim; 5 persons; **Andacia**, 1846

Ruether, Joh. Ch.—s, 24; from Eystrup; **Weser**, 1844
Ruhl, Jacob—s, from Heidesheim; **Hamilton**, 1846
Ruhl, Joh.—from Wettersburg; **Sarah Ann**, 1846
Ruhrenbring, Friedr.—s, 45; **Franziska**, 1846
Rumpf, Aug.—from Reh Nass.; arr. 1845; died 1846, age 17 (NBChR)
Rumpf, Hein.—arr. 1845; † 1846, age 17; heirs: Emilie, Susanna (see also Rompf, Christ. Hein.)
Runge, Henry—s, *Bremen, 1816; New Orleans to Indian Point, (Indianola) March 1846 on ship **Lone Star**; merchant and banker at Indianola, Galveston, New Braunfels
Ruprecht, Andr.—from Olnhausen; 3 persons; **Nahant** 1846, wrecked at sea, then **Timoleon**, 1846
Russ, Georg Simon—38, from Friedelshausen, Meiningen; w—Cath. 38; ch—Anne Elise 7, Anna Christine 4, Anna Maria 1; **Garonne**, 1845
Russer, Alois—s, 23; from Munich, Bavaria; New Braunfels 1845; **Herschel**, 1844
Russmann, Joh. Peter—arr. Nov. 1845; died 1846; heirs.—Caspar, Susanna, Clara, Christiane
Rust, Christ.—New Braunfels 1845

— S —

Saalmueller, Friedr.—s, 22; from Untermassfeld, Meiningen; New Braunfels 1845; **Johann Dethardt**, 1844
Sacherer, Gabriel—38, Marie Anna—33, from Mühlhausen, Württ.; ch—Elise 8, Louise 5, Marie 4, Emil 1; a Castro Colonist; New Braunfels 1845; **Henrich**, 1844
Sachmann, Hermann—s, 49; and Joh.—s, 20; **Apollo**, 1844
Sack, Doctor Ferd.—s, 25; from Prussia; **Weser**, 1844
Saeger, Philip—m, † before 1860; had Verein land grant
Saenger, Marg.—26; **Strabo**, 1845
Sahm, Ludw. Jacob—from Rehe, Nassau; w—Christine nee Goebel; ch—Ludwig, Siegfried; Pauline; Comal Co.; **George Delius**, 1845
Sailer, Lorenz—m, arr. Jan. 1846; died 1846
Salge, Conrad—s, 34; from Gross Mahner, Han.; **Everhard**, 1845
Salge, Hein.—s, 29; from Gross Mahner, Han.; Calhoun Co.; **Everhard**, 1845

Salinger, Christian—† 14.XI.1846, age 34; from Fallersleben, Han.; w—Dor. nee Spauth †1846, age 46; ch—Ad. † 1846 age 2 (NBChR); **Creole**, 1846
Salomon, Dr. Carl—s, from Schwerin, Mklbg; **Weser**, 1846
Salziger, Joh. Georg Jacob—s, 20; Comal Co.; **Joh. Dethardt**, 1845
Salziger, Joh. Gottfried—44, from Patersberg; w—Anna Gertrude nee Kayser † 7.XII.1846, age 48; ch—Cath. Elis. 12, Joh. Gottfried 8, Marie Magda. 4; Comal Co.; **Joh. Dethardt**, 1845
Salzmann, Christoph. Joh.—m, from Mosbach near Eisenach; **Elisa & Charlotte**, 1846
Salzmann, Conrad and wife Johanna—from Farnroda, Weimar; **Elisa & Charlotte**, 1846
Salzmann, Eva Cath.—ch—Johann, Christina; **Everhard**, 1845
Sames, Peter—38, from Werdorf; w—Maria Christine nee Dallas (Donart?), †28.VIII.1846, age 36; ch—Ludw. † 1846, age 12, Peter † 1846, age 5, Friedr. † 1846, age 3 (NBChR); other ch—Johannette 9, Louise 7, Joh. 4; **Neptune**, 1845
Sammet, Joh. Fr.—from Lauxenhoff; 3 persons; **Diamant**, 1846
Samse, Friedr.—s, from Golmbach; **Sophie**, 1846
Sander, Mathias—s; Sander, Mathias—m, died; Kath.—widow with 2 ch.; New Braunfels 1845; to Galveston by land Oct. 1843
Sandrisser, Adam—s, from Herbolzheim; **Diamant**, 1846
Sartor, Alex—from Langen, Schwalbach; w—Sabine nee Dieffenbach, † 24.X.1847, age 42; ch—Carl 20, Friedr. 13, Aug. 11, Bertha 8, Johanne 6, Marie 2; Bexar Co.; **Joh. Dethardt**, 1845
Sartor, Carl—s, 20; New Braunfels; **Joh. Dethardt**, 1845
Sartor, Daniel—**Louise Friedricke**, 1846
Sassmann, Thomas—s, from Kredenbach, Kreis Siegen; **Element**, 1846
Satoni, Jos.—from Oestrich; 2 persons; arr. 1845
Sattelmaier, Jacob—s, from Schluchtern; **Diamant**, 1846
Sattelmeier, J. Hein.—s, from Schluchtern; **Diamant**, 1846
Sattler, Wilh.—36, from St. Goarshausen; w—Sophie 34, ch—Henry 12, Caro. 10, Wilh. 5; Travis Co.; **Strabo**, 1845
Sauer, Joh. Wilh.—s, 22; from Frohnhausen; Gillespie Co.; **Harriet**, 1845

134

Sauer, Wilh.—m, † 22.VIII.1846, age 51; from Ansbach, Bavaria (NBChR); **Strabo**, 1845
Sauer, Wilh.—from Frohnhausen, wife and 6 ch., 4 died; Gillespie Co.; **Harriet**, 1845
Sauerborn, Andreas—s, 29; from Königshofen; † 14.II.1846, age 31; NewBraunfels 1845; **Ferdinand**, 1844
Sauersby, Adolph—m; widower with more than 2 ch.; **Ferdinand**, 1844
Sauerwein, Philipp—from Lierschied; arr. 1845
Sauter, Michael—s, from Weiler; **Talisman**, 1846
Saur, (Sauer) Friedr.—from Gefell; w—Anna nee Mueller; ch—Karl, Lina; **Orient**, 1846
Saur, (Sauer) Georg—s, from Gefell; **Orient**, 1846
Saur, Wilh.—from Trendel, ch—Sibylla 14, Georg. 11, Caro. 7, Julius 7, Louise 5; **Strabo**, 1845
Saviez, von—**Fredericksburg**, 1847
Schaaf, Ph. Hein—† 1852, age 35, from Niederscheld; w—Cath. nee Rees 28; ch. Johanna, Elis., Wilhme, Phillipine; Comal Co.; **Joh. Dethardt**, 1845
Schach, Christian—from Leutenberg, Schwarzbg; w—Christine nee Bergmann, ch—Amalie, Ludwig; **Johanna**, 1846
Schach, Friedr.—s, from Leutenberg, Schwzbg; **Johanna**, 1846
Schade, Kath. Elis.—† 24.III.1846, age 74, from Schwandstedt, Han.; (NBChR); **Ferdinand**, 1844
Schade, Ludwig—from Walsrode; w—Anna nee Monken; **Neptune**, 1845
Schade, N.—from Eisenach; arr. 1845
Schade, Wilh.—28, w—Anna 31, from Walsrode, Han.; Galveston Co.; **Neptune**, 1845
Schader, Auguste—from Frankenhausen; **Elisa and Charlotte**, 1846
Schadt, Carl—from Grumbach; 7 persons; Harris Co.; **Colchis**, 1846
Schaefer, Ad.—from Bonfeld, 6 persons; **Dyle**, 1846
Schaefer, Adam—from Queck; 4 persons and 1 baby; Comal Co.; **Colchis**, 1846
Schaefer, Carl—†11.VIII.1845, age 52; Elisa nee Ackermann † 29.VI.1845, age 47; from Langscheid;orphans—Christiane,Hein., Friedrike, Elis.., Sofia, Friedr., Johanetta; Carl 18; New Braunfels 1845; **Joh. Dethardt**, 1844

Schaefer, Carl—s, 22; **Sarah Ann**, 1845
Schaefer, Franz—s, 22; from Eisleben; Bexar Co.; **Franziska**, 1846
Schaefer, Franz Jos.—32, from Hesselbach; w—Franziska nee Ealm, † 17.IX.1846, age 32(NBChR); son—Franz 9; Comal Co.; **Neptune**, 1845
Schaefer, Friedr.—s, 21; from Hainchen, Comal Co.; **Sarah Ann**, 1845
Schaefer, Georg—s, from Mackensen, Han.; Comal Co.; **Sophie**, 1846
Schaefer, Georg Christian—from Oesede, w—Martha nee Gundermann; ch—Joh., Gottlieb, Bernh., Johanne; **Mathilde**, 1846
Schaefer, Hein.—from Nieder Netphen by Siegen; 4 persons; **Element**, 1846
Schaefer, Hein.—from Queck by Schlitz, Darmstadt; w—Marg. nee Adolph; dau.—Elis. † 1848, age 2; New Braunfels 1845; **Ferdinand**, 1844
Schaefer, Joh. Adam—s, from Ilsfeld; **Diamant**, 1846
Schaefer, Joh. Ernst—from Wengeroth, Nassau; w—Anna Maria; **Leontine**, 1844
Schaefer, Johann Jost, age 41 † 2.VIII.1846; from Manderbach, Nassau; w—Emilie nee Heiser; sister—Martha Heiser; ch—Joh., Wilh., Elisa, Friedr., Hein.; **Auguste Meline**, 1845
Schaefer, Peter—s, from Hartenstein or Schatthausen; Kendall Co.; **Talismann**, 1846
Schaefer, Philipp—s, 19; New Braunfels 1845; **Joh. Dethardt**, 1844
Schaefer, Thomas—s, from NiederNetphen, Kreis Siegen; **Element**, 1846
Schafer, Martin—from Manderbach, Nass.; w—Cath. nee Christ; **Auguste Meline**, 1845
Schake, Hein.—from Hesslingen, Kurh.; w—Friedrike nee Uhde; ch—Hein., Friedrike; **Everhard**, 1845
Schandua, Peter—29; from Frickhofen; w—Marg. 26; Peter 3, Joh. 1; Gillespie Co.; **Washington**, 1845
Schaper, August—s, 19; **Margaretha**, 1845
Schaper, Caro.—from Netze, Waldeck; **Margaretha**, 1845
Schaper, Christoph—from Almstedt; w—Johanna nee Diehle; ch—Ernst, Conrad, Louisa, Johanna; Gillespie Co.; **Weser**, 1845

Schaper, Friedr.—from Sack, Han.; w—Justine nee Flagge; ch—Aug., Friedr., Justine, Hein., Ernst, Ludwig; **Margaretha,** 1845
Schaper, Friedr.—s, 17; from Sack; **Margaretha,** 1845
Schaper, Joh. Chr. Ludw.—from Kleinllde; † 21.VII.1846, age 17 (NBChR); **Margaretha,** 1845
Schaubode, Ludwig—† 31.VIII.1846, age 41 (NBChR); from Peine, Han.; w—Christine nee Ebeling 38; ch—Christine Elisa 15, Carl 6; **Hercules,** 1845
Schaumann, Joh.—from Fischelbach, near Laasphe; **Arminius,** 1845
Scheel, Joh. Gottlob—Galveston Co.; **Anthony,** 1846
Scheele, Herm.—s, from Klein Heins; † 25.V.1846 age 40; Scheele, Cath. † in Indianola; Scheele, mother † in Victoria; Scheele, Fr., † 1846, age 6; **Matador,** 1845
Scheibe, Fr. Wilh.—from Berlin; arr. 1845
Scheidler, Marg.—18, from Trusen, Kurh.; **Garonne,** 1845
Schein, Conrad—from Farnroda, Weimar; w—Friedricke nee Schick; **Elisa & Charlotte,** 1846
Scheler, Peter—1807-1869; from Schleusingen; w—Elisa nee Block; **Orient,** 1846
Schellentraeger, Chr. Peter—arr. 1844; New Braunfels 1845
Schellentraeger, Philip—24, from Eisenach; w—Pauline nee Froebst; **Herschel,** 1844
Scheller, Carl—s, from Perleberg; **Orient,** 1846
Schelper, Hein.—1811-1888; from Kleinschneen; w—Johanna nee Rosenberg; ch—Laura, Hein.; **Joh. Dethardt,** 1845
Schenk, Friedr.—s, **St. Pauli,** 1847
Schenken, Carl—28; **Neptune,** 1845
Scherfius, Chr.—8 persons; from Kiedrich; **Andacia,** 1846
Scherfius, Joh. Anton—from Welgesheim or Kiedrich; 9 persons; Galveston Co.; **Andacia,** 1846
Schertz, Joh.—from Rüdesheim, Ff/M; New Braunfels 1845; a Castro Colonist; **Jean Key,** 1844
Schertz, Joseph—32, from Rüdesheim Ff/M; w—Anna Marie 33; ch—Affre (Alfred?) 16, Marg. 12, Cath. 28; Castro Colonists; New Braunfels 1845; **Jean Key,** 1844
Scherz., Sebastian—22, from Rüdesheim; Ff/M; a Castro Colonist, New Braunfels 1845, **Jean Key,** 1844

Scheurer, Joh. Jac.—s, from Coblenz; **James Edward,** 1846
Schickedanz, Gerhard—† 1846, from Salzdetfurt, Han.; w—Rosalie nee Rothe; ch—Herm.,Anna; **Everhard,** 1845
Schickedanz, Theo.—s, 45; from Salzdetfurt, Han.; **Everhard,** 1845
Schiewetz, Christoph—43, DeWitt Co. 1850
Schiewetz, Georg Jacob—37, from Furfeld; w—Friedricke nee Fumale 34, and female infant; ch—Christine 11, Friedr. 9, Jacob 5, Jane 7, George 3; DeWitt Co.; **Dyle,** 1846
Schiewitz, John Jacob—35, from Fürfeld; w—Margaret G. 30; Phillip 2, Regina 64; **Dyle,** 1846
Schiffbuch, Mrs. Marg.—from Zegartowith; arr. 1846
Schild, Theo. A.—s, from Frankenhausen, Prussia; Gillespie Co.; **Elisa and Charlotte,** 1846
Schildknecht, Adolph—from Wiesbaden; w—Caro.; ch—Aug. 24, Auguste 13; **Bohemia,** 1846
Schillenberg, Albert—from Einbeck; arr. 1845
Schilling, Carl—from Braunschweig; wife and mother; ch—Henriette 14, and baby; Galveston Co.; **Weser,** 1844
Schilling, Christoph Friedr.—m, from Stetten a/Harz; Harris Co.; arr. 1846
Schilling, F.—s, 32; from Preuss-Minden; Galveston Co.; **Weser,** 1844
Schilling, Georg—s, 18; Schilling, G. F.—s, 24; **Franziska,** 1846
Schilling, Gottfried—m, from Osterburg, Prussia; **Joh. Dethardt,** 1846
Schilling, Jacob Friedr.—m, from Tannhausen, Stetten; arr. 1846
Schilling, Kaspar—s, from Stockheim, Württ.; arr. 1846
Schilling, Ludwig—from Halberstadt, Prussia; Austin Co.; **Joh. Dethardt,** 1846
Schilling, Matheus and family—from Stockheim, Württ., Bastrop Co.; arr. 1846
Schink, W. Gustav—† 31.X.1846, age 31 (NBChR); 6 persons; from Dilheim, Wetzlar; **Dyle,** 1846
Schippach, Napoleon—New Braunfels, 1845
Schirmer, Franz—from Tackau, Prussia; w—Friedricke nee Lubbert; **Elisa and Charlotte,** 1846
Schirmer, Fried. Andreas—m, from Neindorf; **Karl Ferdinand,** 1846
Schladoer, F. H.—s, from Iserlohn; Kendall Co.; **Washington,** 1845

Schlaeger, Hein. and sister Maria—from Niendorf, Han.; **Karl Ferdinand,** 1846
Schlager, Chr.—47, from Kiedrich; w—Auguste 48, ch—Anton 19, Joh. 17, Christian 14, Marie 1; **Andacia,** 1846
Schlander, George—wife and 5 children; **Harriet,** 1845
Schlaudt, Christian Georg—† 1851, from Westerburg; w—Christine; ch—Regina, Mathilda, Caro., Charles, John; Gillespie Co.; **Harriet,** 1845
Schleich, Joseph—s, 28; from Bavaria; **Dyle,** 1846
Schleicher, Gustav—from Darmstadt; **St. Pauli,** 1847
Schleicher, Oddur—s, from Görzig bei Köthen; **Margaretha,** 1846
Schlenning, Theo.—s, **St. Pauli,** 1847
Schlichting, Friedr.—† 27.V.1847, age 45; from Limlingerode; w—Friedrike nee Steinmetz; ch—Dor. Wilhelmine † 6.I.1845, age 20; Friedrike † 25.VII.1846, age 14; other ch—Friedrich, Carl; New Braunfels 1845; **Herschel,** 1844
Schlick, Adolph Carl—s, from St. Andreasberg, Han.; **Karl Ferdinand,** 1846
Schlick, Aug. Edward—m, from Silbernaal, Grund a/Harz; **Karl Ferdinand,** 1846
Schliemann, Ferd.—**Albatros,** 1846
Schlobohm, Carl—s, from Luckau, Han.; arr. 1846
Schloesser, Carl—21, from Kleinschneen; **Joh. Dethardt,** 1845
Schloesser, Joh. Peter—from Welschneudorf, Nassau; w—Elis. nee Neurath; **Auguste Meline,** 1845
Schloesser, Michael—s, from Kiedrich; **Nahant**(wrecked 1846), then **Timoleon,** 1846
Schlote(Scholte?), Henriette—New Braunfels, 1845
Schlueigmann, C. F.—s, 29; from Lippe; **Weser,** 1844
Schlueter, Aug.—from Lauenstadt, Han.; w—Sophie nee Kern; ch—Louise, Hein., Wilh.; **Gesina,** 1846
Schlueter, Dor.—from Hildesheim, Han.; **Creole,** 1846
Schlueter, Herm.—from Dungelbeck, near Peine, Han.; † 3.VI.1849; **Weser,** 1845
Schmakl, Christian—from Volkstedt, Rudolstadt; **Margaretha,** 1846
Schmalzen, Franz—from Rüdesheim? or Büdesheim?; **Henry,** 1846

Schmidler, Nicolas—s, 37; from Esch; **Sarah Ann,** 1845
Schmidt, Ad.—from Zimmersrode; arr. 1845
Schmidt, Adam Joh.—s, from Belg; Bexar Co.; arr. 1846
Schmidt, Adolph—from Herborn; arr. 1845
Schmidt, Adolph—from Clausthal; **Anna,** 1846
Schmidt, Adolph—s, 25; from Hartenstein; **Joh. Dethardt,** 1845
Schmidt, Anna—50, Cath.—10; **Herschel,** 1845
Schmidt, Anton—s, 18; Gillespie Co.; **Franziska,** 1846
Schmidt, Anton—50, died; from Offenbach, Nassau; widow Anna 50; ch—Joh. 22, Lorenz 20, Ludwig 18, Cath. 10; Medina Co.; **Herschel,** 1845
Schmidt, Aug.—s, from Biebrich; Gillespie Co.; **Washington,** 1845
Schmidt, Aug.—from Gudensberg by Kassel; **Franziska,** 1846
Schmidt, Aug.—s, 21; from Breslau; Gillespie Co.; **Franziska,** 1846
Schmidt, Casper—s, 20; from Schmalkalden; **Garonne,** 1845
Schmidt, Christian—s, from Oberbandenburg; Comal Co.; **Hamilton,** 1846
Schmidt, Conrad—s, 23; **Apollo,** 1846
Schmidt, D.—s, 25; Gillespie Co.; **Ferdinand,** 1844
Schmidt, Lieut. Edward—from Weilburg, Nassau; w—Anna nee Volk; Comal Co.; **Herschel,** 1844
Schmidt, Edward—from Zimmersrode; **Anna,** 1846
Schmidt, Enoch—wife and 4 ch.; **Ferdinand,** 1844
Schmidt, Ernst—from Tecklenburg; † 11.VIII.1846, age 46; w—Lisette nee Kremer † 8.VIII.1846, age 44;\ (NBChR); arr. 1846
Schmidt, Franz Conrad—s, 27; from Kurhessen; **Washington,** 1845
Schmidt, Friedr.—from Rappenau, 5 persons; **Nahant**(wrecked 1846), then **Timoleon,** 1846
Schmidt, Friedr.—from Neesbach; Galveston Co.; **Washington,** 1845
Schmidt, Friedr.—from Winnen Nassau; †16.VIII.1846, age 33 (NBChR); **Washington,** 1845
Schmidt, Georg—from Veilsdorf, 2 persons; Guadalupe Co.; **Nahant** (wrecked at sea 1846), then **Timoleon,** 1846
Schmidt, Gottlob—from Breslau, **Mathilda,** 1846
Schmidt, Gottlob Friedr.—from Frankenhausen, Prussia; w—Christina nee Ullrich; **Elisa & Charlotte,** 1846

137

Schmidt, Gustav—40, w—Anna B. 38 and 4 ch; **Andacia,** 1846
Schmidt, Hein.—s, from Brotterode; Comal Co.; **Friedrich,** 1846
Schmidt, Hein. Friedr.—from Oste- rode, Han.; †30.VII. 1846, **age 44** (NBChR); w—Lisette nee Teufel; ch—Theo., Friedrike, Henriette; **Neptune,** 1845
Schmidt, Jacob—37, from Brett- hausen; w—Elisa nee Reh † 19.VII. 1846, age 31; ch—Gustav 12, Wilh. 8, Johanna 6, Adolph 2; Comal Co.; **Washington,** 1845
Schmidt, Jacob—Bexar Co.; **George Delius,** 1845
Schmidt, Joh.—from Hannover; † 5.X.1846 age 26 (NBChR)
Schmidt, Joh.—22; **Strabo,** 1845
Schmidt, Joh.—s, 19; **Auguste Me- line,** 1845
Schmidt, Joh.—from Büdesheim, **Hamilton,** 1846
Schmidt, Joh.—s, 22; from Offenbach; **Herschel,** 1845
Schmidt, Johann Ad.—from Belg., Gillespie Co.; **James Edward,** 1846
Schmidt, Joh. Christ.—s, 28; from Berlin; **Apollo,** 1846
Schmidt, Joh. Friedr.—42, from Vöh- rum, Han.; w—Sophie nee Degener 40; ch—Wilhme 20, Ferd. 11, Caro. 6, Dorette 3; Grimes Co.; **Her- cules,** 1845
Schmidt, Joh. Hein. Christoph—s, 22; from Oberg, Han.; Galveston Co.; **Apollo,** 1846
Schmidt, Joh. Hein. Friedr.—s, from Peine, Han.; **Hercules,** 1845
Schmidt, Joh. Jacob—58, † 16.IV.1846, at Indianola; dau—Anna Frederika 37, died at sea; from Weidhausen; **Andacia,** 1846
Schmidt, Joh. Jost—from Langen, Nassau; w—Elisa nee Schmidt; ch—Maria, Rosina, Hein., Lisette; **George Delius,** 1845
Schmidt, Joh. Nic—from Weid- hausen, w—Kunigunde nee Schil- ling 34; ch—Paul 9 mo., died at sea; Christina 2, died, Carl 4, Julius 3; Gillespie Co.; **Andacia,** 1846
Schmidt, Joh. Peter—from Rappach, Bavaria; wife and 4 ch; **Henry,** 1846
Schmidt, Joh. Wilh.—s, 22; from Ren- nerod; **Strabo,** 1845
Schmidt, Julius—s, 30; **Sarah Ann,** 1845
Schmidt, Julius—from Zimmers- rode; Comal Co.; **Anna,** 1846
Schmidt, Leonhard—†6.X.1846, age 33; from Grafenburg, Bavaria; w—Maria Cath. nee Merz; ch

—Leonhard, Magda, Marg., Cath., Carl; New Braunfels 1845; **Her- schel,** 1844
Schmidt, Lorenz—20, from Offenbach; **Herschel,** 1845
Schmidt, Ludwig—s, 18, from Offenbach; Gillespie Co.; **Herschel,** 1845
Schmidt, Mathias—from Belg; w—Elis.; ch—Adam, Peter, Jacob, Cath., Elisa, Nicolas; Gillespie Co.; **James Edward,** 1846
Schmidt, Peter—from Fürth; Gil- lespie Co.; **Golchis,** 1846
Schmidt, Peter—27, and Anna S. 23; **Andacia,** 1846
Schmidt, Peter—from Villmar, 6 per- sons; arr. 1845
Schmidt, Rudolph—s, **Elisa & Charlotte,** 1846
Schmidt, Sebastian and wife—from Zillbach, Weimar; **Everhard,** 1845
Schmidt, Susan Lisette Dor.— widow with 2 ch.; **Neptune,** 1845
Schmidt, Theo. Christian—s, from Winnen, Nassau; † 3.VIII.1846, age 36,(NBChR); **Washington,** 1845
Schmidt, Wilh.—s, from Peine, Han.; Galveston Co.; **Hercules,** 1845
Schmidt, Wilh.—23; Comal Co.; **Dyle,** 1846
Schmidtsinsky, Hein.—s, 29; from Hildesheim, Han.; **Margaretha,** 1845
Schmidtzinsky, Joh.—m, Gillespie Co.; **Neptune,** 1845
Schmitt III, Anna Marie nee Ru- ther—from Büdesheim; arr. 1845
Schmitt, Friedr.—m, from Rap- penau; **Timoleon,** 1846
Schmitt, Joh. Jacob—58, Fried- ricke—37; from Büdesheim; **Anda- cia,** 1846
Schmitt, Joh. Jost—from Lang- enaubach, Nassau; w—Elis nee Schmidt; ch—Maria, Rosina, Hein., Lisette; **George Delius,** 1845
Schmitt, Peter—m, from Lörzen- bach, Hesse; Bexar Co.; arr. 1846
Schmitz, E.—New Braunfels, 1845
Schmitz, Jacob—s, New Braunfels 1845; a Castro colonist; **Ocean,** 1844
Schmitz, Peter—27, and Anna S. 23; from Weinähr; Gillespie Co.; **An- dacia,** 1846
Schmuhl, Christian—s, from Volkstädt, Schwarzburg; arr. 1846
Schnautz, Andreas—s, from Frohn- hausen; **York,** 1846
Schnautz, Joh.—from Frohnhausen; w—Elisa nee Bernhard; ch—Carl, Phillipine, Phillip, Andreas; **George Delius,** 1845

Schnautz, Joh.—m, from Frohnhausen; 5 persons; **York**, 1846
Schnautz, Joh. Wilh.—s, 22; from Frohnhausen; Travis Co.; **George Delius**, 1845
Schneider, Anton—from Hachen; 3 persons; Comal Co.; **Diamant**, 1846
Schneider, Carl—s, from Offenbach a/M; Galveston Co.; later Kerr Co.; **Colchis**, 1846
Schneider, Christian—s, **Diamant**, 1846
Schneider, David—s, from Schluchtern; **Hamilton**, 1846
Schneider, David—from Weidebrunn, Kurh.; **Margaretha**, 1845
Schneider, Franz—from Hachen; w † 25.VIII.1846; 2 ch—†25.VIII.1846 (NBChR); **Diamant**. 1846
Schneider, Georg—s, 18; from Offenbach; **Harriet**, 1845
Schneider, Jacob—arr. 1846; Austin Co.
Schneider, Jacob—s, from Feudinger-Hütte, by Erndtebrück; Bexar Co.; **York**, 1846
Schneider, Jacob—from Welgesheim; 2 persons; **Andacia**, 1846
Schneider, Jacob Daniel—46, from Möhrendorf, Nassau; w—Johannette nee Blum 36; ch—Johannette 22, Caro. 19, Henry 18, Justine 6, Philipp 3; **Garonne**, 1845
Schneider, Joh.—27, from Rumbach, Hesse; New Braunfels, 1845; **Weser**, 1844
Schneider, Joh.—57, and son David 23; from Weidebrunn, Kurh.; **Margaretha**, 1845
Schneider, Joh.—s, from Molsberg; **Timoleon**, 1846
Schneider, Joh.—s, from Welgesheim; **Hamilton**, 1846
Schneider, Joh.—s, 20; from Elz, Nassau; **B. Bohlen**, 1845
Schneider, Ludwig—30, from Pfuhl, Ff/M; w—Anna 38; ch—Wilhme 13, Christ 8, Anna Julianne 3; **Washington**, 1845
Schneider, Wilh.—s, 23; from Offenbach; **Harriet**, 1845
Schneider, Wilh.—from Offenbach; wife and 4 ch.; Austin Co.; **Harriet**, 1845
Schober, Christian—s, 18; from Neckarmühlbach; **Dyle**, 1846
Schoeckel, Wilhelmine—from Wolfenbuttel, Han; **Hamilton**, 1846
Schoenberger, Jacob—s, from Mehren,(IC) † 1.X.1846, age 25; from Wallmerod (NBChR); **Harriet**, 1845
Schoene, H.—New Braunfels, 1845
Schoenewolf, Aug.—died; from Kaltenlengsfeld; widow with 3 ch; **Joh. Dethardt**, 1845

Schoenhuette, Hein.—from Neckarhausen; w—Anna nee Zaune; **Friedrich**, 1846
Schoettler, Aug.—s, from Magdeburg; **Weser**, 1845
Schoke, Joh. H.—died; **B. Bohlen**, 1845
Scholing, Ferd.—s, from Bodenwerder; Comal Co.; **Mercur**, 1846
Scholl, Daniel—33, from Oberasbach; and w—Elise nee Hoff, 31; both †14.IV.1846, buried in Indianola (NBChR); ch—Joh 8, Elis. 3, Anna 18; **Washington**, 1845
Scholl, Edward—s, 26; from Allendorf, Nassau; **George Delius**, 1845
Scholl, Elisa and son Wilhelm; from Allendorf, Nassau; Fredericksberg, 1847; **George Delius**, 1845
Scholl, Joh.—died; from Bergeborbeck, Nassau; wife—Marie nee Petri; ch—Hein. 12, Marg. 15, Adam 12; **Arminius**, 1845
Scholl II, Joh. Hein.—from Allendorf, Nassau; w—Anna nee Becker; ch—Wilh., Hein.; Comal Co.; **George Delius**, 1845
Scholles, Gustav—s, from Nordhausen; **Elisa & Charlotte**, 1845
Scholte, Henriette—from Kleinschneen; **Timoleon**, 1846
Scholzen, Franz—s, from Pelm; **Henry**, 1846
Schonilt, Christian—s, from Oberbandenberg; **Hamilton**, 1846
Schooke, Joh.—s, died; Johanne Marie Langkopf, sole heir; **B. Bohlen**, 1845
Schorer, Christian—from Trunkelsberg; † 1846; widow—Johanna Theresa nee Mueller; **Everhard**, 1845
Schorn, Cath. Elis.—from Stein, Nassau; † 30.V.1846, age 28 (NBChR)
Schorn, Jacob Hein.—died; Sophia Schorn sole heir; **Washington**, 1845
Schorn, Joh. Anton—s, 21, from Stein; **Washington**, 1845
Schorn, Joh. Peter—from Salzburg (near Rennerod); †29.XI.1846, age 38 (from Stein) (NBChR); w—Sophie 29; ch—Wilh. 6, Carl 4, Alwine 2; **Washington**, 1845
Schorre, Julius—s, from Cassel; **Friedrich**, 1846
Schrader, Diedr. Wilh.—from Quarnebeck; w—Maria nee Klaas; ch—Carl, Friedrike, Auguste, Wilhelmina; **B. Bohlen**, 1847
Schrader, Friedr.—s, **Washington**, 1846
Schrader, Friedr.—s, from Westfeld, Han.; **Margaretha**, 1845

Schrader, Hein.—s, 25; from Wedelheine; **B. Bohlen,** 1845
Schrader, Hein.—s, 35; from Hillerse, Han.; **B. Bohlen,** 1845
Schrader, Ludwig—s, from Hesel or Gross Mahner, Han.; **Franziska,** 1846
Schrader, Marianne—from Lüerdissen, Brnschwg; **Sophie,** 1846
Schrader, Wilh.—s, **Cooper,** 1847
Schraub, Phil. Jacob—s, 22; from Rauenthal, Nassau; **Neptune,** 1845
Schroder, Friedr.—s, **Margaretha,** 1845
Schroeder, Friedr.—from Jembke, Han.; w—Anna nee Dierkop; ch—Joh., Friedr., Jakob; **Karl Ferdinand,** 1846
Schroeder, Friedr.—s, 55; **Franziska,** 1846
Schroeder, Georg—from Meissen; w—Regina nee Kleber; **Flavius,** 1846
Schroeder, Gottfried—from Kanitz, w—Dor. nee Schmidt; ch—Ernst, Charl.; Harris Co.; **Flavius,** 1846
Schroeder, Hein.—s, from Daverden, Han.; arr. 1845
Schroeder, Jacob Wilh.—33, from Rötgen; w—Jane L. 36 and baby girl; ch—Elenore 4, Peter 2; Galveston Co.; **Dyle,** 1846
Schroeder, Joh.—s, 19; **Franziska,** 1846
Schubach, Martin—from Erbach; w and 2 ch; **Harriet,** 1845
Schubbert, Dr.—-Gillespie Co.; Fredericksburg, 1847
Schuchardt, Carl Emil—s, from Vehra/Erfurt; Guadalupe Co.; **Elisa & Charlotte,** 1846
Schuchardt, Friedr.—from Hildesheim, w—Sophie nee Stegmaier; ch—Friedr., Cath.; **Gerhard Hermann,** 1846
Schuchardt, Friedr. Ferd.—from Vehra/Erfurt; widower with ch—Carl, Wilh.; Guadalupe Co.; **Elisa & Charlotte,** 1846
Schuchard(t), Julius—s, 23; from Brotterode, Kurh.; Mason Co.; **Garonne,** 1845
Schueler, Aug.—30; Christina 21, Elisa. 50; Gillespie Co.; **Herschel,** 1845
Schueler, Caspar—from Büdesheim, 6 persons; **Andacia,** 1846
Schueler, Elisa, Widow, died 1849; from Dillenburg, Nassau; ch—Aug., Caro.; **Herschel,** 1845
Schuenemann, Friedr.—s, 38; from Meisterhorst; Comal Co.; **B. Bohlen,** 1847
Schuerg, Hein.—32; from Zinnhain;

w—Marie K. 29; Christian 6, Caro. 3; Comal Co.; **Andacia,** 1846
Schuessler, Adam(J.A.)—35; from Bonfeld, w—Eva P. and baby girl, ch—Joh. 9, Conrad 7, Jacob 5, Guillianne 2; **Dyle,** 1846
Schuessler, Joh. Peter—† 28.IX. 1846, age 46; w—Cath. nee Schneider and baby; ch—Ludwig, Wilhme, Caro.; Ferd. † 1846, age 5; Wilh. † 1846, age 9; (NBChR) Comal Co.; **Auguste Meline,** 1845
Schuessler, Joseph—s, from Lohr; **Diamant,** 1846
Schuette, Hein.—s, from Cassel; Comal Co.; **Friedrich,** 1846
Schuette, Wilh.—m, from Bochum; **Diamant,** 1846
Schuetz, Adam—from Fürth, 9 persons; **Colchis,** 1846
Schuetz, Cuno von—from Wiesbaden; **Timoleon,** 1846
Schuetz, Damian von—s, **Timoleon,** 1846
Schuetz, Joh. Peter—s, died 1848; from Langenbach; **Harriet,** 1845
Schuetz, Ludwig—from Langenbach, w and 2 ch; **Harriet,** 1845
Schugerth, Ludwig—m, 25; from Ketten, Weimar; **Garonne,** 1845
Schuhardt, Adam—from Farnroda, Weimar; **Elisa & Charlotte,** 1846
Schuhardt, Pauline—from Frankenhausen, Weimar; **Elisa & Charlotte,** 1846
Schukraft, J.J.—38; from Cleversulzbach; w—Marie 33; Gottlieb 7, Friedr. 6 and baby girl; **Dyle,** 1846
Schukraft, Joh.—25 and Marg. 25; from Cleversulzbach; **Dyle,** 1846
Schukraft, Regina—64, **Dyle,** 1846
Schulenburg, Ludwig—m, **Ferdinand,** 1845
Schulenmeier, Joh. Val.—46; from Menteroda, Sachsen Gotha; w—Susanne; ch—T. Faub 12, T. Leopold 6, Wilhme 2, Johanna 8 weeks; Comal Co.; **Weser,** 1844
Schulke, Henry and wife—**B. Bohlen,** 1845
Schuller, Ferd.—from Altensteig; 5 persons and 1 baby; Harris Co.; **Element,** 1846
Schuller, Wilh.—s, from Stuttgart; **Element,** 1846
Schulte, Diedrich—from Heil, 10 persons; **Colchis,** 1846
Schulte Jr., Diedrich—s, from Heil; **Colchis,** 1846
Schulte, Wilh.—s, from Heil; **Colchis,** 1846
Schulte, W.—from Stockum, 5 persons; ch—Caro., Ferd.; **Diamant,** 1846
Schulter, Gustav—m, from Nordhausen; **Elisa & Charlotte,** 1846

Schultheis, Augusta—16, from Braunschweig; Neptune, 1845

Schultz, Leopold—s, Kendall Co.; St. Pauli, 1847

Schultze, Joh. Hein.—from Armsen, Han.; w—Cath. Adelheid nee Uelzen; New Braunfels 1845; arr. 1844

Schulz, Andreas—60, from Nassau; w—Anna nee Schmidt 53, ch—Elis. 27, Caro. 24, Wilhme 12; Austin Co.; Neptune, 1845

Schulz, Bernard—and 2 ch.; Sarah Ann, 1845

Schulz, Carl Aug.—from Linderode near Sorau, Ff/Oder; w—Christine nee Buchwald; Creole, 1846

Schulz, Carl Aug.—from Golchen near Stettin; Comal Co.; Joh. Dethardt, 1846

Schulz, Carl Gottlieb—from Havelberg, w—Auguste nee Friedrich; Mathilde, 1846

Schulz, Christoph—from Mieste, Prussia; w—Marie nee Miste; ch—Cath., Maria, Elisa, Anna, Friedr.; B. Bohlen, 1847

Schulz, Fried.—18; Neptune, 1845

Schulz, Friedr.—57, from Quarnebek; w—Maria nee Heverkerdel; ch—Friedr., Wilh.; Comal Co.; B. Bohlen, 1847

Schulz, Friedr.—from Grävenitz, Prussia; w—Maria nee Schulze; ch—Jacobina, Friedr., Wilh.; B. Bohlen, 1846

Schulz, Friedr.—s, from Lieberose, Ff/Oder; Franziska, 1846

Schulz, Gottlieb—m; arr. before Sept. 1847, died 1847; heirs—Anna Gesina, Johanna, Gottlieb

Schulz, Gustav—s, from Beuthen, Silesia; Colorado Co.; Flavius, 1846

Schulz, Hein. Wilh.—died; from Nassau; widow—Anna Marie and 3 ch; Neptune, 1845

Schulz, Joh.—s, 29; Fayette Co.; Harriet. 1845

Schulz, Joh. Christian—s, from Triebsees; Apollo, 1846

Schulz, Michael—42; from Birkholz, Prussia; wife and 2 ch; Comal Co.; Joh. Dethardt, 1846

Schulz, Rudolph Wilh.—from Nassau; † 17.IX.1846, age 62 (NBChR)

Schulz, Wilh.—s, from Birkholz, Prussia; Joh. Dethardt, 1846

Schulze, Ferd. Friedr.—from Brettleben; w—Eleanore nee Kossmann; son—Wilh.; Gillespie Co.; Elisa & Charlotte, 1846

Schulze, Friedr.—s, 18; Guadalupe Co.; Neptune, 1845

Schulze, Friedr.—from Wangelstedt, w—Johanne nee Nolten; ch—Justine, Caro., Minna, Johanne; Mercur, 1846

Schulze, Friedr. Aug. Wilh.—s, Mercur, 1846

Schulze, Friedr. Wilh.—from Jeeben, Prussia; wife—Maria nee Jureges; ch—Maria, Johanna; B. Bohlen, 1847

Schulze, Gottlob—m, from Wellersdorf, Prussia; Mathilde, 1846

Schulze, Joh.—Guadalupe Co.; B. Bohlen, 1847

Schulze, Joh. Hein.—from Armsen; Han.; w—Cath. Adelheid Schulze; ch—Herm., Friedke; New Braunfels 1845; Joh. Dethardt, 1844

Schulze, Moritz—from Naumberg, a/Oder; w—Marie nee Starke; Friedrich, 1846

Schumacher, Friedr. Wilh.—from Stromberg; w—Marie E.; ch—Bertha, Gottlieb; Gillespie Co.; Colchis, 1846

Schumacher, Hein.—from Koblens, 2 persons and 1 baby; Fayette Co.; James Edward, 1846

Schumacher, John—25, Marg. 25; from Rostorf; Comal Co.; Strabo, 1845

Schumann, Mrs. Amalie—from Rosslau, Prussia; arr. 1846

Schumann, Aug. Wilh.—s, 32; from Köthen; Comal Co.; Dyle, 1846

Schumann, Ernst—s, 18; Everhard, 1845

Schumann, G.—from Köthen; Dyle, 1846

Schumann, Gustav—s, Gillespie Co.; Margaretha, 1846

Schumann, Hein.—from Hattenheim, w—Cath. nee Klein, ch—Friedr., Jacob, Val. B. Bohlen, 1847

Schumann, Hein.—s, 69; from Kyrburg; Harriet, 1845

Schumann, Joh. Christoph—from Cassel, Han.; w—Maria nee Cramm; ch—Georgine, Ludw., Heinr.; Everhard, 1845

Schumann, Wilh.—s, from Rosslau, Gillespie Co.; Margaretha, 1846

Schupp, Friedr.—27, from Giesenthal, Pomerania; Gillespie Co.; Neptune, 1845

Schupp, Hein.—1792-1869, (FChR); Gillespie Co.

Schupp, Wilhme nee Kollmeier; 1820-1865; (F.Ch.R.)

Schuster, Jacob—from Weidenbach; wife and 4 ch.; Henry, 1845

Schutter, Gustav—from Nordheim; w—Johanna nee Hohne; Elisa & Charlotte, 1846

Schutz, Anton—s, 20; Gesina, 1846

Schutz, Joh.—from Celle; Apollo, 1846

Schwab, Joh.—s, from Rumbach, Hesse; New Braunfels 1845; Weser, 1844
Schwab, Marie—Weser, 1844
Schwab, Thomas—s, 26; from Rumbach, Hesse; New Braunfels 1845; Weser, 1844
Schwalm,---,—from Cassel; Franziska, 1846
Schwanecke, Joh. Georg—s, from Clausthal, a/Harz; Karl Ferdinand, 1846
Schwank, Nicolaus—arr. Dec. 1845; died 1846; Anna Maria Schwank; sole heir (See also Schwenk, Nic.)
Schwarting, Joh.—s, 20; Apollo, 1844
Schwartzhoff, S. von—Lawyer; Comal Co.
Schwarz, Herm.—from Bärenklau, Prussia; 4 persons; Franziska, 1846
Schwarz, Josef—s, from Amorbach; Element, 1846
Schwarze, Edward—s, 18; Franziska, 1846
Schweitzer, Joh. G.—from Waldenbuch; 6 persons; Colorado Co.; Element, 1846
Schweitzer, Wendel—s, from Herbolzheim; York, 1846
Schwenk, Andreas—from Zegartowith, Poland; w—Rosina nee Klett; Johanna, 1846
Schwenk, Nic.—s, from Seelbach; (See also Schwank, Nic.); Andacia, 1846
Schwerdfeger, Franz—s, from Stadtoldendorf; Sophie, 1846
Schwerd(t)feger, Friedr.—m, from Stadtoldendorf; Galveston Co.; Sophie, 1846
Schwerin, Joh. Jacob—from Lupitz, Prussia; w—Anna nee Engers; B. Bohlen, 1847
Schwerin, Rudolph von—s, from Meseritz (Meserich, Rhein Pfalz?); Louise, 1846
Schwind, Jacob—m, from Offenburg; arr. 1846
Sebastian, Jonas—from Hedeper, Brnschwg; w—Regina nee Geyer; Comal Co.; Louise, 1846
Seekatz, Wilh.—m, from Stein, Nassau; Comal Co.; Joh. Dethardt, 1845
Seele, Hermann, s, 20; teacher, from Hildesheim, Han.; oo1862 Mathilde Blum; New Braunfels 1845; arr. Galveston 1843
Seelemann, Gottlieb—s, 35; from Berlin; Franziska, 1846
Segner, Peter—from Eitelborn, Nassau; 3 persons; w—Marg. nee Cabberts; Calhoun Co.; Auguste Meline, 1845

Sehr, Jacob—s, from Hadamar; Bohemia, 1846
Seibel, Joh.—from Oberscheld, Nassau; with 7 persons; w—Cath. nee Arnold; Bexar Co.; Arminius, 1845
Seibert, C. H.—New Braunfels 1845; Joh. Dethardt, 1844
Seidel, Aug.—from Hattingen; w—Friedricke nee Heiden; and daughter; Harris Co.; Flavius, 1846
Seidemann, Peter—32, from Dillenburg, Nassau; w—Anna Marie nee Daum 22; Comal Co.; Herschel, 1845
Seidler, Marg.—from Trusen, Kurh.; Garonne, 1845
Seiger, Friedr.—m, from Lipperode; arr. 1846
Seiler, Jacob—46; w—Elisa nee Hufaus 46; ch—Wilh. 20, Elisa 19, Marg. 18, Jacob 15, Guadalupe Co.; from Manderbach; Herschel, 1845
Seiler, Jacob Christian—s, Herschel, 1845
Seiler, Joh.—24, from Manderbach, Nassau; Herschel, 1845
Seiler, Lorenz and wife—from Rupertshofen; Austin Co.; Riga, 1846
Seiler, Wilh.—s, 20; Guadalupe Co.; Herschel, 1845
Seitmann, Nic.—m, died; from Holler, Nassau; Riga, 1846
Seitz, Ferdinand—s, from Winterbach; arr. 1846
Seitz, Joh. Friedr.—s, 27; from Altensteig; arr. 1846
Selkes, Franz—s, from Coblenz; James Edward, 1846
Sellhorst, Friedr.—s, 21; Franziska, 1846
Selten, Adolph—23; Star Republic from N.Y.; New York from N.O. 1845
Senfloth,Friedr.—from Quarnebeck; w—Dor. nee Henchered; son—Friedr.; B. Bohlen, 1846
Senft, Emil—s, 29; Joh. Dethardt, 1845
Seng, Franz Jacob—w—Maria nee Ullrich, from Böckels, by Fulda; Guadalupe Co.; Neptune, 1845
Settegast, M.W.—from Biebrich; 7 persons; arr. 1845
Seul, Edgar—from Berlin; Franziska, 1846
Seyffarth, Ludwig—s, 20; from Ohrdruff; Galveston Co.; Dyle, 1846
Sickel, Aug. von—s, from Berlin; † 15.VII.1846, age 30; (NBChR); Creole, 1846
Sickfeld, Hein.—from Graste, Han.; arr. 1845
Siebald, Friedr.—from Herrenbreitungen; w—Elisa nee Martin; ch

—Elisa, Maria, Christine, Caro., Friedr.; **B. Bohlen,** 1845
Siebert, Carl Heinr.—s, from Winnenden, Württ.; **Johann Dethardt,** 1844
Siedenstopp, Tine—from Sehlem, Han.; **Margaretha,** 1845
Sieghertner, Joh.—s, 29; **New York** from N.O., 1844
Siegle, Friedr. Joh. Jacob—m, from Schweiberdingen, Württ.; **James Edward,** 1846
Siegman, Friedr.—from Ottensteig, Brnschwg.; w—Charl. nee Wotte; ch—Charl., Justine, Aug., Caro., Hein.; Gillespie Co.; **Mercur,** 1846
Siehn, E.—s, 22; New Braunfels 1845; **Ferdinand,** 1844
Siems, Friedr. and wife—**Apollo,** 1844
Siering, N.—New Braunfels, 1845
Sievers, Carl—s, from Hannover; **Creole,** 1846
Sievers, Friedr.—from Woltwiesche, arr. 1846
Sigmund, Joh.—from Weiler, 5 persons; **Talisman,** 1846
Sigmund, Ludwig—s, from Weiler; **Talisman,** 1846
Simert, Hein. Aug.—arr. 1846
Simon, Ferd.—m, **Strabo,** 1845
Simon, Ferd.—s, from Darmstadt; Comal Co.; **Strabo,** 1845
Simon, Georg—arr. 1845
Simon II. Joh.—from Eitelborn, Nassau; 4 persons; **George Delius,** 1845
Simon, Joh. Hein.—from Eitelborn, Nassau; w—Gertrude nee Zerbach; ch—Maria, Anna Maria; **George Delius,** 1845
Simon, Mathias—from Eitelborn, Nass.; 1815-1867; w—Caro. nee Weber; ch—Georg, Anne, Marg.; Calhoun Co.; **George Delius,** 1845
Simon, Peter—s, 17; **Strabo,** 1845
Simon, Philipp—45; from Gubberath; w—Frederica 36; ch—Conrad 14, Christian 11, Cath. 9, Maria 2; Gillespie Co.; Mason Co. 1859; **Strabo,** 1845
Simon, Sylvester—s, 28; (1817-1883); from Mollau (Mollen?); New Braunfels 1845; a Castro Colonist; **Heinrich,** 1844
Single, Joh.—34, from Winterlingen; w—Barbara 41; ch—Bertha 8, Aug. 9, Wilh. 4; **Andacia,** 1846
Sinz, Joh. Hein.—from Wiesbaden; w—Marg. and 3 ch.; **Riga,** 1846
Sinz, Joseph—from Wiesbaden; w and 3 ch.; **Riga** 1846
Sinz, Marg.—widow with more than 2 ch.; **Riga,** 1846
Sippel, Georg—s, 46; from Schwal-

lungen, Meiningen; **B. Bohlen,** 1845
Sippel, George—s, 47; from Walleshausen, Gotha; **Apollo,** 1846
Sippel, Joh. Christian—from Walleshausen, Gotha; **Apollo,** 1846
Sippel, Valentin—from Wehrda, 6 persons and 1 baby; Comal Co.; **Colchis,** 1846
Sittig, Nic.—28, from Trusen, Kurh.; **Garonne,** 1845
Skerl, Hein.—m, from Cottbus, Lausitz; arr. 1846
Soefge, Hein.—s, 25; from Dölme; Comal Co.; **Mercur,** 1846
Soehn, Jacob—m, from Herborn; **Element,** 1846
Soehn, Wilh.—s, from Herborn; **Element,** 1846
Soergel, Alwin Hein.—s, from Eisleben; Fayette Co.; **Franziska,** 1846
Soergel, Ernst—s, from Perleberg; Fayette Co.; arr. 1846
Solms—Braunfels, Carl Prince of; from Braunfels on the Lahn; founder of New Braunfels 1845; First Commissoner-General of the Verein; arr. July 1, 1844; left May 1, 1845
Sommer, Carl—s, from Culm; **Louise Friedricke,** 1847
Sommer, Ferd.—from Büdesheim; 6 persons; Galveston Co.; **Andacia,** 1846
Sommer, Joh. Traugott—Fayette Co.
Sommer, Julius—s, from Culm; **Louise Friedricke,** 1847
Sondergold, Michael and Anna from Oberschonau, Kurh.; **Everhard,** 1845
Sonderling, Michael—s, 50; **Everhard,** 1845
Sonnenberg, Hein.—s, 38; from Stederdorf; Austin Co.; **Franziska,** 1846
Sonnschein, Hein.—from Osterburg, Prussia; **Joh. Dethardt,** 1846
Sorge, Friedr.—from Markoldendorf; 4 persons; w—Louise nee Kahlem † 6.VI.1846, age 35; Comal Co.; (NBChR); **Talisman,** 1846
Sorrieth, Chr. Franz—from Widdern, 6 persons; **Nahant** (wrecked 1846); then **Timoleon,** 1846
Sowersby, Herm. Robert—s, from Bremen; New Braunfels 1845; **Ferdinand,** 1844
Spangenberg, Christoph—from Ballenhausen, Han.; w—Elis. nee Voigt; ch—Julie, Sophie, Hein., Herm.; Wilh.; Comal Co.; **Johann Dethardt,** 1845
Spangenberg, Friedr.—s, 36; from Nobiskrug, Han.; **Everhard,** 1845

Spangenberg, Joseph—37, from Hannover; **Joh. Dethardt,** 1845
Spath, Elisa.—widow with 2 ch; Gillespie Co.; **Herschel** 1845
Spatz, Edward—20; from Rötgen; **Caro.** 20; Charlotte, mother, 60; **Dyle,** 1846
Spatz, Friedr.—29, from Rötgen; **Dyle,** 846
Spatz, Hein.—died; from Rötgen; Emilie Charl. Foerster, sister and only heir; **Dyle,** 1846
Specht, Christian—s, from Lobach, Brnschwg; Guadalupe Co.; **Sophie,** 1846
Specht, Friedr. Wilh.—24; Caro. 22; Comal Co.; **Matador,** 1845
Specht, Hans von—Comal Co.
Specht, Theodor Zeisig—from Wolfenbüttel, oo Marie Berger 7.II.1847; **Louise,** 1846
Specknagel, Sussanna—from Oberschönau, Kurh.; **Everhard,** 1845
Speier, Friedr.—s, from Cassel; **Friedrich,** 1846
Speier, Joseph—from Wakhausel (Wakenhausen, Wurtt.?); wife † 17.I.1846, age 28 (NBChR); Comal Co.
Spellerberg, F. Albert—s, 37; from Einbeck, Han.; **Franziska,** 1846
Spengler, Christoph—from Wolfenbüttel, Brnschwg; w—Doris nee Lueders; ch—Louise, Hein., Chr., Maria; **Franziska,** 1846
Spernhauer, Wilh.—m, from Salzburg; **Washington,** 1845
Speuerer, Adam—from Obernhausen; **York,** 1846
Speuerer, Josef—from Obernhausen; widower with 2 ch; **York,** 1846
Speyer (Speier), Adam—s, **Harriet,** 1845
Speyer, Ferd.—s, **Friedrich,** 1846
Speyer, Sr., Hein.—m, 54; from Nentershausen; 4 persons; Gillespie Co.; **Harriet,** 1845
Spicker, Christian—**Sophie,** 1846
Spiess, Hermann—successor to John O. Meusebach as Comissioner-General of German Emigration Co.
Spilker, Aug.—s, from Hildesheim, Han.; **Margaretha,** 1845
Spille, Joh.—wife and 2 ch; Colorado Co.; **Franziska,** 1846
Spiller, Hein.—from Wendhausen, Han.; w—Anna nee Hasse; ch—Johanna; **Everhard,** 1845
Spiller, Joh.—s, 23; from Wendhausen; **Everhard,** 1845
Spiller, Joh.—and wife, from Wendhausen; **Everhard,** 1845
Splittgerber, Julius—s, 26; from Rückers; Gillespie Co.; **Arminius,** 1845

Sponring, Caspar with family—from Stockheim, Württ.; arr. 1846
Spornhauer, Wilh.—50, w—Louise; ch—Susanna; **Washington,** 1845
Spyr, Joh. (Jean)—s, from Merll, Luxemburg; **Talsiman,** 1846
Staats, Christian—s, from Harzburg, a/Harz; Gillespie Co.; **B. Bohlen,** 1847
Staats, Hein.—from Heimer, arr. 1845
Staats, Joh. Hein.—s, from Dungelbeck bei Peine, Han.; oo Wilhelmine Busch, 22.II.1847 (NBChR); **Hercules,** 1845
Staedtler, Joh. Casper—from Zillbach, Weimar; w—Elis. nee Ernst; ch—Theo., Carl, Louise, Mathilda, Aug., Emma; Travis Co.; **Everhard,** 1845
Staehler, Pastor Christian—from Schönberg; **Timoleon,** 1846
Staffelmeier, J. H.—from Weiler; **Talisman,** 1846
Staffelmeier, Jacob—from Siegelsbach; **Talisman,** 1846
Stahl, Jacob Hein.—died; Sophie Schorn, sole heir; **Washington,** 1845
Stahl, Joh. Peter—45, from Hainberg.; sons—Leonard 16, Aug. 6; **Washington,** 1845
Stahl, Leonard—s, **Washington,** 1845
Stahlbaum, Christian—from Hammelspringe, arr. 1845
Stahlen, Christof—26, from Ketten, Weimar; **Garonne,** 1845
Staken, Peter—from Helmhof; **Washington,** 1845
Stalp, Hein Wilh.—m, from Reh; Gillespie Co.; **Harriet,** 1845
Stark, Peter—m, from Nassau; **James Edward,** 1846
Starks, Chester B.—m, Gillespie Co.; **Matamoros,** from New Orleans to Corpus Christi 1845
Startz, Hein—s, New Braunfels 1845; **Joh. Dethardt,** 1844
Startz, Joh.—from Stockheim, Württ.; w—Marg. nee Pertsch; ch —Hein., Friedke., Caro.; 3 stepch.; Christian, Cath. and Louise Loeffler; New Braunfels 1845; **Joh. Dethardt,** 1844
Statz, Phillip—s, 20; **Harriet,** 1845
Staudt, Jac.—from Rauenthal; 8 persons; arr. 1845
Staussenberger, Franz—3 persons; from Dörsdorf; arr. 1845
Staussenberger, G. P.—9 persons; from Dörsdorf; arr. 1845
Stecher, Wilh.—s, from Sachsa, Prussia (IC); † 22.IX.1847, age 35; from Tettenborn, Erfurt (NBChR); arr. Dec. 1846

144

Steckel, Aug.—from Berlin; arr. 1845
Steco, Jos.—s, 18; **Sarah Ann,** 1845
Steffen, Carl—s, **Mary** from N.O.; Dec. 1847
Steffen, Dietrich—m, † before 1860; had Verein land grant;
Steffers, Richard—from Rötgen bei Aachen, † 16.III.1847, age 37; 6 persons; widow—Pauline with 2 ch under 17; **Element,** 1846
Stegmann, Joh.—m, from Farnroda bei Eisenach; **Elisa & Charlotte,** 1846
Stehling, Amandus—21, from Fulda; w—Barbara nee Vogel; ch—Christian, Joh.; Gillespie Co.; **Garonne,** 1845
Stehling, Genoveva—from Fulda, Kurh.; **Garonne,** 1845
Stehling, Georg Francis—s, 22; from Fulda; Gillespie Co.; **Garonne,** 1845
Stein, Friedr.—and wife from Clausthal; **Anna** 1846
Stein, Joh. Julius Christoph—20, from Wolfshagen; arr. 1846
Stein, Joseph—from Eitelborn, Nassau; w—Maria nee Marx; ch—Anna Marie, Gertrude; **Auguste Meline,** 1845
Steinebach, Franz Anton—s, died; from Ehrenbreitstein; **Riga,** 1846
Steinbrink, Hein. Ludw.—25, from Weibeck, Nassau; Gillespie Co.; **Apollo,** 1846
Steinbrink, Wilhelmine—52; widow with 2 ch under 17; **Apollo,** 1846
Steiner, Adam—from Flinsbach, 6 persons; **York,** 1846
Steiner, George—s, from Flinsbach; **York,** 1846
Steiner, Mary C.—26, **Dyle,** 1846
Steinmeier, Hein.—s, from Dölme, Brnschwg; Comal Co.; **Mercur,** 1846
Steinmetz, Lorenz—43, from Oestrich, Nassau; w—Sophie nee Schrader 38; **Neptune,** 1845
Steintraeger (Steindreger), Herm.—from Rietberg; w and 5 ch; **Apollo,** 1846
Stellburg, Gottlieb—s, from Isenbüttel, Han.; 1845
Stellter, Cath. Dor—**Ferdinand,** 1844
Stellter, Friedr.—from Reppner, Brnschwg; w—Sophie nee Knopp; ch—Caro.; **Gerhard Hermann,** 1846
Stemke, Henrich—from Wülfinghausen; arr. 1845
Stendebach, Wilh.—† 14.XI.1846, age 51; from Welschneudorf; w—Anna nee Schmidt, † 14.XI. 1846, age 41; Cath. † 1847, age 7 (NBChR); ch—Anna, Cath. "Orphans left behind."; **Auguste Meline,** 1845

Stengel, Conrad—arr. Dec. 1845, died 1847; w—Hannah Stengel
Stengler, Joh.—from Diez; w—Johannette Hankamer; 2 sons, 3 stepsons; Chambers Co.; **Harriet,** 1845
Steppens, Diedrich—wife and 2 ch.; **Franziska,** 1846
Stern, Carl Gustav—from Naugard; w—Helene nee Kauschen; ch—Carl, Herm., Emma, Bertha; Austin Co.; **Franziska,** 1846
Sternberg, Karl—from Marlow, Mecklbg; w—Friedricke nee Schlattner; ch—Wilh., Hulda; **Mathilda,** 1846
Sternheimer, Joh.—s, 29; from Weilbach; **Washington,** 1845
Sterzing, Theo. Friedr.—30, from Wiesbaden; w—Helena 28; ch—Friedr. 2; Caro. † 1846, Bertha † 1849 (NBChR); Comal Co.; **Strabo,** 1845
Stetter, Friedr.—from Reppner, **Apollo,** 1845
Stetz, Conrad—s, from Hennethal; Gillespie Co.; arr. 1845
Steubing, Jacob—† 16.VII.1849, age 42, from Offenbach, Nassau; w—Anna Cath. nee Schaefer, † 27.VII.1846, age 41(NBChR); ch—Wilh. 12, Friedr. 4; **Herschel,** 1845
Steubing, Joh. Jost—from Bicken, Nassau; w—Anna nee Schmidt † 10.VI.1846, age 25; (NBChR); Comal Co.; **Herschel,** 1845
Stiebel, Joh. Hein. Anton—from Kissenbruck near Borsum, Brnschwg.; w—Marie Christine nee Gerloff; ch—Henriette Sophie; Guadalupe Co.; **Louise,** 1846
Stiehl, Christian—s, from Bierstadt; Fayette Co.; **Timoleon,** 1846
Stiehl, Christian—from Heilberscheid; arr. 1845
Stiehl, Heinr.—31, from Oberscheld; w—Cath. nee Arnold 33; ch—Cath. 4, Anna 2, Ludw. 1; Gillespie Co.; **Arminius,** 1845
Stiehler, Carl Julius—from Dresden; w—Rosalie nee Naacke; † 22.VIII.1852, age 36 (NBChR); 2 ch.
Stieren, Wilh.—from Salzdetfurt, Han.; w—Antoinette nee Gehrke; ch—Louise, Emma, Amalie, Auguste, Johanne; **Everhard,** 1845
Stiernberg, Wilhelm von—s, from Cassel, † 1865 at Indianola; **Friedrich,** 1846
Stiffer, Christian, and Friedr.—from Clausthal; **Anna,** 1846
Stilger, Jacob—s, 35; from Lorch by Rüdesheim; **Joh. Dethardt,** 1845

Stinkel, Christian—Everhard, 1845
Stinner, Anton—from Harbach, wife and 5 ch.; arr. 1846
Stisser, F. W.—† before 1860; had Verein land grant
Stock, Carl—† 26.V.1847; wife † 24.V.1847; child † 23.V.1847, (NBChR); New Braunfels 1845; Herschel, 1844
Stock, Peter—from Ort, Bavaria; w—Elisa nee Bauer † 15.IX.1845, age 42 (NBChR); with 5 ch; New Braunfels 1845; Herschel, 1844
Stoeltje, Reinhard—wife and one child; Colorado Co.; Apollo, 1844
Stoer, Heinr.—from Leutkirch; James Edward, 1846
Stoer, Otto—s, from Leutkirch; James Edward, 1846
Stoffers, Franz—s, from Marlow, Mcklbg; Gillespie Co.; Mathilde, 1846
Stolbe, Joh. Hein.—from Hillerse; 1845
Stolte, Christian—s, from Hagen near Pyrmont; arr. 1846; Guadalupe Co.
Stommel, George Karl—s, from Herrnstein; Gillespie Co.; Colchis, 1846
Storch, Joh. George—† 11.X.1846, age 45; from Wahles, Kurh.; w—Eva nee Weihe; ch—Val., Marg., Christiana; Gillespie Co.; Everhard, 1845
Storch, Simon—36, from Schwallungen; Garonne, 1845
Storch, Valentin—s, 24; B. Bohlen, 1845
Strackbein, Hein.—38, from Steinbrücken, Nassau; w—Elis. 35; ch—Elis. 13, Cath. 11, Henry 5, Christian 4; Arminius, 1845
Straehle, Gottlieb—from Eisenach; Timoleon, 1846
Straehler, Joh. Gottlieb—s, from Nagold; Element, 1846
Stranz, Adam—s, 21; from Cassel; Weser, 1844
Straube, Hein.—m, from Dillenburg; York, 1846
Strauss, Aug.—s, St. Pauli, 1847
Strauss, Georg Andreas—from Schwallungen; w—Susanna nee Limpert; Everhard, 1845
Streibelein, Carl Friedr.—s, 47; from Cassel; Franziska, 1846
Stroele, Gottlob—s, from Oberlenningen; Timoleon, 1846
Strotheyn, Salomon and wife; Franziska, 1846
Strube, Hermann—s, from Alferde, Han.; Margaretha, 1845
Strueber, Andreas—from Zellerfeld, Han.; w—Louise nee Shrader;

ch—Wilh., Caro., Friedr., Adolph, Sophie, Louise; Friedrich, 1846
Stucke (Stuecke), Adolph—m, 51; from Schulenburg, Han.; Gillespie Co.; Gesina, 1846
Studemann, Ludw.—from Osterburg, Altmark; Joh. Dethardt, 1846
Stuemke, Aug.—s, Weser, 1846
Stuenkel, Joh. Hein. Conrad—from Metel, Han.; w—Johanna; ch—Dietrich, Maria; Weser, 1845
Stuhn, Cath.—24, Andacia, 1846
Sturhahn, Paul Alexander—s, 26; from Schöttmar, Detmold; Auguste Meline, 1845
Suchart, Georg Friedr.—m, from Hildesheim; 6 persons and 1 baby; Gerhard Hermann, 1845
Sucklap, Fr.—s, 26; from Rosenthal, Bärenklau, Ff/O; Franziska, 1846
Suessler, Jos. Joh.—from Frankfurt a/M; Talisman, 1846
Suessmann, George—from Hamburg, Kurh.; Austin Co.; Creole, 1845
Suessler, Jos.—from Franfurt; Talisman, 1846
Syring(Siering), Christoph—s, by land to Port Lavaca, 24.XII.1844; Siering, N.—New Braunfels 1845

— T —

Talleur,——had lot in Fredericksburg, 1847
Taps, Joh. Fr.—from Fuhrberg, Han.; † 4.I.1847, age 43; with U.S. Army in Mexico; (NBChR); Weser, 1845
Taps, Joh. Hein.—died; from Fuhrberg, Han.; w—Cath. nee Depke; ch—Cath., Sophie, Wilh., Friedr.; Comal Co.; Weser, 1845
Taubert, Wolfgang—from Kaltennordheim, w—Christine nee Kreisel; ch—Anna Martha, Elisa, Eva; Everhard, 1845
Tausch, Joh. Friedr.—s, 26; from Charlottenberg; New Braunfels 1845, Wm. Bryant, 1845
Tegge, Friedr.—from Steinke (Steinegg?), w—Anna nee Darneland; Colorado Co.; B. Bohlen, 1847
Telge, Wilh.—s, from Fallersleben, Han.; Karl Ferdinand, 1846
Tendler, Wilhelm—s, from Heiligendorf, Han.; Karl Ferdinand, 1846
Tewes, Ludwig—s, from Arolsen; Colchis, 1846
Thalheim, Jacob—s, 21; B. Bohlen, 1845
Thalmann, Hein.—from Hoppensen, 1845

Theilmann, Hein.—s, 19; from Ath, Belgium; **Franziska**, 1846
Theis, Hein.—s, from Hellenhahn; **Dyle**, 1846
Theis, Hein.—from Hellenhahn, Nass.; w—Anna nee Mundscheuer ch—Martha, Marg.; **Gerhard Hermann**, 1846
Theis, Joh. Jacob—38, from Offenbach, Nass.; w—Marg. nee Groos 27; ch—Anna Cath. 5; Comal Co.; **Herschel**, 1845
Thelemann, Carl Friedr.—s, from Görsbach, Prussia; arr. 1845
Theohald, Friedr.—s, from Grebenstein, Kurh; **Friedrich**, 1846
Theuerkauf, Joh.—s, from Niederingelheim; † 5.VII.1846, age 40 (NBChR), **Talisman**, 1846
Thiel, Christian—s, 25; **Ferdinand**, 1844
Thiel, Gustav—Galveston Co.; **Franziska**, 1846
Thiel, Wilh.—widower with 2 ch.; from Drinhausen; **Henry**, 1846
Thiele, Aug.—m; from Köhlde (Pöhlde?); **Talisman**, 1846
Thiele, Carl—s, and Carl—m; from Wendessen, Brnschwg; Comal Co.; **Louise**, 1846
Thiele, Hein.—s, from Peine, Han.; **Louise**, 1846
Thiele, Hein.—from Hohenfelde, Weimar; **Margaretha**, 1845
Thiele, Wilh.—s, from Pöhlde; **Talisman**, 1846
Thiel(e)mann, George—from Dillenburg, Nass.; 2 persons and 1 baby; **Element**, 1846
Thielepape, Georg—s, 34, from Wabern, Hesse; New Braunfels, 1845; Calhoun Co.; **Joh. Dethardt**, 1844
Thielepape Herm.—s, 30; from Wabern, Kurh.; Comal Co.; **Franziska**, 1846
Thielepape, Justus C.—New Braunfels 1845; **Johann Dethardt**, 1844
Thielepape, W.—s, 30; from Wabern, Kurh.; Comal Co.; **Franziska**, 1846
Thieman(n), Carl Theo.—s, 36; from Berlin; **Franziska**, 1846
Thieme, Joh. Christian—from Teichröda, Schwzbg.; w—Elis. nee Langenhammer; ch—Auguste, Henriette, Christine, Gustav, Theo., Hein., Joh.; DeWitt Co.; **Margaretha**, 1846
Thier, Henry—25, and Marg. 20; **Dyle**, 1846
Thier, widow and 1 child—**Harriet**, 1845
Thies(Ties), Christian—from Gross Lafferde, Han.; **Hercules**, 1845
Thies, Joh.—w and 4 ch.; **Riga**, 1846

Thies, Michel—from Lierschied, Nass.; † 17.X1846, age 56 (NBChR); **Gerhard Hermann**, 1846
T(h)ies, Wilh.—s, 26; from Gadenstedt, Han.; **Hercules**, 1845
Thiessen, Joh.—s, Bexar Co.; **Franziska**, 1846
T(h)oelke, Aug.—s, 26; from Brüggen, Han.; † 28.XI.1846, age 26 (NBChR); **Margaretha**, 1845
Thomae, Carl Wilh.—New Braunfels 1845; Comal Co.
Thomas, Carl—s, from Reichenbach, Silesia; **Louise**, 1846
Thomas, Daniel—from Oberscheld, 7 persons; **Element**, 1846
Thomas, Michael—s, from Unzenberg; **James Edward**, 1846
Thran, Jacob—from Eydkuhnen, Lithuania; w—Leopoldine nee Hecht; ch—Edward, Franz, Mina; **Margaretha**, 1846
Thullen, Philipp—from Weidenbach, wife and 1 ch; **Henry**, 1846
Thunecke, Aug.—from Salzwedel; **B. Bohlen**, 1846
Thurm, Wilh.—m, from Sorau, Lausitz; Gillespie Co.; **Louise**, 1846
Tillian, Joh.—from Arolsen; **Colchis**, 1846
Timmer, Friedr.—s, from Antwerp; **Diamant**, 1846
Tittler, Adolph—from Oestrich, Nassau; w—Franziska, nee Langer; **Neptune**, 1845
Todd, Wilh.—s, 30; **Franziska**, 1846
Toell, Joh. Adam—from Sachsen-Meiningen; † 6.XII.1846, age 46 (NBChR)
Toll, George—s, 21; **George Delius**, 1845
Tolle, Christopher Aug.—s, 18; Comal Co.; **Joh. Dethardt**, 1845
Tolle, Fried.—s, Comal Co; **Joh. Dethardt**, 1845
Tolle, George Friedr.—48, from Göttingen, Han.; w—Helene nee Mackenrodt 44; ch—Sophie Auguste 19, Joh. Friedr. 8, Friedr. Wilh., Joh. Gottlieb, Dorette; Comal Co.; **Joh. Dethardt**, 1845
Tolle, Gottlieb—21, from Hannover; **Joh. Dethardt**, 1845
Tonndorf, Wilh.—s, from Jena; arr. 1846
Tonnies Hein.—from Clausthal; w—Wilhme nee Ebler; **Anna**, 1846
Torczynsky, Carl Florian von—hunter for Prince Solms, from Lemberg, Galizia; w—Elisa nee Mensching; **Apollo**, 1845
Trachtena, Joseph—m, **Ferdinand**, 1847
Treibs, Gottfried—from Kirchberg, w—Ann Mary; ch—Mary Ann,

Jacob, Gottfried, Georg, Friedr.;
Gillespie Co.; **James Edward**, 1846
Treibs, Jacob—s, from Kirchberg;
Gillespie Co.; **James Edward**, 1846
Trentge, Wilh.—30, **Joh. Dethardt,**
1845
Trieb, Aug.—s, from Pöhlde; **Talisman,** 1846
Trieb, W.—s, from Pöhlde; **Talisman,**
1846
Triesch, Joh. Peter—32, from Hohenroth; w—Henrietta 36, Adolph 11,
William 6, Wilhelmine † 1847, age
4 (NBChR); Comal Co.; **Washington,** 1845
Trochus, L.—from Albachten Münster; 4 persons; **Bohemia,** 1846
Troeste, Anton—m, **Sarah Ann,** 1845
Trost, Bernhard—s, from Mark,
Prussia; **B. Bohlen,** 1845
Trumm, Anton—from Ober Elbert;
arr. 1845
Trum(m), Joh.—57, from Stahlhofen;
w—Sophie 46, ch—Anna 24, Maria
19, Elis. 16, Peter 14, Christian 11,
Joh. 8; **Strabo,** 1845
Trumpf, Ludwig—s, Sprendlingen;
Andacia, 1846
Trunk, Joh. Jos.—from Rauenthal,
† 22.VII.1846, age 43; "His family
is in Antwerp." (NBChR); **Washington,** 1845
Tschache, Adolph—s, from Köben
a/Oder, Silesia; **Flavius,** 1846
Tuerener, Conrad T.—s, 34; **Weser,**
1844
Twehnes, L.—from Albachten Kr.
Münster; 4 persons; **Element,** 1846
Twele, Ludwig—s, from Stadtoldendorf; Comal Co.; **Sophie,** 1846
Twelkemeyer, Phil.—s, 35; **Franziska,** 1846
Twiefel, Harm. Hein.—m, **B. Bohlen,** 1845
Twilkening, Henry—s, 20; **Franziska,** 1846

— U —

Ude, (Uhde) Chas.—w and 5 ch.;
Franziska, 1846
Ude, Julius—from Hachenhausen,
Han.; w—Johanna nee Laue;
Grimes Co.; **Friedrich,** 1846
Ullrich, Georg—from Lindenau,
Meiningen; w—Margaretha nee
Decker; Came to Texas in 1839;
Wagon Master for German Emigration Co.; New Braunfels 1845;
Comal Co.
Ullrich, Michael—from Schatthausen; **Talisman,** 1846
Ulmer, Jacob—s, from Ilsfeld;
Diamant, 1846
Ulrici, Dorette,—21, **Neptune,** 1845

Ulrizi, Aug.—m, from Brome, Han.;
arr. 1846
Uneling, H. and wife—**Franziska,**
1846
Unger, Benjamin—s, from Stendal,
Prussia; **Creole,** 1846
Ungewitter, Joh Michael—from Behringen, Thuringia; w—†3.III.1847;
son—†19.III.1847; **Sophie,** 1846
Ungs, Nicolaus—s, from Beaufort;
Henry, 1846
Urban, Joh.—from Mittelstelle,
Han.; w and 4 ch; Goliad Co.;
Everhard, 1845
Usener, Carl—41, from Dillenburg,
Nass.; w—Catharine nee Hartsfeld 31; ch—Jacob 11, Hein. 9,
Ludw. Wilh. 4; Gillespie Co.; **Arminius,** 1845
Utermoehlen, Aug.—21; Comal Co.;
Joh. Dethardt, 1845
Utermoehlen, Friedr.—from Kleinschneen, by Göttingen, Han.; †
27.XII.1845, age 44 (NBChR); w—
Cath. Sophie nee Otte, †25.XI.1846,
age52;son—Aug.Fried.Ludw.†age
20; Comal Co.; **Joh. Dethardt,** 1845

— V —

Vahldick, Fried.—from Schöppenstedt, Brnschwg; w—Dor. nee Sommerneier;ch—Auguste;GrimesCo.;
Sophie, 1846
Valdick, Theodor—from Schöppenstedt; **Sophie,** 1846
Vahrenhorst—see Fahrenhorst
Valentin, Aug.—from Breslau;
Mathilde, 1846
Valentin, Carl—s, 24; from Beibrich,
Nass.; **Neptune,** 1845
Vasterling, Joh. Hein.—from Siersse, Han.; w—Christine nee Pommarin; ch—Hein., Christian; Gillespie Co.; **B. Bohlen,** 1845
Vechten,(Fechte?), Gustav van der
—30; from Hannover; New Braunfels 1845; **Joh. Dethardt,** 1845
Vennewitz, Berthold—s, 24; from
Ahden; **Dyle,** 1846
Veramskoff, Engelbert—25; **Andacia,** 1846
Verberne, Joh.—m, from Trennfurt;
10 persons; Galveston Co.; **Diamant,** 1846
Vetter, Joh. Martin—s, from
Schwieberdingen; Fayette Co.;
Diamant, 1846
Vetter, Joh. Victor—from Gemmingen; **Talisman,** 1846
Vinzent, Victor—29, and wife **Apollo,** 1844
Vocler, A.—s, 26; from New Orleans,
1844

Voelker, Eugen—s, Comal Co.; **Weser**, 1846
Voelker, Franziska—†10.XI.1846; age 22 (NBChR)
Voelker, Hein. Jos.—s, from Hausen by Orb (Ort?), Bavaria; †8.VIII. 1846, age 22 (NBChR); **Talisman**, 1846
Voelker, Julius—s, 23; New Braunfels 1845; **Wm. Bryant**, 1845
Voelser, H.—**Talisman**, 1846
Vogel, Christian—s, 20; from Niederelbert; Gillespie Co.; **Riga**, 1846
Vogel, G. P.—from Gammelsbach; 3 persons; **Nahant**, 1846, wrecked at sea; then **Timoleon**, 1846
Vogel, H. Chr.—from Wiesbaden; w and 3 ch.; **Harriet**, 1845
Vogel, Joh.—from Niederelbert; w and 4 ch; **Riga**, 1846
Vogel, Julius—New Braunfels, 1845
Vogel, Ludw.—from Breitscheid near Aachen; w—Anna Christina nee Hak; ch—Bertha, Gustav Adolph, Augusta, Carl Herm. and Alexandria; Comal Co.; **Joh. Dethardt**, 1844
Vogel, Ludw.—s, from Lorsch; **Talisman**, 1846
Vogel, Ludw.—Comal Co.; **Riga**, 1846
Vogelsang, Aug.—s, from Lauenburg; Fayette Co.; **Matador**, 1845
Vogelsang, Aug.—from Lauenburg; w and 1 ch; Fayette Co.; **Franziska**, 1846
Vogelsang, Jacob—from Lauenberg; w and 4 ch.; Austin Co.; **Franziska**, 1846
Voges, Chs.—s, 34; Guadalupe Co.; **George Delius**, 1845
Voges, Christoph—from Lauenstadt, Han.; 5 persons; w—Rosine nee Namedorf; ch—Johanna, Aug.; Comal Co.; **Gesina**, 1846
Voges, Conrad Hein.—from Bissendorf, Han.; and mother Catharine; Comal Co.; **George Delius**, 1845
Voges, Diedrich—s, 64; Guadalupe Co.; **George Delius**, 1845
Voges, Friedr.—s, 38; from Bodenwerder; Comal Co.; **George Delius**, 1845
Voges, Friedr.—s, **Mercur**, 1846
Voges, Hein.—36, from Oberg, Han.; w—Sophie nee Ehlers 30; ch—Dor. 9, Henr. 5, Friedr. 3; Comal Co.; **Hercules**, 1845
Voges, Joh.—s, 18; from Lauenstadt; **Gesina**, 1846
Voges, Joh. Friedr.—from Bissendorf; family of 4 persons; w—Cath. nee Meine; **George Delius**, 1845
Voges, Joh. Hein—s, from Bissendorf, Han.; Comal Co.; **George Delius**, 1845
Voges, Ludwig—s, from Bodenwerder; Comal Co.; **Mercur**, 1846
Voges, Martin and son—**George Delius**, 1845
Voges, Sophie—**George Delius**, 1845
Voges, Wilh.—s, **Mercur**, 1846
Vogg, Michael—m, from Gochsen, Württ.; Matagorda Co.; **Sarah Ann**, 1845
Vogt, Adam—s, from Hesse Cassel; **St. Pauli**, 1847
Vogt, Adam.—from Michelstadt, Darmstadt; w—Susanna Maria nee Schmall; ch—Barbara, Hein., Marie, Phil.; New Braunfels 1845; Comal Co.; **Ferdinand**, 1844
Vogt, Friedr.—s, **Joh. Dethardt**, 1846
Vogt, Georg—s, from Brotterode, Kurh.; arr. 1846
Vogt. Hein.—s, 27; from Fischbach, Weimar; Gillespie Co.; **Everhard**, 1845
Vogt, Joh. Gottlieb—s, from Birkholz; Comal Co.; **Johann Dethardt**, 1846
Vogt, Wilh.—s, from Birkholz, Prussia; Kendall Co.; **Johann Dethardt**, 1846
Voigt, Adolph—from Einbeck; arr. 1845
Voigt, Andrew—w—Elis. nee Preiss; **Mathilde**, 1846
Voigt, Carl Fried.—s; from Beutha, Saxony; Comal Co.; **Franziska**, 1846
Voigt, Friedr.—s, from Birkholz, Prussia; Comal Co.; **Joh. Dethardt**, 1846
Voigt, Gottfried—m, from Birkholz, Prussia; Comal Co.; **Joh. Dethardt**, 1846
Voigt, Johanna—from Hildesheim, Han.; **Margaretha**, 1845
Voight, Ludwig—40, from Ballenhausen, Han.; w—Elise nee Becker 38; ch—Wilh. 13, Sophie 9; Comal Co.; **Joh. Dethardt**, 1845
Voigt, Reinhold—s, from Pölzig bei Altenburg; Bexar Co.; **Margaretha**, 1846
Volch, Carl—s, from Schierstein; **Diamant**, 1846
Volk, Carl—s, from Wiesbaden; † 19.VII.1846, age 33; (NBChR)
Volk, Georg Wilh.—s, from Beerfelden; with sister—Elis. 23; Calhoun Co.; **Washington**, 1845
Volkmar, Joh.—s, 18; **Everhard**, 1845
Volkmar, Marg. Elisa—widow, from Oberschönau, Kurh.; 7 persons; **Everhard**, 1845
Volkmar, Philip—22, from Cassel; **Weser**, 1844

149

Vollmann, Joh. Gottfried—m, **Mary,** from New Orleans, 1847
Vollmer, Friedr.—30, from Rosa, Meiningen; **Garonne,** 1845
Vollmer, Hein.—s, had Verein land grant
Vormann, Edward—s, 21; **Weser,** 1845
Voss, Friedr.—from Lippstadt; with Christian, Aug., Christine, Caro., Ernestine; **Flavius,** 1846
Voss, Joh.—m, from Goslar, a/Harz; Colorado Co.; **Flavius,** 1846

— W —

Waase, Joh. Christian—from Tennstedt; 2 persons; **Orient,** 1846
Wachtmann, Friedr.—s, 30; from Wedmershagen, Han.; **B. Bohlen,** 1845
Wadzeck, Friedr.—from Berlin; w—Friedke nee Kleinvogel; ch—Rudolph, Ernst, Albert, Wilhme, **Franziska,** 1846
Waesche, Hein.—from Adenstedt, Han.; w—Dor. nee Bornemann; ch—Friedr., Carl, Josephine, Caro.; **B. Bohlen,** 1845
Wagand(Waigand?), Mathias—from Molsberg; widow—Anna Maria; Weigand, W. H. † 3.I.1847, age 26(NBChR); **Timoleon,** 1846
Wagenfuehr, Friedr.—m, from Rhoden, Prussia; Comal Co.; **Louise,** 1846
Wagg, Chr.—s, 17; **Sarah Ann,** 1845
Wagg, Friedr.—and wife; **Sarah Ann,** 1845
Wagg, Joh. and wife—**Sarah Ann,** 1845
Wagner, Albert—from Waischenfeld, Bavaria; arr. 1845
Wagner, Carl—s, 25; from Gernsbach; Galveston Co.; **Dyle,** 1846
Wagner, Conrad—s, 30; from Dolzbach? (Dolsach?); **Joh. Dethardt,** 1845
Wagner, Hein. Joh.—from Schiermansdorf(?), Oberndorf(?); 3 persons; Austin Co.; **York,** 1846
Wagner, Herm.—from Griesenbach by Siegen; 2 persons; **Element,** 1846
Wagner, Joh.—s, 33; from Manderbach, Nass.; Bexar Co.; **Auguste Meline,** 1845
Wagner, Joh. Georg—s, from Immenhausen, Kurh.; **Fayette** Co.; **Friedrich,** 1846
Wagner, Joh. Jost—from Griesenbach by Siegen; 2 persons; **Element,** 1846
Wagner, Joh. Philipp—48; from Kat-

zenellenbogen; w—Elis. 47; ch—Jacobina 16; Anton † age 14; Christian 12, Jacob 9; **Strabo,** 1845
Wagner, Julius—s, DeWitt Co.; **St. Pauli,** 1847
Wagner, Justin—s, 18; Maria—age 51, Maria 25; **Strabo,** 1845
Wagner, Peter—s, 21; **Strabo,** 1845
Wagner, Wilh.—54, from Göhringen; w—Maria 54, ch—Maria 25, Julius 18, Joh. 14; **Strabo,** 1845
Wahl, Joh. Georg—s, from Oberberken, Württ.; arr. 1846
Wahldick—see Vahldick
Wahnschaffe, Hein—from Watenstedt; Comal Co.; **Louise,** 1846
Wahnschaffe, Rudolf,—from Koldingen, Han.; Comal Co.; **George Delius,** 1845
Wahrmund, Christian—from Wiesbaden; ch—Louis, Susan, Charles; Gillespie Co.; **Talisman,** 1846
Wahrmund, Emil—s, (1828-1872), from Wiesbaden; oo Auguste Sander 1847; Gillespie Co.; **Talisman,** 1846
Wahrmund, Louis—s, from Wiesbaden; Gillespie Co.; **Talisman,** 1846
Wahrmund, Wilh.—from Wiesbaden; w—Amalie nee Schildknecht; Gillespie Co.; **Talisman,** 1846
Walch, Joh. Jos.—s, 17; from Marxheim; Gillespie Co.; **Washington,** 1845
Walch, Peter—46, from Marxheim; ch—Joh. 17, Elis. 11; **Washington,** 1845
Waldburger, Pastor Joh. Jacob—m, from Frankendorf; **James Edward,** 1846
Walder (Walter?), Hein.—from Büdesheim; 3 persons; **Andacia,** 1846
Waldschmidt, George—m, **Bohemia,** 1846; 4 persons; **Wurges**
Waldschmidt, Joh.—from Dornholzhausen; w—Maria Christine nee Metz, † 25.V.1846 age 37 (NBChR); **Sarah Ann,** 1845
Waldschmidt, Joh. Friedr.—from Frohnhausen; w—Elis. nee Mueller; ch—Elisa, Joh.; **George Delius,** 1845
Waldschmidt, Jost Wilh.—from Frohnhausen, Nass.; w—Anna Elis. nee Schmidt; ch—Gottfried, Andreas, Joh., Louise, Johanne, Christine; **George Delius,** 1845
Wallhoefer, Hans Hein.—from Fuhrberg, Han.; w—Louise nee Ranken; ch—Carl, Hein., Justine; Comal Co.; **George Delius,** 1845
Wallhoefer, Hein. W.—from Langenhagen; son—August † 1846 age 9, (NBChR)

Wallsbein, Conrad—m, had Verein land grant
Walt, Johannes—s, 49; from Sachsen-Weimar; **Weser,** 1844
Walter, Aug. Friedr.—died; from Klein Lafferde; w—† 24.XI.1846 age 21, (NBChR); Hein. Aug.— brother and sole heir; **Everhard,** 1845
Walter, Hein.—from Klein Lafferde, Han.; w—Sophie nee Balm; son— Friedr.; Colorado Co.; **Everhard,** 1845
Walter, Hein.—from Rettert, Nass.; w—(Elis) Rosine nee Holzhaeuser; Cath. 18, Elis. 14, Joh. 12, Peter 9, George 6, Friedr 3; **Neptune,** 1845
Walter, Hein.—from Büdesheim; 3 persons; **Andacia,** 1845
Walter, Johannes—from Würzburg; arr. 1845
Walter, Peter—from Appenhofen; Gillespie Co.; 7 persons; **James Edward,** 1846
Walther, Georg—from Bullau, 3 persons; **Nahant,** 1846 wrecked at sea, then **Timoleon,** 1846; also Peter
Walz, Thomas,—s, from Oberschwandorf; **Element,** 1846
Wamel, Franz von—38, from Czarze, Prussia; w—Anna 41; ch—Rafael 9, Ernestine 12, Emilie 6, Rudolph 3; **Neptune,** 1845
Wamel, Julius Hein. von—s, 17; from Czarze bei Culm, Prussia; Bastrop Co.; **Neptune,** 1845
Wanemaker, Hein.—Galveston Co.; **Franziska,** 1845
Wangemann, Adam—s, 18; Austin Co.; **Joh. Dethardt,** 1845
Wangemann, Ernest—s, 21; **Joh. Dehardt,** 1845
Wangemann, Joh. Hein.—from Mihla, Weimar; w—Christine nee Heinz; ch—Adam, Ernst, Joh., Cath.; Austin Co.; **Joh. Dethardt,** 1845
Warbach, Jacob G.—33, w—Caro. 37 and male child; Emilie 9; **Andacia,** 1846
Warnecke, Hein.—from Neindorf, Han.; w—Dor. nee Studt; Fayette Co.; **Karl Ferdinand,** 1846
Warnecke, Hein.—from Volkmarsdorf, Han.; w—Elis. nee Spanth (Spauth?); **Karl Ferdinand,** 1846
Wartenbach, Wilh.—from Hallscheid; w—Caro.; ch—Cath. Wilhme.; Gillespie Co.; **James Edward,** 1846
Wassermann, Elisa—**Everhard,** 1845
Wasterl, Christian—from Wettmershagen; w—Christian nee Trissler; **Creole,** 1846

Weber, Carl Christian—s, 17; **Sarah Ann,** 1845
Weber, Conrad—2 persons; from Kiedrich; **Diamant,** 1846
Weber, David—s, 1823-1899; from Herborn; Galveston Co.; **York,** 1846
Weber, Diedrich—s, 19; **George Delius,** 1845
Weber, Edward—s, 20; **George Delius,** 1845
Weber, Elisabeth—(Elisa nee Weber); from Sieghofen, Nass.; † 21.XI.1846, age 36; husband buried near Pitch Creek, Texas; (NBChR)
Weber, Englehard—had town lot in Fredericksburg, 1847
Weber, Georg Hein.—from Sulzbach; w—Elisa; ch—Joh., Hein., Friedr., Georg; **Washington,** 1845
Weber, H.—m; † before 1860; had Verein land grant.
Weber, Hein.—m, 56; from Hesselbach, Nass.; Bexar Co.; **Arminius,** 1845
Weber, Jacob—from Cappel; † 10.X.1847, age 39; (NBChR); **York,** 1846
Weber, Jacob—Travis Co.; **George Delius,** 1845
Weber, Joh.—with w and 6 ch; from Esch; **Sarah Ann,** 1845
Weber, Joh.—30, from Offdilln, Nass.; Comal Co.; **Arminius,** 1845
Weber, Joh.—s, from Feudingen Hütte; **York,** 1846
Weber II, Johannes—from Herborn, 6 persons; w—Anna nee Weber from Burg; **York,** 1846
Weber, Joh. Conrad—from Fellinghausen, Nassau; **George Delius,** 1845
Weber, Joh. Georg—s, from Frickhofen; Gillespie Co.; **Element,** 1846
Weber, Joh. Phil.—from Sulzbach; † 15.VII.1846 age 46, buried near Victoria; w—Anna nee Hoffmann † 22.VIII.1846, age 32, buried in New Braunfels; ch—Elisa, George; Christine † 1846, age 14; Carl † 1846, age 3; Philip † 1846, age 12; Orphans: Philippine, George, Joh. (NBChR); **Neptune,** 1846
Weber, Martin—from Grumbach; 7 persons; Harris Co.; **Colchis,** 1846
Weber, Nicolaus—from Oberkatz, Mein.; w—Sophie nee Strauch and 3 ch.; **B. Bohlen,** 1845
Weber, Wilhme—from Rössing; **Creole,** 1846
Wechsler, Jos.—s, from Eltville; arr. 1845
Weckert, Jacob Ph.—s, from Büdesheim; **Andacia,** 1845

151

Wecking (Werking?, Welking?), Moritz—s, from Rheda, Prussia; arr. 1846
Wedekind, Conrad—s, 32, and Leonard—from Schulenburg, Han.; **Gesina**, 1846
Wedemeyer, Adolph von—s, 23; from Hannover, Han.; New Braunfels, 1845; **Ferdinand**, 1844
Wedemeyer, Wilh.—from Brunkensen; w—Christina nee Krueger; ch—Louise, Wilh., Christine, Hein., Wilhme; **Margaretha**, 1845
Wedig, Joachim—from Emmerke, Han.; w—Magda. nee Molkers; ch—Magda., Cath.; **Gerhard Hermann**, 1846
Wege, W.—4 persons; from Abbensen; arr. 1845
Wegener, Aug.—s, 26; from Minten, Prussia; **Franziska**, 1846
Weger, Hein.—with wife and 2 ch.; **Harriet**, 1845
Wehle, Georg—s, 18, Fredericksburg; **George Delius**, 1845
Wehmann, Carl—from Jeeben, Prussia; w—Anna nee Schulze; **B. Bohlen**, 1846
Wehmann, Christoph—s, from Jeeben, Prussia; **B. Bohlen**, 1846
Wehmann, Wilh. Hein.—from Pretzier, Saxony; w—Cath. nee Schulze; **B. Bohlen**, 1846
Wehmeyer, Adolph—New Braunfels, 1845
Wehmeyer, Conrad—s, 1816-1898; arr. New Orleans 1846; to Fredericksburg 1847; oo Louise Klingelhoefer in 1851.
Wehr, Hein. and wife—from Lenterode; **B. Bohlen**, 1845
Wehrspann, Christian—s, 26; from Gross Lafferde, Han.; **Hercules**, 1845
Weichold, Hein.—m, from Saxony; Comal Co.; arr. 1845
Weichold, Paul—s, from Hohenfelden; oo Dor. Jahn 5.II.1847 (NBChR); **Margaretha**, 1845
Weidemueller, C.—2 persons; from Cassel; arr. 1845
Weidemueller, Hein—from Cassel; w—Marg. nee Weye; **Franziska**, 1846
Weiershausen, Daniel—from Manderbach, Nass.; w—Christine nee Ankel † 16.V.1846 age 36, buried at Indianola; ch—Hein., Cath., Friedr., Anna; Joh. † 1846 age 1½ Gillespie Co.; **Auguste Meline**, 1845
Weigand, C. W.—from Beerfelden; 9 persons; Fayette Co. 1855;
Weigand, Math.—from Mosberg† 3.I.1847 age 27(NBChR); **Colchis** 1846

Weigel, Conrad—s, 21; Colorado Co.; **B. Bohlen**, 1845
Weihe, Joh.—s, 59; **Everhard**, 1845
Weil, (Weyl) Aug. Jacob—s, 22; from Stein, Nass.; New Braunfels 1845; **Joh. Dethardt**, 1844
Weil(Weyl), Georgine—widow and 2 ch; **Joh. Dethardt**, 1844
Weil, Jacob—s, 22; from Wissenbach; **Harriet**, 1845
Weil, Joh.—40, from Linn; w—Maria 42; ch—Jane 14, Hein. 10; Comal Co.; **Dyle**, 1846
Weil (Weyl) Joh.—w and 2 ch; **Joh. Dethardt**, 1844
Weil, Joh.—from Wissenbach; 3 persons; **Harriet**, 1845
Weil, Joh. Hein.—s, from Wissenbach; † 16.II.1847 age 19 (NBChR); **Harriet**, 1845
Weil, Joh. Jost—from Stein, Nass.; † 11.IX.1850, age 50; and w—Julianne (Stahl) Weil; ch—Ferd., Theo., Wilh., Aug. Jacob, Aug., Adolph; New Braunfels 1845; **Joh. Dethardt**, 1844
Weil, Ph.(Th?)—New Braunfels, 1845
Weil, Theo.—s, 24; from Stein, Nassau; † 24.XII.1845, age 24; New Braunfels 1845; **Johann Dethardt**, 1844
Weil(Weyl), Wilh.—New Braunfels 1845; **Joh. Dethardt**, 1844
Weinert, August—s, 21; from Nassau; oo Henriette Breustedt 16.V.1851(NBChR); **Joh. Dethardt**, 1845
Weinert, Hein.—53, from Nassau; Louise—24; **Johann Dethardt**, 1845
Weinert, Reinhard—from Dillenburg, Nass.; 5 persons; Comal Co.; and Guadalupe Co.; **Joh. Dethardt**, 1845
Weinheimer, Anton—s, 18, and Georg —s, 21; from Lipporn; Gillespie Co.; **Strabo**, 1845
Weinheimer, Jacob—and wife, from Lipporn; ch—Anton 16, Elis. 15, Georg 20, Sophie 9, Anna 3; Gillespie Co.; **Strabo**, 1845
Weinreich, Chr.—(see also Wembrich, Joh C.); from Rudolstadt; 6 persons; **Andacia**, 1846
Weins, Mathias—from Weidenbach; **Henry**, 1846
Weirich, Carl—s, 30, from Creuzburg, Sachsen Weimar; Gillespie Co.; **Joh. Dethardt**, 1845
Weisbach, Aug.—from Osterode, Han.; w—Auguste nee Mahner; ch—Louise, Ludwig, Car., Aug., Conrad; **Karl Ferdinand**, 1846
Weisbach, Hein.—from Osterode, Han.; **Karl Ferdinand**, 1846
Weisheit, Chr.—s, 26; from Erfurt; **Gerhard Hermann**, 1846

Weisheit, Christian—s, 22; from Mittelstille, Kurh.; **Everhard,** 1845
Weisheit, Cornelius—s, 18; Joh., w and 2 ch **Harriet,** 1845
Weisheit, Joh.—s, 21; from Erfurt; **Gerhard Hermann,** 1846
Weisheit, Joh. Hein.—from Erfurt, w—Marg. nee Drawschar; and 2 ch.; **Gerhard Hermann,** 1846
Weisheit, Nic.—from Wiesbaden; 5 persons, **Harriet,** 1845
Weis(s), Anton—from Alken; 6 persons; **James Edward,** 1846
Weiss, Franz Thomas—26, from Fulda, Kurh.; w—Chlotilde 32; **Garonne,** 1845
Weiss, Gunther—s, from Leutenberg, Schwarzburg, Rudolstadt; **Weser,** 1845
Weiss, Peter—from Alken; **James Edward,** 1846
Weissenborn, Wilh.—s, 23; from Alfeld, Han.; **Gerhard Hermann,** 1846
Welge, Conrad—from Barwedel, w—Christine nee Rake; Gillespie Co.; **Gerhard Hermann,** 1846
Welge, Georg. Christian—from Peine, Han.; w—Sophie nee Meyer; ch—Sophie Caro., Rudolf Ludwig, Hein., Minna; Gillespie Co.; **Hercules,** 1845
Welge, Henry—s, 18; from Barwedel; **Gerhard Hermann,** 1846
Welge, Hein.—from Vallstedt, Brnshwg.; Gillespie Co.; **Flavius,** 1846
Welgehausen, Friedr.—from Jeinsen, Han.; w—Judith Elisa.; ch—Conrad, Johanna; Gillespie Co.; **Gesina,** 1845
Welker, Friedr.—s, from Fürstenberg or Arolsen; **Colchis,** 1846
Welking, Moritz—s, from Rheda, Prussia; to Texas 1845
Weller, Hch—s, from Dünabusch; arr. 1846
Wellges, Geo. Christian—from Peine, to Texas 1845
Wellke, Peter Simon—m, from Renzkau (Renzow?), Prussia; Harris Co.; arr. 1846
Welsch, Peter Carl—s, from Alsenz; **Colchis,** 1846
Wembri(c)h, John C.—40, (see also Weinreich, Chr.); w—Dor. M. 42, and female ch.; ch—Aug. 14, Alex 12, Wilh. 9, Bernhard 8; **Andacia,** 1846
Wendel, Peter Jacob—s, from Büdesheim; **Andacia,** 1846
Wenderoth, Wilh.—s, 21; from Cassel; died 1846; **Herschel,** 1845
Wendsoehn, Louis—26, from Hannover; **Joh. Dethardt,** 1845

Wendt (Wundt), Carl—m, **St. Pauli,** 1847
Wengeroth, Joh.—from Berzahn, Rennerod, Nass.; w—Johanna nee Jung; New Braunfels, 1845; **Ferdinand,** 1844
Wengeroth, Johanetta—widow with more than 2 ch; **Ferdinand,** 1844
Wennel, Joh.—from Bruchköbel, Kurh.; w—Marg. nee Greiner; **Louise Friedricke,** 1847
Wen(t)zel, Carl—from Celle; Kendall Co.; **Apollo,** 1846
Wenzel, Georg—† before 1850; from Oberbessenbach, Bavaria; w—Marg. nee Schnautz; ch—Ignaz, Regina, Maria Anna, Hein., Conrad; Comal Co.; **Joh. Dethardt,** 1844
Wenzel, Ignaz—s, 19; New Braunfels 1845; **Johann Dethardt,** 1844
Werber, Joh. Joachim—m, from Cattchne(?), Prussia; arr. 1846
Werder, (Woerter), Lt. Hans von—from Berlin; Comal Co.; **Strabo,** 1845
Werner, Gustav—s, 18; from Liebenscheid, Ff/M; **Joh. Dethardt,** 1846
Werner, Joh. —s, 22, from Cassel; Kendall Co.; **Everhard,** 1845
Werner(Woerner, Worner) Joh. Erstine—s, 23; from Bierstadt; Mason Co.(?); **Harriet,** 1845
Werner, Joh. Peter—from Liebenscheid, Ff/M; w—Elisa nee Simon; ch—Gustav, Hein.; **Johann Dethardt,** 1846
Werner, Wilh.—from Liebenscheid; Bastrop Co.; **Joh. Dethardt,** 1846
Werscheweh, Friedr.—from Rudolstadt, Schwzbg; **Johanna,** 1846
W(o)ersdoerfer, Jos.—from Hahn, Nassau; w—Anna nee Schmidt; and 2 ch; New Braunfels 1845; **Ferdinand,** 1844
Werthenbach, Jost.—from Nenkersdorf; **Element,** 1846
Werthing, Andrew F.—23, **Dyle,** 1846
Wertmann, D.—s, 18; from Abbesbüttel, Han.; **Everhard,** 1845
Wertmann, Hein.—died; from Abbesbuttel, Han.; w—Marie nee Hoppen; Gillespie Co.; **Everhard,** 1845
Wesch, Hein.—w—Dor. and 5 ch.; New Braunfels 1845
Wescowy, Emanuel,—s, from Lemburg; **Orient,** 1846
Wessel, Edw.—New Braunfels 1845
Wessel, Joh. Christian Christoph—from Gross Denkte; to Texas 1846
Wessel, Wilh.—s, 21, from Hannover; **Ferdinand,** 1845
Wesselroth, Hry—s, 20; **Gerhard Hermann,** 1846

Wessinger, Jacob—from Bonfeld bei Heilbronn; † 6.VIII.1846 age 47(?); 6 persons of family already buried (NBChR); Wessinger, John,—age 7, orphan (NBChR), **Dyle**, 1846
Wessler, John—30; **Dyle**, 1846
Westerling, Joh. Hein.—from Siersee; to Texas 1845
Westphal, Friedr.—s, from Rhoden, Waldeck; Colorado Co.; arr. 1846
Wetz, Conrad—from Offenbach; † 14.X.1846, age 58 (NBChR); **Herschel**, 1845
Wetz, Joh. Georg—s, 26; from Offenbach, Nass.; oo 18.XII.1845 to Anna Marg. Meckel (NBChR); Comal Co.; **Herschel** 1845
Wetzel, Christian Friedr.—from Hartmannsdorf, Thuringia; w—Johanna nee Weisse; **Margaretha**, 1846
Wetzel, Wilh.—s, 20; New Braunfels, 1845; Comal Co.; **Herschel**, 1844
Wetzler, Henrich—27, **Andacia**, 1846
Weyel, Weyl, Weil—see also Weil
Weyl, Wilhelmine Georgine—widow with 3 ch. under 17; **Johann Dethardt**, 1844
Weyrich, Carl—s, from Creuzburg, Weimar; Gillespie Co.; **Joh. Dethardt**, 1845
Weyse, Wilh.—wife and 1 child, **Franziska**, 1846
Wichmann, Joh.—s, from Rendsburg; **Emily**, 1847
Wichmann, Joh. and wife—Colorado Co.; **Apollo**, 1844
Wicke, Christian—died; from Hamelspringe, Han.; w—Wilhelmine and 2 ch.; **Gesina**, 1846
Wideburg, Hugo—s, **St. Pauli**, 1846
Wiecker, Christoph—s, from Bühne, Prussia; **Louise**, 1846
Wiedenfeld, Theo.—s, 20; from Göttingen; Kendall Co.; **Joh. Dethardt**, 1845
Wiedenfeld, Wilh. Friedr.—54, from Göttingen; w—Henriette nee Giesecke; † 29.IV.1851, age 45(NBChR); ch—Theo. 20, Franziska 12; **Joh. Dethardt**, 1845
Wiederstein, Ludwig—s, 24; from Stein; **Washington**, 1845
Wiegand, Gustav—s, 19; from Gudensberg, Kurh.; DeWitt Co.; **Franziska**, 1846
Wiegand, Mat.—from Molsberg(?); **Timoleon**, 1846
Wiegand, Wilh.—34; 5 persons; from Fulda, Kurh.; **Garonne**, 1845
Wiemann, Anton—36, from Prussia; wife and ch—Maria Rogena 5, Joseph 1; **Weser**, 1844
Wienges, Moritz—s, from Brotterode, Kurh.; **Friedrich**, 1846

Wienstroh, Friedr.—s, 35; **Franziska**, 1846
Wiese, Carl—Harris Co.; **Creole**, 1845
Wilheine, Jacob—from Jembke, Han.; w—Marie nee Schaper; Harris Co.; **Karl Ferdinand**, 1846
Wilhelm, Christian—s, from Frankenberg, Württ; **Element**, 1846
Wilhelm, Ferd.—27, from Schmalkalden; w—Cath. nee Ullrich 26; Maria Elisa Auguste ½; **Garonne**, 1845
Wilke, Peter—w—Ernestine nee Blaske; ch—Robert, Emil, Mathilde, Johanna, Leopold, Ernst, Laura, Hermine; **Johanna**, 1846
Wilken, Joh.—s, 45; San Antonio; **Gesina**, 1846
Wilkin, Joh. Leonhard—s, from Breverce near Malmedy; **Timoleon**, 1846
Willeges, Carl—s, † 5.IX.1846, age 38 (NBChR); from Vollbüttel, Han.; **Everhard**, 1845
Willer(Weller?), Joh. and family—from Thomashardt; Württ.; arr. 1846
Will(i)gerodt, Georg—s, from Clausthal; **Talisman**, 1845
Willke, Conrad Hein.—s, from Berlin; went to Fisher-Miller grant with Meusebach; New Braunfels 1845, Comal Co.; **Ferdinand**, 1844
Willke, Friedr—s, from Berlin; **Margaretha**, 1846
Willke, Hermann—s, 22; Surveyor for German Emigration Company—from Collberg on the Baltic Sea; Comal Co.; **Ferdinand**, 1844
Willke, Louis—m, from Collberg on Baltic Sea; appointed by Prince Solms as overseer of depot at Indianola; New Braunfels 1845, Kendall Co. later; came to Texas by land on Oct. 1, 1843
Willmann, Mathias—from Heilberscheid, 8 persons and 1 baby; **Colchis**, 1846
Willms, Jacob—and 5 ch, from Weidenbach; Austin Co.; **Henry**, 1846
Winch, Conrad—20, **Neptune**, 1845
Windisch, Gottfried—from Gefell, w—Sophie nee Kammerschmidt; ch—Caro., Edward, Hein., Maria; **Orient**, 1846
Windwehen, Ludwig—from Kleinschneen; **Timoleon**, 1846
Wink, Ludwig F.—m, from Büdesheim; Austin Co.; **Andacia**, 1846
Winkel, Aug. Hein.—† 1.VII.1846, age 43 (NBChR); from Stederdorf, Han.; w—Dor. nee Wilken 36, ch—

Henriette 9, Ernestine 7, Louise 5, Friedr. 1; **Hercules, 1845**
Winkel, Friedr.—33, from Peine, Han.; w—Ilse Marg. nee Sievers 33; ch—Friedr. 11, Hein. 9, Wilh. 5; Gillespie Co., **Hercules, 1845**
Winkel, Hein. Franz—from Peine, Han.; w—Cath. nee Brandes; ch —Friedr., Elise Marie, Sophie, Joh.; **Hercules, 1845**
Winkel, Ludwig—died; from Peine, Han.; w—Sophie nee Barthels; **Hercules, 1845**
Winkler, Jacob—32, Francoise—35, Francoise—8, Marie Anne—1½; from Ransbach; New Braunfels, 1845; a Castro colonist; **Heinrich, 1844**
Winsch, Conrad—from Werdorf/ Braunfels; †29.VI.1847, age 32 (NBChR); **Neptune, 1846**
Winter, Hein. and wife Sophie— from Luerdissen; Comal Co.; **Sophie, 1846**
Wiskeman, David (Daniel)—Colorrado Co.; **Diamant, 1846**
Witte, Bernhard and Victor—Latium, Washington Co., 1848
Witte, Cath.—from Oberg, Han.; **Margaretha, 1845**
Witte, Christoph and wife—from Oberg, Han.; **Margaretha, 1845**
Wittekop, Christian—s, from Uehrde, Brnschwg; **Louise, 1846**
Wittenberg, Hein.—s, from Wöhle, Han.; arr. 1845
Witting, Georg—s, from Morschen, Kurh.; Victoria Co.; **Neptune, 1846**
Wittneben, Conrad—40, from Peine, Han.; w—Christina nee Stadtmann 39; ch—Hein. 16, Wilh. 10; **Hercules, 1845**
Wittneben, Friedr.—s, from Gadenstedt, Han.; **Hercules, 1845**
Wittnebert, Ernst—s, 25; from Erfurt, Prussia; **Auguste Meline, 1845**
Wode, Ludwig—with wife and 1 ch; from Hattorf; arr. 1846
Woehler, Christoph—m, **Creole, 1846**
Woehler, Ernst Christian—m, **Neptune, 1845**
Woehler, Joh. E.—40; from Greene, Brnschwg; w—Johanna nee Regenhardt 32; ch—Caro. 10, Johanne 10, Hein. 8, Wilhm 5, Ernst 2; **Neptune, 1845**
Woehler, Wilh.—s, from Stadttoldendorf; †1.VI.1847, age 23 (NBChR); **Sophie, 1846**
Woehlert, Christian—from Wettmershagen, Han.; 4 persons; to Texas 1845
Wohlfahrt, J.—from Berlin, to Texas; 1845

Wolf(f), Aug.—from Ringleben or Frankenhausen; Bastrop Co.; **Elisa & Charolotte, 1846**
Wolf, Carl—s, 38; from Stein, Nass.; Fayette Co.; **Joh. Dethardt, 1845**
Wolf, Caro.—from Gehsdorf; **Louise, 1846**
Wolf, Georg—s, from Erndtebrück; Austin Co.; **York, 1846**
Wolf, Leo.—s, 23; **George Delius, 1845**
Wolf, Peter—from Hünfeld; **York, 1846**
Wolff, Joh.—from Lindenberg; 2 persons; **James Edward, 1846**
Wolfgang, Theo.—s, from Clausthal, a/Harz; **Karl Ferdinand, 1846**
Wolfshohl, Aug.—from Dillenburg, Nass.; w—Cath. nee Eberling; ch—Jacobine, Carl; **Joh. Dethardt, 1845**
Wolken, Marie—from Norden; **Timoleon, 1846**
Wolter, Conrad—from Hillerse; wife died on ship; to Texas 1845
Worff, Peter—widower from Ebersheim by Mainz; 5 persons and 1 baby; Comal Co.; **York, 1846**
Worff, Peter—widower with 2 ch; **York, 1846**
Wrede, Friedr. Wilh. von—from Oberndorf; came to Texas in 1836; travelled in U.S., wrote book about U.S. and Texas, killed by Indians at Manchaca Springs Oct. 25, 1845, age 52 (NBChR); was official of Verein
Wrede, Jr., Fried. Wilh. von—Secretary to Prince Solms; from Oberndorf; a founder of New Braunfels 1845; married Sofia Bonzano; was County Clerk of Gillespie Co.; 1850-1859; was in 8th Texas Legislature; returned to Germany 1865; ch—Margaret, Friedrich, Max
Wrede, Joachim—s, from Triebsees; arr. 1846
Wuest, Joh. Adam—from Berghahn, Nass.; w—Philippine † 13.VI.1846, age 43; ch—Emma, Herm., Gustav, August; married 1847 to Cath. Kempel; New Braunfels 1845; **Ferdinand, 1844**
Wulle, Anna—23, **Washington, 1845**
Wullfcrona, Aug.—s, 28, from Sweden; **Apollo, 1844**
Wunderlich, Peter—from Volkholz by Erndtebrück; 2 persons; Gillespie Co.; **York, 1846**
Wunderly, Edward, Dr. Med.—s, 26; arr. 1846
Wurzbach, Fr. Gustav—from Winterlingen; Bexar Co.; **Dyle, 1846**
Wurzbach, Jacob Daniel—m; Bexar Co.; **Andacia, 1846**

Zabel, Charles—23, from Kokocko, Kulm; Comal Co.; **Neptune,** 1845

Zabel, Peter—45, from Kokocko, Kulm; w—Elisa nee Rosente 43, Karl 23; **Neptune,** 1845

Zahm, W. H.—from Emmerichenhain, 6 persons; **Harriet,** 1845

Zahn, Carl—from Wiesbaden; to Texas 1845

Zahn, G.—from Berlin; arr. 1845

Zammert, Joh. Dan.—died?; from Neunkhausen, wife and 4 ch.; Gillespie Co. 1850 Census: "Fried., Wilh., Cath. Zammert living with Conrad Hahn;" **Harriet,** 1845

Zapp, Robert—s, from Elberfeld; Fayette Co.; **James Edward,** 1846

Zavisch, Karl von—from Olmütz, w—Maria nee Kaszye; ch—Bertha, Herbert; step-daughter—Marie Katzke; Fayette Co.; **Orient,** 1846

Zech, Conrad—s, 24; from Werdorf; Mason Co.; **Neptune,** 1845

Zefferer, Anton—s, from Neckarsulm, Württ.; **Element,** 1846

Zeisig, Theo.—see Specht, Theo. Zeisig

Zeller, G.—from Eltville, 3 persons; 1845

Zeller, Valentin—s, † 16.VII.1846, age 32, (NBChR); from Berncastel; **Talisman,** 1846

Zentner, Franz—s, **St. Pauli,** 1847

Zerbach, Antony—26, **Dyle,** 1846

Zerbach, Hein.—† 1846, age 53; from Eitelborn, Han.; w—Gertrude nee Metzger † 1846, age 52; ch—Elize 24; Maria 21; Johanna † 1846, age 14, (NBChR); **Dyle,** 1846

Zerbach, Joh.—23, **Dyle,** 1846

Zerbach, Joh. and wife—3 persons; from Eitelborn; **Riga,** 1846

Zeuner, Axel von—s, from Wiesbaden; **Neptune,** 1846

Zickler, Carl Emil—m, from Cassel; Grimes Co.; **Diamant,** 1846

Zieger, George Adam—s, **York,** 1846

Ziegler, Wilh.—30, from Prussia; **Joh. Dethardt,** 1845

Ziehle, Carl—m; see also Zuehl, Carl Christ.; **Mercur,** 1846

Zimmer, Fr.—from Burghausen; **Talisman,** 1846

Zimmermann, Eduard—m, 13 persons; from Rötgen; **Dyle,** 1846

Zimmermann, Georg—s, 28; from Gedern, Gross Hessen; **Garonne,** 1845

Zimmermann, Hein. G.—s, from Wiesbaden; **Bohemia,** 1846

Zimmermann, widow—had town lot in Fredericksburg 1847

Zimpel, Joh.—s, from Schweidnitz; to Texas 1845

Zink, Nicolaus and wife—from Neuenberg, former Lt. Col. Bavarian Army; Civil engineer for Verein, surveyed town lots for New Braunfels; New Braunfeks 1845; Gillespie Co.; Kendall Co. later; **Herschel,** 1844

Zink, W.—s, **Herschel,** 1844.

Zinke, Carl—s, from Berlin or Frankenhausen; Cameron Co.; **Elisa & Charlotte,** 1846

Zipp, Joh.—from Klein Cziste, Kulmsee; w—Christine nee Pettinger; ch—Joh, Eva, Cath., Marg., Christian, Christina; Comal Co.; **Johanna,** 1846

Zipprian(Zyprian), Joh.—from Weiler, 6 persons; Matagorda Co.; **Talisman,** 1846

Zobel, Adolph—s; **New York** from New Orleans, 1845

Zoeller, Phil.—s; **St. Pauli,** 1847

Zoellner, Jost. Hein.—from Rabenscheid, Nassau; w—Wilhme nee Kusser; ch—Friedr.; **George Delius,** 1845

Zoellner, Martin—s, 18 and Anna; **George Delius,** 1845

Zsckoche, Carl Gottlieb—s, from Dresden; arr. 1846

Zuch, Fried.—from Arendsee, Prussia; **Joh. Dethardt,** 1846

Zuehl, Carl Christian—from Tribsees, w—Johanna (Marie) nee Wrede † 25.V.1849 (NBChR); ch—Friedr., Wilh., Wilhme; see also Ziehle, Carl; **Mercur,** 1846

Zuehl, Wilh.—s, Guadalupe Co.; **Mercur,** 1846

Zuercher, Nic.—38, from Mühlhausen; w—Magda 36 from Colmar †9.IV.1846, age 36 (NBChR); oo Elis. nee Loos; New Braunfels 1845; a Castro colonist; **Heinrich,** 1844

Zum Berge, Hermann—from Sülfeld, Han.; w—Sophie nee Sturm, Gillespie Co.; **Creole,** 1845

Zuschlag, Conrad—New Braunfels 1845; **Ferdinand,** 1844

Zuschlag, Hein.—from Cassel; w—Anna Martha nee Appel † 23.VII.1852, age 43; dau—Helene †15.VII.1852, age 15 (NBChR); son—Conrad; New Braunfels 1845; **Ferdinand,** 1844

Zuspann, Chas—s, 25 and Christ.—s, 22; from Hannover, Han.; **Weser,** 1845

Zuspann, Hein. Ludw.—from Hannover; w—Wilhelmine nee Koch; Grimes Co.; **Weser,** 1845

Appendix I

EINWANDERUNGS-VERTRAEGE
Immigration Contracts

The German Immigration Contracts, made between 1844 and 1847, are in the General Land Office in Austin, Texas. There are 2650 contracts bound into nineteen volumes and indexed. These contracts are of importance in the United States since they contain facts about the immigrants; such as his residence in Europe, whether single or married, often the number in his family, his signature, and the date and port of departure from Europe. These facts were copied from each contract and incorporated in the information about each emigrant in the indexed list of over four thousand emigrants who came to Texas under the auspices of the Verein.

Shown in Plates 10 and 11 is the Immigration Contract of Christian Gollmer, together with a translation of it. Each male emigrant over the age of seventeen signed one of these at the port of embarkation, usually Bremen or Antwerp. Except for a few handwritten contracts these were printed forms bearing the insignia of the Verein and the signature of a representative of the Consulate of the Republic of Texas.

See Plates No. 10 and 11.

Appendix II

Contracts in the General Land Office
in Austin, Texas for the sale of land to the
German Emigration and Railroad Company

There are about one thousand contracts for the transfer of land by immigrants to the German Emigration and Railroad Company. These were found and indexed by Mrs. Virginia H. Taylor, Curator of the Spanish Archives of the State of Texas. They are of value genealogically since they give information on an immigrant; such as the name of the ship and port of departure from Europe, the date of arrival at Galveston, and his marital status (indicated by the fact that he received 640 acres if married and 320 acres if single).

When the Verein acquired an interest in the Fisher-Miller contract, it also acquired the right to one-half of an immigrant's land. Perhaps this explains the discrepancy between the 640 acres (if married) and 320 acres (if single) given him as a conditional grant and the 320 and 160 acres mentioned in his German Immigration Contract.

A photostatic copy of one of the land transfer contracts (that of Heinrich Staats) is shown in Plate 12. It was witnessed by Henry F. Fisher and notarized by DeCordova for the State of Texas.

Appendix III

SHIP LISTS

The names of immigrants on sixty-one ships from Europe and fourteen ships from ports in the United States were indexed in an effort to get as complete a list as possible of the Germans who came to Texas during the years 1844-1847. Of the ships that sailed from Bremen, all reached Texas except the *Nahant* which was shipwrecked on the coast of England. Its passengers continued their voyage on other Verein ships, most of them coming to Texas on the *Timoleon*. A list of these ships has been compiled from two main sources:

A. in Texas, from
1. The Colonization and Fisher-Miller Papers in the State Archives.
2. Microfilm records of ship lists of the U. S. Bureau of Customs.
3. Ship lists in the *New Braunfels Zeitung Year-book for 1936*.
4. Ship lists in the *New Braunfels Zeitung* issue for August 18, 1938 and the 100th Anniversary issue of the *New Braunfels Zeitung*, 1952.

B. in Texas, from
1. German records in the Solms-Braunfels Archives.
2. German records in the "Verein zum Schutze deutscher Einwanderer in Texas" Collection in the University of Texas Archives.

Important information to be found about an immigrant in a ship list includes: port and date of departure, port and date of arrival in Texas; his residence in Europe, often his age and profession, the maiden name of his wife and names of his chil-

158

dren, if known, and sometimes the record of his death when this occurred en route.

A copy of the German list (partial) of passengers on the *Riga* and also a copy of the Republic of Texas list (partial) may be found in Plates 14 and 15.

List of ships from Europe with Verein immigrants to Texas, 1844-1847

N.B.—In a date, Roman numeral indicates **month**. Name of ship is in boldface. Date named is date of ship's arrival at Galveston. Gal. = Galveston; imm. = immigrants.

Albatross—from Hamburg; Gal. XII.1847

Andacia—from Antwerp 5.XII.1845; Gal. 29.III.1846; 188 imm.

Anna—from Bremen 5.IV.1846; Gal. 25.VI.1846; 65 imm.

Anthony—from Hamburg; Gal. 1.IX.1846 and 27.XII.1847

Apollo—from Bremen; Gal. 20.XII.1844; 62 imm.

Apollo—from Bremen 3.XI.1845; Gal. 20.I.1846; 94 imm.

Arminius—from Bremen 18.VIII.1845; Gal. 15.X.1845; 124 imm.

Auguste Meline—from Bremen 16.IX.1845; Gal. 9.XII.1845; 150 imm.

Bohemia—from Antwerp 4.VIII.1846; Indianola 9.XII.1846; 115 imm.

B. Bohlen—from Bremen 9.X.1845; Gal. 22.XII.1845; 188 imm.

B. Bohlen—from Bremen 2.XI.1846; Gal. 2.I.1847; 133 imm.

Carl Wilhelm—from Bremen; wrecked at Gal. 23.V.1846

Colchis—from Antwerp 1.IX.1846; Gal. 29.X.1846; 167 imm.

Chas. N. Cooper—from Hamburg; Gal. 23.X.1847

Cranstadt—from Antwerp; Gal. 3.VI.1846; 107 imm.

Creole—from Bremen 13.XI.1845; Gal. 23.IV.1846; 122 imm.

Diamant—from Antwerp 19.I.1846; Gal. 20.IV.1846; 116 imm.

Dyle—from Antwerp 18.XI.1845; Gal. 15.III.1846; 134 imm.

Dr. Syntax—from Antwerp; Gal. 24.IV.1846; 58 imm.

Element—from Antwerp; 25.VIII.1846 Gal. 22.X.1846; 170 imm.

Emily—from Hamburg; Gal. 24.VIII.1847

Elisa & Charlotte—from Bremen 26.VIII.1846; Gal. 20.X.1846; 120 imm.

Everhard—from Bremen 27.IX.1845; Gal. 9.XII.1845; 287 imm.

Ferdinand—from Bremen 7.X.1844; Gal. 21.XII.1844; 61 imm.

Ferdinand—from Bremen, 1845; Gal. 24.VI.1845

Flavius—from Bremen 2.X.1846; Gal. 26.XII.1846; 118 imm.

Franziska—from Bremen 28.X.1845; Gal. 11.I.1846; 107 imm.

Friedrich—from Bremen 13.VIII.1846; Gal. 24.X.1846; 129 imm.

Fyen—from Bremen; Gal. 1.X.1846.

Garonne—from Bremen 21.VIII.1845; Gal. 6.XII.1845; 131 imm.

George Delius—from Bremen 21.IX.1845; Gal. 25.XI.1845; 140 imm.

Gerhard Hermann—from Bremen 13.XI.1845; Gal. 10.I.1846; 153 imm.

Gesina—from Bremen 15.X.1845; Gal. 2.I.1846; 89 imm.

Hamilton—from Antwerp 22.XII.1845; Gal. 8.IV.1846; 159 imm.

Harriet—from Antwerp 31.X.1845; Gal. 18.I.1846; 186 imm.

Henry—from Antwerp 1846; Gal. 10.IX.1846; 112 imm.

Hercules—from Bremen 25.VIII.1845; Gal. 23.XI.1845; 170 imm.

Herschel—from Bremen 23.IX.1844; Gal. 5.XII.1844; 102 imm.

Herschel—from Bremen 14.VIII.1845; Gal. 16.X.1845; 138 imm.

Israelio—from Antwerp; Gal. 18.X.1845.

James Edward—from Antwerp 17.IX.1846; Gal. 30.XI.1846; 172 imm.

Johann Dethardt—from Bremen 16.IX.1844; Gal. 23.XI.1844; 129 imm.

159

Johann Dethardt—from Bremen 18.IV.1845; Gal. 20.VI.1845; 115 imm.
Johann Dethardt—from Bremen 25.IX.1845; Gal. 18.XII.1845; 140 imm.
Johann Dethardt—from Bremen 18.IX.1846; Gal. 23.XI.1846; 101 imm.
Johanna—from Bremen 12.X.1846; Gal. 22.XII.1846; 125 imm.
Karl Ferdinand—from Bremen 1.IX.1846; Gal. 20.XII.1846; 122 imm.
Leo—from Bremen; Gal. 25.VI.1846; 70 imm.
Leontine—from Bremen 22.X.1844; Gal. date?
Louise—from Bremen 8.IX.1846; Gal. 2.XI.1846; 118 imm.
Louise Friedrike—from Bremen 4.XI.1846; Gal. 8.I.1847; 73 or 99 imm.
Margaretha—from Bremen 1.VIII.1845; Gal. 25.XI.1845; 129 imm.
Margaretha—from Bremen 21.VIII.1846; Gal. 21.X.1846; 90 imm.
Mathilda—from Bremen 1.VIII.1846; Gal. 3.X.1846; 114 imm.
Matador—from Bremen 1.X.1845; Gal. 22.XII.1845.
Mercur—from Bremen 27.VIII.1846; Gal. 26.X.1846; 66 imm.
Natchez—from Hamburg; Gal. 26.X.1847
Nahant—from Antwerp 25.XI.1845;

wrecked on English coast 18.III.1846; 130 imm.
Neptune—from Bremen 2.X.1845; Gal. 23.XI.1845; 214 imm.
Neptune—from Bremen 15.X.1846; Gal. 23.XII.1846; 43 imm.
Orient—from Bremen 30.IX.1846; Gal. 31.XII.1846; 85 imm.
Richard—from Antwerp; Gal. 6.I.1846.
Riga—from Antwerp; 11.XI.1845; Gal. 8.I.1846; 138 imm.
St. Pauli—from Hamburg; Gal. 4.VII.1847; ca 100 imm.
Sarah Ann—from Hamburg; Gal. 9.XII.1845; 127 imm.
Sophie—from Bremen 23.VIII.1846; Gal. 31.X.1846; 80 imm.
Strabo—from Antwerp 11.IX.1845; Gal. 20.XI.1845; 169 imm.
Talisman—from Antwerp 2.I.1846; Gal. 18.IV.1846; 143 imm.
Timoleon—from Antwerp 25.XI.1845; 167 imm.; left Torbay, England 5.V.1846 after taking on board passengers from ship wrecked Nahant; arr. Gal. 8.VIII.1846
Washington—from Antwerp 25.IX.1845; Gal. 25.XI.1845; 187 imm.
Weser—from Bremen 10.V.1844; Gal. 8.VII.1844; 85 imm.
Weser—from Bremen 8.IX.1845; Gal. 27.XI.1845; 93 imm.
York—from Antwerp 14.VIII.1846; Gal. 23.X.1846; 136 imm.

List of ships from the United States with Verein immigrants to Texas, 1844-1847

Agnes—from New Orleans; Gal. I.1846
Alabama—from New Orleans; Gal. 4.I.1845
Bryan—from New Orleans; Indianola 15.III.1845
Cincinnatti—from New Orleans; Gal. 7.II.1846 and 15.X.1846
Constitution—from New Orleans; 1845
Galveston—from New Orleans 22.I.1846 and 15.VI.1846
Lone Star—from New Orleans 3.IV.1846

Mary—from New Orleans; Indianola XII.1845 and VIII.1847
Matamoros—from New Orleans: Corpus Christi 11.XII.1845
New York—from New Orleans; Gal. 26.XI.1843; VIII.1844; 21.IV.1845
Robert—from New Orleans IX.1844
Sam Ingham—from New Orleans; Gal. 29.V.1844; 31.I.1846; 15.XII.1845
Star Republic—from New York; Gal. II.1845; 15.III.1846

List of ships sent by Henry Castro to Texas

Heinrich—from Strassburg 28.XI.1843; Gal. 8.IV.1844
Jean Key—from Antwerp 25.X.1843; Gal. 2.I.1844

Ocean—from Antwerp 9.IV.1844; Gal. 29.V.1844

Maiden Names (when known) of German Immigrants' Wives

Wives	Husbands

— A —

Wives	Husbands
Abbethern, Betty	Holekamp, Georg Fried
Abecke, Ernestine	Lehmann, Gottlieb
Ackermann, Elisa	Schaefer, Carl
Ahrens, Wilhme	Schaefer, Hein.
Aht, Elis.	Behrens, Christoph
Albers, Johanne	Petri, Joh. Hein.
Albrecht, Doris	Mueller, Andreas
Ankel, Christine	Brumme, Ludw.
Appel, Anna	Weiershausen, Daniel
Armgard, Elisa	Zuschlag, Hein.
Arnold, Cath.	Bode, Hein.
Arnold, Catharina	Seibel, Joh.
Aul, Cath.	Stiehl, Heinrich
	Dickhut, Wilh.

— B —

Wives	Husbands
Badenstadt, Dor. (Meta)	Pape, Conrad
Bader, Christine	Moehle, Conrad
Balm, Sophie	Walter, Hein.
Bartel, Eva	Kliewer, Peter
Bartels, Cath.	Hook, Fried. Lud. Wilh.
Bartels, Maria	Dedeke, Joh. Hein.
Barthels, Sophie	Winkel, Ludwig
Basemann, Anna	Heinrich, Joh.
Bauer, Elis.	Stock, Peter
Baumgaertner, Anna	Koch, Wilhelm
Bause, Elenore	Pfannenschmid(t), Georg
Becker, Anna	Scholl II, Joh. Hein.
Becker, Cath.	Brinkrolf, Christoph
Becker, Cath. Caro.`	Fritze, Georg
Becker, Elise	Voigt, Ludw.
Becker, Marg.	Hemmerle, Franz
Behl, Maria	Bertling, Hein.
Behr, Julie	Laue, Wilh.
Behrends, Sophie	Eimcke, Hein.
Behrens, Doris	Kutscher, Ludw.
Bergmann, Christine	Schach, Christian
Berger, Marie	Specht, Theo. Zeisig
Bergmann, Wilhme	Andreae, Carl
Bernhard, Cath.	Kirchner, Joh. E.
Bernhard, Elisa	Schnautz, III, Joh.
Betsch, Amelia	Hemme, Dietr. H.
Betz, Maria	Jung I, Joh. Martin
Beusshausen, Regina	Grobecker, Berthold
Bick, Antonie	Besch, Ferd.
Biedenbrink, Louise	Hauer, Christ
Bierschwale, Cath.	Henniger, Hein.
Bindewald, Auguste	Dieffencach, Carl
Bischoff, Augusta Caro.	Letsch, Daniel
Blaske, Ernestine	Wilke, Peter
Blieder, Catharina	Groos, Johann Jacob
Block, Elisa	Scheler, Peter
Blum, Johanneta	Schneider, Joacob Dan.

Blum, Johanna
Bockelmann, Auguste
Bolz, Marg.
Bolzer, Elis.
Bormann, Caro.
Botte, Friedricke
Botte, (Wotte?) Char.
Braeutigam, Cath.
Braeutigam, Eva
Brandenburg, Wilhme
Brandenberger, Christine
Brandes, Cath. Maria
Brandes, Dor.
Braun, Mathilde
Brehmeyer, Henriette
Breitenstein, Johanna (Rosa Elis.)
Bremer, Elisa
Briel, Eva
Britting, Margaretha
Brockenfeld, Johanne
Brockhoff, Theresa
Buchtenkirchen, Elisa
Buchwald, Christine
Burkhard, Marie

Moeller, Christian
Kammlah, Hein.
Langer, Joh
Halm, Wilh.
Mehrmann, Fried
Dammann, Carl
Siegmann, Fried
Anschuetz, Georg
Marschall, Caspar
Meyer, Hein.
widow of Diehl, Christian
Winkel, Hein.
Heine, Joh. Hein.
Moye, Albert
Kensing, David
Nix, Hein. Ludw.
Bade, Ludwig
Meyer, Franz
Merz, Johannes
Roebbeln, Hein
Herting, Wilh.
Isensee, Hennig
Schulz, Carl Aug.
Mertz, Carl Conrad

— C —

Cabberts, Marg.
Christ, Elisa
Clas, Elisa.
Classen, Johanne
Conrad, Anna
Cordes, Wilhme
Cra(e)mer, Anna Marg.
Cramm, Maria

Segner, Peter
Schafer, Martin
Hof, Joh. Jost
Beckshoeft, Joh. Simon
Henrich, Erasmus
Koch, Andreas
Doell, Joh. Adam
Schumann, Joh. Christoph

— D —

Dallas (Donart?), Maria Christine
Danburg, Anna Maria
Dannsmann, Christine
Darneland, Anna
Dauer, Caro.
Daum, Maria
Debke (Depke?), Marie
Degener, Anna Sophie
Dennings, Dor.
Depke, Cath.
Depke, Cath.
Deppe, Henriette Louise
Deuslake, Maria
Dieffenbach, Sabine
Diehle, Johanna
Dier, Sibella
Dierkens, Cath.
Dierkop, Anna
Dierks, Anna
Diester, Johanne
Dietrich, Cath.
Dietzel, Maria
Dietzel, Ottilie
Dismer, Sophie
Dittmar, Martha

Sames, Peter
Faber, Anton
Becker, Fried..
Tegge, Joh. Fr.
Breustedt, Andreas.
Seidemann, Peter
Luessmann, Geo. Hein.
Schmidt, Joh. Fried.
Backhaus, Hein.
Engelke, Conrad.
Taps, Joh. Hein.
Henne, Joh. Ludw.
Brinkhof, Franz
Sartor, Alex
Schaper, Christoph
Oehring, Joh.
Becker, Fried.
Schroeder, Fr.
Koehler, Hein.
Brandes, Ludw.
Eberts, Joh.
Hohmann, Val.
Hohmann, Val.
Holzhausen, Georg
Hohlefeld, Phil.

Dobke, Sophie
Donart (Dallas?), Maria Christine
Droege, Caro.
Drawschar, Marg.
Dreyer, Charlotte
Durlan, Cath.

Hemme, Fried.
Sames, Peter
Fischer, Hein.
Weisheit, Joh. Hch
Hausmann, Fried.
Dornemann, Christoph

— E —

Ealm, Franziska
Ebeling, Christiana
Eberling, Cath.
Eberling, Tina
Ebert, Cath.
Eberts, Maria
Ebler, Wilhme
Ehlers, Sopha
Eicher, Margarethe
Eisenkraut, Elisa.
Engel, Ilse
Engers, Anna
Erbelein, Maria Elisa.
Erdmann, Eva
Erdmuth, Johanne
Ernst, Elis.
Ernst, Maria
Ernst, Sophie (Cath. Ilse)
Ettling, Caro.
Every, Johanna

Schaefer, Franz Jos.
Schaubode, Ludw.
Wolfshohl, Aug.
Evers, Bernhard
Hoffmann, Joh. Peter V
Fries, Peter
Tonnies, Hein.
Voges, Hein.
Herber, Justus
Mueller, Michael
Ottens, Joh. Hein.
Schwerin, Joh. Jacob
Phannstiehl, Justus Dav.
Hohmann, Val.
Lehmann, Daniel
Staedler, Joh. Caspar
Ranzau, Ludwig
Butte, Fried.
Eggeling, Hein. Julius.
Dreier, Hein.

— F —

Fasch, Elisa
Feldmann, Gesina
Fey, Juliane
Ficht, Johanna
Fink, Anna Barbara
Fischer, Elisa
Fischass, Friedrike
Fischer, Elisa
Flagge, Justine
Fohlmann, Cath.
Freitag, Theresa
Fricke, Anna
Fricke, Dor.
Fricke, Louise
Friedrich, Auguste
Fritsche, Dorette
Froebst, Pauline
Froelich, Marie
Fuellbach, Marg.

Jung I, Jacob
Moellring, Andreas
Hirth, Fried.
Ebers, Christian
Er(c)k, Georg
Behrens, Peter
Gollmer, Christian
Frank, Joh. Georg
Schaper, Fried.
Kothmann, Hein. Conrad
Herburg, Fried.
Koether, Christoph
Kreibaum, Christoph (Christian?)
Funk, Wilh.
Schulz, Carl Gottlieb
Lange, Wilh. G.
Schellentraeger, Phil.
Ludewig, Joh. Justus
Dernt, Jos.

— G —

Gebuchs, Rosina
Gehrke, Antoinette
Geibel, Anna M.
Gerkens. Dor.
Gerloff, Marie Christine
Geruker, Caro.

Meyer, Fried.
Stieren, Wilh.
Orth, —.
Pipo (Piepho), Christ.
Stiebel, Joh. Hein Anton
Koepsel, Gottfried

163

Gesser, Cath.
Geyer, Anna Marie Regine
Giesecke, Henriette
Giesecke, Emma
Glas, Cath.
Glindelmann, Sophie
Gochig, Caro.
Goebel, Christine
Goebel, Maria
Gold, Marie, Dor.
Goldbeck, Judith
Goldbeck, Maria
Goling, Elisa
Goll, Dor.
Gotthardt, Marie
Graf, Cath.
Gramm, Johanne
Greiner, Marg.
Grethe, Christina
Grimm, Eva
Groos, Marg.
Gruen, Cath.
Grundgrieper, Caro.
Guenke, Eva
Guenther, Cath.
Gundermann, Martha
Guttermann, Sophie

Blum, Casper Jr.
Sebastian, Jonas
Wiedenfeld, Wilh. Fried.
Jahn, Hermann
Kneiber, Joh.
Huebner, Hein.
Klinge, Fried
Sahm, Ludw. Jacob
Post III, Joh Peter
Kirchner, (Hein) Christian
Bremer, Hein. Christian
Rewoldt, Joh.
Moos, Joh.
Heinemann, Fried.
Leih(e)ner, Wilh.
Meckel, Joh. Georg
Rolle, Fried. Lud.
Wennel, Joh.
Gehrke, Dan.
Maurer, Christoph
Theis, Joh. Jacob
Arhelger, Wilh.
Muecke, Hein
Broegger, Casper
Klasing, Hein.
Schaefer, Geo. Chr.
Deppermann, E.H. Gust.

— H —

Habfurtes, Friedricke
Haerter, Martha
Hagedorn, Adele
Hagemann, Elisa
Hak, Anna Christina
Halm, Maria
Hansemann, Justine
Harmme, Dor.
Harmsen, Dor.
Hartzfeld, Cath.
Hasper, Ernestine
Hasse, Anna
Hauer, Sophie
Hausmann, Helene
Haustein, Ernestine (Georgia)
Hecht, Leopoldine
Heiden, Friedke
Heiland, Elisa
Heine, Marie Caro.
Heinemann, Caro.
Heinz, Christine
Heise, Dor.
Heise, Elis.
Heiser, Emilie
Helhne (Hehlne?), Charlotte
Helmhold, Louise
Henchered, Dor.
Herbst, Rosa
Hermes, Bernhardine
Herzog, Caro.
Hess, Sophie
Heuris, Caro.
Heverkerdel, Maria
Hillner, Amalie

Cramer, Ernst
Holzmann, Wilh.
Bieberstein, Herm. von
Coers, Joh. Hein.
Vogel, Ludw.
Pitton, Georg
Ebert, August
Hornburg, Christoph
Otte, Fried. Joh.
Usener, Carl
Pape, Joh. Hein.
Spiller, Hein.
Conrad, Behrens
Klemm, Joh.
Rompf, Christ. Hein.
Thran, Jacob
Seidel, Aug.
Klingelhoefer, Joh. Jost.
Hagedorn, Hein. Con.
Hahne, Hein.
Wangemann, Joh. Hein.
Kreibaum, Conrad
Fromme, Georg
Schaefer, Joh. Jost
Gerloff, Carl
Middelege, Conrad
Senfloth, Fried.
Krauskopf, Engelbert
Broegger, Joh.
Rompel, Joh.
Eggeling, Fried.
Reppien, Carl
Schulz, Fried.
Habenicht, Hein.

Hinz, Maria
Hitker, Amailie
Hoessel, Sophie
Hoffmann, Anna
Hoffmann, Christine
Hoffmann, Margaretha
Hofmann, Johanna
Hohmeier, Wilhme
Hohne, Johanna
Hollaender, Friedke
Holz, Elis.
Holzhaeuser, (Elis.?) Rosina
Hombach, Franziska
Hombach, Magda.
Hombach, Marg.
Hoppen, Marie
Hosch, Marg.
Huebner, Anne
Huebner, Elisa.
Hufaus, Elisa
Hundertmark, Johanne

Klaas, Joh.
Kolmeyer, Conrad
Guenther, Jacob
Weber, Joh. Ph.
Goerg. Joh. Goerg
Klein, Stephan
Maier, Wilh.
Henke, Hein.
Schutter, Gustav
Becker, Fried.
Driver, Eduard
Walter, Hein.
Riedel, Anton
Riedel, Nicolaus
Koller, Christoph
Wertmann, Hein.
Baumann, Conrad
Petmecky, Jos. Gottfried
Freudenthal, Fried. Aug.
Seiler, Jacob
Grote, Hein.

— J —

Jaco, Louise
Jacobi, Friedrike
Jaeger, Charl.
Jaeger, Marie
Jaeger, Wilhelmine
Jahr., Elisa.
Jaupen, Johanne
Jesinicke, Sophie
Jordan, Christine
Jordan, Maria
Jung, Anna Maria
Jung, Cath.
Jung, Johanna
Jureges, Maria
Just, Johanna

Dauer, Christian
Kage, Ludw.
Koehler, Ludw.
Lock, Fried.
Lockstedt, Fried.
Geffers, Wilh.
Biere, Bernh.
Assmann, Ferd.
Kuckuck, Joh. Hein.
Mueller, Phil.
Noll, Johannes
Baumsche, Peter
Wengeroth, Joh.
Schulze, Fried. Wilh.
Hesse, Aug. Wilh.

— K —

Kahle, Friedricke
Kahlem, Louise
Kalberlein, Juliana
Kalinowska, Marie
Kammerschmidt, Sophie
Kappell, Ida
Karge, Elisa
Karsten, Elisa.
Kaszye, Marie
Kaupitz, Christine
Kauschen, Helene
Kayser, Anna Gertrude
Keese, Christine
Kehr, Anna
Kern, Sophie
Keune, Henriette
Kilper, Caro.
Kirchner, Marie
Klaas, Maria
Klause, Sophie
Kleber, Regina

Rosenthal, Hein.
Sorge, Fried.
Dannheim, Ernst. Fried.
Iwonsky, Leopold von
Windisch, Gottfried
Kapp, Dr. Ernst
Meyer, Aug.
Meinecke, Albert
Zavisch, Karl von
Hackbarth, Fried.
Stern, Carl Gustav
Salziger, Joh. Gottfried
Deppe, Carl Philipp
Kreid, Jacob
Schlueter, Aug.
Bart(h)els, Hein.
Krause, Christoph
Lange, Gottfried
Schrader, Wilh.
Kampe, Christian
Schroeder, Georg

165

Klein, Cath.
Kleinvogel, Friedke.
Klemm, Maria
Klett, Rosina
Klier, Josephine
Klingelbe, Cath.
Klingstein, Sibille
Kloepper, Antoinette
Knoesel, Johanna
Knopp, Sophie
Kobbe, Dor.
Kobiuska, Anna
Koch, Wilhelmine
Koehler, Marie
Ko(e)necke, Henriette
Koerner, Anna Elise
Kolb, Anna Maria
Kossmann, Eleanora
Kraemor, Christine
Kramm, Sophie
Krause, Anna
Krause, Henriette
Kreinsen, Johanne
Kreisel, Christine
Krek, Maria
Kremer, Lisette
Kresch, Elisa
Kretzmeier, Charlotte
Kreusser, Therese von
Kring, Anna Marie
Kropp, Caro.
Krueger, Christina
Kuemmel, Wilhme
Kuenicke, Johanna
Kuhn, Wilhme
Kusser, Wilhelmine

Schumann, Hein.
Wadzeck, Fried.
Ewald, Johannes
Schwenk, Andreas
Ransleben, Julius Joh. Ludw.
Lange, Christ.
Reiss, Valentin
Gruene, Ernst
Reese, Conrad
Stellter, Fried.
Koenemann, Fried.
Pawski, Mathias
Zuspann, Hein. Ludw.
Ottens, Joh.
Luetze, Hein.
Joerns (Joerdens), Christoph
Goebel, Jr., Jost Hein.
Schulze, Ferd. (Fried.)
Rieck (Rieg.), Joh.
Kavelmacher, Joachim
Koepsel, Daniel
Luedke, Peter
Kiehne, Fried.
Taubert, Wolfgang
Nuettelmann, Joh. Hein.
Schmidt, Ernst
Anding, Hein.
Laesecke, Joh. Hein.
Roeser, Hein.
Behrns, Joh. Hein.
Luessmann, Geo. Hein.
Wedemeyer, Wilh.
Elmendorf, Carl
Holzgrefe, Conrad
Palm, Joachim
Zoellner, Jost Hein.

— L —

Lange, Amalie
Langer, Franziska
Lange, Henriette
Langhamma, Elis.
Lask, Theresa
Laue, Johanna
Leissner, Caro.
Lemm, Charlotte
Lenz, Anna Maria (Meta?)
Leyendecker, Cath.
Limpert, Susanna
Liss, Anna
Loos, Elis.
Lottmann, Dor.
Lubbert, Friedke.
Luecke, Caro.
Luedecke, Theresa
Lueders, Doris
Lueders, Leonora

Fenski, Wilh.
Tittler, Adolf
Bruns, Christian
Thieme, Joh.
Hartscher, Jos.
Ude, Julius.
Hoffmann, Aug.
Gerbert, Wilh.
Pehl, Joh. Adam
Metzger, Fried.
Strauss, Georg Andreas
Holzhauser, Christ.
Kimmel, Georg
Holtermann, Juergen Hein.
Schirmer, Franz
Basson (Baston), Hector
Gramme, Conrad
Spengler, Christoph
Luebky, Christian

— M —

Mack, Marg.
Mackenrodt, Helene

Halm, Joh.
Tolle, Georg Fried.

Mahner, Auguste
Martin, Elisabeth
Marx, Anna Marg.
Marx, Maria
Mattheus, Auguste
Max, Mathilde
Meier, Wilhme.
Meine, Cath.
Meine, Maria
Mener, Gertrude
Mensching, Anna D.
Mensching, Elisa
Merz, Marie Cath.
Metz, Maria Christine
Metzger, Gertrude
Mewe, Marie Caro.
Meyer, Henriette
Meyer, Josephine
Meyer, Maria
Meyer, Regina
Meyer, Sophie
Miste, Marie
Moeller, Cath.
Moeller, Wilhme
Moellring, Dor. (Cath.)
Moellring, Sophie (Marie)
Mohr, Anna Maria
Molkers, Magda.
Molle, Auguste
Monken, Anna
Moos, Marg.
Mueller, Anna
Mueller, Auguste
Mueller Dor.
Mueller, Elis.
Mueller, Elisa
Mueller, Elis.
Mueller, Elis.
Mueller, Elis.
Mueller, Johanna
Mueller, Johanna
Mueller, Marie
Muench (Monch), Luise
Muench, Maria
Mundscheuer, Anna
Munk, Dor.
Munn, Johanna

Weisbach, Aug.
Reede, Fried. von
Pelzer, Adam
Stein, Jos.
Doebbler, Ferd. Fried.
Dangers, Pastor Burchard
Lessmann, Hein.
Voges, Joh. Fried.
Penshorn, Joh. Hein.
Juffrig, Christian
Luehrs, Hein.
Torezynsky, Carl Florian
Schmidt, Leonhard
Waldschmidt, Joh.
Zerbach, Hein.
Karbach, Fried. David
Rauch, Joh. Fried.
Hebgen, George
Metz, Phil, Hein.
Juencke, Joh. Hein. Ludw.
Welge, Geo. Christian
Schulz, Christoph
Klingemann, Joh. Hein.
Martens, Fried. Wilh.
Lochte, Friedr.
Newig, Hein.
Keller, Peter
Wedig, Joachim
Luenert, Aug.
Schade, Ludwig
Kretzer, Hein.
Sauer, Fried.
Eickenroth, Fried.
Knigge, Juergen
Arhelger, Jacob
Jatho, Joh.
Kring, Joh. Hein.
Richter, Hein.
Waldschmidt, Joh. Fried.
Krause, Hein.
Schorer, Christian
Franke, Joh. Ludw.
Ervendberg, Pastor L.L.
Peper, Christian
Theis, Hein.
Koenig, Geo.
Kleinecke, Carl Aug.

— N —

Naber, Marg.
Namedorf, Rosina
Neurath, Elis.
Nickel, Cath. Wilhme.
Nickel, Elisa
Nickel, Sophie
Nolten, Johanne
Nussbaum, Elisa.

Buchholz, Michael
Voges, Christoph
Schloesser, Joh. Peter
Froelich, Joh. Jost
Aurand, Jacob
Knetsch, Joh.
Schulze, Fried.
Dechert, Hein.

— O —

Ockner, Eva
Offermann, Friedke

Lindemann, Joh.
Reinar(t)z, Joh. Wilh.

Ohse, Marie Cath.
Oschweiler, Cath. (Elis?)
Otte, Friedke
Otte, Cath. Sophie

Muehlbrecht, Geo. Hein.
Dittmar, Martin
Bussmann, Daniel
Utermoehlen, Fried.

— P —

Pabst, Elisa.
Packbusche, Dor.
Pape, Dor.
Pape, Friedricke
Pascut, Anna
Paul, Charlotte
Pertis(c)h, Johanna
Pertsch, Marg.
Peter, Cath.
Petri, Cath.
Petri, Anna
Petri, Marie
Petsch, Johanna Elisa.
Pettinger, Christina
Pfeiffer, Maria
Pflug, Henriette
Poehlert, Marianna
Pommarin, Christine
Praehler, Anna Maria
Preiss, Elis.

Hoch, Val.
Herber, Joh.
Metzing, Hein.
Bengener, Christoph
Lindenberg, Fried.
Rotsch, Franz Wenzel
Niebeling, J.C.A.
Startz, Joh.
Philippus, Jost Hein.
Petri, Philipp
Braun, Joh. Hein.
Scholl, Johannes
Meurer, Theo.
Zipp, Joh.
Braeutigam, Val.
Hetzer, Hein.
Meixner, Andreas
Vasterling, Joh. Hein.
Heim, Jacob
Voight, And.

— Q —

Quintel, Frederika Char.

Basse, Pastor Hein.

— R —

Rabe, Wilhme.
Radeke, Friedricke
Rake, Christine
Ranken, Louise
Re(e)b, Charlotte
Re(e)b, Maria
Reeh, Anna
Re(e)h, Cath. Luisa
Rees, Cath.
Regali, Friedke
Regenberg, Sophie
Regenhardt, Johanne
Reinhard, Barbara
Reininger, Anna Maria
Reinken, Anna (Cath. M.)
Reise, Martha
Reipe, (Reisse?) Anna Marg.
Resslingen, Sophie
Richter, Johanna
Riedel, Cath.
Riemenschneider, Elisa
Rinkel, Maria
Rodemann, Elise
Rodemann, Louise
Rodenbach, Anna
Rodscheid, Marie Elise
Rose, Anna

Lue(c)ke, Hein. Wilh.
Fritzsche, Carl
Welge, Conrad
Wallhoefer, Hans Hein.
Bitter, Heinrich
Braum, Joh. Fried.
Hahn, Christ. Aug.
Peter, Gerlach
Schaaf, Phil. Hein.
Rabke, Aug.
Knibbe, Hans Dietr.
Woehler, Joh. E.
Fuchs, Georg
Horne, Peter
Lorenz, Joh. Hein.
Martin, Conrad
Bering, Joh.
Loehmann, Hein.
Kuhfuss, Carl Hein.
Arnold, Peter
Ewald, Conrad
Bremer, Hein.
Leissner, Joh.
Oelker, Hein.
Reinhard, Georg
Kreitz, Joh. Mathias
Boettcher, Joh.

Rosenberg, Johanna
Rosente, Elisa
Roth, Angela
Rothacker, Sophie
Rothe, Caro.
Rothe, Rosalie
Ruebsamen, Justina
Ruencker, Luise J.
Ruff (Russ?) Cath.

Schelper, Hein.
Zabel, Peter
Boeddeker, Anton
Ernest, Conrad
Engelmann, Martin
Schickedanz, Gerhard
Luckenhach, Jacob
Fuchs, Adolph
Blumberg, Carl

— S —

Saal, Cath.
Salari, Maria
Salzmann, Elis.
Sandhorst, Ernestine
Sauder, Wilhme
Sauer, Marg.
Schader, Louise
Schader, Christine
Schaefer, Anna Cath.
Schaefer, Maria
Schalm, Charlotte
Schaper, Marie
Scheidler, Catharina
Schenck, Anna
Scherschmidt, Catherine
Schick, Friedricke
Schickedanz, Elisa
Schickerlein, Magda
Schildknecht, Amalie
Schilling, Kunigunde
Schirmer, Friedke
Schirmer, Maria
Schlattner, Friedke
Schleger, Marg.
Schliepler, Marg.
Schlosser, Josephe
Schmall, Susanna Marie
Schmidt, Anna
Schmidt, Anna
Schmidt, Anna
Schmidt, Anna Elisa
Schmidt, Cath.
Schmidt, Dor.
Schmidt, Marg.
Schmidt, Marg.
Schmidt, Martha
Schmidt, Sophie
Schnautz, Marg.
Schneider, Cath. (Wilhme)
Schoen, Ernestine
Schoeniger, Auguste
Schorn, Cath. Elis.
Schrader, Caro.
Schrader, Louise
Schrader, Sophie
Schraeddor, Cath.
Schraeder, Sophie
Schramm, Johanne
Schroeder, Friedke
Schuetten, Dorette
Schultheis, Elisa
Schulz, Johanne, Christine

Best, Joh. Hein.
Hoffmann, Fried.
Danz, Caspar
Brueger, Ludw.
Martin, Christian
Kuhlmann, Joh. Peter
Strueber, Andreas
Lindmueller, Wilh. Christ.
Steubing, Jacob
Immel, Joh.
Habich, Julius Mart.
Wilheine, Jacob
Luck, Philipp
Mueller, Alex.
Preiss, Joh. Christ.
Schein, Conrad
Lambrecht, Fried.
Bielstein, Aug.
Wahrmund, Wilh.
Schmidt, Joh. Nic.
Nehrlich, Fried.
Kneese, Hein. Fr.
Sternberg, Karl
Hohmann, Hein.
Baumeister, Michael
Koerner, Val.
Vogt, Adam
Schulz, Andreas
Steubing, Joh. Jost
Stendebach, Wilh. Joh.
Waldschmidt, Jost. Wilh.
Mohr, Joh.
Schroeder, Gottfried
Geyer, Edward
Hirschhauser, Conrad
Holzapfel, Joh.
Pluenneke, Conrad
Wenzel, Georg
Schuessler, Joh. Peter
Alves, Fried.
Menger, Joh. Simon Nic.
Reis, Joh. Peter
Graf, Wilh.
Strueber, Andreas
Steinmetz, Lorenz.
Cornelius, Christian
Bothe, Carl Ernest Aug.
Blum, Hein.
Hartung, Joh. Christ.
Mueller, Hein.
Brecher, Joh. Jacob
Kaulvers. Gottlieb

Schulz, Maria
Schulze, Anna
Schulze, Anna
Schulze, Cath.
Schumm, Maria
Schwiegendeck, Wilhme
Seehaus, Christine
Segner, Gertrude
Segner, Marg.
Seifert, Anna
Seifferth, Anna, Cath.
Selig, Barbara
Selzer, Susanna
Siebels, Johanne
Siebert, Anna
Sievers, Ilse Marg.
Simon, Elisa
Sommer, Cath.
Sommerneier, Dor.
Sondergold, Anna
Spandau, Friedke.
Spangenberg, Ernestine
Spannagel, Maria
Spanth (Spauth?), Elis.
Spatz, Emily
Spauth, Dor.
Spritzhorn, Anna Maria
Staace, Louise
Stadtmann, Christine
Stahrenberg, Friedke
Starke, Christine
Starke, Marie
Startz, Caroline
Stauder, Marie
Stede, Marg.
Stegmaier, Sophie
Stein, Marg.
Steinbring, Sophie
Steingut, Bertha
Steinkel, Marie
Steinmetz, Friedricke
Stetter, Cath. Dor. Marie
Stemener, Dorothea
Stiebler, Auguste
Stieping, Anna
Stieren, Emilie
Stiffer, Meta
Stolzer, Henriette
Strackbein, Elisa
Straube, Cath.
Strauch, Sophie
Strauss, Caro.
Streber, Bernadine
Stubberg, (Strubberg?), Dor.,
Studt, Dor.
Stump, Cath.
Stumpf, Adelheid
Sturm, Sophie
Suge, Christine
Suthoff, Dor.

Hevekerdel, Friedr.
Mertens, Joh.
Wehmann, Carl
Wehmann, Wilh. Hein
Preiss, Joh. Theo.
Herrmann, Chr. Ludw.
Meyer, Conrad
Knopp, Joh.
Knopf (Knopp), Peter
Dietzel, Joh.
Doell, Georg Adam
Imhof, Heinr.
Lenz, Andreas
Kiesewetter, Ernst.
Damm, Dittmar
Winkel, Fried.
Werner, Joh. Peter
Hild, Joh. Peter
Vahldick, Fried.
Menz, George
Richter, Fried.
Giesecke, Joh. Wilh.
Ransleben, Julius Joh. Ludw.
Warnecke, Hein.
Foerster, Edward
Salinger, Christian
Klein, Joh.
Brandes, Fried.
Wittneben, Conrad
Giesecke, Christian
Franz, Carl
Schulze, Moritz
Coers, Heinrich
Daum, Joh.
Nugetter, Joh.
Schuchardt, Fried.
Peter, Peter
Hagemann, Ch. Wilh.
Adams, Jacob
Kretzmeier, Fried. Aug.
Schlichting, Fried.
Bevenroth, Hein.
Ellebracht, Fried. Albr.
Reiche, Gottlieb
Bachmann, Ludw.
Mylius, Dr. Adolph
Behrends, Carl
Johannes, Joh. Michael
Franz, Joh. Conrad
Gerhard, Wilh.
Weber, Nic.
Beckel, Joh. Georg Chr.
Kirchner, Ludw.
Eickler, Wilh.
Warnecke, Hein.
Hoffmann, Val.
Moris, Aug.
Berge, Hermann zum
Christ, Joh. Aug.
Wahnschaffe, Hein.

— T —

Tauss, Maria
Tendler, Anna

Kimpel, Joh. Georg
Mueller, A.

Teufel, Lisette
Theis, Sophia
Theiss, Cath.
Tilly, Henriette
Trappe, Marie
Triesch, Wilhelmine
Trissler, Christine

Schmidt, Hein. Fried.
Cramm, Christian
Gruen, Jost Hein.
Juenke, Wilh.
Dettmer, Conrad
Knetsch, Wilh.
Wasterl, Chr.

— U —

Uberech, Marg.
Uflaker, Wilhelmine
Uhde, Friedke
Ullrich, Cath.
Ullrich, Christina
Ullrich, Maria

Kempenich, Joh.
Jordan, Ernst Chr. Franz
Schake, Hein. Ludw.
Wilhelm, Ferd.
Schmidt, Gottlob Fried.
Seng, Franz Jac.

— V —

Vahldick, Anne Dor. Sophie
Verleben, Anna
Vogel, Barbara
Vogeler, Sophie
Voges, Friedke (Cath.)
Voges, Cath.
Voges, Johanna
Vogt, Cath.
Voigt, Anna
Voigt, Elisabeth
Volk, Anna
Vollmer, Ottilie

Geier (Geyer), Andreas
Rinkel, Joachim
Stehling, Amandus
Kretzmeier, Joh.
Pape, Fried.
Heine, Hein.
Langkopf, Carl Hein.
Knopf (Knopp), Jac.
Malsch, Ulrich
Spangenberg, Christoph
Schmidt, Edward (Lieut.)
Herbst, Andreas

— W —

Waechter, Dorothea
Waldmann, Sabine
Walforth, Caro.
Walken, Dor.
Walter, Maria
Warnecke, Elisa
Weber, Anna Maria
Weber, Caro.
Weber, Christine Philippine
Weber, Louise
Webner, Henriette
Weihe, Eva
Weiher, Anna
Weimar, Ernestine
Weisse, Johanna
Wense, Louise
Weye, Marg.
Weymann, Auguste
Wiethers, Dor.
Wilken, Dorothea
Willach, Anna Sophie
Witte, Dor.
Wittmann, Auguste
Wolf, Maria
Wolbers, Maria Cath.
Woltern, Dor.
Wotte, Charlotte

Droege, Fried.
Oppermann, Gottfried
Mueller, Wilh.
Otte, Hein. Friedr.
Heimann (Heymann), Gottfried
Elze, David
Berns, Joh. Hein.
Simon, Mathias
Kaiser, Christian
Laade, Christian
Peter, Wilh.
Storch, Joh. Georg
Gross, Adam Val.
Barthelmes, Hein. Gustav
Wetzel, Chr. Fried.
Behne, Ludw.
Weidemueller, Hein.
Kott, Fried. Wilh.
Hornburg, Hein.
Winkel, August
Bickenbach, Daniel
Ahrens, Conrad
Cabanis, Albert
Cordes, Harm
Grobe, Hein.
Pepper, Fried.
Siegmann, Fried.

Wunn, Johanna

Kleinecke, Carl Aug.

— Z —

Zahrberg, Caro.
Zaune, Anna
Zerbach, Cath.
Zerbach, Gertrude
Zimmermann, Cath.

Johr, Ludwig.
Schoenhuette, Hein.
Mueller, Peter Jos.
Simon, Joh. Hein.
Hilge, Justus David

BIBLIOGRAPHY
Books

Barkley, Mary Starr. *History of Travis County and Austin, 1839-1899.* Waco, Texas, Texian Press, 1963

Batte, Lelia M. *History of Milam County, Texas.* San Antonio, Texas, Naylor, 1956

Biesele, Rudolph Leopold. *The History of the German Settlements in Texas 1831-1861.* Austin, Texas, von Boeckman-Jones, 1930

Biggers, Don H. *German Pioneers in Texas.* Fredericksburg, Texas, Fredericksburg Publishing Co., 1925

Boethel, Paul C. *The Big Guns of Fayette.* Austin, Texas, von Boeckmann-Jones, 1965

Bracht, Viktor. *Texas in 1848.* Trans. by Charles Frank Schmidt, San Antonio, Texas, Naylor, 1931

Day, James M. *Maps of Texas 1527-1900.* The Map Collection of the Texas State Archives, Austin, Texas, Pemberton Press, 1964

Dresel, Gustav. *Houston Journal. Adventures in North America and Texas 1837-1841.* Trans. and edited by Max Freund. Austin, Texas, University of Texas Press, 1954.

Gillespie County Historical Society, Compilers. *Pioneers in God's Hills: A History of Fredericksburg and Gillespie County People and Events.* Austin, Texas, von Boeckmann-Jones, 1960

Haas, Oscar, Compiler. *The First Protestant Church: Its History and Its People 1845-1955.* New Braunfels, Texas, *The Zeitung,* 1955; *History of New Braunfels and Comal County,* Austin, Texas, The Steck Company, 1970

Lotto, F. *Fayette County: Her History and Her People.* Schulenburg, Texas, Sticker Steam Press, 1902

Meusebach, John O. *Answer to Interrogatories.* Austin, Texas, Pemberton Press, 1964. Reprint.

Olmsted, Frederick Law. *Journey Through Texas. A Saddle-Trip on the Southwestern Frontier.* New York, Dix, Edwards & Co., 1857

Polk, Stella Gipson. *Mason and Mason County: A History.* Austin, Texas, Pemberton Press, 1966

Ransleben, Guido E. *A Hundred Years of Comfort in Texas.* San Antonio, Texas, Naylor, 1954

Roemer, Ferdinand. *Texas, with Particular Reference to German Immigration.* Trans. by Oswald Mueller. San Antonio, Texas, Standard Printing Co., 1935

Solms-Braunfels, Prince Carl of, *Texas 1844-1845.* Trans. from the German. Houston, Texas, Anson Jones Press, 1936

Tiling, Moritz. *German Element in Texas from 1820-1850.* Houston Texas, Moritz Tiling, 1913

Trenckmann, W. A. *Austin County.* Bellville, Texas, 1899

Webb, Walter P. and H. Bailey Carroll, Editors. *Handbook of Texas.* In 2 vols., Austin, Texas, Texas State Historical Association, 1952

PAMPHLETS

First Evangelical Lutheran Church. Galveston, Texas, 1950
History of Hilda (Bethel) Methodist Church [Mason County],
   1862 — Centennial — 1962. Historical Committee, San Marcos,
   Texas, *Record* Print
New Braunfels Zeitung Yearbook for 1916. New Braunfels, Texas,
   Zeitung
New Braunfels Yearbook for 1936. New Braunfels, Texas, *Zeitung*
New Braunfels Zeitung, 100th Anniversary Edition. New Braun-
   fels, Texas, New Braunfels Publishing Co. 1952
Raeke, Herman H. W. *One Hundred Years of Methodism at In-
   dustry, Texas.* Industry, Texas, 1948
Sadler, Jerry, *History of Texas Land.* General Land Office, Aus-
   tin, Texas, 1964

BIBLIOGRAPHY

Primary Sources

Original transcripts and records

I. For information about emigrants' departure from Germany:
   1. German Immigration Contracts—2650 contracts in 19 vol-
      umes, indexed, in General Land Office, Texas State Library
      and Archives Building, Austin, Texas
   2. German Emigration Company land transfer contracts—1000
      contracts in office of Mrs. Virginia H. Taylor, General
      Land Office
   3. Immigrants who sailed for Texas in 1845—850 names. List
      in Verein Collection, University of Texas Archives, Austin,
      Texas
   4. Ship lists—16 lists in Verein Collection in University of
      Texas Archives
   5. Wied Collection in University of Texas Archives—docu-
      ments
   6. Solms Braunfels Archives. Copies of, in 70 volumes in
      State Archives, University of Texas Archives, and Sophien-
      burg Museum in New Braunfels, Texas
   7. Colonization Papers and Fisher-Miller Papers in State Ar-
      chives, Austin, Texas
   8. Ship lists—*Neu Braunfelser Zeitung Jahrbuch fuer* 1936.
   9. Ship lists—*Neu Braunfelser Zeitung* 100th Anniversary Issue
   10. German Gazetter: *Ortsverzeichnis I* and Müeller's
   11. Julius Kaufmann Collection, Rosenberg Library, Galveston,
      Texas
II. For information about German immigrants in Texas:
   1. County histories for Austin, Bastrop, Fayette, Lavaca, Ma-
      son, Milam, and Travis counties
   2. Naturalization and deed records in Texas county court-
      houses
   3. Microfilm records of United States Census reports of Texas
      counties for 1850 and 1860
   4. Protestant church registers for deaths of immigrants—New
      Braunfels and Fredericksburg, Texas
   5. Fredericksburg Church Book

INDEX
of Story and Eleven Reports of Prince Solms